Composing Model-Based Analysis Tools

Robert Heinrich • Francisco Durán •
Carolyn Talcott • Steffen Zschaler

Editors

Composing Model-Based Analysis Tools

 Springer

Editors
Robert Heinrich (iD)
Karlsruhe Institute of Technology
Karlsruhe, Germany

Francisco Durán
University of Málaga
Málaga, Spain

Carolyn Talcott
SRI International
Menlo Park, CA, USA

Steffen Zschaler (iD)
King's College London
London, UK

ISBN 978-3-030-81917-0   ISBN 978-3-030-81915-6   (eBook)
https://doi.org/10.1007/978-3-030-81915-6

This Springer imprint is published by the registered company Springer Nature Switzerland AG.
The registered company address is: Gewerbestrasse 11, 6330 Cham, Switzerland

Foreword by Jeff Gray

The composition of software tools to support a task-specific process is a need that often arises in projects of all sizes. Engineers, scientists, and others who have expertise in a certain domain often depend on the integration of a tool pathway to complete work-related tasks. For example, a business analyst may export data from a company-specific dashboard to conduct some analysis using a specialized secondary tool, with visualization of the results then handled by a third tool that best serves the particular requirements of a project.

The need to compose software tools is not new. Over a quarter-century ago, the "software component" wars between standardization efforts like OpenDoc, with direct competition from Microsoft's Object Linking and Embedding (OLE)/Component Object Model (COM), rivalled that of the fervor of a religious debate. The need to compose and analyze information from different sources of origin has been a common need in computer-based solutions.

Engineers use models to abstract properties of a system, which can then be analyzed by different tools for various purposes. For example, avionics engineers may have a model that one division of a company uses for reliability analysis, and a separate model and supporting tool used by colleagues on another team for failure modes effect analysis. These two separate models and tools represent the same targeted system, but are created and maintained by different groups, for different objectives. In such a common scenario, each tool is a highly specialized package that contributes to a critical step in the engineering process.

Although tool vendors offer what they advertise as all-encompassing tool suites, many of the tools used in practice are very rarely integrated across the engineering process. Often, the tools were not designed with composition in mind, resulting in isolated stovepipes. In such cases, engineers must force integration in a human intensive and error-prone manner. Solving the model composition problem across diverse tools is not easy and requires consideration of both *syntax* (e.g., file formats, APIs) and *semantics* (i.e., what is the meaning of a concept in each individual tool and how do concepts map across tools?). The different abstractions used in separate models may also lead to topics of uncertainty and ambiguity, such as when one model captures more detail than another model, leading to a lossy situation during a round-trip translation between models. Simple composition solutions are insufficient in the case of complex engineering tools and processes. The composition solution must also account for the evolution of the system, as tools and processes change over time. Scalability is also a concern. Adding a new tool to the analysis tools ecosystem should not break the process or require exponential effort.

The editors and authors of this book recognize that the same challenges exist for software and systems engineers who use different models and (often independent) tools to analyze desired system properties (e.g., functional correctness, performance, and reliability). They wrote, "The composition of systems, their models and analyses is a challenging but unavoidable issue for today's complex systems" (Chap. 1). At the "Composing Model-Based Analysis Tools" Dagstuhl seminar in November 2019, they assembled an impressive cohort of experts in both software engineering and formal methods to discuss the challenges and potential solutions for analysis tool composition. The various chapter authors cover a range of foundational topics (e.g., modeling language composition, tool integration, uncertainty, and ambiguity) from the perspectives of formal methods and software engineering, with representation from both industry and academia. Readers are also offered a series of case studies that concretize the most important challenges and issues faced in applying model-based composition to analysis tools in different domains and contexts.

This book is recommended to anyone who is involved in the important decisions that emerge when composing multiple analysis tools during software and systems modeling. The book is suitable for both practitioners and researchers, and may also serve as a textbook for a graduate course on model-based analysis tools.

Tuscaloosa, AL, USA   Jeff Gray
May 2021

Foreword by Antonio Vallecillo

It is essential to have good tools, but it is also essential that the tools should be used in the right way

Wallace D. Wattles

Conceptual modeling aims at raising the level of abstraction at which systems are described to cope with their increasing complexity. To this end, precise languages are used to represent the elements of the system that are relevant to the purposes of the modelers, abstracting away those that are not. These high-level representations of a system are known as software models, and their role in software engineering has been gaining relevance as soon as they were considered, stored, and managed like any other software artifacts.

Based on these principles, model-based engineering (MBE) is the software engineering discipline that advocates the use of these software models as primary artifacts for the software engineering process. In addition to the initial goals of being useful to capture user requirements and architectural concerns, and to generate code from them, software models are proving to be effective for many other engineering tasks. Model-based engineering approaches, such as model-driven modernization, models-at-runtime, or model-based testing, already provide useful concepts, mechanisms, and tools for the engineering of complex systems at the right level of abstraction. Software engineers have also realized the extensive possibilities that models offer when treated as actual software artifacts, and how they enable, for example, the development of powerful software engineering tools.

It was more than a decade ago, when MBE was starting to gain acceptance as a software engineering discipline, that Jean Bézivin contacted me because he was happy to see the remarkable developments, artifacts, and tools produced by the modeling community, but worried about the lack of interoperability between them. At that moment in time I was working on tools for the RM-ODP framework, and I was facing similar problems for integrating the separate analysis tools available for each viewpoint language. As a visionary, Jean thought that such interoperability was key to the successful development and adoption of MBE, and that models were again the essential elements to achieve it. Therefore, he coined the term "model-driven interoperability" to refer to this approach.

We were fully aware that interoperability implies much more than simply defining a common serialization format, for example, XMI. This would just resolve the syntactic (or "plumbing") issues between models and modeling tools. Interoperability should also involve further aspects, including the integration of different behavioral specifications, reaching agreements on names and concepts (ontologies), overcoming the differences between separate models of operation (e.g., discrete vs. continuous), or handling other semantic issues such as inconsistency management or exception handling. Furthermore, interoperability not only means being able to exchange information, but also to exchange services and functions to effectively operate together.

We soon realized that the best way to proceed was to set up a forum for the modeling community to discuss all these issues, because it was not a one-person effort (or even two). So, we contacted Richard Mark Soley from OMG, who at the time was also concerned about the same issues, and the three of us decided to organize a workshop at the MODELS 2010 conference in Oslo, on "Model-Driven Interoperability",[1] where the community could meet to exchange ideas and problems about these topics. The workshop was a great success, and more than 30 people participated by presenting their contributions, proposing problems and challenges, and exploring possible solutions. We all discovered there that the subject entailed more complexity than expected, that the relevance to industry was higher than anticipated, but at the same time that successful solutions could be possible if MBE concepts and techniques were used.

Unfortunately, and despite the interest raised by the first edition, the workshop was not continued and no other dedicated forum took its place to allow the software engineering community discuss about making tools interoperate using MBE technologies and artifacts. This is why I was so glad to learn about the Dagstuhl seminar on "Composing Model-based Analysis Tools" and, even more, about this book!

I believe that this initiative fills an existing gap in current research on this fundamental topic by compiling the main concepts and issues related to the composition of model-based analysis tools and, more importantly, by describing a set of concrete case studies that illustrate successful implementations of the book's central ideas. I am sure that the software engineering community, both researchers and practitioners, will truly appreciate the efforts made by the editors and authors to put together such a useful and valuable compilation of concepts, results, and case studies into a coherent body of work.

Finally, I am very grateful to the editors for inviting me to write the foreword to this book, especially when the authors are all the world's best-known experts on model-based concepts and tools. This is undoubtedly the best book that could have been written on this topic, and I look forward to the next Dagstuhl seminar,

---

[1] Bézivin J., Soley R.M., Vallecillo A. (2011) Model-Driven Interoperability: MDI 2010. In: Dingel J., Solberg A. (eds) Models in Software Engineering, MODELS 2010. Lecture Notes in Computer Science, vol 6627. Springer. https://doi.org/10.1007/978-3-642-21210-9_14.

which I hope will be held soon to further discuss about this fascinating subject and to produce the continuation of this excellent book!

Málaga, Spain   Antonio Vallecillo
May 2021

Preface

Modelling and analysis are key to managing the increasing complexity and heterogeneity of today's software-intensive systems. Historically, different research communities have studied the modelling and analysis of different software quality properties (e.g., performance or security) for different types of systems. As a result, the tools available for designing and maintaining software that meets such properties are also distinct, using different languages and techniques, making interaction difficult. This leads to a significant amount of unnecessary development work when building modern applications that must meet combinations of these properties—for example, it may be necessary to construct redundant models in different formalisms and using different tools to support analyses for different quality properties.

We, the editors of this book, have been working on modelling and analysing software-intensive systems for a long time. In our work, we faced the need for more flexibility in model-driven engineering and for decomposing and composing models and analyses in several areas. Addressing this need provokes fundamental questions—for example, on validity, uncertainties, behaviour and property preservation, and termination of analyses. Traditionally, research on these topics has been conducted in different communities isolated from each other. This is why we organised the Dagstuhl seminar 19481 on "Composing Model-based Analysis Tools", held in 24–29 November 2019, at Schloss Dagstuhl, Leibniz Center for Informatics, Germany, to bring together researchers and industry experts from the software engineering and formal methods communities to leverage synergy effects and make progress towards establishing the foundations for a common understanding on composing model-based analysis tools.

This book is an outcome of this Dagstuhl seminar. As such, it presents current challenges, background on those challenges, and concepts to address those challenges in the broad area of the composition of model-based analysis tools, based on the discussions initiated during the seminar. The book also illustrates and underpins the challenges and concepts by discussing case studies.

We are grateful to the participants of Dagstuhl seminar 19481, who were kind enough to accept the challenge of participating in the seminar and later writing this book. We hope that the seminar and the book will make a small contribution towards bringing these communities together into this joint endeavour.

Karlsruhe, Germany   Robert Heinrich
Málaga, Spain   Francisco Durán
Menlo Park, CA, USA   Carolyn Talcott
London, UK   Steffen Zschaler
May 2021

Contents

Contributors

Sofia Ananieva FZI Research Center for Information Technology, Karlsruhe, Germany

Kyungmin Bae POSTECH, Gyeongbuk, South Korea

Simona Bernardi University of Zaragoza, Zaragoza, Spain

Erwan Bousse University of Nantes, Nantes, France

Arvid Butting RWTH Aachen, Aachen, Germany

Benoit Combemale IRISA – University of Rennes, Rennes, France

Jesús Sánchez Cuadrado Universidad de Murcia, Murcia, Spain

Juan De Lara Autonomous University of Madrid, Madrid, Spain

Francisco Durán University of Málaga, Málaga, Spain

Michalis Famelis Université de Montréal, Montréal, QC, Canada

Anas Fattouh Mälardalen University, Västerås, Sweden

Martin Gogolla Universität Bremen, Bremen, Germany

Esther Guerra Autonomous University of Madrid, Madrid, Spain

Jörg Henß FZI Research Center for Information Technology, Karlsruhe, Germany

Robert Heinrich Karlsruhe Institute of Technology, Karlsruhe, Germany

Mark Hills East Carolina University, Greenville, NC, USA

Katrin Hölldobler RWTH Aachen, Aachen, Germany

Jean-Marc Jézéquel IRISA – University of Rennes, Rennes, France

Kenneth Johnson Auckland University of Technology, Auckland, New Zealand

Narges Khakpour Linnaeus University, Växjö, Sweden

Ehsan Khamespanah University of Tehran, Tehran, Iran

Sandro Koch Karlsruhe Institute of Technology, Karlsruhe, Germany

Raffaela Mirandola Polytechnic University of Milan, Milan, Italy

Pavle Mrvaljevic Mälardalen University, Västerås, Sweden

Diego Perez-Palacin Linnaeus University, Växjö, Sweden

Fiona A. C. Polack Keele University, Newcastle, UK

Daniel Ratiu CARIAD, Wolfsburg, Germany

Arend Rensink University of Twente, Enschede, Netherlands

Ralf Reussner Karlsruhe Institute of Technology, Karlsruhe, Germany

Elvinia Riccobene Università degli Studi di Milano, Milano, Italy

Bernhard Rumpe RWTH Aachen, Aachen, Germany

Houari Sahraoui Université de Montréal, Montréal, QC, Canada

Patrizia Scandurra University of Bergamo, Bergamo, Italy

Marjan Sirjani Mälardalen University, Västerås, Sweden

Carolyn Talcott SRI International, Menlo Park, CA, USA

Catia Trubiani Gran Sasso Science Institute, L'Aquila, Italy

Hans Vangheluwe University of Antwerp, Antwerp, Belgium

Dániel Varró McGill University, Montreal, QC, Canada

Arthur Vetter Dr. Ing. h.c. F. Porsche AG, Stuttgart, Germany

Andreas Wortmann Universität Stuttgart, Stuttgart, Germany

Marc Zeller Siemens AG, Munich, Germany

Steffen Zschaler King's College London, London, UK

Chapter 1
Introduction

Robert Heinrich, Francisco Durán, Carolyn Talcott, and Steffen Zschaler

Abstract This chapter sets the scene, describes the context, and motivates the need for more detailed research on composing model-based analysis tools. We give a general motivation of the topic of the book and a high-level overview of the area. We then describe the goals of the book, its target audience, and the structure of the remainder of the book. Furthermore, we give suggestions for how to read the book.

1.1 Motivation and Context

Software is an essential part in various facets of our daily life. Mobility, energy supply, economics, production, and infrastructure, for example, strongly depend on software which is not always of high quality. Critical issues that arose from poor software quality can be found manifold in the press. For example, Denver International Airport opened, delayed, and over budget, due to a dysfunctional automated baggage-handling system [Don02]; a new online banking system at TSB Bank led to access and confidentiality issues for its customers, and eventually forced the CEO to step down [Mon18]; and a supply-chain attack against SolarWinds inserted a Trojan Horse into installation packages enabling attackers to access customers' systems running the affected products [Int21].

R. Heinrich (✉)
Karlsruhe Institute of Technology, Karlsruhe, Germany
e-mail: robert.heinrich@kit.edu

F. Durán
University of Málaga, Málaga, Spain
e-mail: duran@lcc.uma.es

C. Talcott
SRI International, Menlo Park, CA, USA
e-mail: clt@csl.sri.com

S. Zschaler
King's College London, London, UK
e-mail: szschaler@acm.org

1

Besides functional correctness, highly relevant quality properties for today's systems include, for example, performance, as directly perceived by users, confidentiality, as important legal constraint for system design, and maintainability, as important decision factor for system evolution.

Ensuring these properties is a major challenge for design engineers. Several techniques have been developed to effectively model and analyse different facets of software quality, such as response time or failure rate of systems. However, the very different nature of quality properties has led to the use of different analysis techniques and mostly independent tools for modelling and analysing different quality properties. For instance, while some of the properties (e.g., performance, reliability, and availability) are quantitative, other ones (e.g., confidentiality and safety) are essentially qualitative.

Depending on the size and complexity of the systems and the available details, different tools and techniques must be used for modelling and analysing quality. For modelling dependability, for example, techniques like fault trees [Ves+81], Markov chains [Gil05], and reliability block diagrams [Čep11] are available. Similarly, a range of techniques are available for dependability analysis, including simulations—using numerical, analytical, or graphical techniques—and analytical methods.

Although methods and procedures are not standardised for most industries, and there are several open questions, known techniques, both for the modelling and analysis, are successfully used in cases such as defence, transportation, and space industries.

For when rigorous and precise methods are required, different formal methods have been used to provide mathematical reasoning, so that once the system's intended behaviour is modelled, one can construct a proof that the given system satisfies its requirements. For example, for dependability analysis, we can find proposals using Petri nets, model checking, and higher-order logic theorem proving. A survey on the use of formal methods for dependability modelling and analysis is given in [AHT16].

Model-driven engineering (MDE) seems a promising technique to efficiently designing and reasoning about behaviour and quality of systems in various disciplines. Indeed, it has been very successfully applied to improve the efficiency of software development and analysis, including the representation and analysis of quality properties. In the context of performance and dependability analysis, tool-supported approaches like Palladio [Reu+16], Modellica [Mod13] or AADL [FGH06], are good examples of the possibilities.

Recent innovations, like the Internet of Things, production automation, and cyber-physical systems, combine several domains such as software, electronics, and mechanics. Consequently, also the analyses for each of these individual domains need to be combined to predictively analyse the overall behaviour and quality. The composition of systems, their models, and analyses is a challenging but unavoidable issue for today's complex systems. We believe MDE techniques can help in such composition. Or at least, that these techniques may contribute to the improvement of the situation in these regards.

Existing MDE approaches to modelling and analysis are not sufficient to compose modular analyses combining *domain-specific modelling languages* (DSMLs). Indeed, an approach like Palladio already provides a modelling language for the analysis of performance, reliability, maintainability, and other quality properties of systems. However, it, like other similar approaches, relies on a monolithic modelling language and monolithic analysis tools, making the extension of the language and tools, so that they provide support for new properties, challenging. Thus, the internal structure of Palladio's modelling language and analysis tools eroded over time due to uncontrolled growth of dependencies, instance incompatibility, and incompatible extensions [Str+16]. Furthermore, there is no way to verify the non-interference between the analyses provided. On the other hand, we have witnessed interesting advances in some of these issues, for example, in the fields of graph rewriting, algebraic specification, or tree automata. First attempts towards composable modular models have been developed in recent years, attempting to compose, not only the structure of models and DSMLs, but also their dynamic aspects (behaviour and semantics). These indeed may be good foundations for building composable modular analyses.

Furthermore, since models are abstractions of reality, they are not a faithful representation of the system but they contain uncertainties [KO01, Wal+03]. Identifying and handling these uncertainties is a challenge for the research community [EM13, PM14] that is, at present, only partially addressed. The combination of models from different domains and usage perspectives may exacerbate the effect of such uncertainties by creating, for instance, model inconsistencies, incoherence, mismatches in granularities of models, mismatches in the underlying assumptions made when creating the different models, etc. The study of the existence, quantification, and management of the new uncertainties created during the combination of models is an unaddressed task that should be tackled to trust the results of the subsequent model-based analysis.

1.2 Goals of the Book

This book fills a gap in the existing research literature. There is a wide literature on software engineering, model-driven engineering, analysis tools, and formal methods. We, however, do not know of any publication that presents solutions to the challenges raised in the previous section.

This book was created with the belief that sharing specific challenges and advances in some of the aforementioned fields might lead to new approaches and alternative views so some of these challenges may be tackled.

We target more flexibility in MDE by decomposing and composing models and analyses, a topic whose challenges have been the focus of research in software engineering and formal methods, respectively. Traditionally, research on this topic is conducted in these communities in isolation. This book presents joint works of members of the software engineering and formal methods communities and representatives from industry with the goal of establishing the foundations for a common understanding.

We envision an environment in which modelling languages and analysis techniques for the different quality properties are independently provided, and where one can pick up the desired ones at will. In addition to being able to perform such a composition of models and analyses, the combined analysis would allow us to analyse the trade-offs between different properties (e.g., performance vs. security). Furthermore, it allows to share the analysis effort between computation resources as much as possible. This leads to the following interesting questions, relevant for research and industry, for which we provide a common understanding and first answers in this book.

- How can different analysis formalisms be composed safely and correctly?
- How can different analysis tools be composed efficiently, effectively, and correctly?
- How does composition of analyses interact with the need for continuously updated and incremental analysis?
- How are analysis results from composed analysis best presented to users in an actionable form?
- How does analysis composition affect analysis uncertainty and vice versa?

1.3 Target Audience

Central to the book is to provide more flexibility in MDE by enabling the decomposition and composition of models and analyses, a fundamental question in software engineering. This also provokes questions in the field of formal methods—for example, on validity, uncertainties, behaviour and property preservation, and termination of analyses. Traditionally, research on these topics is conducted in the formal methods community isolated from the software engineering community.

This book addresses readers from research and industry in the software engineering and formal methods communities to make progress towards establishing the foundations for a common understanding.

We do not expect any specific knowledge from potential readers, but the book is mainly targeted to researchers in the field of software engineering and formal methods as well as to software engineers from industry with basic familiarity with quality properties, model-driven engineering, and analysis tools. No specific technical knowledge is required, and most terminology used is either widely known by the software engineering/formal methods communities, or will be introduced in the book. The focus is mainly on providing an introduction to the concepts and commonalities.

Readers of the book should expect to learn about concepts fundamental for the composition of model-based analysis tools, a detailed description of technical and research challenges, as well as a description of case studies addressing some of these challenges. More specifically, researchers in the field will receive an overview of the state of the art and current challenges, research directions, and recent concepts, while practitioners will be interested to learn about concrete tools and practical applications in the context of case studies.

1.4 Structure of the Book

The book is structured in two parts and organised around five fundamental core aspects of the subject:

1. The composition of languages, models, and analyses;
2. The integration and orchestration of analysis tools;
3. The continual analysis of models;
4. The exploitation of results; and
5. The way to handle uncertainty in model-based developments.

After a chapter on foundations and common terminology and a chapter on challenges in the field, a chapter is devoted to each of the above five core aspects in the first part of the book. These core chapters are accompanied by additional case-study chapters, in the second part of the book, in which specific case studies are presented in further detail to illustrate the concepts and ideas previously introduced.

When talking about the composition of languages, models, and analyses, we need to understand the different elements impacting analysis compositionality, their different classes, and specific conditions of composition. This is the main focus of Chap. 4. Chapter 5 addresses the challenge of how to orchestrate the composition of analyses implemented in different tools, and how to combine and integrate them. Of course, the possible solutions are diverse. The chapter introduces a reference architecture and orchestration strategies for the integration of existing analysis tools into modelling environments. Independently of whether analyses are performed by isolated tools or in coordination, they must be ready to repeat such analyses after input-system changes. In many cases, systems must be analysed after each change during both design and runtime phases. Continual model-based analysis must be performed efficiently and ideally in a modular way without re-assessing the complete system whenever analysing a specific part of the system is sufficient. Chapter 6 presents techniques to address this challenge. Of course, when discussing interconnection and coordination as well as provision of inputs and communication of results, data and interfaces come into play. In this regard, the last two core chapters elaborate on two key aspects, namely using the results of the analyses (Chap. 7) and their associated uncertainty (Chap. 8). Chapter 7 classifies the different ways of using and presenting the results of analyses, and demonstrates these with several real-world examples. The last core chapter, Chap. 8, is devoted to uncertainty. It discusses the different forms of uncertainty we may find in models, analyses, and results, and describes the importance of recognising its presence and relevance. It also explores the main different forms currently used to include uncertainty in the models of systems and how existing tools can use them, with a particular focus on analysis composition.

The case-study chapters in the second part of the book illustrate the core concepts and provide further details by discussing specific tools. Software should be developed in problem-specific languages rather than general-purpose programming languages. However, most existing analysis tools are tied to a specific representation of the software to be analysed. Chapter 9 discusses how to model a language's semantics explicitly to make it possible to reason about semantics when developing and composing analysis tools. Composing modelling languages and analysis tools still requires significant efforts to properly consider syntax and semantics as well as related analyses and syntheses. Chapter 10 demonstrates object-oriented language engineering concepts that enable composing models of heterogeneous languages. Evolving modelling languages and analysis tools over time may cause design smells. These design smells are structures that require refactoring. Decomposition is key for refactoring design smells in modelling languages and analysis tools. Chapter 11 presents a case study for the evolution of a historically-grown model-based analysis approach. The chapter discusses how techniques for decomposition and purpose-oriented composition can help refactoring modelling languages and analysis tools. Design issues may not only occur in modelling languages and analysis tools but also in model transformations. Chapter 12 presents a tool for the static analysis of the ATL model transformation language. The tool also serves as a case study for result representation, as it focuses on how transformation developers can exploit analysis results to understand and fix transformation problems and achieve higher quality transformations. Chapter 13 presents a case study on how to use different tool-orchestration strategies to combine various tools for the analysis of actor models.

1.5 How to Read This Book

This book can of course be read sequentially from start to finish. However, depending on your goals, different strategies may be more suitable:

- *Researchers in software engineering or formal methods*, and in particular PhD students, may find it useful to focus on a particular challenge in the composition of model-based analysis tools. In this case, you may wish to start by reading Chap. 2 to understand the fundamental terminology used before delving more deeply into the specific core chapter corresponding to your challenge of choice. You may wish to first read Chap. 3 to get an overall overview of the challenges and help you pick the right core chapter to start from. Each of the case-study chapters in the second part of the book is linked to one or more of the challenges and provides a concrete instantiation of the challenges and some solutions.
- As a *practitioner in software engineering*, you may find it more useful to start directly with one of the case-study chapters in the second part of the book. From there, you can always link back to the corresponding core chapters.

- If you are a *master's student* studying software analysis, then the foundations chapter (Chap. 2) will be your best starting point. You will likely then find it useful to read the chapters in the first part of the book (Chaps. 4–8) to gain an overview of the key challenges in the field and the general solution approaches. Depending on your specific focus, you may then want to read specific case-study chapters from the second part of the book.

References

[AHT16] Waqar Ahmad, Osman Hasan, and Sofiène Tahar. "Formal Dependability Modeling and Analysis: A Survey". In: *9th International Conference Intelligent Computer Mathematics, CICM*. Vol. 9791. 2016, pp. 132–147. https://doi.org/10.1007/978-3-319-42547-4_10.

[Čep11] Marko Čepin. "Reliability Block Diagram". In: *Assessment of Power System Reliability: Methods and Applications*. 2011, pp. 119–123. https://doi.org/10.1007/978-0-85729-688-7_9.

[Don02] John Donaldson. *A Case Narrative of the Project Problems with the Denver Airport Baggage Handling System (DABHS)*. Tech. rep. Software Forensics Centre Technical Report TR 2002-01, 2002.

[EM13] Naeem Esfahani and Sam Malek. "Uncertainty in Self-Adaptive Software Systems". In: *Software Engineering for Self-Adaptive Systems II - International Seminar, Dagstuhl Castle, Germany, October 24–29, 2010 Revised Selected and Invited Papers*. Vol. 7475. 2013, pp. 214–238. https://doi.org/10.1007/978-3-642-35813-5_9.

[FGH06] Peter Feiler, David Gluch, and John Hudak. *The Architecture Analysis & Design Language (AADL): An Introduction*. Tech. rep. CMU/SEI-2006-TN-011. Software Engineering Institute, Carnegie Mellon University, 2006. http://resources.sei.cmu.edu/library/asset-view.cfm?AssetID=7879.

[Gil05] Walter Gilks. *Markov chain Monte Carlo*. 2005. https://doi.org/10.1002/0470011815.b2a14021.

[Int21] Center for Internet Security. *The SolarWinds Cyber-Attack: What You Need to Know*. Mar. 2021. https://www.cisecurity.org/solarwinds/.

[KO01] M. Kennedy and A. O'Hagan. "Bayesian calibration of computer models". In: *Journal of the Royal Statistical Society* 63 (2001), pp. 425–464.

[Mod13] Modelica Association. Modelica - *A Unified Object-Oriented Language for Physical Systems Modeling*. 2013.

[Mon18] Angela Monaghan. *Timeline of trouble: how the TSB IT meltdown unfolded*. The Guardian, UK. June 2018. https://www.theguardian.com/business/2018/jun/06/timeline-of-trouble-how-the-tsb-it-meltdownunfolded.

[PM14] Diego Perez-Palacin and Raffaela Mirandola. "Uncertainties in the modeling of self-adaptive systems: a taxonomy and an example of availability evaluation". In: *ACM/SPEC International Conference on Performance Engineering, ICPE*. 2014, pp. 3–14. https://doi.org/10.1145/2568088.2568095.

[Reu+16] Ralf H. Reussner, Steffen Becker, Jens Happe, Robert Heinrich, Anne Koziolek, Heiko Koziolek, Max Kramer, and Klaus Krogmann. *Modeling and simulating software architectures: The Palladio approach*. MIT Press, 2016.

[Str+16] Misha Strittmatter, Georg Hinkel, Michael Langhammer, Reiner Jung, and Robert Heinrich. "Challenges in the Evolution of Metamodels: Smells and Anti-Patterns of a Historically-Grown Metamodel". In: *Proceedings of the 10th Workshop on Models and Evolution*. Vol. 1706. 2016, pp. 30–39. http://ceur-ws.org/Vol-1706/paper5.pdf.

[Ves+81] William E. Vesely, Francine F. Goldberg, Norman H. Roberts, and David F. Haasl. *Fault tree handbook*. Tech. rep. NUREG-0492. U.S. Nuclear Regulatory Commission, 1981. https://www.nrc.gov/docs/ML1007/ML100780465.pdf.

[Wal+03] Warren Walker, Poul Harremoës, Jan Rotmans, Jeroen van der Sluijs, Marjolein van Asselt, Peter Janssen, and Martin Krayer von Krauss. "Defining Uncertainty: A Conceptual Basis for Uncertainty Management in Model-Based Decision Support". In: *Integrated Assessment* 4.1 (2003), pp. 5–17. https://doi.org/10.1076/iaij.4.1.5.16466.

Chapter 2
Foundations

Carolyn Talcott, Sofia Ananieva, Kyungmin Bae, Benoit Combemale, Robert Heinrich, Mark Hills, Narges Khakpour, Ralf Reussner, Bernhard Rumpe, Patrizia Scandurra, Hans Vangheluwe, Francisco Durán, and Steffen Zschaler

Abstract This chapter gives an introduction to the key concepts and terminology relevant for model-based analysis tools and their composition. In the first half of the chapter, we introduce concepts relevant for modelling and composition of models and modelling languages. The second half of the chapter then focuses on concepts relevant to analysis and analysis composition. This chapter, thus, lays the foundations for the remainder of the book, ensuring that readers can go through the book as a coherent piece.

C. Talcott (✉)
SRI International, Menlo Park, CA, USA
e-mail: clt@csl.sri.com

S. Ananieva
FZI Research Center for Information Technology, Karlsruhe, Germany
e-mail: ananieva@fzi.de

K. Bae
POSTECH, Gyeongbuk, South Korea
e-mail: kmbae@postech.ac.kr

B. Combemale
IRISA – University of Rennes, Rennes, France
e-mail: benoit.combemale@irisa.fr

R. Heinrich · R. Reussner
Karlsruhe Institute of Technology, Karlsruhe, Germany
e-mail: robert.heinrich@kit.edu; ralf.reussner@kit.edu

M. Hills
East Carolina University, Greenville, NC, USA
e-mail: hillsma@ecu.edu

N. Khakpour
Linnaeus University, Växjö, Sweden
e-mail: narges.khakpour@lnu.se

B. Rumpe
RWTH Aachen, Aachen, Germany
e-mail: rumpe@se-rwth.de

2.1 Models, Modelling Languages, and Their Composition

In this section, we give an overview of core concepts that must be considered when composing semantics, languages, and models, and discuss how these core concepts are interrelated.

Scientists as well as engineers (including software engineers) use models to address complexity. Given this, it is worthwhile to precisely clarify what a model is. A commonly agreed-upon general definition, given by Stachowiak [Sta73], states that a *model* has three main characteristics:

- There is (or will be) an original.
- The model is an abstraction of the original.
- The model fulfils a purpose with respect to the original.

A model can be called *valid* if it fits for its purpose with respect to the original within certain *validity boundaries*. Interestingly, engineers and scientists differ in their viewpoint here [Com+20]: A scientist regards the model as invalid (or bad), if it does not describe the real world. An engineer regards the produced artefact as bad if it does not fit to the model.

We may have explicit representations of models, which can be defined using natural language or a more formal modelling language. Existing modelling languages can be classified as general-purpose modelling languages, such as the *unified modeling language* (UML) [BRJ98], and *domain-specific modelling languages* (DSML) [Kle08]. For example, software developers regularly use class diagrams to define data structures, concepts of the real world and their relations, and also technical architectures within the software.

The advantage of such *explicit* models is that they can be used as documentation, be subjected to different forms of analysis, or even be used as a source to produce some output, including code generation or 3-D printing. The specific focus that a modelling language usually has may be a burden for the modeller, because of the restrictions that it imposes, but also enables many smart constructive and analytic algorithms based on that language. For example, state machines can be checked for completeness and determinism, the *structured query language* (SQL) provides efficient database retrieval and storage based on E/R-models, etc.

P. Scandurra
University of Bergamo, Bergamo, Italy
e-mail: patrizia.scandurra@unibg.it

H. Vangheluwe
University of Antwerp, Antwerp, Belgium
e-mail: hans.vangheluwe@uantwerp.be

F. Durán
University of Málaga, Málaga, Spain
e-mail: duran@lcc.uma.es

S. Zschaler
King's College London, London, UK
e-mail: szschaler@acm.org

It is also possible that models, instead of being expressed in a certain modelling language, are encoded directly within a general-purpose programming language, like C++, Python, or Java. These models are typically used, for example, in simulations, such as of phenomena in climate and weather, at the atomic level, in cell biology, or in the wider universe. In this case, the sole and only form of analysis is through direct execution and an examination of the resultant execution trace. The availability of code also allows the possibility of checking certain coding properties, as type consistency or the correct handling of exceptions. Tools like Coverity [Syn] or CodeSonar [Gra] provide quite sophisticated forms of what is typically called (static) program analyses. The following discussions concentrate on modelling languages and their use for the definition of models. A discussion of the use of modelling languages in the construction of simulation models can be found in [ZP20].

2.1.1 Types of Models and Their Role in Analysis

Various types of models [Lee18] and the roles they can play [Küh16] are described in the literature. Here, we adopt the distinction made by Combemale et al. [Com+20], who consider three types of models: engineering, scientific, and machine learning models.

An *engineering model* is used to specify and represent a targeted system [Lee18]. It drives the development of the system to be built by specifying concerns such as, e.g., braking and obstacle avoidance in on-board control systems for autonomous vehicles, traffic management models, information systems, or business rules. Engineering models are typically used as a means to develop a physical system, a software-based system (including behaviour, structure, and the interaction of the system with its context), or both (e.g., cyber-physical systems). Engineering models can be described using both domain-specific and general-purpose languages.

A *scientific model* is a representation of some aspects of a phenomenon of the world [GL16]. Scientific models are applied to describe, explain, and analyse the phenomenon based on established scientific knowledge defining a theory. A theory provides a framework with which models of specific phenomena and systems can be constructed. Scientific models are used in various application areas ranging from climate change models, to electromagnetic models, protein synthesis models, or metabolic network models. Typical examples include continuous, equation-based formalisms like differential equations, or discrete-event models.

A *machine learning model* is created by automated learning algorithms based on sample data (i.e., training data) to make predictions or decisions without being explicitly programmed for the task at hand. It approximates the conceptual relationship between a given input and the expected, or a priori unknown, target output. Machine Learning models can be applied in various application areas such as image classification, feature extraction, defect density prediction, language translation, or motion planning of robots. Common formalisms include neural networks, Bayesian classifiers, and statistical models.

According to [Com+20], a model can play several roles with respect to its purpose: It can be descriptive, prescriptive, or predictive.

- A model plays a *descriptive role* if it describes some current or past properties of the system under study, facilitating understanding and enabling analysis.
- A model plays a *prescriptive role* if it describes properties of the system to be built, driving the constructive process—including runtime evaluation in the case of self-adaptive systems.
- A model plays a *predictive role* if it is used to predict properties of the system that one cannot or does not want to measure.

Each type of model can play several roles, which determine whether and how the model is used in analysis. A scientific model is descriptive first and then may become predictive, e.g., to support what-if analyses [Bru+15]. The model may also become prescriptive, e.g., if embedded into a socio-technical system. For example, a prescriptive model of a decision-making tool for climate change using a predictive simulator based on a descriptive scientific model of the earth's water cycle [Com+20].

An engineering model typically starts by being descriptive and then, at design time, is refined and transformed into a prescriptive model. Then, once the system is built as prescribed, the model becomes descriptive again as a kind of documentation [Hei+17]. An engineering model may also be used as a predictive model. For example, a system architecture model can be applied to predict the performance of a specified system configuration [Reu+16].

A machine learning model is typically used in a predictive role to infer new knowledge based on some hypothetical input data. It might also be descriptive of a current or past relationship, or prescriptive if machine learning results are used for decision-making [Com+20]. For example, we may have a prescriptive model of a smart factory where a predictive model is used to make decisions about production plans based on descriptive historical data.

2.1.2 What Is a Modelling Language?

According to [Com+16], a *modelling language* defines a set of models that can be used for modelling purposes. Its definition consists of

- Syntax, describing how its models appear,
- Semantics, describing what each of its models means, and
- Pragmatics, describing how to use its models according to their purpose.

This is a rather general definition which can be realised in various ways. Graphical, tabular, and textual forms of syntax are possible. The semantics can, for example, be defined in denotational form [Sto77], where a semantic domain is mathematically defined and a mathematical function relates syntactic elements to elements of the semantic domain. The semantics could also be defined by explaining the execution effect of model elements, for example, using abstract machines.

Models need a precisely defined semantics. Semantics describes the precise *meaning* [HR04] of each well-formed model in terms of the *semantic domain*, which is generally well understood. We also speak of a *formalism* or *formal language* instead of a *modelling language*. Such a semantics is the formal foundation for understanding whether a model is correct; that is, whether desired properties are satisfied. For example, the set of words over an alphabet can be used as a semantic domain for state machines. A concrete state machine can then be mapped to the subset of accepted words.

There are different formalisms and formal methods for the specification of well-defined semantics, such as rewriting logic semantics [MR04], small-step/structural-operational semantics [Plo04], or big-step/natural semantics [Kah87] or their extensions to distributed, event driven systems [BS01]. In many cases, however, no explicit semantics is available, or we may say that there are different forms of ad hoc semantics. For instance, despite different attempts to provide a formal semantics, the semantics of Python continues to be defined primarily by the behaviour of the Python interpreter, just as the semantics of Java is provided by its virtual machine.

The main purpose of software is "to do". Therefore, many modelling languages concentrate on software and the behaviour it specifies. However, it is worthwhile to mention that semantics should not be confused with behaviour as such, because purely structural languages, such as class diagrams, also have semantics, which in this case is the set of possible object structures.

It is also worthwhile to note that the semantics should not be confused with a *real world interpretation*. For a precise study of the phenomena of a formal language, the semantic domain should be a mathematically well understood, precisely defined construction. It is then up to us to *interpret* this in the real world. For example, words over an alphabet may be interpreted as sequences of human actions in workflows, sequences of messages over a communication channel, or sequences of produced physical component parts in a production line.

A *sound* semantic definition is very helpful to understand what shall be analysed and what the desired outcomes of analysis techniques are. This is true for binary results of analyses, but also for quantifiable results that rely, for example, on statistical considerations. In practice, an explicitly defined semantics is not always needed. Sometimes the language designers already have a good informal understanding and can directly encode the desired properties into algorithmically executable analysis techniques. However, if the domain is complicated, not very well understood, or if the DSML is newly defined, then an intermediate step consisting of mapping the syntax of the language into a semantic domain, before designing executable analysis techniques, has proven very helpful in practice. Such a mapping into a semantic domain can indeed explain the desired and technically implemented results of an analysis technique much better. This even holds if it is not formally defined, but used as a shared understanding for a formal language. The following examples illustrate the use of semantic domains (traces, object-diagram structures, or Petri nets) for different analysis problems.

- The failure rate of state machines can be well explained using a set of traces. In this case the syntax is the state machines, and the semantics its traces. The analysis technique needed is the efficient examination of a representative finite set of traces or a BDD-like[1] integrated representation of all traces.
- The coverage of test sets can be well explained over an appropriate minimal set of object structures that can be derived from a class diagram. In this case the syntax is the class diagrams, and the semantics its object structures. The analysis technique needed is a monitoring of the tests and a finite grouping of relevant object structures into equivalence classes.
- The set of reachable states of a machine can be understood using a mapping from state machines into Petri nets. In this case the syntax is the state machines, and the semantics its Petri net representation. The wide range of tools available for Petri nets provide the needed analysis technique.

According to the above definition of models, a model has a purpose with respect to its original. In practice, a model can be used for more than one purpose, typically associated with the above-mentioned model roles, and such purposes may change during the model's use in various activities of a development process. For example:

(a) A business analyst uses a model to capture and convey requirements and other related information known about the system to be developed.
(b) A developer uses the same model to constructively implement a system fitting to the model.
(c) Quality assurance may use the same model to analyse different quality properties.
(d) Testers use that model both to identify potential problems and derive tests.
(e) Engineering models might be used to realise a digital twin that collects data, provides services and, to some extent, also controls the physical twin [Bib+20].

While for all those the semantics of a model is the same, they use the model in rather different ways and therefore also need rather different functionality centred around the model.

2.1.3 Metamodels

Tools need a suitable representation of models to manage them. An approach that has proved itself useful for constructive as well as analytical tools is metamodelling technology [Gro06].

---

[1] BDD stands for Binary Decision Diagram.

It is a core idea of *model-driven engineering* (MDE) to also use models for explicitly defining modelling languages: this is called *metamodelling*. Let us borrow the following definitions of metamodel and conformance from [Com+16].

A *metamodel* is a model describing the abstract syntax of a language. It is commonly agreed that a metamodel is usually defined as a class diagram, very similar to UML class diagrams. A metamodel therefore describes a set of object structures, where each of these object structures describes the abstract syntax and therefore the essence of a model, which is needed for analysis, code synthesis, or other development activities.

A model *conforms* to a given metamodel if each model element is an instance of a metamodel element. Such a model is considered valid with respect to the language represented by the metamodel. It is a big advantage of the metamodelling approach that exactly the same metamodel can be used within a tool both to represent the abstract syntax and to operate on such model, for example, for code generation or for the application of some analysis technique (see Chap. 11 of this book [Hei+21] for an example). A metamodel therefore serves a dual purpose, defining the language and all the models in that language (i.e., the syntax), and serving as basic infrastructure for tooling. The class diagram however only captures the abstract syntax, which needs to be augmented by a concrete representation, usually in diagrammatic, tabular, or textual form.

2.1.4   Property Models

In model-based analysis, we are interested in understanding certain properties of the system under study. When the property of interest can vary, such properties must be made explicit by the developers and then provided to the tooling. Given this, it is necessary to give the desired properties a precise semantics in addition to the models. For that purpose, we distinguish between *properties* that talk about the semantic domain of the model, e.g., the set of possible system runs, reachability of states in a model, or climate behaviour, versus pure *syntactical properties*, such as readability or cyclomatic complexity of code.

As a consequence of these considerations, a semantic property is itself a kind of model, which we call a *property model*. The property is then the set of all elements of the semantic domain that satisfy the property. Formulated in set-theoretical form: A model fulfils a property, exactly if the semantics of the model is contained in the semantics of the property. Or, formulated in logical form: The semantics of the model implies the semantics of the property.

2.1.5   Two Dimensions of Model Compositionality

Models need to be compositional along two dimensions, namely concerns and subsystems. To tackle the complexity of systems development, it is often necessary to use diverse models describing different aspects or viewpoints of the system as a whole or of subsystems.

The separation of concerns is important for enabling contributions by different subject-matter experts, and enables parallel development and evolution. This is why modern modelling languages, such as UML [BRJ98] and SysML [Gro12], provide a number of different sublanguages, allowing the modeller to concentrate only on certain aspects of the system.

Model reuse is only possible if the models are developed in independent, relatively encapsulated pieces. Building models as encapsulated pieces implies a mechanism and opportunity for composition, and building up a description of the overall system. For example, we may use state charts to describe the behaviour of individual components, and then combine them into a model of the system as a whole. These behavioural descriptions of components can then be reused to build models of different systems.

In summary, the two dimensions of model composition are:

(a) Within the modelling language, models are semantically composed to produce larger specifications. This form of composition usually goes along with the composition of the system components.
(b) Models of different aspects of the same component are composed to give a more complete description of this component.

2.1.6   Models of Context

In many cases, in addition to the models of the system or component to be built, we require a model of the *context* of the system or component.

In systems modelling, the term "context" refers to models which are needed for system construction and analysis but which do not describe entities to be built. Instead they describe the environment of the system. Considering contexts is important as they affect the system to be built for two reasons:

(a) If the implementation of the system can rely on certain *assumptions* about how it is being used, then certain internal optimisations become possible.
(b) When using the implemented subsystem/component, the context model actually gives restrictions on how it can be composed into a larger system.

If we lift this understanding of context to the metamodel (the language definition level, Sect. 2.1.3), we also have to draw a line between the artefacts to be manipulated and the additional *context* information. As an example, given all potential executions of a system, a context model may define the subset of executions that need to be analysed. In addition, one could also consider platform-specific parts of the semantics definition (like scheduling policies) as a context model which act as a parameter to the analysis. Alternatively, such information could have also been considered as part of the model's semantics. The choice depends on the specific questions to be studied and on the available analysis tools.

In the case of security analysis, for example, the context model may include an attack model (e.g., the Dolev–Yao model [DY83]), giving the capabilities of attackers of concern. When analysing robustness or resilience against faulty or inaccurate sensors or actuators, a context model might include fault models. In the case of a multi-agent system, analysis might focus on a single agent to reduce analysis complexity, using a context model that includes a model of the remaining agents, suitably abstracted.

2.1.7 Model and Language Composition

Composition of models and the languages used to describe them is key to coping with the complexity inherent in modelling diverse aspects of large systems, possibly modelled in models expressed in heterogeneous languages. This, therefore, implies that also languages need to be composed.

In general, when composing languages, we need to understand what to compose, given as shown in Sect. 2.1.2, that a language is defined by syntax, semantics, and pragmatics. Assume you have one syntax definition and two different semantic definitions. For the purpose of composition, we might view these as two different languages. However, having one syntax and semantics definition, and two pragmatics descriptions, we would still consider this to be one language, with two ways of using it. Consequently, when considering composition, we would treat syntax and semantics definitions as constitutional parts of the language (any change of either will change the language), while the pragmatics description would not be part of the language and, hence, not subject of language composition.

Looking at the efforts to standardise UML in recent years, we can observe that a clear, precise, and well integrated semantics for such a language is not easy to achieve. This is partially due to the complexity of UML itself, partially due to political problems, because different driving forces have different understandings and interpretations, but also partly due to the overwhelming desire that UML should cover every domain of software systems. Actual realisations of components may differ in multiple details, for example in communication forms, timing, interaction of threads, sharing of memory, etc. If UML is mainly used for communication between developers in the form of "paper-based" models, this lack of semantics is not necessarily harmful. For sophisticated analysis techniques, however, this is a strong impediment.

For an advanced and potentially integrated form of composite semantics, it is necessary, as a consequence of the above discussion, to also think of composition of models of different aspects and, therefore, as well on the modelling languages used for describing these aspects. Instead of a one-size-fits-all language, such as UML, a feasible alternative could be to use small individual modelling languages, allowing us to describe small and focused models, and then integrate the models by integrating the analysis techniques or the results of the analysis algorithms as described in Sect. 4.4.2 of this book [Hei+21].

Knowing that to manage complexity it is important to decompose the problem, so different aspects can be addressed individually, as well as to decompose system models into models of subsystems, it is clear that we also need mechanisms to compose models, including those written in different heterogeneous languages.

Forms of Model Composition Although there is work on model composition, coming up with a complete classification of forms of model composition is challenging, because the form of composition very often depends on the form of the models and the aspects they describe. For example:

- Class diagrams can be merged (see, e.g., [Obj17, DDZ08]).
- State machines can be composed using the cross product for synchronous communication, but there are also other forms of composition when allowing asynchronous communication or feedback (see, e.g., [LV03, Chapter 4]).

For software code written in typical programming languages (e.g., Java or C), composition of different code components is typically not performed at the source-code level. Instead, composition is normally delayed to the binding stage. For example, in virtual machines this only happens when loading the compiled code. Composition is conceptually clearly understood on the source-code level, but modularity allows to defer the actual composition to a very late stage, which supports agility of development. In contrast, state machines have composition techniques that are applied directly on the state machine models. This is true for many other modelling languages, too.

It is important that analysis techniques are designed to be as modular as possible. They can then be applied to certain model subsets, for example, the models of a subsystem, independently of other subsystems. This will lead to more efficient analysis execution, delivering results more quickly, potentially even immediate feedback during editing, and to a better reuse of the analysis results when composing the overall system (see also Chap. 7 of this book [Hei+21]). However, some analyses cannot be modularised. These analyses need a holistic view of the overall system model and an understanding of how the system will be used in its context, which therefore also needs to be explicitly modelled.

Forms of Language Composition Composition of models within a given language is already a challenge, but has been addressed at least in formal methods and also by a variety of tools. Composition of models expressed in different languages is equally important, in particular in the context of holistic analysis techniques.

When composing models expressed using different languages, some consistency checks are necessary. One needs to ensure that symbols defined in one language, for example, classes in class diagrams, are consistently used in the other languages, for example, in object diagrams or performance models. These checks can in many cases be executed automatically.

Composition of models may be interpreted as the integration of models into one single uniform model, but it may also mean that models of subsystems or concerns are somehow coordinated. For example, state machines that describe the behaviour of individual components of a component diagram may be connected through component diagram channels [SGW94] in various ways, and their composition is of course dependent on the component diagram structure.

An alternative to coordinating models in different languages is to compose the languages and then compose models within the resulting language. Given that metamodels are class diagrams, we have several alternatives for language composition:

- We can use merging algorithms for class diagrams to get an integrated meta-model. This, however, involves a lot of design choices, especially when the language concepts that should be the same are technically realised in different forms in the different metamodels. See, e.g., [Cla11], and works on Concepts, Templates and Mixin Layers by de Lara and Guerra [LG10], Melange [WTZ10], model amalgamation [Dur14, Dur+17] or the GTS Morpher in Chap. 9 of this book [Hei+21].
- We can define mappings between metamodels that would allow to translate the complete model of one language or at least certain parts of one model into a model of the other language. This approach is more decentralised, because it does not need a one-fits-all integrated metamodel. However, it leads to redundancy on the model level, which in turn leads to issues when evolving models. Changes in the different models need to be synchronised. See, e.g., [Hu+11, GS18, Hid+16] for an overview on bidirectional model transformations.
- We can define consistency relations between the metamodels. These relations can, however, only be used to check consistency, but are not helpful in constructive adaptations.

These forms of composition may also be mixed in different ways. And of course, we may have cases in which neither the metamodels nor the models are integrated at all. In these cases, the execution of the models may still be synchronised both in time and events and potentially also in shared data. Chapter 9 of this book [Hei+21] describes a form of metamodel composition that includes a composition of the semantics.

2.1.8 Model Transformations and Transformation Models

In order to explicitly capture relations between models, we need to establish a *transformation model* [Béz+06], which, in turn, obeys its own *transformation language*, often specified in form of a *transformation metamodel*.

Transformation metamodels typically connect a source and a target language (metamodel) through explicit constructs for expressing relations (e.g., QVT-Relational [OMG16]) or algorithmic translations (e.g., QVT-Operational [OMG16] or ATL [Jou+08]). A transformation model specifies a set of *model transformations*, one for each acceptable combination of input models. It is, therefore, sometimes referred to as a *model transformation specification*.

Relational transformation models can potentially specify model transformations in different directions, including transformations used to bi-directionally synchro-nise different models [Hu+11, GS18, Hid+16]. Algorithmic transformation models typically fix a particular transformation direction.

Many transformation languages come with dedicated engines for efficiently "ex-ecuting" a given transformation model; that is, for instantiating the corresponding model transformation for a given set of input models.

Model transformations have been used in many different areas, including model translation, model composition, refinement, etc. Surveys [CH06, REP12, Men13] provide classifications of model transformation approaches and languages, showing the features of the most prominent ones. More recently, in [Kah+19], Kahani et al. provide a detailed overview of the state of the art in model transformation techniques and tools by presenting a catalogue of 60 metamodel-based transformation tools, which are categorised in accordance with several attributes.

The correctness of model transformations is key for MDE. Their correctness is even more important if model transformations are used to compose models and interoperate analysis tools, since the validity of such analysis rely not only on the analyses or analysis tools themselves but also on the translations to which models and analysis results are subjected. [CS12] and [Amr+15] present exhaustive reviews of the literature on the verification of model transformations analysing the types of transformations, on the properties that the different existing techniques verify, and the verification techniques that have been applied to validate such properties. [RW15] also surveys research on model transformation verification by classifying existing approaches based on the techniques used (testing, theorem proving, model checking, etc.), level of formality, transformation language used, and properties verified.

Related to the verification of model transformations, we have testing and static analysis of such transformations. For example, surveys such as [Mus+09, Bau+10, SCD12] present views on the state of the art in the area of model transformation testing. Sánchez Cuadrado, Guerra, and de Lara make an interesting proposal in [CGL17] for the static analysis of model transformations. They present a method for the static analysis of ATL model transformations (also discussed in Chap. 12 in this book [Hei+21]). Their goal is to discover typing and rule errors using static analysis and type inference.

Formally and systematically defining the semantics of transformation languages is important to ensure consistent and predictable execution of transformations. Different approaches have been taken for defining the semantics of model trans-formations. For example, in [TV10, TV11], Troya and Vallecillo give a formal semantics of the ATL 3.0 model transformation language [Jou+08] using rewriting logic and Maude. [RN08] translates model transformation definitions in the QVT (Query/View/Transformation) [OMG16] language to a graph production system, thus providing a graph transformation-based semantics to it. Guerra and de Lara propose in [GL12] a formal, algebraic semantics for QVT-Relations check-only transformations, defining a notion of satisfaction of QVT-Relations specifications by models. In [CS13], Calegari and Szasz present a formal semantics for the meta-object facility (MOF) and QVT-Relations languages based on the Theory of Institutions. With this approach, the semantics given reflects the conformance relation between models and metamodels, and the satisfaction of transformation rules between pairs of models. Indeed, the theory facilitates the definition of semantic-preserving translations between the given institutions and other logics which will be used for verification.

2.2   Analysis and Analysis Composition

The essence of analysis is to answer questions about properties of interest of a system under study. However, an analysis generally does not reason directly about such a system, but instead about a model of the system. An analysis that reasons about a model of a system under study is called a *model-based analysis* in this book. To allow a model to be used to answer questions about the system it represents, the properties of the model need to adequately reflect those of the system under study. Models can be used to represent the structure of a system (i.e., its parts and how they are connected), the behaviour of a system (i.e., what it actually does when it is executed), the interaction of the system with its context (i.e., other systems, the physical environment, or humans), quality aspects of the system (e.g., performance, code complexity, or energy consumption), or a combination of these. Similarly, properties can target structure (e.g., to reason about connectivity or potential flow of information), behaviour (e.g., to reason about the correctness of what the system does, or how it interacts with other components or its environment), or quality aspects (to determine if the system guarantees a desired quality).

From a semantically and precisely defined relation between models and properties, we need to derive practical algorithmic analysis techniques, that effectively compute the answer to a query on the composition of a system model and its context. We define an analysis as the following judgement:

$$M, C \vdash_T Q \rightsquigarrow A$$

stating that the query Q on a system model M in the context C leads to the answer A using the technique T. The *satisfaction relation*, often denoted by $M, C \models Q$ is an instance of such entailment where $A = \text{true}$. From the literature, we know a number of such precisely defined satisfaction relations, such as

(a) Logical implication for various forms of logic [Tom99],
(b) Refinement and various forms of (bi)-simulation relations [Mil89],

(c) Satisfaction of temporal logic formulas by automata [CES83], and
(d) consistency checks for object structures with respect to given data structure definitions (e.g., class diagrams) [RG00].

Analysis techniques can be categorised along different dimensions, including automation degree, time, result type, purpose, quality, and composition of analysis, that we will discuss in the following.

2.2.1 Automation Degree

The first dimension for categorising analysis techniques is the degree by which they can be automated by tools. An analysis can be carried out fully automatically by a tool, semi-automatically (i.e., interactively or tool-assisted), or manually, depending on the kind and complexity of the analysis problem. The reason for its level of automation is diverse. While some analyses can be performed in a fully automatic way, others are computationally expensive or undecidable, which makes them less amenable to full automation. Software that partially or fully automates an analysis is called *analysis tool* in this book. There are multiple alternatives for analysis automation, including:

- Typically, analysis such as type checking and well-formedness checking can be carried out fully automatically.
- In the formal methods community, there are several techniques and their supporting tools such as model checking [CES83, KNP11, Ben+95], symbolic execution [Kin76, How77], automated theorem proving (e.g., Hoare logic-based verifiers [Hoa69]), and satisfiability modulo theories and solvers [Bar+09] to analyse a system automatically.
- In some cases, we may perform analysis on specific aspects of systems. For example, at the programming level, data-flow and control-flow analyses are techniques that allow the user to perform checks on the dynamic aspects of our programs, checking, for example, whether a storage location has been initialised before it is being used, or whether a program leaks information.
- Simulation is another example of automated analysis. Simulation typically works with specific scenarios and supports detailed analysis of functional and non-functional (e.g., performance) aspects of a system's behaviour.
- While the satisfaction of many properties can, in principle, be checked automatically, this is not always possible efficiently, for example, when using backtracking-based exponential algorithms. Model checking of large models is a prominent example. Large models cannot be model-checked automatically due to the state explosion problem [Cla+11]. As a result, analysis algorithms sometimes stop with an undetermined result. In some cases, a combination of various techniques might be used to perform the analysis, such as abstract interpretation, refinement checking, and modular or incremental analysis. Another alternative is to provide a partial analysis result. For example, *bounded model checking*

explores the system's state space up to a specific depth, and provides a valid result only up to that depth.

- It may be that the analysis judgement cannot be automatically established, but needs help from the developers/designers. For example, in program verification, analysis users provide explicit hints and assertions, such as loop invariants, to support the analysis. In general, verification systems based on theorem proving—for example, Isabelle [NPW02] or PVS [OS08]—fall into that category where the tool can often provide semi-automatic proof assistance, but active proving effort is needed. Another common example are verification tools driven by developer-provided annotations, written using notations such as the *Java Modeling Language* (JML) [Bur+03] or Spec# [BLS05].
- Finally, there are informal but systematic methodological techniques. In this case, explicit reviews of models according to the defined properties are carried out— for example, certification processes in which the properties are met if all the reviewing criteria are determined to hold. Of course, certifiers may be assisted by all kinds of analysis tools to do this.

2.2.2 Design Time vs. Runtime Analyses

The time at which the analysis takes place is another dimension to categorise analysis techniques. In this dimension we consider *design-time*, *runtime*, or *hybrid* analysis techniques.

Design-time analysis techniques deal with analysing models of the system at design and compile time. Such analyses can be done either at the program level or using an abstract model of the system for analysis. Design-time analysis is helpful to identify violations before they occur, and can help to find design problems early, when they are easier or less expensive to fix. However, in some cases, analyses must be postponed to runtime. This is due to (i) the nature of the analysis, e.g., in case of undecidable satisfaction relations or the state explosion problem in model checking, or (ii) the lack of detailed information at design time, as a design-time model often describes the system at an abstract level. Although analysis can be done ad hoc, design-time analysis is often done using more formal, semantics-based techniques. This includes the semantics techniques already mentioned above, as well as others, such as abstract interpretation [CC77] or matching logic [RES10]. Model-based software development is an example where various model transformation and analysis techniques are employed to design and analyse a software system [Voe+13, Kus+17].

A *runtime analysis* is based on a notion of *execution* of the model or system. To this end, execution traces or similar elements are included in the semantic domain of the modelling formalism, which may be augmented with information needed for the analysis (e.g., security properties in a security analysis). At runtime, the desired properties can be checked against individual system executions, against an abstract model of the system, which is maintained and updated at runtime to reflect the changing behaviour of an adaptive system (called models@runtime) [BGS19], or against the events that occurred during execution. Runtime verification [LS09] is an example of runtime analysis where an execution of the system is analysed— for example, to check simple assertions, temporal logic formulas, automaton-based properties, etc. Testing is another example of dynamic analysis [Bin00].

In a *hybrid* approach, the results of design-time analysis are used to generate a monitor that runs along with the system, observes its behaviour, analyses it, and possibly dynamically adapts itself (see, e.g., [GS02, Ald+19, KS18]).

2.2.3   Quantitative vs. Qualitative Analyses

As a third dimension, we may categorise analysis techniques according to whether the answer to the query is binary (true or false), or quantifiable. Queries about whether a given predicate holds of a system under study are the main example of qualitative analysis. The predicate can concern a specific scenario, or it can concern "all" executions in some class of contexts. A simple example is analysis of the function computed, such as the *isSorted* property of the list returned. Another example is an analysis to check that a system rejects illegal input (that is formally specified). Checking that specified state invariants hold is another example.

While many types of analyses can be formulated as satisfaction relations that are binary, in practice there are also a lot of queries that deal with quantifiable properties. For example, the quality of service needs to be measured by the up-time of the system, by behaviour under load, or by meantime of delay for transport of data, video and speech. Properties are then often defined using probabilities, intervals, or numbers (representing measurements).

Quantifiable properties usually lead to analysis techniques that also produce quantified results, that can be thought of as a degree of satisfaction. This opens the possibility for different system models to be compared by *how well* they satisfy a certain property, enabling an optimisation-based approach to software design, such as is explored in the field of search-based software engineering [HMZ12] or, in the modelling context, search-based model-driven engineering [BSA17, Joh+19].

Often, the quantities are expressed in the property, using, for example, interval ranges for some quantity or bounds on probabilities, while the checking itself is binary. For example, timing can be modelled using formalisms including timed automata [AD94], or timed transition rules [ÖM07], with properties expressed with timed temporal logics that are checked by model checkers such as UP-PAAL [BDL04] or Maude [Cla+07]. To model properties about performance, or check the probability of events occurring or conditions holding, probabilistic models can be used. Properties of such models can be expressed in probabilistic variants of temporal logics and checked by stochastic model checkers such as Prism [KNP11]. Precision of analysis can be traded for scalability by using statistical model checking using tools such as PVeStA [AM11]. Statistical methods rely on sampling the execution space, for example, using simulators. Simulation is a technique for quantifying satisfaction executing the system model on exemplary input data and simulated interaction with the system's context. The analysis collects aggregated data about the overall system behaviour in the form of traces, which are then used to quantify satisfaction.

2.2.4 Purpose of Analysis

A further dimension for categorising analysis techniques is their *purpose*. Seeing "analysis" as answering queries about systems under study, we identify the following possibilities:

Structural analysis is concerned with analysing the system at the structural level. A *structural model* describes the elements of the system and their relationships, e.g., a call graph describes the methods of a program and their invocation relationships, or a component model (e.g., BIP [BBS06]) allows us to express the architecture of a system as a set of modules and their interactions. From such models, dependency relations can be derived. Coordination models often work at the level of components, organising the interactions. The underlying graph structure may give useful insights, for example, identifying hubs or components that mediate interactions. Graph rewriting and transformation systems [Roz97] is a class of techniques often used to analyse the systems structure.

Behavioural analysis is concerned with properties of system executions. A *behavioural model* allows analysing a system's runtime behaviour—its interactions and results—by reasoning about properties of the model's semantics. For example, "does the light go on when the door opens?"; "does the data store correctly save and retrieve data?"; or "does a warehouse robot pick the correct packages?" The analyst may only be interested in behaviour in a specific set of conditions, such as a particular set of data, or a particular region of the warehouse. These restrictions can be expressed as a context model to compose with the system model, or simply specified in a configuration file. The first question above might be analysed, e.g., using a dynamic dependency analysis of sensor and actuator events. The second question might be treated as a verification problem: The analyst would develop a formal model of the data store, express the properties as formulas, and use a model checker or theorem prover to show that the model satisfies the corresponding formulas. For answering the third question, the analyst might choose testing, providing a variety of tasks to test the robots capability.

Quality analysis is concerned with assurance of quality properties of a system (often also called non- or extra-functional properties, as for example defined in the ISO/IEC 25010 [25011] standard). Quality properties include performance, reliability, or availability. Similar to testing, the analysis of such quality properties depends on the expected usage of the system. For example, in the analysis of security aspects, attack models describe the "usage" of the system by an attacker. Safety analysis requires a definition of states deemed unsafe and conditions that could lead to safety violations if the system is not properly designed and implemented. Effects of a successful security attack could lead to unsafe conditions, unavailability, or other quality failures. Thus, combining analysis of, e.g., security with other quality properties is important.

In addition, information about the execution environment is needed to interpret executions regarding the quality property under analysis. Examples are the speed of hardware resources in case of performance, or the security guarantees provided in case of security analysis. In principle, such models of the execution environment could be seen a part of specific semantic models for quality analyses. However, as they describe environmental factors, not being part of the system being built, and as their change does not change the system (but the analysis results), we consider these environment models also as context [Zsc09].

Structural/behavioural co-analysis   The system's structure and behaviour can affect each other, e.g., if component interaction is constrained by the system structure, this will affect component's internal executions and, consequently, the whole system's execution. While structural analyses may operate only on syntactical elements and behavioural analyses concern system executions, co-analyses of structure and behaviour consider both aspects. HPobSAM [KKS19] is a model to co-specify the system's behaviour and structure using graph transition systems. Chapter 9 of this book [Hei+21] presents a tool for the composition of DSMLs defined with both structure and behaviour (defined with graph transformation rules). Other formalisms, e.g., graph grammars [Roz97] and rewriting logic [Mes92, Mes12], can also nicely express both structure and behaviour.

Table 2.1 summarises, for each kind of analysis, which kind of models are required. Table 2.2 shows, for different analysis types, the information to be provided by context models.

2.2.5   Correction and Counterexamples

Knowing that a satisfaction relation has not been met, or that the degree of satisfaction is not high enough, is only half of the solution. We also need to understand how to improve the model and the implemented system in such a way that the desired properties are met. Again, we can see different categories of assistance here:

Table 2.1 Kinds of analyses and their required model kinds

	Syntax	Semantics	Context
Structural	x		
Behavioural	x	x	(x)
Quality	x	x	x

Table 2.2 Examples of different analyses and their required context models

Analysis	Kind	Required information in context models
Simple dependency analysis (e.g., static component dependencies)	structural	–
Advanced dependency analysis (e.g., slicing, points-to)	Behavioural	start item for analysis
Verification	Behavioural	Fixation of parameters in semantic specification, e.g., platform-specific scheduling policies
Testing	Behavioural	execution environment, test case specification
Performance, reliability	Quality	Usage profile, deployment and resource descriptions, description of external service quality
Safety	Quality	Definition of set of safe/unsafe states
Security	Quality	Attacker model, model of platform security
Maintainability	Quality	Change propagation rules, seed modification

- The analysis technique tells us that the satisfaction relation is not met, but gives no hint beyond that.
- If the satisfaction relation is not met, we at least get hints where the problem is located. This may be, for example, specific elements in the model which contributed to the problem, or the places where certain desired invariants have not been met the first time. Another example is counterexample generation by model checkers [HKB09], where when a property is not satisfied, a counterexample is usually generated and provided to the user that can help identify the reason of violation. A counterexample is usually an execution trace that violates the property.
- As a result of the analysis, we not only get the location where the problem arises, but also a list of suggestions, what can be done to correct the problem. This is typically the case in an integrated development environment (IDE) that checks context conditions already while source code is being edited, and suggests a list of possible corrections on the fly. This, however, is more effective if the problem can be relatively easily localised. There is a lot of experience on what the typical error sources are in many different cases: wrong type chosen for a variable in a program; unsatisfiable trigger condition of a transition in an automaton; or not enough redundancy on the available compute nodes in a performance model.
- The last category of analysis techniques not only identifies flaws, but also automatically corrects them. *Automatic program repair* techniques (see [GMM19] for a survey) fit in this category, where several techniques are used, e.g., a generate-validate-test approach to generate a fix that will be tested before being accepted (e.g., GenProg [Gou+12]), or a semantics-driven approach where formal approaches are used to synthesise a patch (e.g., Angelix [MYR16]).

See Chap. 7 of this book [Hei+21] for an in-depth discussion of how analysis results can be used.

2.2.6 Quality of Analyses

Two important concepts related to the quality of an analysis are *soundness* and *completeness*. Recall that analysis was earlier defined as the judgement $M, C \vdash_T Q \rightsquigarrow A$, where analysis technique T is used to answer query Q over the model M in context C. Here, we focus just on those cases where the answer A is either *true* or *false*. Thus, the analysis is answering the question whether the property Q holds of M in context C. To determine the soundness or completeness of T, a "ground truth" is needed. One form of ground truth is a semantics of both models and properties. Thus we assume a mapping $[[M]]_C$ giving the meaning of M in context C as an element of a semantic domain D, and a mapping $[|\ Q\ |]$ of properties to subsets of D.

T is *sound* if T derives *true* as the answer to Q only when Q is *actually true* of M in context C. That is, $[[M]]_C \in [|\ Q\ |]$. An analysis technique T that incorrectly derives *true* in this case—that is, that says that the answer to Q is *true* when it is actually *false*—is *unsound*. To ensure soundness, T will answer *false* in cases where T cannot prove *true*. Another option is for T to only answer *false* when Q is definitely *false* for M in C. Such an analysis is said to be *complete*. For instance, if T is an analysis technique that checks for deadlocks, M is a model of a concurrent system, and Q is the property "M is deadlock-free in context C", a sound version of T will not answer *true* when it cannot prove that M is deadlock-free in context C, meaning it may potentially answer *false* in some cases where M actually is deadlock-free. A complete version of T will not answer *false* when M is deadlock-free in context C, but may potentially answer *true* when M is not deadlock-free (i.e., when it may deadlock). For some properties, it may be difficult or even impossible to fully establish ground truth. Measuring reliability or performance are examples. How does one know if a real system satisfies 99.9% up-time, or if the system responds within 1 s with probability 0.95?

Most analysis techniques T cannot be both sound and complete, due to the undecidability of the problem, or its complexity. Because of this, the *precision* and *recall* of T are also both important. Precision measures how often T derives *true* correctly, in comparison to how often it derives *true* overall. For instance, a precision of 0.75 would indicate that, in 3 out of 4 cases, T answers *true* for query Q when Q is actually true, while in 1 out of 4 cases it incorrectly answers *true* when the proper answer is *false*. A sound analysis will have a precision of 1.0 since it never incorrectly answers *true*. Recall instead measures how often T answers *true* when it could, correctly, answer *true*. For instance, a recall of 0.6 means that, given M and C where Q is *true*, T correctly answers *true* 60% of the time and otherwise answers *false*. A complete analysis has a recall of 1.0. Since computation of both precision and recall require knowledge of the correct answers to Q across the input M and

C, these values would generally be computed as a benchmark across an existing collection of known inputs as a way to test the quality of the analysis.

Note that, along with what has been discussed above, an analysis also needs to satisfy some more basic requirements. For instance, the results of running an analysis should be both repeatable and reproducible. By *repeatable*, we mean that an analysis set up under identical conditions will yield the same results. By *reproducible*, we mean that, given the proper instructions, an analysis set up and conducted by different operators on the same models or systems of interest will yield the same results.

2.2.7 Analysis Composition

It is not always possible to answer a query using a single model or a single property or one analysis technique. There are various reasons for this, such as

(i) The high computational complexity of an analysis technique to handle large and complex models and queries, e.g., model checking of large models is still a major issue due to the state explosion problem,

(ii) The lack of expressiveness of the modelling or property language to express any model or query, for instance a temporal property cannot be expressed using propositional logic, or

(iii) Infeasibility of designing techniques (both, modelling and analysis techniques) to answer all queries, as each technique can be used to answer a specific class of queries.

Different modelling and analysis techniques can be composed to answer a query properly. For instance, to ensure that a large-scale system is trustworthy, several aspects of security and safety should be checked and analysed, where each aspect itself needs different techniques to be analysed, possibly at different levels of abstraction, at different stages of the system life-cycle, with various classes of properties, etc. Security consists of three main aspects, namely confidentiality, integrity, and availability. Confidentiality can concern confidentiality of communications, computations, or storage, and different methods can be used to specify, enforce, and ensure each case. For example, encryption can be used to ensure confidentiality of data during communication while information flow control mechanisms can be used to ensure that computations will not leak information.

We may formulate analysis composition in terms of the following general rule using the judgement introduced earlier in this section:

$$\frac{M_1, C_1 \vdash_{T_1} Q_1 \rightsquigarrow A_1 \qquad M_2, C_2 \vdash_{T_2} Q_2 \rightsquigarrow A_2 \qquad \psi}{M, C \vdash_T Q \rightsquigarrow A}$$

where $M = M_1 ||_m M_2$ is the composition of models using the composition operator $||_m$, $C = C_1 ||_c C_2$ is the result of composing the contexts using the operator $||_c$, T is the composed analysis technique, $Q = Q_1 ||_Q Q_2$ is the new query as the result of composing Q_1 and Q_2, and A is the final answer result of the composition of partial answers A_1 and A_2. This rule informally states that if the query Q_i on the model M_i with the context C_i using the analysis technique T_i leads to the answer $A_i, i \in \{1, 2\}$, the query Q using a combination of techniques T_1 and T_2 under the condition ψ will lead to the answer A on the composed model M in the composed context C. The side-condition ψ specifies the conditions under which this composition can be performed, as it is not always possible to arbitrarily compose analyses.

Establishing the composed judgement using this rule can be done in a mathematically sound way, or informally based on some heuristics or expert knowledge. This depends on several factors, such as the existence of a formal definition of the semantics of the prerequisite judgements, the existence of a suitable algorithm or procedure to divide the problem into smaller problems in a sound way (i.e., basic judgements by decomposing the model, context, and query), etc. As an example, the query "Is this system secure?" can be decomposed into three subqueries, each query stating that the system is secure in terms of confidentiality, integrity, and availability. Similarly, these subqueries can be decomposed further into simpler properties, each of which is possibly analysed using a different technique. This means that basic judgements might be established using different methods, such as verification, performance modelling, model-based testing, simulation, penetration testing, etc. The models or properties of the composed judgements could be specified using a multi-view modelling language or an ordinary single-view language.

We proceed by instantiating this general rule with two classic examples: the assume-guarantee verification [AL95] and Hoare logic. In the case of assume-guarantee verification of concurrent systems/programs, let $M, S \models G$ state that a system with the model M will guarantee the relation G (guarantee), if it runs in an environment ensuring the relation S (assumption) on the states. The model is usually specified using a state transition system and the relation is a predicate that specifies some conditions on the transitions (i.e., a pair of states). A simple assume-guarantee verification rule looks like the following:

$$\frac{M_1, S \cup G_2 \models G_1 \qquad M_2, S \cup G_1 \models G_2 \qquad \psi}{M_1 || M_2, S \models G_1 \cup G_2}.$$

The rule informally states that if a module M_i runs in an environment $S \cup G_j$ and guarantees $G_i, i, j \in \{1, 2\}, i \neq j$, then, if the two modules run concurrently in the environment S, they will together guarantee $G_1 \cup G_2$. The notation $\cup$ is used to show the union of two relations. This entailment relation $M, S \models G$ can be expressed as $M, S \vdash_V G \rightsquigarrow \mathsf{True}$ using our above judgement. The model composition operator $||_m$ is a formal well-defined parallel composition operator that computes the product of the two models. The context composition operator returns the intersection of two relations. Such assume-guarantee judgements should be used with caution as they have subtle conditions for validity [AL93].

As the second instantiation, let $\{p\}c\{q\}$ be a Hoare logic's judgement for sequential programs that informally states that if a program c starts in a state that satisfies the precondition p, if it terminates, the final state will satisfy the post-condition q. The rule for sequential composition of two programs is specified using the following rule:

$$\frac{\{p\}c_1\{q\} \qquad \{q\}c_2\{r\}}{\{p\}c_1; c_2\{r\}}.$$

The judgement $\{p\}c\{q\}$, in terms of our judgement, is specified as $c, p \vdash_V q \rightsquigarrow$ True, where the model is the program semantics usually described using a state transition system, the context is the precondition p, the query is the satisfaction of q on termination, and the composition operator of models is the ordinary sequential composition ";". The composition operator on the contexts returns the context of the first judgement.

References

[25011] ISO/IEC 25010. *ISO/IEC 25010:2011, Systems and software engineering—Systems and software Quality Requirements and Evaluation (SQuaRE)—System and software quality models*. 2011.

[AD94] Rajeev Alur and David L. Dill. "A Theory of Timed Automata". In: *Theor. Comput. Sci.* 126.2 (1994), pp. 183–235. https://doi.org/10.1016/0304-3975(94)90010-8.

[AL93] Martin Abadi and Leslie Lamport. "Composing Specifications". In: *ACM Transactions on Programming Languages and Systems* 15.1 (1993).

[AL95] Martin Abadi and Leslie Lamport. "Conjoining Specifications". In: *ACM Trans. Program. Lang. Syst.* 17.3 (1995), pp. 507–534. https://doi.org/10.1145/203095.201069.

[Ald+19] Jonathan Aldrich, David Garlan, Christian Kästner, Claire Le Goues, Anahita Mohseni-Kabir, Ivan Ruchkin, Selva Samuel, Bradley R. Schmerl, Christopher Steven Timperley, Manuela Veloso, Ian Voysey, Joydeep Biswas, Arjun Guha, Jarrett Holtz, Javier Cámara, and Pooyan Jamshidi. "Model-Based Adaptation for Robotics Software". In: *IEEE Softw.* 36.2 (2019), pp. 83–90. https://doi.org/10.1109/MS.2018.2885058.

[AM11] Musab AlTurki and José Meseguer. "PVeStA: A Parallel Statistical Model Checking and Quantitative Analysis Tool". In: *4th International Conference on Algebra and Coalgebra in Computer Science, CALCO*. Vol. 6859. 2011, pp. 386–392. https://doi.org/10.1007/978-3-642-22944-2_28.

[Amr+15] Moussa Amrani, Benoît Combemale, Levi Lucio, Gehan M. K. Selim, Jürgen Dingel, Yves Le Traon, Hans Vangheluwe, and James R. Cordy. "Formal Verification Techniques for Model Transformations: A Tridimensional Classification". In: *J. Object Technol.* 14.3 (2015), 1:1–43. https://doi.org/10.5381/jot.2015.14.3.a1.

[Bar+09] Clark W. Barrett, Roberto Sebastiani, Sanjit A. Seshia, and Cesare Tinelli. "Satisfiability Modulo Theories". In: *Handbook of Satisfiability*. Vol. 185. 2009, pp. 825–885. https://doi.org/10.3233/978-1-58603-929-5-825.

[Bau+10] Benoit Baudry, Sudipto Ghosh, Franck Fleurey, Robert B. France, Yves Le Traon, and Jean-Marie Mottu. "Barriers to systematic model transformation testing". In: *Commun. ACM* 53.6 (2010), pp. 139–143. https://doi.org/10.1145/1743546.1743583.

[BBS06] Ananda Basu, Marius Bozga, and Joseph Sifakis. "Modeling Heterogeneous Realtime Components in BIP". In: *Fourth IEEE International Conference on Software Engineering and Formal Methods, SEFM*. 2006, pp. 3–12. https://doi.org/10.1109/SEFM.2006.27.

[BDL04] Gerd Behrmann, Alexandre David, and Kim G. Larsen. "A Tutorial on Uppaal". In: *4th International School on Formal Methods for the Design of Computer, Communication, and Software Systems*. 3185. Sept. 2004, pp. 200–236.

[Ben+95] Johan Bengtsson, Kim G. Larsen, Fredrik Larsson, Paul Pettersson, and Wang Yi. "UPPAAL—a Tool Suite for Automatic Verification of Real–Time Systems". In: *Workshop on Verification and Control of Hybrid Systems III*. 1066. 1995, pp. 232–243.

[Béz+06] Jean Bézivin, Fabian Büttner, Martin Gogolla, Frédéric Jouault, Ivan Kurtev, and Arne Lindow. "Model transformations? transformation models!" In: *International Conference on Model Driven Engineering Languages and Systems*. 2006, pp. 440–453.

[BGS19] Nelly Bencomo, Sebastian Götz, and Hui Song. "Models@run.time: a guided tour of the state of the art and research challenges". In: *Software & Systems Modeling* 18.5 (2019), pp. 3049–3082. https://doi.org/10.1007/s10270-018-00712-x.

[Bib+20] Pascal Bibow, Manuela Dalibor, Christian Hopmann, Ben Mainz, Bernhard Rumpe, David Schmalzing, Mauritius Schmitz, and Andreas Wortmann. "Model-Driven Development of a Digital Twin for Injection Molding". In: *Advanced Information Systems Engineering*. 2020, pp. 85–100.

[Bin00] Robert V. Binder. *Testing Object-Oriented Systems - Models, Patterns, and Tools*. Addison-Wesley, 2000.

[BLS05] Mike Barnett, K. Rustan M. Leino, and Wolfram Schulte. "The Spec# Programming System: An Overview". In: *International Workshop on the Construction and Analysis of Safe, Secure, and Interoperable Smart Devices, CASSIS*. Vol. 3362. 2005, pp. 49–69.

[BRJ98] Grady Booch, James Rumbaugh, and Ivar Jacobson. *The Unified Modeling Language User Guide*. Addison-Wesley, 1998.

[Bru+15] Jean-Michel Bruel, Benoit Combemale, Ileana Ober, and Hélène Raynal. "MDE in Practice for Computational Science". In: *Procedia Computer Science* 51 (2015). International Conference On Computational Science, ICCS, pp. 660–669. https://doi.org/10.1016/j.procs.2015.05.182.

[BS01] Manfred Broy and Ketil Stølen. *Specification and Development of Interactive Systems. Focus on Streams, Interfaces and Refinement*. Springer, 2001.

[BSA17] Ilhem Boussaïd, Patrick Siarry, and Mohamed Ahmed-Nacer. "A survey on search-based model-driven engineering". In: *Automated Software Engineering* 24.2 (2017), pp. 233–294. https://doi.org/10.1007/s10515-017-0215-4.

[Bur+03] Lilian Burdy, Yoonsik Cheon, David R. Cok, Michael D. Ernst, Joseph Kiniry, Gary T. Leavens, K. Rustan M. Leino, and Erik Poll. "An overview of JML tools and applications". In: *8th International Workshop on Formal Methods for Industrial Critical Systems, FMICS*. Vol. 80. 2003, pp. 75–91. https://doi.org/10.1016/S1571-0661(04)80810-7.

[CC77] Patrick Cousot and Radhia Cousot. "Abstract Interpretation: A Unified Lattice Model for Static Analysis of Programs by Construction or Approximation of Fixpoints". In: *4th ACM Symposium on Principles of Programming Languages, POPL*. 1977, pp. 238–252. https://doi.org/10.1145/512950.512973.

[CES83] Edmund M. Clarke, E. Allen Emerson, and Aravinda Prasad Sistla. "Automatic Verification of Finite State Concurrent Systems Using Temporal Logic Specifications: A Practical Approach". In: *Tenth Annual ACM Symposium on Principles of Programming Languages*. 1983, pp. 117–126. https://doi.org/10.1145/567067.567080.

[CGL17] Jesús Sánchez Cuadrado, Esther Guerra, and Juan de Lara. "Static Analysis of Model Transformations". In: *IEEE Trans. Software Eng.* 43.9 (2017), pp. 868–897. https://doi.org/10.1109/TSE.2016.2635137.

[CH06] Krzysztof Czarnecki and Simon Helsen. "Feature-based survey of model transformation approaches". In: *IBM Syst. J.* 45.3 (2006), pp. 621–646. https://doi.org/10.1147/sj.453.0621.

[Cla+07] Manuel Clavel, Francisco Durán, Steven Eker, Patrick Lincoln, Narciso Martí-Oliet, José Meseguer, and Carolyn L. Talcott. *All About Maude - A High-Performance Logical Framework, How to Specify, Program and Verify Systems in Rewriting Logic*. Vol. 4350. Springer, 2007. https://doi.org/10.1007/978-3-540-71999-1.

[Cla+11] Edmund M. Clarke, William Klieber, Milos Novácek, and Paolo Zuliani. "Model Checking and the State Explosion Problem". In: *International Summer School on Tools for Practical Software Verification, LASER*. Vol. 7682. 2011, pp. 1–30. https://doi.org/10.1007/978-3-642-35746-6_1.

[Cla11] Mickael Clavreul. "Model and Metamodel Composition: Separation of Mapping and Interpretation for Unifying Existing Model Composition Techniques". PhD thesis. University of Rennes 1, France, 2011. https://tel.archives-ouvertes.fr/tel-00646893.

[Com+16] Benoit Combemale, Robert France, Jean-Marc Jézéquel, Bernhard Rumpe, Jim R.H. Steel, and Didier Vojtisek. *Engineering Modeling Languages*. Chapman and Hall/CRC, 2016, p. 398. http://mdebook.irisa.fr/.

[Com+20] Benoit Combemale, Jörg Kienzle, Gunter Mussbacher, Hyacinth Ali, Daniel Amyot, Mojtaba Bagherzadeh, Edouard Batot, Nelly Bencomo, Benjamin Benni, Jean-Michel Bruel, Jordi Cabot, Betty H C Cheng, Philippe Collet, Gregor Engels, Robert Heinrich, Jean-Marc Jézéquel, Anne Koziolek, Sébastien Mosser, Ralf Reussner, Houari Sahraoui, Rijul Saini, June Sallou, Serge Stinckwich, Eugene Syriani, and Manuel Wimmer. "A Hitchhiker's Guide to Model-Driven Engineering for Data-Centric Systems". In: *IEEE Software* (2020).

[CS12] Daniel Calegari and Nora Szasz. "Verification of Model Transformations: A Survey of the State-of-the-Art". In: *XXXVIII Latin American Computer Conference, CLEI*. Vol. 292. 2012, pp. 5–25. https://doi.org/10.1016/j.entcs.2013.02.002.

[CS13] Daniel Calegari and Nora Szasz. "Institution-Based Semantics for MOF and QVT-Relations". In: *16th Brazilian Symposium on Formal Methods: Foundations and Applications, SBMF*. Vol. 8195. 2013, pp. 34–50. https://doi.org/10.1007/978-3-642-41071-0_4.

[DDZ08] Jürgen Dingel, Zinovy Diskin, and Alanna Zito. "Understanding and improving UML package merge". In: *Softw. Syst. Model.* 7.4 (2008), pp. 443–467. https://doi.org/10.1007/s10270-007-0073-9.

[Dur+17] Francisco Durán, Antonio Moreno-Delgado, Fernando Orejas, and Steffen Zschaler. "Amalgamation of domain specific languages with behaviour". In: *J. Log. Algebraic Methods Program.* 86.1 (2017), pp. 208–235. https://doi.org/10.1016/j.jlamp.2015.09.005.

[Dur14] Francisco Durán. "Composition of Graph-Transformation-Based DSL Definitions by Amalgamation". In: *10th International Workshop on Rewriting Logic and Its Applications, WRLA, Revised Selected Papers*. Vol. 8663. 2014, pp. 1–20. https://doi.org/10.1007/978-3-319-12904-4_1.

[DY83] Danny Dolev and Andrew Chi-Chih Yao. "On the Security of Public Key Protocols". In: *IEEE Transactions on Information Theory* 29.2 (1983), pp. 198–207. https://doi.org/10.1109/TIT.1983.1056650.

[GL12] Esther Guerra and Juan de Lara. "An Algebraic Semantics for QVT-Relations Check-only Transformations". In: *Fundam. Informaticae* 114.1 (2012), pp. 73–101. https://doi.org/10.3233/FI-2011-618.

[GL16] Philip Gerlee and Torbjörn Lundh. *Scientific Models*. Springer, 2016.

[GMM19] Luca Gazzola, Daniela Micucci, and Leonardo Mariani. "Automatic Software Repair: A Survey". In: *IEEE Trans. Software Eng.* 45.1 (2019), pp. 34–67. https://doi.org/10.1109/TSE.2017.2755013.

[Gou+12] Claire Le Goues, ThanhVu Nguyen, Stephanie Forrest, and Westley Weimer. "GenProg: A Generic Method for Automatic Software Repair". In: *IEEE Trans. Software Eng.* 38.1 (2012), pp. 54–72. https://doi.org/10.1109/TSE.2011.104.

[Gra] GrammaTech. *CodeSonar: Static Code Analysis*. https://www.grammatech.com/products/source-code-analysis (visited on 04/24/2021).

[Gro06] Object Management Group. *MOF Specification Version 2.0*. http://www.omg.org/docs/ptc/06-05-04.pdf. Jan. 2006.

[Gro12] Object Management Group. *OMG Systems Modeling Language (OMG SysML), Version 1.3*. 2012. http://www.omg.org/spec/SysML/1.3/

[GS02] David Garlan and Bradley R. Schmerl. "Model-based adaptation for self-healing systems". In: *First Workshop on Self-Healing Systems, WOSS*. 2002, pp. 27–32. https://doi.org/10.1145/582128.582134.

[GS18] *International Summer School on Bidirectional Transformations, Tutorial Lectures*. Vol. 9715. 2018. https://doi.org/10.1007/978-3-319-79108-1.

[Hei+17] Robert Heinrich, Reiner Jung, Christian Zirkelbach, Wilhelm Hasselbring, and Ralf Reussner. "Software Architecture for Big Data and the Cloud". In: 2017. Chap. An Architectural Model-Based Approach to Quality-aware DevOps in Cloud Applications, pp. 69–89.

[Hei+21] Robert Heinrich, Francisco Durán, Carolyn L. Talcott, and Steffen Zschaler (eds.) *Composing Model-Based Analysis Tools*. Springer, 2021. https://doi.org/10.1007/978-3-030-81915-6.

[Hid+16] Soichiro Hidaka, Massimo Tisi, Jordi Cabot, and Zhenjiang Hu. "Feature-based classification of bidirectional transformation approaches". In: *Softw. Syst. Model.* 15.3 (2016), pp. 907–928. https://doi.org/10.1007/s10270-014-0450-0.

[HKB09] Tingting Han, Joost-Pieter Katoen, and Damman Berteun. "Counterexample Generation in Probabilistic Model Checking". In: *IEEE Transactions on Software Engineering* 35.2 (2009), pp. 241–257.

[HMZ12] Mark Harman, S. Afshin Mansouri, and Yuanyuan Zhang. "Search-based software engineering: Trends, techniques and applications". In: *ACM Comput. Surv.* 45.1 (2012), 11:1–11:61. https://doi.org/10.1145/2379776.2379787.

[Hoa69] Charles A. R. Hoare. "An Axiomatic Basis for Computer Programming". In: *Commun. ACM* 12.10 (1969), pp. 576–580. https://doi.org/10.1145/363235.363259.

[How77] William E. Howden. "Symbolic Testing and the DISSECT Symbolic Evaluation System". In: *IEEE Trans. Software Eng.* 3.4 (1977), pp. 266–278. https://doi.org/10.1109/TSE.1977.231144.

[HR04] David Harel and Bernhard Rumpe. "Meaningful modeling: what's the semantics of "semantics"?" In: *Computer* 37.10 (2004), pp. 64–72.

[Hu+11] Zhenjiang Hu, Andy Schürr, Perdita Stevens, and James F. Terwilliger. "Bidirectional Transformation "bx" (Dagstuhl Seminar 11031)". In: *Dagstuhl Reports* 1.1 (2011), pp. 42–67. https://doi.org/10.4230/DagRep.1.1.42.

[Joh+19] Stefan John, Alexandru Burdusel, Robert Bill, Daniel Strüber, Gabriele Taentzer, Steffen Zschaler, and Manuel Wimmer. "Searching for Optimal Models: Comparing Two Encoding Approaches". In: *12th Int'l Conf. on Model Transformations, ICMT*. 2019.

[Jou+08] Frédéric Jouault, Freddy Allilaire, Jean Bézivin, and Ivan Kurtev. "ATL: A model transformation tool". In: *Sci. Comput. Program.* 72.1-2 (2008), pp. 31–39. https://doi.org/10.1016/j.scico.2007.08.002.

[Kah+19] Nafiseh Kahani, Mojtaba Bagherzadeh, James R. Cordy, Juergen Dingel, and Dániel Varró. "Survey and classification of model transformation tools". In: *Software and Systems Modelling* 18.4 (2019), pp. 2361–2397. https://doi.org/10.1007/s10270-018-0665-6.

[Kah87] Gilles Kahn. "Natural Semantics". In: *4th Annual Symposium on Theoretical Aspects of Computer Science, STACS*. Vol. 247. 1987, pp. 22–39.

[Kin76] James C. King. "Symbolic Execution and Program Testing". In: *Commun. ACM* 19.7 (1976), pp. 385–394. https://doi.org/10.1145/360248.360252.

[KKS19] Narges Khakpour, Jetty Kleijn, and Marjan Sirjani. "A Formal Model to Integrate Behavioral and Structural Adaptations in Self-adaptive Systems". In: *8th International Conference on Fundamentals of Software Engineering, FSEN*. Vol. 11761. 2019, pp. 3–19. https://doi.org/10.1007/978-3-030-31517-7_1.

[Kle08] Anneke Kleppe. *Software Language Engineering: Creating Domain-Specific Languages using Metamodels*. Pearson Education, 2008.

[KNP11] Marta Z. Kwiatkowska, Gethin Norman, and David Parker. "PRISM 4.0: Verification of Probabilistic Real-Time Systems". In: *23rd International Conference on Computer Aided Verification, CAV*. Vol. 6806. 2011, pp. 585–591. https://doi.org/10.1007/978-3-642-22110-1_47.

[KS18] Narges Khakpour and Charilaos Skandylas. "Synthesis of a Permissive Security Monitor". In: *23rd European Symposium on Research in Computer Security, ESORICS, Part I*. Vol. 11098. 2018, pp. 48–65. https://doi.org/10.1007/978-3-319-99073-6_3.

[Küh16] Thomas Kühne. "Unifying Explanatory and Constructive Modeling: Towards Removing the Gulf between Ontologies and Conceptual Models". In: *ACM/IEEE 19th International Conference on Model Driven Engineering Languages and Systems*. 2016, pp. 95–102. https://doi.org/10.1145/2976767.2976770.

[Kus+17] Evgeny Kusmenko, Alexander Roth, Bernhard Rumpe, and Michael von Wenckstern. "Modeling Architectures of Cyber-Physical Systems". In: *13th European Conference on Modelling Foundations and Applications, ECMFA*. Vol. 10376. 2017, pp. 34–50. https://doi.org/10.1007/978-3-319-61482-3_3.

[Lee18] Edward A. Lee. "Modeling in Engineering and Science". In: *Commun. ACM* 62.1 (2018), pp. 35–36. https://doi.org/10.1145/3231590.

[LG10] Juan de Lara and Esther Guerra. "Generic Meta-modelling with Concepts, Templates and Mixin Layers". In: *13th International Conference on Model Driven Engineering Languages and Systems, MODELS, Proceedings, Part I*. Vol. 6394. 2010, pp. 16–30. https://doi.org/10.1007/978-3-642-16145-2_2.

[LS09] Martin Leucker and Christian Schallhart. "A brief account of runtime verification". In: *J. Log. Algebraic Methods Program*. 78.5 (2009), pp. 293–303. https://doi.org/10.1016/j.jlap.2008.08.004.

[LV03] Edward A. Lee and Pravin Varaiya. *Structure and interpretation of signals and systems*. Addison-Wesley, 2003.

[Men13] Tom Mens. "Model Transformation: A Survey of the State of the Art". In: *Model-Driven Engineering for Distributed Real-Time Systems*. 2013. Chap. 1, pp. 1–19. https://doi.org/10.1002/9781118558096.ch1.

[Mes12] José Meseguer. "Twenty years of rewriting logic". In: *J. Algebraic and Logic Programming* 81 (2012), pp. 721–781.

[Mes92] José Meseguer. "Conditional Rewriting Logic as a Unified Model of Concurrency". In: *Theoretical Computer Science* 96.1 (1992), pp. 73–155.

[Mil89] Robin Milner. *Communication and concurrency*. Prentice Hall, 1989.

[MR04] José Meseguer and Grigore Rosu. "Rewriting Logic Semantics: From Language Specifications to Formal Analysis Tools". In: *Second International Joint Conference on Automated Reasoning, IJCAR*. Vol. 3097. 2004, pp. 1–44. https://doi.org/10.1007/978-3-540-25984-8_1.

[Mus+09] Mohamed Mussa, Samir Ouchani, Waseem Al Sammane, and Abdelwahab Hamou-Lhadj. "A Survey of Model-Driven Testing Techniques". In: *Ninth International Conference on Quality Software, QSIC*. 2009, pp. 167–172. https://doi.org/10.1109/QSIC.2009.

[MYR16] Sergey Mechtaev, Jooyong Yi, and Abhik Roychoudhury. "Angelix: scalable multiline program patch synthesis via symbolic analysis". In: *38th International Conference on Software Engineering, ICSE*. 2016, pp. 691–701. https://doi.org/10.1145/2884781.2884807.

[NPW02] Tobias Nipkow, Lawrence C. Paulson, and Markus Wenzel. *Isabelle/HOL - A Proof Assistant for Higher-Order Logic*. Springer, 2002.

[OMG16] Object Management Group. *OMG Unified Modeling Language (OMG UML), Version 2.5.1*. 2017. https://www.omg.org/spec/UML/2.5.1/.

[ÖM07] Peter C. Ölveczky and José Meseguer. "Semantics and Pragmatics of Real-Time Maude". In: *Higher-Order and Symbolic Computation* 20.1-2 (2007), pp. 161–196.

[Obj17] OMG - Object Management Group. MOF Query/View/Transformation. Version 1.3. 2016. https://www.omg.org/spec/QVT/.

[OS08] Sam Owre and Natarajan Shankar. "A Brief Overview of PVS". In: *21st International Conference on Theorem Proving in Higher Order Logics, TPHOLs, Proceedings*. Vol. 5170. 2008, pp. 22–27. https://doi.org/10.1007/978-3-540-71067-7_5.

[Plo04] Gordon D. Plotkin. "A structural approach to operational semantics". In: *Journal of Logic and Algebraic Programming* 60–61 (2004), pp. 17–139.

[REP12] Davide Di Ruscio, Romina Eramo, and Alfonso Pierantonio. "Model Transformations". In: *12th International School on Formal Methods for the Design of Computer, Communication, and Software Systems, SFM*. Vol. 7320. 2012, pp. 91–136. https://doi.org/10.1007/978-3-642-30982-3_4.

[RES10] Grigore Rosu, Chucky Ellison, and Wolfram Schulte. "Matching Logic: An Alternative to Hoare/Floyd Logic". In: *13th International Conference on Algebraic Methodology and Software Technology, AMAST*. Vol. 6486. 2010, pp. 142–162. https://doi.org/10. 1007/978-3-642-17796-5_9.

[Reu+16] Ralf H. Reussner, Steffen Becker, Jens Happe, Robert Heinrich, Anne Koziolek, Heiko Koziolek, Max Kramer, and Klaus Krogmann. *Modeling and Simulating Software Architectures – The Palladio Approach*. MIT Press, 2016.

[RG00] Mark Richters and Martin Gogolla. "Validating UML Models and OCL Constraints". In: «*UML*» *2000 - The Unified Modeling Language, Advancing the Standard, Third International Conference*. Vol. 1939. 2000, pp. 265–277. https://doi.org/10.1007/3-540-40011-7_19.

[RN08] Arend Rensink and Ronald Nederpel. "Graph Transformation Semantics for a QVT Language". In: *Electron. Notes Theor. Comput. Sci. 211* (2008), pp. 51–62. https://doi. org/10.1016/j.entcs.2008.04.029.

[Roz97] *Handbook of Graph Grammars and Computing by Graph Transformations, Volume 1: Foundations*. World Scientific, 1997.

[RW15] Lukman Ab. Rahim and Jon Whittle. "A survey of approaches for verifying model transformations". In: *Softw. Syst. Model.* 14.2 (2015), pp. 1003–1028. https://doi.org/10.1007/s10270-013-0358-0.

[SCD12] Gehan M. K. Selim, James R. Cordy, and Juergen Dingel. "Model transformation testing: the state of the art". In: *First Workshop on the Analysis of Model Transformations, AMT*. 2012, pp. 21–26. https://doi.org/10.1145/2432497.2432502.

[SGW94] Bran Selic, Garth Gulkeson, and Paul Ward. *Real-Time Object-Oriented Modeling*. John Wiley and Sons, 1994.

[Sta73] Herbert Stachowiak. *Allgemeine Modelltheorie*. Springer, 1973.

[Sto77] Joseph E. Stoy. *Denotational semantics: the Scott-Strachey approach to programming language theory*. MIT Press, 1977.

[Syn] Synopsys. *Coverity Scan Static Analysis*. https://scan.coverity.com/ (visited on 04/24/2021).

[Tom99] Paul Tomassi. "An Introduction to First Order Predicate Logic". In: 1999, pp. 205–280.

[TV10] Javier Troya and Antonio Vallecillo. "Towards a Rewriting Logic Semantics for ATL". In: *3rd International Conference on Theory and Practice of Model Transformations, ICMT*. Vol. 6142. 2010, pp. 230–244. https://doi.org/10.1007/978-3-642-13688-7_16.

[TV11] Javier Troya and Antonio Vallecillo. "A Rewriting Logic Semantics for ATL". In: *J. Object Technol.* 10 (2011), 5: 1–29. https://doi.org/10.5381/jot.2011.10.1.a5.

[Voe+13] Markus Voelter, Daniel Ratiu, Bernd Kolb, and Bernhard Schätz. "mbeddr: instantiating a language workbench in the embedded software domain". In: *Automated Software Engineering* 20.3 (2013), pp. 339–390. https://doi.org/10.1007/s10515-013-0120-4.

[WTZ10] Christian Wende, Nils Thieme, and Steffen Zschaler. "A Role-based Approach Towards Modular Language Engineering". In: *2nd Int'l Conf. on Software Language Engineering, SLE*. Vol. 5969. 2010, pp. 254–273.

[ZP20] Steffen Zschaler and Fiona Polack. "A Family of Languages for Trustworthy Agent-Based Simulation". In: *13th International Conference on Software Language Engineering, SLE*. 2020.

[Zsc09] Steffen Zschaler. "Formal Specification of Non-functional Properties of Component-Based Software Systems: A Semantic Framework and Some Applications Thereof". In: *Software and Systems Modelling* 9.2 (2009), pp. 161–201. https://doi.org/10.1007/s10270-009-0115-6.

Part I
Challenges and Concepts

Chapter 3
Overview of Challenges in Composing Model-Based Analysis Tools

Francisco Durán, Robert Heinrich, Carolyn Talcott, and Steffen Zschaler

Abstract This chapter introduces the key challenges in composing model-based analysis tools, giving references to book chapters discussing each challenge in more detail.

The composition of model-based analysis tools is a broad area of research with a range of different challenges. In the first part of this book [Hei+21], we will discuss the main challenges in detail. This chapter gives a first overview of these challenges. It is meant to serve as an orientation for readers and a guide to the chapters that follow.

The first two challenges we will discuss in this book are about what is required to make the composition of model-based analysis tools feasible. We will need to discuss:

Challenge 1. *The theoretical foundations*—how to compose the underlying languages, models, and analyses, and

Challenge 2. *The practical implications*—how to integrate and orchestrate existing analysis tools.

Clearly, there are interactions between these challenges: how to integrate and orchestrate analysis tools will be informed by the choices made in composing the

F. Durán (✉)
University of Málaga, Málaga, Spain
e-mail: duran@lcc.uma.es

R. Heinrich
Karlsruhe Institute of Technology, Karlsruhe, Germany
e-mail: robert.heinrich@kit.edu

C. Talcott
SRI International, Menlo Park, CA, USA
e-mail: clt@csl.sri.com

S. Zschaler
King's College London, London, UK
e-mail: szschaler@acm.org

underlying languages, models, and analyses. Chapter 4 discusses the theoretical foundations, introducing the notion of composition and a mathematical character-isation of what composition of analyses involves. In the course of this discussion, the chapter will discuss subchallenges such as the composition of semantics and formalisms, and the composition of analysis techniques vs. the composition of analysis results (cf. also Chap. 7). The chapter also provides brief descriptions of some examples of analysis composition in the real world. Chapter 5, then, builds on Chap. 4 by discussing the challenges involved in integrating and orchestrating existing analysis tools into modelling environments and proposing a reference architecture to highlight key concepts. This helps to address subchallenges such as interoperability between different analysis tools, and bridging different levels of abstraction between modelling environments and analysis tools. The chapter provides an overview of different orchestration strategies and real-world examples where these strategies have been used.

Once we have discussed these foundational challenges, we are ready to discuss other challenges that are orthogonal, but that fundamentally affect the composition of analyses and analysis tools. We will discuss three such additional high-level challenges:

Challenge 3. *Continual model-based analysis.* Continual and incremental analysis is increasingly more important: On the one hand, the systems and properties we want to analyse become more complex. On the other hand, we are aiming for increasingly tight feedback loops in the system development process, requiring analyses to run fast and efficiently. Chapter 6 discusses the challenges that this brings. The chapter introduces an abstract framework for capturing the key components of continual analysis and shows how this can be used to describe real-world analysis systems, through several case studies. The chapter then goes on to describe how continual analysis can benefit from, but can also complicate the composition of analysis tools and formalisms.

Challenge 4. *Exploiting analysis results.* Analysis is done to get results that can inform the use or improvement of a modelled system. But how are these results affected by the composition of different analyses and analysis tools? And, conversely, how can the results of analysis be used to inform the composition of analyses? Chapter 7 discusses this challenge and offers a general model and terminology of results exploitation in the context of analysis composition. The terminology is exemplified through nine case studies of different forms of analysis composition.

Challenge 5. *Living with uncertainty.* Any system development involves a substan-tial amount of uncertainty: For example, requirements may be incomplete or only partially known, or there may not be enough information about real-world impacts of a system's behaviour. An interesting question is, then, how uncertainty is affected by analysis composition and, conversely, how it can affect analysis composition. For example, composing different analyses may re-duce overall uncertainty. However, at the same time, analysis composition may lead to a compounding of uncertainty. Chapter 8 discusses these subchallenges in more detail, including the error quantification under analysis composition; the combination of different analyses to reduce overall uncertainty; and the handling of uncertainty/incompleteness in underlying models.

Following these detailed discussions of challenges, the chapters in the second part of this book [Hei+21] will build on these challenges and give examples in the context of specific case studies and tools.

Reference

[Hei+21] Robert Heinrich, Francisco Durán, Carolyn L. Talcott, and Steffen Zschaler (eds.) *Composing Model-Based Analysis Tools*. Springer, 2021. https://doi.org/10.1007/978-3-030-81915-6.

Chapter 4
Composition of Languages, Models, and Analyses

Carolyn Talcott, Sofia Ananieva, Kyungmin Bae, Benoit Combemale,
Robert Heinrich, Mark Hills, Narges Khakpour, Ralf Reussner,
Bernhard Rumpe, Patrizia Scandurra, and Hans Vangheluwe

Abstract This chapter targets a better understanding of the compositionality of analyses, including different forms of compositionality and specific conditions of composition. Analysis involves models, contexts, and properties. These are all expressed in languages with their own semantics. For a successful composition of analyses, it is therefore important to compose models as well as the underlying languages. We aim to develop a better understanding of what is needed to answer questions such as "When I want to compose two or more analyses, what do I need to take into account?" We describe the elements impacting analysis compositionality, the relation of these elements to analysis, and how composition of analysis relates to compositionality of these elements.

This core chapter addresses Challenge 1 introduced in Chap. 3 of this book (*the theoretical foundations*—how to compose the underlying languages, models, and analyses).

C. Talcott (✉)
SRI International, Menlo Park, CA, USA
e-mail: clt@csl.sri.com

S. Ananieva
FZI Research Center for Information Technology, Karlsruhe, Germany
e-mail: ananieva@fzi.de

K. Bae
POSTECH, Gyeongbuk, South Korea
e-mail: kmbae@postech.ac.kr

B. Combemale
IRISA – University of Rennes, Rennes, France
e-mail: benoit.combemale@irisa.fr

R. Heinrich · R. Reussner
Karlsruhe Institute of Technology, Karlsruhe, Germany
e-mail: robert.heinrich@kit.edu; ralf.reussner@kit.edu

45

4.1 Introduction and Problem Statement

To tackle the complexity of systems design and development, it is necessary to use a multitude of models describing certain aspects, or viewpoints, of the system as a whole or of its subsystems. These models may be expressed using formalisms that provide multiple sublanguages, or special purpose formalisms, or both. Understanding the prerequisites for model composition helps to solve challenges in system design. If the models are specified in different languages describing a variety of views, language composition is required. Even if the models are only augmented with variants of extra properties, compositionality of these kinds of properties must be addressed.

Thus language, semantics, and model composition are an important basis to address the question of how to compose analyses. One main question discussed in this chapter is when and how language, semantics, or model composition is in accordance with, or orthogonal to, analysis composition.

For analysis of behavioural and/or quantitative aspects of a model of a system or system component, it is important to also provide (a model of) the execution context—information about patterns of use, and about elements that affect the behaviour but are not part of the modelled system. Thus, we need to understand the ways context can be composed with other contexts and with models of the system under study, and how this relates to the properties being analysed (see also Sect. 2.1.6 of this book [Hei+21]).

This chapter addresses a better understanding of what is needed to answer questions such as "When I want to compose models or analyses, what do I need to take into account?"; "What are the key relations among models of systems, contexts, and properties and their underlying formalisms?" and "What do these relations tell us about composing analyses?".

The chapter begins with a discussion of core concepts and their interrelations. Sections 4.2 and 4.3 recall the key aspects concerning the concepts of model and

---

M. Hills
East Carolina University, Greenville, NC, USA
e-mail: hillsma@ecu.edu

N. Khakpour
Linnaeus University, Växjö, Sweden
e-mail: narges.khakpour@lnu.se

B. Rumpe
RWTH Aachen, Aachen, Germany
e-mail: rumpe@se-rwth.de

P. Scandurra
University of Bergamo, Bergamo, Italy
e-mail: patrizia.scandurra@unibg.it

H. Vangheluwe
University of Antwerp, Antwerp, Belgium
e-mail: hans.vangheluwe@uantwerp.be

analysis discussed in detail in Chap. 2 of this book [Hei+21]. Section 4.4 takes a broad view of composition and the relations of composition to the elements of analysis, and identifies several forms of composition. Section 4.5 builds on the discussion of core concepts and presents a mathematical framework characterising the relations between models, analyses, and results: how analyses compose, and how composition of the models analysed relates to the analysis results. Section 4.6 presents a diverse sample of formalisms, composition issues, and current practice, to illustrate the ideas presented in the earlier sections. Section 4.7 concludes with a summary of the concepts and challenges and suggests promising research directions.

4.2   Brief Overview of Models and Their Composition

Chapter 2 of this book [Hei+21] already contains a detailed definition of the basic concepts that are needed to understand this chapter. We therefore just repeat some core concepts here. We refer to the definition by Stachowiak [Sta73] to describe what a *model* is. General purpose languages, such as the *Unified Modeling Language* (UML) [BRJ98], become complex and require analysis techniques to better handle the complexity both of the language and systems described. Unfortunately, also analysis techniques become complex and therefore require to be decomposed.

By definition, a model has a purpose with respect to the original [Sta73], and can play one or several roles with respect to this purpose. An engineering model typically starts by being descriptive, and then, at design time, is viewed as prescriptive.

According to [Com+16], a modelling language defines a set of models that can be used for modelling purposes. Various forms of syntax are possible. The semantics can, for example, be defined in the denotational form [HR04]. As discussed in Chap. 2 of this book [Hei+21], a sound semantic definition is very helpful to understand what shall be analysed and what the desired outcomes of analysis techniques are.

In model-based analysis, interesting properties can vary. Thus, we use property models in an explicit language with their own precise semantics. In the very same spirit, we use context models to describe entities of the context, outside of the system to be built.

Composition of models in various forms is a key to cope with complexity, but not easily achievable. Furthermore, advanced and potentially integrated forms of composite semantics, need composition of models of different aspects, their modelling languages, and finally also their associated analysis techniques.

We use metamodelling technology [Gro06] in constructive as well as analytical tools to manage models in an accessible form. [Com+16] defines: "A *metamodel* is a model describing the abstract syntax of a language". Composing models described in heterogeneous languages requires a composition of the metamodels in a useful way. Assuming that metamodels are class diagrams, we therefore have several alternatives for integration: merging algorithms, mappings between metamodels, and consistency relations between the metamodels. Constructive algorithmic translations as well as relations between models can be defined explicitly using a *transformation model*.

4.3   Brief Overview of Analysis

Analysis is the process of answering questions about a system under study. The system may be too complex to reason directly about it, or it may not yet exist. Thus, analysis techniques work with models: models of (some aspect of) the system of interest, of its context, and of the question being asked, i.e., a property.

As proposed in Sect. 2.2 of this book [Hei+21], the idea of analysis can be captured formally by the relation

$$M, C \vdash_T Q \rightsquigarrow A$$

where M, C, Q, and A are (respectively) models of the system, context, question, and answer domains, and T is an analysis technique.

Analysis can be characterised along multiple dimensions. One dimension is the *level of automation*. At one end of the spectrum, determining whether a property holds may be a fully automatic process, while at the other it may involve informal social processes. Many techniques involve user guided automation. Another dimension is whether the analysis is *static* or *dynamic*. A static analysis works over the syntax of the input models, and usually happens at design time. A dynamic analysis occurs during system or model execution, and may be online (monitoring) or offline (analysis of traces from logged information). Simulation sits on the borderline.

The answer domain of an analysis can be simply a two-element set reflecting success or failure. This is referred to as *Qualitative analysis* and includes checking satisfaction of a given property. Alternatively, in a *Quantitative analysis*, the answer domain is richer: real numbers, a probability distribution, or even tables and other structured data are used. Performance analysis is an example of quantitative analysis.

Similarly to a model having a purpose, an analysis also has a purpose. We distinguish three main *kinds* of purpose: analysis of model/system structure; analysis of functional aspects of behaviour; and analysis of quality aspects of behaviour. The analysis of structure works with syntactic descriptions, while the analysis of behaviour requires a semantic domain (and possibly other information). The purpose of a specific analysis may be a mixture of these basic kinds of purpose. Tables 2.1 and 2.2 of Chap. 2 of this book [Hei+21] summarise the different purposes and the elements (e.g., model, context) required for analysis.

Analysis techniques can be characterised by how helpful they are. When the answer produced by an analysis is different from what is expected/desired (e.g., type inference fails, safety or security property fails, or a performance measure is out of desired bounds), does the analysis technique provide a reason for failure? Does it help to locate the cause? Does it help to correct the problem? See Chap. 7 of this book [Hei+21] for more discussion of tools' outputs and their use.

Finally, an important consideration is the *quality* of an analysis. This includes different notions of soundness: Does the analysis always give an answer? Is the answer an over- or under-approximation? Does it produce false positives or false negatives? These represent trade-offs of complexity and accuracy. Another quality issue is whether the analysis is repeatable (by the same analyst) or reproducible (by an independent analyst).

4.4 What Is Composition?

Figure 4.1 shows a holistic vision of composition of analyses across different syntactic and semantic domains and corresponding properties of interest. In particular, disparate models of different aspects are the main subjects to be composed/decomposed on the syntax and semantic level and also at the metamodel level. These models include: system models, context models, property models, and models of analysis results. Composition of analyses relates to compositionality on the syntax and semantic level of the underlying formalisms to represent (sub)system models and contexts (F_i) and property models (PF_i). The act of such compositions (the operation *COMP*) forms a composite model formalism ($COMP(F_1, F_2)$) and a

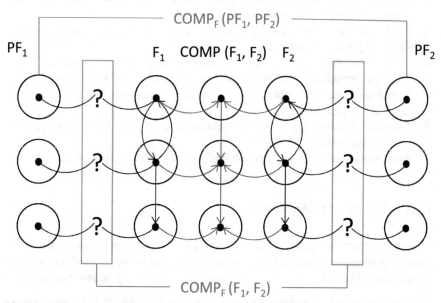

Fig. 4.1 Multiple dimensions of composition. The three central columns represent two modelling formalisms, F_1 and F_2 and their composition. Think of the top row as a metamodel, the middle row as a system or component (syntactic) model, and the bottom row as a semantic model. The outer columns represent properties, at each level. The question marks ("?") stand for satisfaction relations. The arrows connecting nodes (dots or question marks) represent relations such as refinement, abstraction, satisfaction, instanceof, meaningof, etc.

property formalism ($COMP_F(PF_1, PF_2)$). The composition of model formalisms and property formalisms enables *global analysis* [Cla+14]. Given a system model composed with an intended environment of use, one can formulate analysis questions that apply to a certain set of the individual submodels. These analysis questions can be managed at the level of the submodels and contexts involved, by defining and applying appropriate composition/decomposition relational operators (e.g., merge, union, focus, restriction, etc.). These operators are grounded on the semantic domains of the composed formalisms and their supported analysis techniques.

In Sect. 4.4.1 we give examples of targets of composition, and in Sect. 4.4.2 we characterise different forms of composition.

4.4.1 Targets of Composition

Based on the concepts described in the previous sections, for the purpose of composing modelling languages and formalisms to enable global analysis, it is necessary to think about the elements that are the targets of composition. These include:

1. Components (of the system under study): architectural, functional, behavioural
2. Models of aspects of the system or its components
3. Application domain—communications, image processing, manufacturing, chemical process control, . . .
4. User-facing language composed of several elements from sublanguages
5. Analysis formalisms and techniques (possibly made of several subanalyses formalisms and techniques) such as constraint solving, unification, model checking, or simulation
6. Syntactic domains and semantic domains of all specification languages/formalisms involved
7. Tools composed of several subtools dealing with sublanguages (or subanalyses)

4.4.2 Forms of Composition

Considering that the modelling languages and formalisms can be integrated on the syntax and semantics level, and that analysis techniques or the results of the analysis algorithms can be combined, we conceive three general composition approaches:

1. *Model composition (white-box composition)* is the analysis input-model composition realised by language integration (i.e., the definition of a new language from a set of individual languages, for example, by metamodel unification or weaving) [Cla+14, GRS09]. The internals of the composed individual models are exposed at an arbitrary level of detail and open for modifications and for analysis. Note that language composition is not always necessary for model

composition. If there is a joint language for both models, or a transformation to a joint language, there is no need for language composition. For example, see "composition by transformation into a joint formalism" in Chap. 11 of this book [Hei+21].

2. *Result composition (black-box composition)* is the composition of the analysis results. The internals of the models remain encapsulated, only explicitly defined interoperability interfaces are used to access the target analysis and render back the results. Usually, a user-facing model is translated or mapped (e.g., by a model transformation realising *semantic translation* [HR04]) into a concrete model of the target analysis formalism, and then the results of the analysis are lifted back to the level of the user-facing model. Various types of black-box composition are possible, ranging from single analysis orchestration over combined analysis orchestration to sequential analysis orchestration of black-box analysis tools by exchanging results. (cf. Chap. 5 of this book [Hei+21]).

3. *Analysis composition (grey-box composition)* is the composition of the analysis techniques by orchestrating the steps of two or more analysis algorithms. Internal knowledge of models may be partially exposed through interfaces to guide the coordination, but the composition remains modularised. For example, see "composition by co-simulation" in Chap. 11 of this book [Hei+21].

In the white-box approach, the integration of two or more languages may require additional information in the form of a correspondence between the syntax and/or semantics of the constituent languages. It accommodates highly customised composition semantics, but it is not easily extensible, and it is easily applicable only if we have a high overlap between languages. The UML is a well known exemplar of a compound language resulting by the integration of several modelling formalisms properly revisited.

There has also been significant work in the language semantics community on creating modular language definitions that can be combined to form new languages. This includes work related to algebraic specification [Bra+01], rewriting logic semantics [MB04, BM05], modular structural operational semantics (MSOS) [Mos99, Mos02], implicitly-modular structural operational semantics (I-MSOS) [MN08], monads in denotational semantics [Mog89, Mog91, Esp95], abstract state machines [KP97], and the K framework [HȘR07, RS10]. This work has tended to focus on methods for defining reusable language feature modules (e.g., the ability to elide unused parts of the configuration in MSOS, the use of context completion in K), which can then be reused in the construction of a new or extended language. These would also qualify as white-box approaches since they work directly over the formal definitions of the languages.

Black-box composition keeps the composition highly modular, allowing arbitrary analysis tasks to be carried out and the results lifted back to the user-facing domain level as long as they conform to the interfaces. A typical example of this approach is the common practice of translating a user-facing model (including some temporal logic properties) into a model checker input, and then translating back the counterexample into concepts of the user-facing model language. However, because black-box composition cannot rely on internal structure of models, it can only support a fixed composition semantics that is dictated by the corresponding semantic mapping(s) and that might be too restrictive.

The grey-box approach represents a whole spectrum of grey shades in between the white-box and black-box approaches realised via model-based analysis coordination [Cla+14]. Coordination can be achieved implicitly (*implicit coordination*), via sharing concepts with the same semantics; the corresponding models do not exchange information explicitly, but reason about artefacts related to shared semantic concepts. Coordination can also be achieved via sharing of concepts with different semantics; in this case, the corresponding models have to exchange information explicitly via interfaces (*explicit coordination*). The information exchanged can be data or control based, and requires an orchestration model (and therefore an orchestration formalism). A typical example of coordinated analysis is co-simulation where the coupled and possibly interacting simulations of two or more models up to a fixed point can create more detailed results. Hence, grey-box composition takes the best of the first two approaches and works well for highly heterogeneous languages, but requires sophisticated technicality of language orchestration engines.

In order to combine together multiple analysis tools and, therefore, combine multiple results, these forms of composition can be concretely realised by adopting specific orchestration strategies of the analysis tools involved (see Chap. 5 of this book [Hei+21] for more details). Chapter 11 of this book [Hei+21] illustrates how to implement the different forms of composition by discussing examples of concrete composition operators.

4.5 A Mathematical Characterisation of Models, Analyses, and Composition

Many of the concepts we have described in the previous subsections are rather well known, and have all been dealt with in the practical realisation of modelling processes and engineering tools. However, to our knowledge, a general and unifying view on how to deal with composition of analysis, and how composition of analysis relates to compositionality of models and their semantics, contexts, and analysis algorithms, does not exist yet.

In order to provide a precise understanding of how to put all these elements in relation, this section provides a reference conceptual framework for the classes of composition we have identified so far. For that purpose, we use mathematical constructs that allow us to precisely define the effects, but of course need to be embellished in very individual forms in the various domains of software systems, analysis techniques, etc. Here we only give very short examples.

4.5.1   *Model*

Section 2.1.2 of this book [Hei+21] describes the concept of models where modelling formalisms provide a syntax, here called *Syn*, and a semantic domain, here called *Sem*, that provides meaning for syntactic elements. We formalise meaning as a semantic mapping [HR04]:

$$M : Syn \rightarrow Sem.$$

In a mathematical setting, the semantic domain describes an infinite set of possible realisations. For simplicity, one might think of all possible "implementations". As the semantic domain is infinite, usually that semantic mapping is just a mathematical construction and has no algorithmic executability. Semantics in that sense serves as background for a precise definition of the desired properties that can then be proven either precisely or approximately through appropriate algorithmic analysis techniques.

Modelling languages are usually designed to describe or constrain the set of possible implementations. Therefore, by definition, a modelling language differs in its purpose from a programming language, where usually a deterministic execution is desired. The mathematical semantics of the model should therefore reflect that it is a constraint on the set of implementations. To capture this, the semantics definition is refined to a set based approach:

$$M : Syn \rightarrow \mathcal{P}(Sem).$$

One model therefore describes a set of possible implementations. For example, a nondeterministic automaton describes a set of accepted words, a class diagram describes a set of valid object structures, and usually a behavioural description, such as an activity diagram or a Petri net describes a set of traces. If the mapping M is appropriately defined, then mathematically a number of constructs can be easily defined. For example, a model $m \in Syn$ is *consistent*, exactly if $M(m) \neq \emptyset$. Or a model m_2 is a *refinement* of another model m_1, if $M(m_2) \subset M(m_1)$.

As a consequence, it is also relatively easy to define the semantics of two (and thus arbitrary many) models m_1, m_2, that describe different aspects of a system simply by using the set of implementations that obey both models (i.e., intersection): $M(m_1 + m_2) = M(m_1) \cap M(m_2)$. This property allows us to, in the following discussion, only look at the single model, instead of the usually existing set of individual artefacts developed during the project.

This general principle of semantic definitions can be applied to each kind of syntactic artefact that is used during the development process, even if the artefacts are described in different languages. This in particular includes *property* definitions and *context models* as well as models of the system itself. For simplicity, we assume that for each language Syn_i at hand, we have an appropriate mapping M_i:

$$M_i : Syn_i \to \mathcal{P}(Sem).$$

This also serves as a nice mathematical integration of different modelling languages on a semantic level. Please note that if, e.g., in an industrial setting, various different models of different modelling languages are used, an integrated semantic domain is not easy to construct. In [Bro+09a, Bro+09b], such an effort was made for object-oriented systems as a basis for UML models.

4.5.2 Analysis

Mathematically, an analysis technique A has the very same signature as a semantic mapping M. It analyses a model from the modelling language Syn and produces a result R of an appropriate *result domain Res*:

$$A : Syn \to Res.$$

As we discussed already, the purpose of an analysis, however, differs from the semantic mapping M: usually the result domain *Res* is a rather simple domain, covering a huge abstraction of what the original model described. Typical semantic domains for *Res* are:

- Boolean, which means that the analysis checks whether a property is true or false,
- Real Numbers $\mathcal{R}$, which means that the analysis measures some kind of fitness,
- A visual representation of Boolean or real numbers, which means that the analysis is mainly dedicated for exhibiting certain information to the user.

Of course, more forms of analysis techniques are possible, especially if one analysis technique produces only a subresult used in another analysis technique.

Because *Res* usually consists of finite, computable objects, we are interested in algorithmically executable analysis techniques A as well. In complex situations, this interest in algorithmic execution often prevents to directly use the semantics domain *Sem*. In that sense, we might see analysis techniques to be algorithmic executable abstractions of the semantics, and it then makes sense to have several analysis techniques for different purposes available.

We furthermore might be interested in extending an analysis algorithm by an explicit definition of the desired *properties* (in language Syn_2):

$$A : Syn \times Syn_2 \rightarrow Res.$$

Chapter 9 of this book [Hei+21] provides examples of this form of analysis.

The correctness of an analysis technique can be reasoned about. For example, a model $m \in Syn$ fulfils a binary property definition $p \in PL$ of a property language PL exactly if $M(m) \subseteq M_{PL}(p)$. An analysis technique A is sufficient if, for all models $m \in Syn$ and for all properties $p \in PL$, it holds that $A(m, p) \Rightarrow (M(m) \subseteq M_{PL}(p))$. Please note that this definition only demands an implication, because it may be that the property holds, but the analysis technique may fail to verify this. Based on these considerations we may even compare the quality of analysis techniques according to their results. Assuming that both A_1 and A_2 are correct as defined above: A_2 is better than A_1, if it is more accurate, i.e., $\forall m, p : A_1(m, p) \Rightarrow A_2(m, p)$.

4.5.3   Composition

Composition has many different facets. Therefore, we need to be clear on what is to be composed: Components in the system, models about the system, languages that describe different viewpoints on the system, and finally analyses that calculate parts of the results about models.

In this chapter, we concentrate on the composition of analyses and therefore at first ignore that typically the system itself is also composed. In the following, we simply assume that all models and property definitions describe the same component. This simplification avoids the necessity to compose semantic domains as well as semantic mappings. As a remark: Otherwise we would need a composition technique on the semantics of the domain as well, which is of course possible but complicates the following considerations unnecessarily. We simply assume that all semantic mappings directly go to the same semantic domain *Sem*.

We also keep the above described simplification, that we look only at one model, because we assume that we know how to semantically compose models. The discussion below includes all forms of models, i.e., models describing the system, models describing the context of the system, and potentially also models describing interaction between both.

In the following, we give examples and mathematically define the notion of composition of analyses according to the three forms of composition informally introduced in Sect. 4.4.

Simple Result Composition

Given two analysis techniques A_i, $i \in \{1, 2\}$ producing individual results in their own domains Res_i based on the same model m, we can define a *result composition* if an appropriate operator $\odot$ is available:

$$A : Syn \rightarrow Res_1 \odot Res_2$$

by

$$A(m) = A_1(m) \odot A_2(m).$$

As each analysis is conducted in isolation in a black-box manner and only the results are composed, this adheres to the form black-box composition.

Model Decomposition and Result Composition

We decompose a model $m = m_1 \odot m_2$ and then can define

$$A(m_1 \odot m_2) = A_1(m_1) \odot A_2(m_2).$$

This black-box composition together with the decomposition of models is very powerful, but potentially difficult to achieve in practice. It may be that in practice, a mixture may apply: Instead of decomposing a model into disjoint elements, it may be helpful to use algorithmically executable abstraction functions $\alpha_i : Syn \rightarrow Syn$, e.g., slicers, forget functions etc., and apply the following composition:

$$A(m) = A_1(\alpha_1(m)) \odot A_2(\alpha_2(m)).$$

This however works best if all available information is used, which means that no information should be lost under the two abstractions, i.e., $M(m) = M(\alpha_1(m)) \cup M(\alpha_2(m))$.

Please note that it may of course be possible for each A_i to be parameterised with its own property definition language, then obviously different properties can be considered.

Sequential Composition

Parameterisation can also be used to embed the results of one analysis technique into the computation of another analysis technique. We can speak of *sequential composition* of analysis techniques when the following applies:

$$A(m) = A_2(m, A_1(m)),$$

where the second analysis A_2 consumes the results of the first and produces the overall result. From a functional point of view, we might also argue that the analyses themselves are composed by $A = \lambda m.A_2(m, A_1(m))$. Sequential composition, however, still adheres to the form black-box composition, if only results are exchanged between black-box analyses. If there is internal knowledge exposed by orchestrating the steps of the analyses, this is considered grey-box composition. It might even be that several analysis techniques depend mutually on their results.

Mutually Improving Analysis Composition

This shows a technically very interesting dependency, that in practice happens quite often. An example is analysis coupling until a fixpoint is reached (cf. Sect. 5.7 of this book [Hei+21]). The formal definitions would have the form:

$$A_i : Syn \times Res_{3-i} \rightarrow Res_i \quad (i \in \{1, 2\})$$

$$A : Syn \rightarrow Res$$

$$A(m) = (r, s) \; where \; (r, s) = (A_1(m, s), A_2(m, r)).$$

This is an equational definition for the results r and s that needs a careful consideration to understand what the possible solutions are. Typically the mutual dependencies need to be handled in an iterative, potentially approximating manner.

This works particularly well when, for example, an analysis technique A_1 can already deliver initial results with an "empty" input r^0 and further iterations improve the result in a desired direction. Formally, we derive an approximation using a series of results r^n, s^n, where for each iteration step $n \in \mathcal{N}$ the next step is computed by $s^n = A_2(m, r^n)$ and $r^{n+1} = A_1(m, s^n)$ until the iteration can stop.

Again, mutually improving analysis composition adheres to the form black-box composition, if only results are exchanged between black-box analyses. If there is internal knowledge exposed by orchestrating the steps of the analyses this is considered grey-box composition.

Simulation Composition

Simulation with time progress can be seen as a very special case of the above definition, where the analysis techniques are not iteratively rerun, but the results r^n, s^n are iteratively constructed in a stepwise manner.

In this grey-box composition, we probably have a timed structure on the result domain, either in a stepwise manner $Res = (\mathcal{N} \rightarrow X)$ or in a continuous manner $Res = (\mathcal{R}^+ \rightarrow X)$, where both use a set X of messages or events or values. Furthermore, the analysis techniques must be compositional in the sense that they do not use input of a specific time point t to produce output of a time point t_2 that is earlier or equal to t, i.e., $t_2 > t$ must hold. Mathematical theories for this kind of timing behaviour are for example given in Ptolemy [Eke+03], Focus [BS01, RR11], or Abadi/Lamport's TLA [AL90].

4.5.4   Composition of Contexts

As one of the components of an analysis, a context can appear as parameter to the analysis tool, or a context model C can be composed with the system model M, for example, to turn an open system model into a closed system model $C[M]$ for behavioural analysis. In the case of a composed system model $M = M_1 \otimes M_2$, we can consider contexts C_1, C_2 for the component models M_1, M_2, or a composite context $C = C_1 \otimes_c C_2$, and form the analysis model in two ways:

$$(C_1 \otimes_c C_2)[M_1 \otimes M_2]$$

or

$$C_1[M_1] \otimes C_2[M_2].$$

A challenge for future research is to identify conditions under which to choose one form over the other.

A context may only provide part of the information needed to describe operating conditions. Thus, composition with a context can be iterated, incrementally adding contextual information. This is illustrated in Fig. 4.2. Here, component models m_1 and m_2, with respective interfaces M_1 and M_2, are enclosed in contexts C_1 and C_2, respectively, forming models represented by $C_1[M_1]$ and $C_2[M_2]$ (context model composition). Then, model $M = C_1[M_1] \otimes C_2[M_2]$ is formed by composing the resulting models (model–model composition). M may still have undetermined contextual elements. These can be provided by further composition with context C to obtain

$$C[(C_1[M_1] \otimes C_2[M_2])].$$

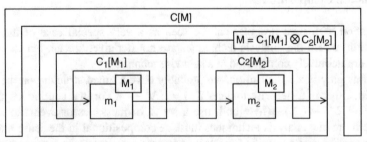

Fig. 4.2 Context composition

4.5.5 Compositionality of Property Satisfaction

A challenging question about all of these compositions is understanding conditions under which properties are preserved. A related challenge is designing an analysis technique in such a way that no potential forms of use of a model, i.e., no forms of composition with other models, invalidate the analysis result.

We can formalise that as follows: Given an analysis result $r = A(m)$, composition with any other model m_2 should retain (or even improve) the result, e.g., in a simplified form, it holds $r = A(m \odot m_2)$.

This, however, is often not the case in practice. For example, for performance models, adding additional components usually reduces the performance of the already deployed components. To some extent this has to do with difficulties of decomposing certain kinds of analysis techniques without pre-defining certain additional knowledge, for example, dedicated slots of computing time attached to each of the submodels.

It is also possible to consider an alternative direction, by using analysis techniques that do not only produce results, but also clarify the necessary conditions for the context of a modelled component in order to operate according to the desired properties. In this case, the analysis technique is potentially also parameterised by a property definition used as a parameter and produces as a result another property definition for the context, which then can be fed as a necessary property for the models of the context. Thus, for an existing property definition language PL we have analysis techniques of the form:

$$A : Syn \times PL \rightarrow PL$$

successively or iteratively applied to the various models as described above producing improved property definitions over time.

The nice thing with analysis techniques delivering property conditions about a modelled component is that, for example, reusable library components can be documented with this kind of usage conditions and newly defined components can be checked for compliance.

All these general considerations may work for certain kinds of properties, but certainly not for all. For example, security properties are usually not easily compositional.

4.6 Examples of Formalisms, Composition Issues, and Current Practice

To give a concrete idea of the concepts and relations discussed in the previous sections, we give an overview of several formalisms and associated modelling and analysis tools. The formalisms range from general purpose modelling systems (rewriting logic, abstract state machines), formalisms designed for modelling specific aspects (hybrid automata, Palladio), and formalisms for coordination and composition (BCOoL). Rewriting logic is a general purpose formalism that supports language and model composition, and all three forms of composition introduced in Sect. 4.4, especially for concurrent/distributed systems. Abstract state machines is a general purpose formalism for functional behaviours, supporting black-box (result) composition. Palladio is an approach and toolset for software architecture modelling and analysis of quality properties, supporting model, result, and analysis composition. Hybrid automata is a formalism composed from discrete and continuous models of behaviour that can be considered as model composition. Grey-box (analysis) composition of hybrid systems is supported by multiple tools. GEMOC Studio is a framework for developing and composing *domain-specific modelling languages* (DSMLs). Analysis composition in GEMOC Studio is provided by coordination mechanisms specified in BCOoL.

4.6.1 Rewriting Logic and Its Realisation in the Maude Language and System

Rewriting logic [Mes92, Mes12] is a logic for reasoning about change over time using rewrite rules. Maude [Cla+07, Dur+19] is a rewriting logic language and toolset providing an efficient implementation that supports executable specification and analysis of concurrent and distributed systems.[1] Similar to programming languages, Maude is a general purpose modelling language with models that can be used for simulation or answering the simple question "Does the model run?". Being based on a formal logic, many other analyses are available as well.

Rewrite theories (Maude modules) can be used for specifying many aspects. For system models the structure/architecture is represented by terms of an equational theory and the dynamics/behaviour is specified by local rewrite rules that specify how a system in a given state evolves. Context models can be represented using terms with "holes", by adding constraints to execution states, or by adding an explicit context component such as an environment or intruder model. Properties are specified using equationally defined Boolean functions. Properties of state/system structure can be specified for static analysis, or for use as state properties in *linear temporal logic* (LTL) formulas for the model checker. Execution traces can be captured using reflection or by instrumenting execution states (and augmenting the rewrite rules to collect information). This allows properties of traces to be equationally defined, and checked by evaluation.

The metatheory of rewriting logic gives a foundation for analysis algorithms implemented in Maude. Static/structural analysis tools include the Church–Rosser checker, the coherence checker [DM12], and the termination tool [DLM08]. Maude

---

[1] Maude is available at http://maude.cs.uiuc.edu/.

directly supports several forms of dynamic/behaviour analysis. Prototyping/testing is supported by executing rules (modulo strategies) using the rewrite engine. The search command provides reachability analysis (can a state satisfying a given property be reached, and if so how). The built-in function modelCheck allows the user to check a system specification for satisfaction of LTL formulas where state properties are arbitrary equationally defined Boolean functions. The Maude LTLR model checker [BM15] is an explicit state model checker supporting analysis of *linear temporal logic of rewriting* (LTLR) properties that involve both events (rule applications) and state predicates, including mixed properties such as fairness. The Real-Time Maude language and tool [ÖM07] supports specification and analysis of real-time and hybrid systems. Available analysis techniques include timed rewriting for simulation purposes, search, time-bounded and unbounded LTL model checking, and *timed computation tree logic* (TCTL) model checking.

Rewriting logic supports the formalisation of many forms of composition of models and of analyses, including the forms discussed in Sects. 4.4 and 4.5. The following are some examples:

1. *Composition of theories by inclusion, parameterised module instantiation, or terms in a module algebra.* Here is an example from the Soft Agent modelling framework [Tal+16]. The parameterised module {SOLVE-SCP{Z :: VALUATION} defines a soft constraint solver solveSCP using a valuation function specified in modules realising the parameter theory VALUATION. The module VAL-Y-PATROL-ENERGY imports two VALUATION modules VAL-ENERGY and VAL-Y-PATROL and forms a lexicographic composition of their valuation functions. A module SCENARIO imports a module defining a model of patrolling bots and the module SOLVE-SCP{val2ypatrolenergy} with the valuation parameter Z instantiated to VAL-Y-PATROL-ENERGY. val2ypatrolenergy is a view mapping elements of the theory VALUATION to their instantiation in VAL-Y-PATROL-ENERGY. In the SCENARIO module configurations to be tested and analysed are defined.
2. *Composition of models (syntax level) by term formation.* In [NT20], the operation [app ; intruder] is used to compose an application model, app, with an intruder model, intruder, to enable search for possible attacks. We can use this composition to illustrate the general analysis judgement,

$$M, C \vdash_T Q \rightsquigarrow A$$

of Sect. 2.2. Here M is the application model app and C is context model intruder. The technique T is search parameterised by the form of answer desired. The query Q is a predicate characterising attack states. The answer A can be either a Boolean (yes, an attack state is reachable), a witness attack state, or an execution trace leading to an attack state. If the search space is finite, the answer could also be the number of (unique) attack states, the set of attack states, or a set of execution traces containing a trace for each reachable attack state.

3. *Algebraic and logical composition of properties.* Assume $P_1(m)$ and $P_2(m)$ are properties of models ranged over by m. Then, $P(m) = P_1(m) @ P_2(m)$ defines the composition of the results of evaluating the properties using operation $@$.

4. *Composition of rule rewriting with external simulators.* An example is a (co)-simulation of a cyber-physical agent behaviour where the cyber (planning) behaviour is simulated in Maude and the physical behaviour (drone or autonomous vehicle) is simulated using a special purpose flight or vehicle simulator [Mas+17]. Simulators are coordinated by meta-level rules and a message passing protocol. In this composition rewriting and simulation steps are interleaved with rewriting results passed to the simulator and simulation results passed back to the Maude. This interleaving with exchange of information can be viewed as an instance of the *Mutually improving results composition* discussed in Sect. 4.5.3. Recall the equation to solve is

$$A(m) = (r, s) \ where \ (r, s) = (A_1(m, s), A_2(m, r)).$$

In our example, m is the system model, s a command, r the system state, A_1 is the simulator which updates the state according to the new command, A_2 is the cyber/Maude simulate that decides the next command given the current state. So with r_0 the initial state, we have $s_0 = A_2(m, r_0)$, $r_1 = A_1(m, s_0)$, and so on. With a log in the state, this can incrementally generate a trace, or performance measures such as average or minimum distance between vehicles, (average) energy used per task, etc.

5. *Symbolic search (narrowing) composes rewriting and unification (equation solving).* Here unification is used to match rule premises with state patterns that represent potentially infinitely many specific states. The Mauda NPA protocol analysis tool [EMM06] uses this composition to determine if a given attack pattern can be realised in a system running one or more instances of given cryptographic security protocols.

6. *Rewriting modulo constraints composes rewriting with* satisfiability modulo theories *(SMT) constraint solving.* In this case, states are pairs consisting of a pattern and a constraint that finitely represent all pattern instances that satisfy the constraint. Constraints are accumulated as rewrite rules are applied. An SMT solver is invoked to check that a constrained state is consistent. An example use is to model timing properties of distance bounding and other protocols as constraints rather than concrete numbers [NTU19].

In the above, 1–2 are examples of white-box composition, 3 exemplifies black-box composition, and 4–6 are examples of grey-box composition.

4.6.2   Abstract State Machines and the ASMETA Analysis Toolset

Abstract state machines (ASMs) [BS03, BR18] are an extension of *finite state machines* (FSMs) where unstructured control states are replaced by *states* comprising arbitrary complex data (i.e., domains of objects with functions defined on them), and *transitions* are expressed by named parameterised transition rules (or simply rules) describing how the data (state function values saved into *locations*) change from one state to the next. ASM models can be read as "pseudocode over abstract data" with a *well-defined semantics*: At each computation step, all transition rules are executed in parallel, leading to simultaneous (consistent) updates of a number of locations. This basic notion of ASM has been extended to synchronous/asynchronous multi-agent ASMs for the design and analysis of distributed systems.

ASMs are primarily tailored to the formalisation and analysis of functional system behaviour via an iterative design process based on model refinement. Tools supporting the process are part of the ASMETA (ASM mETAmodeling) toolset[2] and provide different V&V activities (such as model simulation, scenario-based simulation, property verification by model checking and runtime verification to name a few). Most of these tools provide analysis support for ASMs by *semantic mapping* [GRS09, HR04], i.e., via model transformations that realise semantic mappings from ASM models (edited using the textual language AsmetaL [GRS08]) to the input formalism of the target analysis tool, and then lift back the results of the analysis to the ASM level. Thus, the type of composition commonly realised in the ASMETA analysis toolset is *black-box*. More details on the specific composition strategies adopted in the ASMETA toolset are given in Chap. 5 of this book [Hei+21].

4.6.3   Palladio

Palladio is a tool-supported approach to modelling and analysing software architectures for various quality properties [Reu+16]. Details on Palladio's modelling language *Palladio Component Model* and toolset Palladio-Bench are given in Chap. 11 of this book [Hei+21]. In the context of Palladio, different forms of composition as introduced in Sect. 4.4 are applied. For example, IntBIIS [Hei+17] is an approach for extending Palladio architectural models by business process models to simulate the mutual performance impact of software systems and business processes. IntBIIS therefore conforms to model composition. The *Power Consumption Analyzer* (PCA) [Sti18] uses the results of Palladio's software architecture simulation (mainly utilisation of resources) to forecast power consumption of software

---

[2] ASMeta is available at http://asmeta.sourceforge.net/ and https://asmeta.github.io/.

systems at the architecture level. PCA therefore conforms to results composition. OMPCM [HMR13] integrates the OMNeT++-based network simulation framework INET with the architecture-level software performance prediction of Palladio. OMPCM therefore conforms to analysis composition.

4.6.4 Hybrid Automata

Hybrid automata [Hen00, LSV03] are finite state machines extended with continuous variables. Hybrid automata are widely used to specify cyber-physical systems that exhibit both discrete and continuous behaviour. Such systems include automotive, avionics, robotics, and medical systems. In a hybrid automaton, the discrete part of the system is specified using a finite state machine with discrete states (called *modes*) and transitions (called *jumps*), and the continuous part of the system is modelled using continuous real functions or *ordinary differential equations* (ODEs) over continuous state variables. The values of continuous variables can also be changed (or reset) when jumps happen. The parallel composition of hybrid automata is defined by synchronising jumps with common "actions" in a way similar to the case of finite state machines.

Figure 4.3 shows a hybrid automaton modelling a simple thermostat system, adapted from [Hen00]. Two (continuous) variables x and t represent the temperature and the timer, respectively, and three (discrete) modes off, on, and turbo represent the status of the heater. Initially, the mode is off, the timer t is 0, and the temperature x is any value between 18 and 20. The values of x and t change according to the ODEs for each mode, while satisfying the *invariant* conditions of the mode. For example, in the turbo mode, x and t change according to $\dot{x} = 8 - 0.1x$ and $\dot{t} = 1$ as long as the invariant conditions $x \leq 22$ and $t \leq 2$ hold. A jump between two modes can be taken if the guard condition is satisfied: e.g., a jump from on to turbo can happen whenever $x < 20$ holds, and in this case the value of t is reset to 0.

The behaviour of a hybrid automaton is given by continuous trajectories of modes and variables over time. Formally, each state of a hybrid automaton is a pair $(q, \vec{v})$ of a mode $q \in Q$ and a real-valued vector $\vec{v} \in \mathbb{R}^n$, where Q denotes a finite set of modes and $\vec{v} = (v_1, \ldots, v_n)$ denotes the values of the continuous variables $x_1, \ldots, x_n$. A finite trajectory of length $d \geq 0$ is then a function $\tau : [0, d] \rightarrow Q \times \mathbb{R}^n$

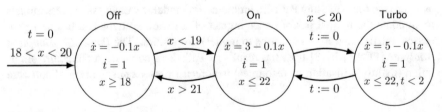

Fig. 4.3 A hybrid automaton H

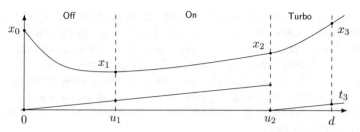

Fig. 4.4 A trajectory

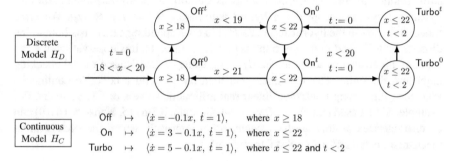

Fig. 4.5 A composition $H = H_D \otimes H_C$

that describes the continuous changes of the states in the time interval $[0, d]$. Excluding Zeno behaviour (with infinitely many jumps in a finite amount of time), a finite trajectory only involves a finite number of discrete jumps in the interval $[0, d]$. For example, a trajectory τ for the thermostat system is shown in Fig. 4.4. Initially, $\tau(0) = (\text{off}, (x_0, 0))$. It involves a jump from off to on at time u_1, and a jump from on to turbo at time u_2.

A hybrid automaton can be considered as the *model composition* of a finite state machine and a continuous dynamical system. Consider the thermostat hybrid automaton H above. As shown in Fig. 4.5, the discrete part is the nondeterministic state machine H_D that abstracts from the continuous dynamics. Each mode m in the hybrid automaton H is separated into two states m^0 and m^t in H_D, where m^0 and m^t correspond to the beginning and the end, respectively, of a trajectory fragment with mode m. Any trajectory of H corresponds to a path in the state machine H_D. For example, the trajectory in Fig. 4.4 corresponds to the path: $(\text{off}^0, x_0, 0)$, (off^t, x_1, u_1), (on^0, x_1, u_1), (on^t, x_2, u_2), $(\text{turbo}^0, x_2, 0)$, $(\text{turbo}^t, x_3, t_3)$. The continuous part is the continuous dynamical system H_C that abstracts from the transition structure. As expected, each trajectory fragment with mode m for H is a valid signal of H_C.

The safety verification problem is to check whether there exists an "error" trajectory that violates safety requirements. As usual, there are different ways to specify the safety requirements of hybrid automata, such as invariant properties of reachable states [Hen00], temporal logic properties of continuous trajectories [MN04], etc.

The safety verification problem is in general undecidable for hybrid automata [Hen00]. Nevertheless, there exist several tools that can approximately verify the absence of error trajectories up to given bounds for different classes of safety properties, including SpaceEx [Fre+11], HyComp [Cim+15], Flow* [CÁS13], dReach [Kon+15], StlMC [BL19], etc. Each of those tools provides its own modelling language to specify hybrid automata. It is worth noting that these modelling languages usually have different syntaxes but have the same semantics, namely, hybrid automata.

Safety verification algorithms for hybrid automata sometimes exploit this composition relation to combine different analysis techniques for discrete and continuous dynamical systems. Consider a hybrid automaton $H = H_D \otimes H_C$. An error trajectory exists in the hybrid automata H, if a corresponding path exists both in the discrete part H_D and in the continuous part H_C. Based on this observation, we can first find an erroneous sequence in H_D, e.g., using an SMT-based model checking algorithm for finite state machines, and then try to build a concrete continuous trajectory, e.g., using linear/non-linear real arithmetic solvers or ODE solvers. For example, SMT-based techniques for hybrid automata [Cim+15, Kon+15, BL19] can be characterised as this *analysis composition* approach, where the orchestration mechanism is the DPLL($\mathcal{T}$) SMT framework.

4.6.5   The GEMOC Studio and BCOoL

The GEMOC Studio[3] provides generic components through Eclipse technologies for the development, integration, and use of heterogeneous executable modelling languages [Bou+16]. This includes

- Metaprogramming approaches and associated execution engines to design and execute the behavioural semantics of executable modelling languages,
- Efficient and domain-specific execution trace management services, model animation services,
- Advanced debugging facilities such as forward and backward debugging and a comprehensive timeline, and
- Coordination facilities to support concurrent and coordinated execution of heterogeneous models.

In particular, the GEMOC studio comes with *Behavioral Coordination Operator Language* (BCOoL) [Lar+15], a metalanguage to explicitly specify coordination patterns between heterogeneous languages. It actually reifies coordination patterns between specific domains by using coordination operators between the DSMLs used in these domains. These patterns are captured at the language level, and then used to derive a coordination specification automatically for models conforming to

---

[3] GEMOC Studio is available at http://gemoc.org/studio.

the targeted DSMLs. The coordination at the language level relies on a so-called language behavioural interface (making the composition *grey-box*). This interface exposes an abstraction of the language behavioural semantics in terms of *events*. Finally, an heterogeneous execution engine, integrated to the GEMOC studio, can be configured by the coordination specification between the models in order to coordinate the execution of each of the dedicated execution engines.

BCOoL provides support for co-simulation. Using BCOoL, the know-how of an integrator is made explicit, stored, and shared in libraries and amenable to analysis.

4.7 Conclusion and Outlook

In this chapter, we explored how to explicitly address the compositionality of analysis and specific forms of composition. Analysis involves models, contexts, and properties. These are all expressed in languages with their own semantics. We first gave a detailed overview of these important concepts as they are fundamental and need to be managed when composing analyses and the underlying formalisms. We have distinguished three main forms of composition: (i) model composition (white-box composition), (ii) result composition (black-box composition), and (iii) analysis composition (grey-box composition). According to such classes, we then introduced a preliminary conceptual framework that defines abstract operations for analyses composition to be implemented explicitly and managed in modelling environments. We have proceeded towards this goal both with a conceptual reasoning and practical examples of their application with real-world analysis formalisms and their supported tools.

An open research challenge is characterisation of the compositionality of the analysis satisfaction relations and property definitions along the three forms of composition we have proposed in this chapter. Additional challenges are: to identify conditions under which to choose one form of composition over the other; and to support the specification of composition by executing relations in operative workflows that may build upon the concepts proposed in this chapter.

References

[AL90] Martin Abadi and Leslie Lamport. "Composing Specifications". In: *ACM Transactions on Programming Languages and Systems* 15.1 (1990), pp. 73–132.

[BL19] Kyungmin Bae and Jia Lee. "Bounded model checking of signal temporal logic properties using syntactic separation". In: vol. 3. 2019, 51:1–51:30. https://doi.org/10.1145/3290364.

[BM05] Christiano Braga and José Meseguer. "Modular Rewriting Semantics in Practice". In: *International Workshop on Rewriting Logic and Its Applications, WRLA, Proceedings*. Vol. 117. 2005, pp. 393–416. https://doi.org/10.1016/j.entcs.2004.06.019.

[BM15] Kyungmin Bae and José Meseguer. "Model checking linear temporal logic of rewriting formulas under localized fairness". In: *Science of Computer Programming 99* (2015), pp. 193–234.

[Bou+16] Erwan Bousse, Thomas Degueule, Didier Vojtisek, Tanja Mayerhofer, Julien DeAntoni, and Benoît Combemale. "Execution framework of the GEMOC studio (tool demo)". In: *International Conference on Software Language Engineering, SLE, Proceedings*. 2016, pp. 84–89.

[BR18] Egon Börger and Alexander Raschke. *Modeling Companion for Software Practitioners*. Springer, 2018. https://doi.org/10.1007/978-3-662-56641-1.

[Bra+01] Mark van den Brand, Arie van Deursen, Jan Heering, H. A. de Jong, Merijn de Jonge, Tobias Kuipers, Paul Klint, Leon Moonen, Pieter A. Olivier, Jeroen Scheerder, Jurgen J. Vinju, Eelco Visser, and Joost Visser. "The ASF+SDF Meta-environment: A Component-Based Language Development Environment". In: *Proceedings of CC'01*. Vol. 2027. 2001, pp. 365–370.

[BRJ98] Grady Booch, James Rumbaugh, and Ivar Jacobson. *The Unified Modeling Language User Guide*. Addison-Wesley, 1998.

[Bro+09a] Manfred Broy, María Victoria Cengarle, Hans Grönniger, and Bernhard Rumpe. "Considerations and Rationale for a UML System Model". In: *UML 2 Semantics and Applications*. Nov. 2009, pp. 43–61.

[Bro+09b] Manfred Broy, María Victoria Cengarle, Hans Grönniger, and Bernhard Rumpe. "Definition of the UML System Model". In: *UML 2 Semantics and Applications*. 2009, pp. 63–93.

[BS01] Manfred Broy and Ketil Stølen. *Specification and Development of Interactive Systems. Focus on Streams, Interfaces and Refinement*. Springer, 2001.

[BS03] Egon Börger and Robert Stärk. *Abstract State Machines: A Method for High-Level System Design and Analysis*. Springer, 2003.

[CÁS13] Xin Chen, Erika ábrahám, and Sriram Sankaranarayanan. "Flow*: An Analyzer for Non-linear Hybrid Systems". In: *Computer Aided Verification - 25th International Conference, CAV*, Proceedings. Vol. 8044. 2013, pp. 258–263. https://doi.org/10.1007/978-3-642-39799-8_18.

[Cim+15] Alessandro Cimatti, Alberto Griggio, Sergio Mover, and Stefano Tonetta. "HyComp: An SMT-Based Model Checker for Hybrid Systems". In: *Tools and Algorithms for the Construction and Analysis of Systems - 21st International Conference, TACAS, Proceedings*. Vol. 9035. 2015, pp. 52–67. https://doi.org/10.1007/978-3-662-46681-0_4.

[Cla+07] Manuel Clavel, Francisco Durán, Steven Eker, José Meseguer, Patrick Lincoln, Narciso Martí-Oliet, and Carolyn Talcott. *All About Maude – A High-Performance Logical Framework*. Vol. 4350. Springer, 2007.

[Cla+14] Tony Clark, Mark van den Brand, Benoît Combemale, and Bernhard Rumpe. "Conceptual Model of the Globalization for Domain-Specific Languages". In: *Globalizing Domain-Specific Languages - International Dagstuhl Seminar, Revised Papers*. Vol. 9400. 2014, pp. 7–20. https://doi.org/10.1007/978-3-319-26172-0_2.

[Com+16] Benoit Combemale, Robert France, Jean-Marc Jézéquel, Bernhard Rumpe, Jim R.H. Steel, and Didier Vojtisek. *Engineering Modeling Languages*. Chapman and Hall/CRC, 2016, p. 398. http://mdebook.irisa.fr/.

[DLM08] Francisco Durán, Salvador Lucas, and José Meseguer. "MTT: The Maude Termination Tool (System Description)". In: *Automated Reasoning, 4th International Joint Conference*. Vol. 5195. 2008, pp. 313–319.

[DM12] Francisco Durán and José Meseguer. "On the Church-Rosser and coherence properties of conditional order-sorted rewrite theories". In: *Journal of Logic and Algebraic Programming* 81.7–8 (2012), pp. 816–850.

[Dur+19] Francisco Durán, Steven Eker, Santiago Escobar, Narciso Martí-Oliet, José Meseguer, Rubén Rubio, and Carolyn L. Talcott. "Programming and Symbolic Computation in Maude". In: *Journal of Logical and Algebraic Methods in Programming* (2019).

[Eke+03] Johan Eker, Jorn W. Janneck, Edward A. Lee, Jie Liu, Xiaojun Liu, Jozsef Ludvig, S. Neuendorffer, Sonia Sachs, and Yuhong Xiong. "Taming heterogeneity - the Ptolemy approach". In: *Proceedings of the IEEE* 91.1 (2003), pp. 127–144. https://doi.org/10. 1109/JPROC.2002.805829s.

[EMM06] Santiago Escobar, Cathy Meadows, and José Meseguer. "A Rewriting-Based Inference System for the NRL Protocol Analyzer and its Meta-Logical Properties". In: *Theoretical Computer Science* 367.1–2 (2006), pp. 162–202.

[Esp95] David A. Espinosa. "Semantic Lego". PhD thesis. 1995.

[Fre+11] Goran Frehse, Colas Le Guernic, Alexandre Donzé, Scott Cotton, Rajarshi Ray, Olivier Lebeltel, Rodolfo Ripado, Antoine Girard, Thao Dang, and Oded Maler. "SpaceEx: Scalable Verification of Hybrid Systems". In: *Computer Aided Verification - 23rd International Conference, CAV, Proceedings.* Vol. 6806. 2011, pp. 379–395. https:// doi.org/10.1007/978-3-642-22110-1_30.

[Gro06] Object Management Group. *MOF Specification Version 2.0 (2006-01-01).* http://www. omg.org/docs/05-04.pdf. Jan. 2006.

[GRS08] Angelo Gargantini, Elvinia Riccobene, and Patrizia Scandurra. "A Metamodel-based Language and a Simulation Engine for Abstract State Machines". In: *J. UCS* 14.12 (2008), pp. 1949–1983. https://doi.org/10.3217/jucs-014-12-1949.

[GRS09] Angelo Gargantini, Elvinia Riccobene, and Patrizia Scandurra. "A semantic framework for metamodel-based languages". In: *Autom. Softw. Eng.* 16.3-4 (2009), pp. 415–454. https://doi.org/10.1007/s10515-009-0053-0.

[Hei+17] Robert Heinrich, Philipp Merkle, Jörg Henss, and Barbara Paech. "Integrating business process simulation and information system simulation for performance prediction". In: *Software & Systems Modeling* 16.1 (2017), pp. 257–277. https://doi.org/10.1007/ s10270-015-0457-1.

[Hei+21] Robert Heinrich, Francisco Durán, Carolyn L. Talcott, and Steffen Zschaler (eds.) *Composing Model-Based Analysis Tools.* Springer, 2021. https://doi.org/10.1007/978- 3-030-81915-6.

[Hen00] Thomas A. Henzinger. "The theory of hybrid automata". In: *Verification of digital and hybrid systems.* 2000, pp. 265–292.

[HMR13] Jörg Henss, Philipp Merkle, and Ralf H. Reussner. "The OMPCM Simulator for Model-Based Software Performance Prediction: Poster Abstract". In: *6th International ICST Conference on Simulation Tools and Techniques, Proceedings.* 2013, pp. 354–357.

[HR04] David Harel and Bernhard Rumpe. "Meaningful modeling: what's the semantics of "semantics"?" In: *Computer* 37.10 (2004), pp. 64–72.

[HŞR07] Mark Hills, Traian Florin Şerbănuţă, and Grigore Rosu. "A Rewrite Framework for Language Definitions and for Generation of Efficient Interpreters". In: *6th International Workshop on Rewriting Logic and its Applications, WRLA, Proceedings.* Vol. 176. 2007, pp. 215–231. https://doi.org/10.1016/j.entcs.2007.06.017.

[Kon+15] Soonho Kong, Sicun Gao, Wei Chen, and Edmund M. Clarke. "dReach: δ-Reachability Analysis for Hybrid Systems". In: *Tools and Algorithms for the Construction and Analysis of Systems - 21st International Conference, TACAS, Proceedings.* Vol. 9035. 2015, pp. 200–205. https://doi.org/10.1007/978-3-662-46681-0_15.

[KP97] Philipp W. Kutter and Alfonso Pierantonio. "Montages Specifications of Realistic Programming Languages". In: *J. UCS* 3.5 (1997), pp. 416–442.

[Lar+15] Matias Ezequiel Vara Larsen, Julien DeAntoni, Benoît Combemale, and Frédéric Mallet. "A Behavioral Coordination Operator Language (BCOoL)". In: *18th ACM/IEEE International Conference on Model Driven Engineering Languages and Systems, MoDELS, Proceedings.* 2015, pp. 186–195. https://doi.org/10.1109/MODELS.2015. 7338249.

[LSV03] Nancy A. Lynch, Roberto Segala, and Frits W. Vaandrager. "Hybrid I/O automata". In: *Inf. Comput.* 185.1 (2003), pp. 105–157. https://doi.org/10.1016/S0890- 5401(03)00067-1.

[Mas+17] Ian A. Mason, Vivek Nigam, Carolyn Talcott, and Alisson Brito. "A Framework for Analyzing Adaptive Autonomous Aerial Vehicles". In: *1st Workshop on Formal Co-Simulation of Cyber-Physical Systems*. 2017.

[MB04] José Meseguer and Christiano Braga. "Modular Rewriting Semantics of Programming Languages". In: *10th International Conference on Algebraic Methodology and Software Technology, AMAST, Proceedings*. Vol. 3116. 2004, pp. 364–378.

[Mes12] José Meseguer. "Twenty years of rewriting logic". In: *J. Algebraic and Logic Programming* 81 (2012), pp. 721–781.

[Mes92] José Meseguer. "Conditional Rewriting Logic as a Unified Model of Concurrency". In: *Theoretical Computer Science* 96.1 (1992), pp. 73–155.

[MN04] Oded Maler and Dejan Nickovic. "Monitoring Temporal Properties of Continuous Signals". In: *Formal Techniques, Modelling and Analysis of Timed and Fault- Tolerant Systems, Joint International Conferences on Formal Modelling and Analysis of Timed Systems, FORMATS, and Formal Techniques in Real-Time and Fault- Tolerant Systems, FTRTFT, Proceedings*. Vol. 3253. 2004, pp. 152–166. https://doi.org/10.1007/978-3-540-30206-3_12.

[MN08] Peter D. Mosses and Mark J. New. "Implicit Propagation in Structural Operational Semantics". In: *Proceedings of SOS'08*. Vol. 229.4. 2008, pp. 49–66.

[Mog89] Eugenio Moggi. An Abstract *View of Programming Languages*. Tech. rep. ECSLFCS-90-113. Edinburgh University, Department of Computer Science, June 1989.

[Mog91] Eugenio Moggi. "Notions of Computation and Monads". In: *Information and Computation* 93.1 (1991), pp. 55–92.

[Mos02] Peter D. Mosses. "Pragmatics of Modular SOS". In: *Proceedings of AMAST'02*. Vol. 2422. 2002, pp. 21–40.

[Mos99] Peter D. Mosses. "Foundations of Modular SOS". In: *Proceedings of MFCS'99*. Vol. 1672. 1999, pp. 70–80.

[NT20] Vivek Nigam and Carolyn Talcott. "Automated Construction of Security Integrity Wrappers for Industry 4.0 Applications". In: *The 13th International Workshop on Rewriting Logic and its Applications*. 2020.

[NTU19] Vivek Nigam, Carolyn Talcott, and Abraão Aires Urquiza. "Symbolic Timed Trace Equivalence". In: *CathyFest2019*. 2019.

[ÖM07] Peter Csaba Ölveczky and José Meseguer. "Semantics and Pragmatics of Real-Time Maude". In: *Higher-Order and Symbolic Computation* 20.1-2 (2007), pp. 161–196.

[Reu+16] Ralf H. Reussner, Steffen Becker, Jens Happe, Robert Heinrich, Anne Koziolek, Heiko Koziolek, Max Kramer, and Klaus Krogmann. *Modeling and Simulating Software Architectures – The Palladio Approach*. MIT Press, 2016.

[RR11] Jan Oliver Ringert and Bernhard Rumpe. "A Little Synopsis on Streams, Stream Processing Functions, and State-Based Stream Processing". In: *International Journal of Software and Informatics* (2011).

[RS10] Grigore Rosu and Traian-Florin Serbanuta. "An overview of the K semantic framework". In: *J. Log. Algebraic Methods Program.* 79.6 (2010), pp. 397–434. https://doi.org/10.1016/j.jlap.2010.03.012.

[Sta73] Herbert Stachowiak. *Allgemeine Modelltheorie*. Springer, 1973.

[Sti18] Christian Stier. "Adaptation-Aware Architecture Modeling and Analysis of Energy Efficiency for Software Systems". PhD thesis. Karlsruher Institut fur Technologie (KIT), 2018. https://doi.org/10.5445/IR/1000083402.

[Tal+16] Carolyn Talcott, Vivek Nigam, Farhad Arbab, and Tobia Kappe. "Formal Specification and Analysis of Robust Adaptive Distributed Cyber-Physical Systems". In: SFM 2016: *Formal Methods for the Quantitative Evaluation of Collective Adaptive Systems*. Vol. 9700. 2016, pp. 1–35.

Chapter 5
Integration and Orchestration of Analysis Tools

Robert Heinrich, Erwan Bousse, Sandro Koch, Arend Rensink, Elvinia Riccobene, Daniel Ratiu, and Marjan Sirjani

Abstract This chapter addresses the integration and orchestration of external analysis tools into modelling environments. We first give a detailed overview of the considered context and problem statement. Then, a solution in the form of a reference architecture for the integration of analysis tools into modelling environments is presented. We collect a set of requirements that analysis tools must satisfy in order to enable (a) the integration of these analyses into modelling environments and (b) the orchestration of these analysis tools to produce overall results. Finally, we give an overview of different orchestration strategies for the integration of analysis tools and show examples.

This core chapter addresses Challenge 2 introduced in Chap. 3 of this book (*the practical implications*—how to integrate and orchestrate existing analysis tools).

R. Heinrich (✉) · S. Koch
Karlsruhe Institute of Technology, Karlsruhe, Germany
e-mail: robert.heinrich@kit.edu; sandro.koch@kit.edu

E. Bousse
University of Nantes, Nantes, France
e-mail: erwan.bousse@ls2n.fr

A. Rensink
University of Twente, Enschede, Netherlands
e-mail: arend.rensink@utwente.nl

E. Riccobene
Università degli Studi di Milano, Milano, Italy
e-mail: elvinia.riccobene@unimi.it

D. Ratiu
CARIAD, Wolfsburg, Germany
e-mail: ratiud@googlemail.com

M. Sirjani
Mälardalen University, Västerås, Sweden
e-mail: marjan.sirjani@mdh.se

5.1   Introduction

Sophisticated modelling environments, often based on the principles of *model-driven engineering* (MDE) and *software language engineering* (SLE), are becoming increasingly ubiquitous. More and more disciplines, may it be avionics, automotive, constructional engineering, automation engineering, or natural sciences, rely on such tools. These tools become all the more valuable if they provide deep insights into the correctness and fitness-for-purpose of the models[1] used and apply model-based analysis to forecast properties of the things to be built. At the same time there is a community of analysis tool builders who distil mathematical and logic experience into analysis tools (cf. Chap. 2 of this book [Hei+21]) that rely on formalisms such as *satisfiability modulo theories* (SMT) formulae, transition systems, or discrete-event systems. Many of these analysis tools can be used beneficially in the aforementioned modelling environments if they are suitably integrated. In practice this usually means that user-facing models must be translated to the input formalism of the analysis tool, and the result of the analysis must be lifted back to the domain level. In addition, there are many use cases like in portfolio solvers, model checkers, simulation coupling, model-based testing, and runtime verification where multiple existing analysis tools must be orchestrated to deliver value in the context of the modelling environment.

This chapter addresses the challenge of how to integrate and orchestrate external analysis tools into modelling environments. We first give a detailed description of the considered context and problem statement in Sect. 5.2. The state of the art of integrating and orchestrating model-based analysis tools is discussed in Sect. 5.3. Then, we provide a solution in the form of a reference architecture for the integration of analysis tools into modelling environments in Sect. 5.4. Based on our professional experience, both in academia and industry, with building and using modelling environments and integrating analysis tools into existing modelling environments, we collect a set of requirements in Sect. 5.5 that analysis tools must satisfy in order to enable (a) the integration of these analyses into modelling environments and (b) the orchestration of analysis tools to produce overall results. Tools that apply the reference architecture may adhere to different orchestration strategies. We give an overview of several orchestration strategies for the integration of analysis tools into modelling environments in Sect. 5.6 and show examples of existing tools to illustrate the application of these orchestration strategies in Sect. 5.7. The chapter concludes with a summary and outlook in Sect. 5.8.

---

[1] Note, while Chap. 2 of this book [Hei+21] postulates analysis input as three kinds of models—of system, of property, and of context—we stay with the term model in this chapter since a distinction of the kind of model is not relevant here.

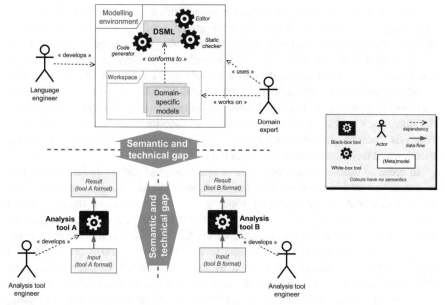

Fig. 5.1 Overview of the context and problem statement

5.2   Context and Problem Statement

To give a better global understanding of the focus of this chapter, Fig. 5.1 depicts
the considered context and problem statement. First, at the top half of the figure,
the key roles and concepts of a typical modelling process are shown. We assume
that a *modelling environment* is used by the *domain expert* in order to work on one
or multiple *domain-specific models*. While the models are being worked on by the
domain expert, the models are stored in a *workspace* provided by the modelling
environment. A classical modelling environment provides one or several[2] *domain-
specific modelling languages* (DSMLs), along with a set of tools—editor, checker,
code generator, etc.—to create, manipulate, or verify models conforming to these
DSMLs. The development and maintenance of the modelling environment and the
DSMLs it uses are taken care by one or several *language engineers*.

Then, at the bottom half of the figure, a common choice to gain insight[3] into
the models is to rely on existing proven and powerful *analysis tools*, such as
model checkers, solvers, or theorem provers. Analysis tools can even be expertly
combined in order to bring more interesting, more complete, or faster results. In this
chapter, we make the assumption that the considered analysis tools are *external*—

---

[2] Note that Figs. 5.1 and 5.2 only show a single DSML for better readability.

[3] We may be interested in insights into models such as correctness and well-formedness of models,
or quality properties of the modelled system.

i.e., developed by different persons and communities than the ones involved in the modelling process shown in the top half—and *black-boxes*—i.e., they are taken off-the-shelf and their internals are not known. An analysis tool typically takes an *input* conforming to a specific input format, and produces a *result* in either a loose (e.g., raw textual description) or a well-defined format. Some tools may also simultaneously require multiple different sources of input (e.g., a configuration file and a model), produce multiple different result artefacts (e.g., a counterexample and the state space used to discover it), or may even function in an incremental fashion. Analysis tools are developed by *analysis tool engineers*, which are experts in the theories and techniques implemented in the tools.

In order to enable the use of single or combined external tools for the analysis of models created in the modelling environment, there are at least two compelling prerequisites that must be fulfilled. First, we call *tool integration* the problem of actually being able to make use of each separate analysis tool (i.e., exchange data, make queries, start and stop tasks, etc.) within the modelling process. For instance, using a model checker requires at least to be able to (1) send it the model and the property to be checked, (2) ask it to start the analysis, and (3) retrieve the result. Second, we call *tool orchestration* the problem of configuring *when* and *how* analysis tools should be used and/or combined in a considered modelling process, which includes how these analysis tools should interact with each other. For instance, it must be possible to drive a sequence of actions such as "give the model in a certain format to the model checker, start the analysis, get the counterexample, translate it to a second format, feed it to a second tool to replay the trace, translate the replay result back to the domain expert".

Unfortunately, both, in between a modelling environment and analysis tools, and in between analysis tools themselves, there are *semantic gaps*—i.e., differences between their semantics— and *technical gaps*—i.e., differences between the technical spaces where each environment and tool operates, such as runtime environments, *application programming interfaces* (APIs), or frameworks—to take into account. Consequently, there are many obstacles to overcome in order to solve the tool integration and tool orchestration problems, such as:

1. A model created in the modelling environment conforms to a DSML that may entirely differ from the input format expected by a given analysis tool, thus first requiring a *model transformation* to make the model understandable by the tool.
2. Since a given analysis tool is not aware of the DSML and of the domain of expertise of the modeller (i.e., the domain expert), the result it produces is likely to be written in "words" that the domain expert cannot easily understand, thus requiring a second model transformation to *lift* the low-level result back into a format fitting the domain of interest, and thus the domain expert.
3. When combining analysis tools, the input and output formats that they use are rarely compatible among themselves, and thus require model transformations as well.
4. Each analysis tool may expose a specific *interface* (e.g., Java API, command line interface, network socket, etc.) for programmatically interacting with it, and

possesses its own explicit or implicit *protocol* to use this interface (i.e., which sequences of actions provided by the interface are valid to achieve certain tasks).

5. The modelling environment and analysis tools may work in very different *technical spaces*, such as different data representations (e.g., graphs *vs.* trees), execution environments (e.g., Java *vs.* Python), or file formats (e.g., XMI *vs.* JSON). These differences add technical complexity over the task of defining sound transformations, both towards and from analysis tools.

All these concerns are rather well known, and have all been dealt with in the past in an ad hoc basis in a great number of modelling environments—AF3, ASMETA, mbeddr, or Palladio to name a few (all described in Sect. 5.3.2). However, to our knowledge, little work has been made to provide *general and systematic* answers that could help dealing with the integration and the orchestration of analysis tools. Hence, as an exploratory attempt to address this issue, we present the following three contributions in this chapter. First, we propose a *reference architecture*— along with important concepts—that can be used to methodically integrate and orchestrate analysis tools into a modelling process. Second, we propose a set of *requirements* that qualify which analysis tools can be properly integrated in such an architecture. Third and last, we propose and formalise a first set of *strategies* that can be used to answer common integration and orchestration cases, especially when multiple analysis tools are combined together to provide one or multiple results. These strategies are illustrated using a selection of real-world examples of existing ad hoc integrations and orchestrations of analysis tools.

5.3 State of the Art

This section provides a discussion of the state of the art of integrating and orchestrating model-based analysis tools before we propose our concepts in the sections that follow. We first give an overview of related research on integrating and orchestrating tools and then give examples of existing modelling environments with integrated analysis tools that may serve as inspiration and illustration for the concepts proposed in this chapter.

5.3.1 Research on Integrating and Orchestrating Tools

A first step to systematically deal with the integration and orchestration of black-box analysis tools is to define how to generically interact with tools. To this end, significant work has been done in different research communities to consider tools as *first-class entities*.

Two early endeavours from the late 1990s are ToolBus [BK96] and the *electronic tool integration* (ETI) platform [SMB97, BMW97] (with some extensions made in the 2000s [MNS05, Mar05]). Both these approaches have assumptions and goals rather similar to what we stated in the previous section: Being able to integrate existing tools into foreign processes is an important challenge, which requires proper data exchange and communication mechanisms with said tools. These approaches already sketch important concepts such as tool adapters, type transformers, tool coordination, or coordination universe. However, these approaches try to tackle a more generic problem, as they make no assumptions on the context in which tools are integrated and combined. They notably do not discuss the problem of lifting analysis results to the domain of interest. While we do take inspiration from these early generic proposals, the present chapter specifically focuses on the integration and orchestration of analysis tools into a modelling environment. Moreover, our proposal also aims at providing a set of requirements for integrating analysis tools, along with a set of interesting re-usable strategies for orchestrating them.

In the 2000s, a slightly similar proposal was made, called Model Bus [BGS05]. In a pure MDE context, this approach aims at providing an environment where both a set of metamodels and a set of services built for these metamodels—such as model transformations and code generators—can be registered. These services can then easily be called and chained thanks to a communication bus called the Model Bus. This approach is mostly targeting MDE practitioners who need to organise a set of model manipulation services, and does not discuss the case of external tools, or the problem of lifting back analysis results.

More recently, some approaches solely focus on the problem of combining the analysis tools. Dwyer et al. [DE10] proposed a vision where tools can be combined using the notion of *evidence* as a pivotal concept. In other words, the authors advocate for a common representation and storage of analysis results, and means to compose these results in a meaningful way. Rather aligned with this vision, and following a proposal from Rushby [Rus05], Cruanes et al. [Cru+13] designed the *evidential tool bus* (ETB), a "distributed framework for integrating diverse tools into coherent workflows for producing claims supported by explicit evidence". While the approach is very interesting, and in some ways in the steps of ETI, it mostly focuses on the problem of storing and sharing analysis results between distributed formal analysis tools. Questions such as the lifting of results back to the domain, or how to soundly transform domain-specific models for analysis tools, or what common orchestration strategies can be used, are not considered.

5.3.2 Examples of Modelling Environments with Integrated Analysis Tools

In the following, we provide examples of modelling environments that integrate various external analysis tools. All our examples are based on open-source and freely available environments. However, commercial environments (e.g., Simulink[4] and SCADE[5]) face the same challenges when integrating external analysis tools. These examples can be seen as existing ad hoc applications of the general concepts presented in this chapter.

AF3[6] [Ara+15] is an environment for modelling and specification of embedded systems. It offers support for modelling requirements, the logical and technical architectures and deployment. AF3 integrates NuSMV [Cim+02] for verifying models and Z3 [MB08] for generating optimal deployments.

ASMETA[7] [Arc+11, GRS08] (ASM mETAmodeling) is a modelling environment for the *abstract state machines* (ASMs) formal method. It is based on the integration of different tools for performing validation and verification activities on ASM models; it integrates different external analysis tools such as the NuSMV [Cim+02] model checker for performing property verification and SMT solvers to support correct model refinement verification [AGR16] and runtime verification [AGR14].

FASTEN[8] [RGS19] is a modelling environment for the specification and design of safety-critical systems. Regarding formal analyses, the main focus of FASTEN is to experiment with usability of formal specification and transition between informal to formal specifications. FASTEN integrates various external analysis tools such as NuSMV [Cim+02], Spin [Hol03], Z3 [MB08], and PRISM [KNP11].

mbeddr[9] is a modelling environment for the development of embedded systems. It integrates various formal analysis tools that work at model level as well as those that work on C code. Examples of model-level analyses are checking for consistency and completeness of decision tables [Rat+12a, Rat+12b] using Z3 [MB08]; examples of code-level analyses are checking assertions from C programs [Rat+13, MVR14] using CBMC [CKL04] or applying the model-driven code checking method [RU19] using Spin [Hol03].

OpenCert[10] is an integrated environment for specification and certification of *cyber-physical systems* (CPS). OpenCert uses modelling languages based on SysML [Obj12] and integrates the OCRA [CDT13] and NuXmv [Cav+14] formal verification tools for checking properties expressed using temporal logic.

Palladio is a tool-supported approach to modelling and analysing software architectures for various quality properties [Reu+16]. It integrates various analysis tools to predict and reason about these quality properties into a modelling environment.

---

[4] Simulink: https://www.mathworks.com/products/simulink.html.

[5] SCADE: https://www.ansys.com/products/embedded-software/ansys-scade-suite.

[6] AF3: https://download.fortiss.org/public/projects/af3/help/index.html.

[7] ASMETA: http://asmeta.sourceforge.net/.

[8] FASTEN: https://sites.google.com/site/fastenroot/home.

[9] mbeddr: http://mbeddr.com.

[10] OpenCert: https://www.eclipse.org/opencert/.

Details on the Palladio approach and the associated tooling are described in Chap. 11 of this book [Hei+21].

VCES[11] [GLO11] is an Eclipse-based environment for the modelling and analysis of software-intensive systems. It includes an implementation of a higher-level modelling language (named SAML—*system analysis and modelling language*) that is an intermediate, automata-based language between arbitrary high-level engineering languages like SysML [Obj12] and the input languages of analysis tools. VCES features model transformations from SAML to the input of verification tools like NuSMV [Cim+02] and PRISM [KNP11]. Results of the verification are lifted in the VCES *integrated development environment* (IDE) and presented in a user-friendly manner.

Why3[12] [FP13] is a platform for deductive program verification for the WhyML language. It integrates a wide range of both automatic and interactive external theorem provers (more than 19 as of today), and any prover can be chosen to perform any of the proofs. While Why3 is not a modelling environment per se— since WhyML is a programming language mostly used as an intermediate language to verify programs written in C, Java, or Ada—it directly deals with the problem of integrating and orchestrating a great number of homogeneous external tools, here using an abstraction layer dedicated to theorem provers.

TOPCASED[13] [Far+06] is an environment for critical applications and systems development, using modelling languages such as UML [Obj15], SysML [Obj12], or AADL [FGH06]. The environment relies on the Fiacre language [Ber+08] as an intermediary language to translate models to analysis tools—such as model checkers—and to lift verification results back to the domain expert. While TOP-CASED is not maintained since 2013, it was one of the first successful attempts to bridge MDE and formal verification in a single environment.

5.4 A Reference Architecture for Integrating Analysis Tools

A *reference architecture* is known in software engineering as a general structure for applications in a particular domain, which may partially or fully implement the reference architecture [Som15]. We transferred the notion of a reference architecture to the problem of integrating analysis tools into modelling environments. The reference architecture for the integration of one or multiple analysis tools into a modelling environment is depicted in Fig. 5.2. Note, in the figure we depict two

---

[11] VCES: https://cse.cs.ovgu.de/cse/researchareas/vecs/.

[12] Why3: http://why3.lri.fr/.

[13] TOPCASED: http://www.topcased.org/.

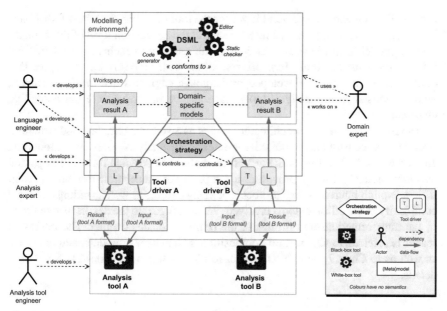

Fig. 5.2 Reference architecture for the integration of analysis tools into a modelling environment

analysis tools to indicate that multiple analysis tools can be integrated, while the number of analysis tools to be integrated is not limited.

The modelling environment is responsible for both, interacting with analysis tools and interacting with the domain expert wishing to perform analyses based on domain-specific models. The modelling environment comprises four components: (a) the DSMLs, (b) a set of tools—e.g., editors, checkers and code generators— to create, manipulate or verify models conforming to these DSMLs, (c) a set of orchestration strategies to manage the interaction with and combination of analysis tools, and (d) the tool drivers that are responsible for actually interacting with the specific analysis tools.

The modelling environment, the DSMLs it uses, and the tools to work on models, are developed and maintained by language engineers. Often, the development and maintenance of tools to work on models is supported by tool developers which are not depicted in the figure as they are not in the focus of this chapter. The modelling environment follows some *orchestration strategy* that defines which analysis tools should be used for a given analysis task, how these tools should be used for a given analysis task, in which order these tools should be used, and how the analysis results they produce should be combined or exchanged. Analysis tools are assumed to already exist and to have been created externally by analysis tool engineers to satisfy specific analysis tasks. The integration of analysis tools into the modelling environment is accomplished by a set of *tool drivers*, each tool driver being responsible for interacting with one external analysis tool. This includes how to use the interfaces of the analysis tool, how to translate a domain-specific model

used by domain experts in a valid input for the tool (T in Fig. 5.2), how to lift back
the analysis result in a form that makes sense at the abstraction level of the domain-
specific model (L in Fig. 5.2),[14] as well as the protocol to exchange messages and
information with the tool. Tool drivers, along with orchestration strategies that
control them, are jointly developed by language engineers and *analysis experts*,
who are versed in the analysis tools that must be integrated into the modelling
environment.

The proposed reference architecture serves as a solution template and structural
overview of constituents required for integrating analysis tools into modelling
environments. It therefore addresses aforementioned obstacles for tool integration
and tool orchestration by providing a template for model transformation, result
lifting, explicit interfaces, and protocols of analysis tools as well as hiding technical
complexity of the different tools involved. We do not go into the details of soundness
of the transformations and liftings in the reminder of this chapter. The interested
reader is referred to Chap. 4, on composition of languages, models, and analyses,
as well as to Chap. 7, on exploiting tool results, of this book [Hei+21] for further
details.

5.5   Requirements for Analysis Tool Integration
and Orchestration

The reference architecture described in the previous section presumes that several
requirements are satisfied by the considered analysis tools. In this section, we
describe such a set of requirements, such that analysis tools satisfying these
requirements can be easily integrated and orchestrated into modelling environments.
We base these requirements on our experience as authors—both in academia and in
industry—with building and using modelling environments and integrating analysis
tools. We categorise these requirements along two dimensions: requirements for the
integration of analysis tools (Sect. 5.5.1), and requirements for the orchestration of
analysis tools (Sect. 5.5.2). The first set of requirements is about the integration of
individual tools, the second set is focused on orchestrating complex use cases with
one or more analysis tools.

---

[14] Note that while Fig. 5.2 does show the analysis results lifted at the domain level by the L
transformation, the figure does not show what language such domain-level results conform to,
for the sake of brevity. Yet, an important task here is to provide domain-level concepts that are able
to represent analysis results in a domain-specific fashion, if possible through explicit relationships
with concepts of the DSMLs.

5.5.1   Integration Requirements

The following are basic requirements to analysis tools which are essential to enable their integration into modelling environments.

R1.1 Explicit Input Language In order to enable the integration of an analysis tool into a modelling environment, it shall have a precisely defined input language (both when the analysis tool consumes textual files as well as when it exposes its functionality via APIs).

R1.2 Explicit Output Language While most analysis tools have a well-defined input language (i.e., to specify models to analyse), much fewer have an explicitly defined language (syntax and semantics) in which analysis results are presented. We need the syntactic definition of the result representation (aka. "output format") in order to enable parsing—e.g., having XML or JSON format for the output of the analysis tool dramatically helps in parsing the results. Besides the syntax, the semantics of the output needs to be precise enough in order to enable interpretation of analysis results.

R1.3 Explicit Protocol to Interact with the Analysis Tool We have identified three scenarios when an explicit protocol is needed for the integration. (1) Many analysis tools can be used in an interactive fashion, and in these cases the protocol of commands accepted by the tools shall be explicitly defined—e.g., the NuSMV model checker [Cim+02] offers an interactive mode that is superior to the automated interaction mode by providing a finer granular interaction protocol (i.e., sequence of NuSMV commands) that can be used to guide the analysis. (2) In the case when the analysis tool provides an API, the order in which the API functions should be called is essential for the integration—e.g., the Z3 solver [MB08] comes with a Java API that specifies the order of function calls and this eases the integration into modelling environments. (3) Many analysis tools can be called several times for performing a certain analysis, each call using some information provided in a previous call—e.g., *C bounded model checker* (CBMC) [CKL04], a bounded model checker for C and C++, can be called first to collect the properties to analyse and subsequently to analyse certain properties of interest.

R1.4 Robustness in Handling Long-Running Analyses Many times the analyses to be performed are complex and, such as the case of formal verification, they might take hours, days, or more to complete. From a tool-integrator perspective, an analysis tool needs to provide mechanisms to handle such situations either by, e.g., setting timeouts, giving feedback about the analysis progress, or enabling a "nice" cancel of analyses—e.g., the Z3 solver enables its users to specify timeouts for managing long-running analyses.

R1.5 Witness for Certification and Assurance When an analysis tool is used for checking properties of safety-critical systems, it shall provide an independently checkable witness of all analysis results. In this manner, the confidence in the correct functioning of analysis tools can be drastically increased—e.g., the software verification competition requires competing tools to provide both correctness and violation witnesses.[15]

5.5.2   Orchestration Requirements

In the following, we present a set of requirements for analysis tools that aim to facilitate their orchestration in modelling environments. Orchestration is often about result exchange and coordination which brings us to these requirements.

R2.1 Reuse Partial Results Between Analyses   Many uses of analysis tools via an IDE imply the integration of the analysis tool into a modelling workflow. Modelling happens today in an incremental and agile fashion, with continuous changes. The interested reader is referred to Chap. 6 of this book [Hei+21]. Ideally, the efforts required to re-analyse a model once changes are performed shall be proportional with the size of the change and not the size of the input model—e.g., caching partial verification results which make subsequent analyses faster or more tractable; another example is the ordering of *binary decision diagrams* (BDDs) variables can be saved by NuSMV [Cim+02].

R2.2 Provide Partial Results   In case when the analysis is incomplete, partial results about what has been successfully covered are essential for the users—e.g., there are tools like CPAChecker [Bey16] that support their users by providing partial verification results for the cases when, e.g., the verification is untractable.

R2.3 Coordination of Portfolio Analysers   In case of portfolio solvers, several tools can be started simultaneously to analyse the same property. Coordinating these tools needs to be done today at low level. Furthermore, depending on the kind of the input models and the checked property, one or another of the integrated solvers in a portfolio might be more efficient. Having explicit information about the strengths of the different solvers (with respect to the model under analysis and the checked property) could be used to increase the analysis efficiency at high-level. A notable example of portfolio solvers is, e.g., Why3 [Bob+12], that offers a unified interface for integrating and coordinating portfolios of SMT solvers.

5.6   Orchestration Strategies

A modelling environment may require the use of a single analysis tool or the coordinated use of a number of analysis tools. In the reference architecture presented earlier in this chapter, such coordination is achieved using so-called orchestration

---

[15] SV-COMP 2020: https://sv-comp.sosy-lab.org/2020/rules.php.

strategies, each one responsible for controlling the different tool drivers and exchanging data between tool drivers and the workspace of the modelling environment. In this section, we describe and define a selection of orchestration strategies that, from our own experience, are both, common and relevant, for composing analysis tools.

5.6.1 Orchestration Strategy Overview

An overview of the different types of strategies marked by capital letters is depicted in Fig. 5.3 and introduced in an informal way hereafter before we give precise definitions. Note that, when multiple analysis tools can be involved, we merely use two tools in the figure and the text for the sake of brevity. Furthermore, in practical settings combinations of these orchestration strategies are possible and orchestration strategies may be nested.

Single Analysis Orchestration (A) For this orchestration strategy, in order to perform a model-based analysis, the modelling environment uses a tool driver to translate a domain-specific model into a valid input for an external black-box analysis tool. Then, the modelling environment translates back (lifts) the result of the analysis tool by using the tool driver again. An example of this strategy is to translate a model conforming to a DSML into a model checker input, and then translate back the response into DSML concepts.

Separate Parallel Analysis Orchestration (B) This strategy is similar to (A), but with multiple different tools. These tools are getting the same input model, but they can run completely separately. This way we obtain separate results (both expressed in terms of the same DSML) which we can compare and from which we can select the most appropriate one. Portfolio solvers are an example of strategy B where we

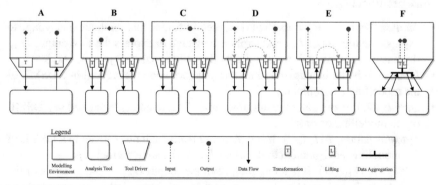

Fig. 5.3 Different types of orchestration strategies

can run the same analysis in different tools, and we make them compete, and we keep the most interesting result (e.g., fastest, more precise, etc.).

Combined Analysis Orchestration (C) In this strategy, the results of different tools that may use different input models are combined into a single output model. This strategy can be used to obtain a more comprehensive result (by combining results) than a single analysis could provide. Combination of qualitative and quantitative results of analysis tools is an example for which the combined analysis strategy can be applied.

Cooperating Analysis Orchestration (D) With this strategy the modelling environment invokes one tool, then translates the result into an input of another tool, and then translates the result of the second tool back into an input of the first tool to run another analysis. This cooperation between analysis tools can be repeated until a certain stop criteria is reached. Coupled simulations are an example of strategy D where the combination of interacting black-box simulations can create a more precise result.

Sequential Analysis Orchestration (E) With this strategy the modelling environment invokes one tool, then translates the result into an input of another tool, and then translates the result of the second tool back to a domain-specific model to provide it to the domain expert. Refining the result of one analysis tool by another is an example of the sequential analysis orchestration strategy.

5.6.2 Orchestration Strategy Definition

After giving an overview and introduction to different orchestration strategies, we now give a precise definition of each strategy.

Elements We identify the following primitives in order to define the orchestration strategies from Fig. 5.3.

- *Analysis Tool*, A_T. It has explicit (i.e., precise format and semantics) language to express the tool input I_{A_T} and explicit language to express the tool output O_{A_T} (by basic requirements); we can define $A_T = (I_{A_T}, activity(A_T), O_{A_T})$;
- *Input*, I. It is the input given to an analysis tool and is expressed in a DSML of the modelling environment;
- *Output*, O. It is the output result of an analysis tool and is expressed in a DSML of the modelling environment;
- *Transformation*, $T(I, I_{A_T})$. It is a mapping from the input I given in a DSML of the modelling environment to the input I_{A_T} of the analysis tool A_T;
- *Lifting*, $L(O_{A_T}, O)$. It is a mapping from the output O_{A_T} of the analysis of the tool A_T to the output O expressed in a DSML of the modelling environment;
- *Tool Driver*, $TD(A_T)$. It is a software component that defines how to make use of a specific analysis tool, including how to translate a domain-specific model

into a valid input for the tool, how to lift back the analysis result into a form
that makes sense at the abstraction level of a domain-specific model, as well as
the protocol to exchange messages and information with the tool; therefore, it is
defined as a tuple

$$TD(A_T) =< T(I, I_{A_T}), L(O_{A_T}, O), protocol(A_T) >$$

where $T(I, I_{A_T})$ is the transformation to provide adequate input to the analysis
tool A_T, $L(O_{A_T}, O)$ is the lifting to make the analysis result useful at the
abstraction level of a domain-specific model, and $protocol(A_T)$ is the protocol
to exchange messages and information with the tool A_T. Transformation T and
lifting L may be the identity mapping in case the tool A_T uses/returns a model
in the same language that the modelling environment uses.

A tool driver can make use of a number of different transformations and
liftings, not necessarily coupled, since the supported tool A_T may require more
than one input model and may return more than one result model. Therefore,
we can extend the definitions of transformation and lifting in the aforementioned
definition of tool driver as follows while $m, n \in \mathbb{N}_{>0}$:

$$T(I, I_{A_T}) =< T_1(I, I_{1 A_T}), \ldots, T_n(I, I_{n A_T}) >$$

$$L(O_{A_T}, O) =< L_1(O_{1 A_T}, O), \ldots, L_m(O_{m A_T}, O) > .$$

Further, the input to a given analysis tool may comprise more than one domain-
specific model. Also the output of a given analysis tool may comprise more than
one domain-specific model. In this chapter, we consider input and output each to
be a single domain-specific model to not overly complicate the explanations and
definitions given.

Orchestration Strategies We define the orchestration strategies depicted in
Fig. 5.3 as follows while $i \in \mathbb{N}_{>0}$, $j, k, m, n \in \mathbb{N}_{>1}$ and $m \leq n$.

- *Single analysis orchestration (A):* a single tool driver $TD(A_T)$ is used, which
  provides input I to a tool A_T by applying transformation $T(I, I_{A_T})$ and gets the
  output O by applying the lifting $L(O_{A_T}, O)$.
- *Separate parallel analysis orchestration (B):* a number n of (not necessary different) tool drivers $TD(A_{T_1}), TD(A_{T_2}), \ldots, TD(A_{T_n})$ are used in parallel; each
  $TD(A_{T_i})$ provides input to the analysis tool A_{T_i} by applying the transformation
  $T(I_i, I_{A_{T_i}})$ and lifts back the output O_i to the modelling environment by applying
  the lifting $L(O_{A_{T_i}}, O_i)$. The input I_i can be the same input I for all $TD(A_{T_i})$,
  or suitably customised by applying $protocol(A_{T_i})$ of $TD(A_{T_i})$. It is up to the
  domain expert to decide about the use of the outputs $O_1, O_2, \ldots, O_m$ (m can be
  equal to n): to keep all of them, to select one of them, etc.
- *Combined analysis orchestration (C):* a number n of (not necessary different) tool drivers $TD(A_{T_1}), TD(A_{T_2}), \ldots, TD(A_{T_n})$ are used in parallel; each

$TD(A_{T_i})$ provides input to the analysis tool A_{T_i} by applying the transformation $T(I_i, I_{A_{T_i}})$ and gets the output O_i by applying the lifting $L(O_{A_{T_i}}, O_i)$. The modelling environment assembles the output O as the result of the (internal) operation combine $(O_1, O_2, \ldots, O_m)$ for a number m of outputs (m can be equal to n).

- *Cooperating analysis orchestration (D):* a number n of (not necessary different) tool drivers $TD(A_{T_1}), TD(A_{T_2}), \ldots, TD(A_{T_n})$ are used in a cooperating way. The modelling environment provides input I to a first analysis tool A_{T_1} by a tool driver $TD(A_{T_1})$ which applies the transformation $T(I, I_{A_{T_1}})$. According to a cooperation schema of the modelling environment, at each cooperation step, the output of a tool A_{T_i} is then given as input to another tool A_{T_j} (even if already used in previous steps) by applying the transformation $T(L(O_{A_{T_i}}, O_i), I_{A_{T_j}})$ which involves also the cooperation between $protocol(TD(A_{T_i}))$ and $protocol(TD(A_{T_j}))$; upon a stop criteria (e.g., a fixed point)—defined in the cooperation schema—is reached, the modelling environment gets the output O by applying the lifting $L(O_{A_{T_k}}, O)$ of the tool driver $TD(A_{T_k})$ for a given k.

- *Sequential analysis orchestration (E):* a number n of (not necessary different) tool drivers $TD(A_{T_1}), TD(A_{T_2}), \ldots, TD(A_{T_n})$ are used in sequence. By $TD(A_{T_1})$ the modelling environment provides input I to a first analysis tool A_{T_1} (the transformation $T(I, I_{A_{T_1}})$ is applied); at each sequential step, the output of the tool A_{T_i} is then given as input to the subsequent tool $A_{T_{i+1}}$ by applying the transformation $T(L(O_{A_{T_i}}, O_i), I_{A_{T_{i+1}}})$ in a cooperation between $protocol(TD(A_{T_i}))$ and $protocol(TD(A_{T_{i+1}}))$; upon end of the sequential use of the orchestrated tools, the modelling environment gets the output O by applying the lifting $L(O_{A_{T_n}}, O)$.

Combinations or nested compositions of the above orchestration strategies are possible in order to perform complex model-based analyses that require tools orchestrated in a more sophisticated way. Combined strategies might also require more powerful tool drivers that can share transformations towards specific formats and are able to combine output results. Indeed, in case different tools are used according to a complex schema such as the orchestration strategy F in Fig. 5.3, where a number n of (not necessary different) analysis tools $A_{T_1}, A_{T_2}, \ldots, A_{T_n}$ are used, the unique tool driver needs a complex transformation able to transform the input model (or suitable parts of it) into the inputs of specific tools, and combine/aggregate (in a suitable way) all or some output results before lifting the analysis result back to the modelling environment.

However, orchestration strategies whose transformation and lifting require to share information and combine results are not in the focus of this chapter, and therefore the formalisation of orchestration strategies such as the case F is an open topic that needs to be addressed in future research.

5.7 Examples of Orchestration Strategy Application

This section provides examples for each of the strategies defined in the previous section to illustrate their application in existing modelling environments.

Single Analysis Orchestration (A) Model-based simulation is an example of the application of the single analysis orchestration strategy. For example, the Palladio [Reu+16] software architecture modelling and analysis approach (cf. Chap. 11 of this book [Hei+21]) uses various analysis techniques to predict quality properties of software systems. The Palladio-Bench corresponds to the modelling environment. To conduct a quality analysis of a software system, an architectural model of the system is created by domain experts in the Palladio-Bench. Several analysis tools can be selected to be executed based on the model. One of these analysis tools is the performance simulator SimuCom [Bec08]. The Palladio-Bench transforms the domain-specific model (i.e., architectural model) into simulation code of SimuCom, which is executed for performance simulation. After the simulation has been finished, the result is lifted back to the Palladio-Bench. The Palladio-Bench in turn displays the result to the domain experts.

Similarly, the single analysis orchestration strategy is used in the ASMETA modelling environment [Arc+11] to perform model-based analysis of the ASM specifications. The ASMETA modelling environment can invoke a number of tools for model validation (e.g., interactive or random simulation by the simulator AsmetaS, animation by the animator AsmetaA, scenario construction and validation by the validator AsmetaV) and verification (e.g., static analysis by the model reviewer AsmetaMA, proof of temporal properties by the model checker AsmetaSMV, proof of correct model refinement [AGR16]). All these tools are orchestrated in a similar way: An ASM model is given as input to a given tool by means of a transformation that translates the input model into an adequate input for the target tool; the result of the analysis is then lifted back in a way that it is understandable by the domain expert.

The modelling environments mbeddr [Voe+12], FASTEN [RGS19], and AF3 [Ara+15] all also use this orchestration strategy. Domain-specific models are translated into the input language of analysis tools, let them run and subsequently lift the results at model level so that they are understandable to domain experts.

Separate Parallel Analysis Orchestration (B) Typical examples of strategy B are portfolio solvers which use multiple solver tools to run in parallel in order to tackle computationally difficult problems. A well known modelling environment for different analysis tools—e.g., SMT solvers—is Why3 [Bob+12]. Why3 takes input models described in a high-level language which aims at maximal expressiveness without sacrificing efficiency of automated proof search. Based on the input models, Why3 applies transformations that will gradually translate Why3's logic into the logic of different provers (e.g., Z3 [MB08], CVC4 [Bar+11], Yices [Dut14]). The transformations are controlled by a configuration file, called a driver, associated with any prover supported by Why3. The results of the external provers are then interpreted and (to some extent) lifted at the level of the input language.

The ASMETA modelling environment also implements the separate parallel analysis orchestration strategy for ASM model validation. The domain expert can invoke the parallel execution of the simulator AsmetaS and the animator AsmetaA on a same input model; results of these analysis tools are lifted back to the modelling environment to show possible states where inconsistent updates (i.e., the same location is simultaneously updated to different values) or invariant violations are detected.

mbeddr features analyses both at model level [Rat+12a] and at code level [MVR14]. Model-level analyses such as checking the consistency and completeness of decision tables are faster but less precise than analyses on code level since they do not take into account the C language semantics with respect to arithmetic, floating points or pointers. Tools that implement these analyses can be run in parallel to combine the advantages of analyses on both levels. Results of the analysis tools can be collected and presented at the level of the domain-specific model.

Combined analysis orchestration (C) CoMA [AGR11] is a tool for runtime verification of Java code with respect to its ASM specification. It observes the behaviour of a Java object O and checks whether it conforms to the expected behaviour captured by an ASM specification M_O. CoMA works as modelling environment having two languages: Java for specifying the structure and the behaviour of the object O, and AsmetaL to model the ASM M_O. Code annotation in O is used for establishing a suitable link between fields and methods of O and the state signature (i.e., a set of locations) of M_O. The operation of CoMA exploits the orchestration strategy C on two tool drivers: that of the *Java virtual machine* (JVM) and that of the AsmetaS simulator. Transformations T are the identity mappings in both cases, while lifting L of the JVM tool driver reports back the state (i.e., a set of memory values) of a Java object and that of the AsmetaS tool driver lifts back the state of an ASM (i.e., a set of locations' values). At a generic step of the runtime verification, CoMA invokes the simulation of O on the JVM. When a changing method (i.e., a method that the domain expert wants to observe and that has been linked to the model) of O is executed, the tool driver of JVM lifts back the current state s_O of O, and the modelling environment invokes the simulator AsmetaS on the model M_O to perform a computation step. The tool driver of AsmetaS lifts back the current model state s_{M_O}. The modelling environment then checks whether a conformance relation holds between current states s_O and s_{M_O}. If they conform, the simulation of the Java object can continue and the orchestration of the two tools starts again, otherwise a lack of conformance between code and specification is reported, so concluding the runtime monitoring. According to our formal definition of the orchestration strategy C, the function combine is the conformance checking predicate since its truth value is computed by combining information from the outputs of the tool drivers of the JVM and the AsmetaS simulator.

Further, the IDE VCES [GLO11] follows the combined analysis orchestration strategy. VCES can be used for both qualitative and quantitative analyses by using two analysis tools, namely NuSMV [Cim+02] and PRISM [KNP11]. Results of these analysis tools are lifted back to and can be combined in VECS.

Cooperating Analysis Orchestration (D)   An example of the cooperating analysis orchestration strategy is simulation coupling. For instance, *Maritime Simulation* (MariSim) [TO17] comprises several simulation tools that are related to Navy and maritime scenarios. These simulation tools can interact, for example, in order to analyse tactical formations at sea. The MariSim modelling environment is used to model and control the interaction between the simulation tools. Simulation parameters (e.g., time of day or wind direction) are described in a domain-specific model in the MariSim modelling environment and transformed for the corresponding simulation tools by tool drivers. Simulation results are lifted back to the modelling environment and passed on to another simulation tool for interaction purposes. Simulating tactical formations at sea requires continuous interaction among the simulation tools, i.e., exchange of information by transformation and lifting, until a certain stop criteria is reached.

Another example of exploiting the cooperating analysis orchestration strategy is CoMA-SMT [AGR14], which has been developed for runtime verification of Java code with respect to an ASM model in case of nondeterministic behaviour. Coma-SMT is a modelling environment using, as languages, Java for specifying the structure and the behaviour of an object, and Yices for representing (initial state and transitions of) a nondeterministic ASM capturing the code behaviour as context of the SMT solver. Coma-SMT orchestrates the tool driver of the JVM for the simulation of Java code and that of the SMT solver Yices for satisfiability checking of a context theory. Transformations T are the identity mappings in both cases, while lifting L of the JVM tool driver reports back the state (i.e., a set of memory values) of a Java object and that of the Yices tool driver lifts back the result of a context satisfiability checking. At a generic step of the runtime verification, the CoMA-SMT modelling environment invokes the Java simulation on the JVM. When a changing method (i.e., a method that the domain expert wants to observe) is invoked, the tool driver of the JVM lifts back the current state of the Java object, and the SMT solver is triggered by the modelling environment: The transformation consists in extending the (current) Yices logical context by asserting a set of formulas stating the values of the observed elements in the current state of the Java object. Yices is then used to check satisfiability of the logical context. If the context is unsatisfiable, then the implementation does not conform with the model and the runtime verification stops (failure fixed point is reached, see definition of strategy D); otherwise the modelling environment continues the runtime verification by invoking a new computation step of the Java program (in this case the transformation from the output model of Yices to the input model of JVM is empty) until an end point of the computation (successful fixed point) is reached.

Sequential Analysis Orchestration (E)   The ASMETA modelling environment also exploits this kind of strategy to orchestrate the sequential use of two different tools to implement an approach for the automatic generation of scenarios (or abstract test cases) for refined ASM models starting from abstract scenarios of abstract ASM models [AR19]. This approach is extremely useful to allow reuse of artefacts in model refinement, and is based on a classical test generation technique by exploiting counterexample generation by model checking. In this approach, the ASMETA modelling environment first invokes a tool that transforms the abstract scenario S_A of the abstract ASM model A into a suitable temporal logic formula ψ; $\not\psi$ (usually called *trap property*) is then model checked against the refined model R of A, and a counterexample c_{ex} is returned to the modelling environment. The counterexample c_{ex} represents a simulation trace of R characterised by ψ. c_{ex} is then transformed into a scenario S_R and given as input to the validator tool AsmetaV on the refined model R. AsmetaV then reports back the result of the scenario execution to the modelling environment.

The sequential analysis orchestration strategy is also used in ASMETA for model-based testing of Java code [AGR18]. The modelling environment invokes the ASM-based test generator *ASM tests generation tool* (ATGT) to derive a test suite T from an ASM specification model of a piece of Java code. Tests in T are then instrumented as JUnit tests by suitable transformation. The results of running JUnit tests on the Java code are then lifted back to the modelling environment. A similar orchestration strategy has been used in [BGM20] to implement an approach that translates abstract test sequences, either generated randomly or through model checking, and scenarios to concrete C++ unit tests using the Boost library.[16] In this case, the orchestrated tools are ATGT or AsmetaV on one side, and the platform to run C++ test drivers on the other side.

Nested Orchestration Strategies AdaptiveFlow [Sir+19, For+20] is a modelling environment for flow management in track-based systems. In AdaptiveFlow, we have nested orchestration strategies; a smaller step using single analysis orchestration (strategy A) within a sequential analysis orchestration (strategy E), together being executed in a loop. AdaptiveFlow can be used in different application domains like for fleet management of collaborating heavy machines in a quarry, coordinating robots in factory aisles, and resource management of smart transport hubs in a city.

Figure 5.4 shows AdaptiveFlow and two analysis tools, the *Rebeca model checker* (RMC) and the *state space analyzer* (SSA). RMC [Reb19] is a customised analysis tool for the Rebeca language and its timed extension [Sir+04, SK16]. SSA [For+20] is developed specifically for AdaptiveFlow but can be reused in other modelling environments as well. The input to SSA is the exact same output from RMC.

As shown in Fig. 5.4, the modelling environment invokes one analysis tool (RMC), and then the output of RMC is fed into another analysis tool (SSA). Here no translation between the output of RMC and the input of SSA is necessary, because SSA is designed in a way to accept the output of RMC. The initial model is revised iteratively and automatically, and in each iteration the revised model is fed as an input to the first tool (RMC), and the output of RMC is fed to the second tool (SSA). This is an instance of orchestration strategy E executed in a loop. Within each instance of the strategy E in the loop, there is a smaller step using the orchestration strategy A, this is debugging of Rebeca models using RMC which may come back

---

[16] Boost library: https://www.boost.org/.

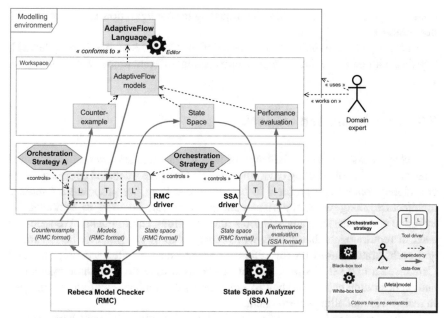

Fig. 5.4 AdaptiveFlow example

by creating a counterexample and jump out of the sequential orchestration (shown as the dashed box in Fig. 5.4).

The RMC driver is responsible for the transformation of AdaptiveFlow models to Rebeca models (RMC format). The driver receives the AdaptiveFlow model as input, generates the output as a Rebeca model, and feeds the Rebeca model to RMC. The AdaptiveFlow model consists of three files including information about the environment, points of interests, and configuration of the system and the moving objects. There is no well-defined DSML for modelling this information, but the specified format of the inputs can be considered as the language. The content and the terminology are selected based on the specific domain of flow management of track-based systems. The Rebeca model is generated by model transformation based on these inputs. RMC receives the Rebeca model and generates the state space and checks the correctness properties. The correctness properties include the safety (lack of collision) and progress (guarantee of no deadlock). The lifting here is an identity mapping, the semantic gap between the Rebeca model and the problem domain is not large, and the domain expert can understand and use the counterexample for debugging. When the correctness of the model is verified, the state space is fed into the SSA tool for performance evaluation of the system. The output of this tool shows the performance measures for different configurations that are checked in different iterations. This output is lifted to be usable for the domain expert once a certain stop criteria is reached. The output is checked by the domain expert, and helps the domain expert in decision making for adjusting the configuration and improving the performance.

This example is explained in more detail in Chap. 13 of this book [Hei+21], together with other similar examples representing different orchestration strategies.

5.8 Conclusion and Outlook

This chapter discussed the challenge of how to integrate and orchestrate external analysis tools into modelling environments. We first gave a detailed overview of the considered context and problem to be addressed. Then, we proposed a reference architecture along with important concepts that can be used to methodically integrate and orchestrate analysis tools into modelling environments. We specified a set of requirements that qualify which analysis tools can properly be integrated and orchestrated based on the reference architecture. Finally, we proposed and formalised a first set of strategies that can be used to answer common integration and orchestration cases and showed examples of the application of these strategies in real-world modelling environments.

Further investigation on additional ways of tool integration and orchestration is needed. These include strategies whose transformations and liftings require to share information and combine results like we sketched for case F in this chapter. The formalisation of orchestration strategies as the case F needs to be addressed in the future. Another open topic is to support the specification of new orchestration strategies by providing primitives, languages, and processes for defining orchestration strategies that may build upon the concepts proposed in this chapter. Furthermore, the soundness of the transformations and liftings proposed in this chapter may be examined in the future. Work on language engineering is required to precisely define the transformation of analysis inputs and the lifting of analysis results.

References

[AGR11] Paolo Arcaini, Angelo Gargantini, and Elvinia Riccobene. "CoMA: Conformance Monitoring of Java Programs by Abstract State Machines". In: *Runtime Verification— Second International Conference*. 2011, pp. 223–238. https://doi.org/10.1007/978-3-642-29860-8_17.

[AGR14] Paolo Arcaini, Angelo Gargantini, and Elvinia Riccobene. "Using SMT for dealing with nondeterminism in ASM-based runtime verification". In: *Electronic Communications of the EASST* 70 (2014), pp. 1–15. https://doi.org/10.14279/tuj.eceasst.70.970.

[AGR16] Paolo Arcaini, Angelo Gargantini, and Elvinia Riccobene. "SMT-Based Automatic Proof of ASM Model Refinement". In: *Software Engineering and Formal Methods - 14th International Conference*. 2016, pp. 253–269. https://doi.org/10.1007/978-3-319-41591-8_17.

[AGR18] Paolo Arcaini, Angelo Gargantini, and Elvinia Riccobene. "Closing the gap between the specification and the implementation: the ASMETA way". In: *Models: Concepts, Theory, Logic, Reasoning and Semantics - Essays Dedicated to Klaus-Dieter Schewe on the Occasion of his 60th Birthday*. 2018, pp. 242–263.

[AR19] Paolo Arcaini and Elvinia Riccobene. "Automatic Refinement of ASM Abstract Test Cases". In: *IEEE International Conference on Software Testing, Verification and Validation Workshops*. 2019, pp. 1–10. https://doi.org/10.1109/ICSTW.2019.00025.

[Ara+15] Vincent Aravantinos, Sebastian Voss, Sabine Teufl, Florian Hölzl, and Bernhard Schätz. "AutoFOCUS 3: Tooling Concepts for Seamless, Model-based Development of Embedded Systems". In: *8th International Workshop on Model-based Architecting of Cyber-Physical and Embedded Systems*. 2015, pp. 19–26. http://ceurws.org/Vol-1508/paper4.pdf.

[Arc+11] Paolo Arcaini, Angelo Gargantini, Elvinia Riccobene, and Patrizia Scandurra. "A model-driven process for engineering a toolset for a formal method". In: *Software: Practice and Experience* 41.2 (2011), pp. 155–166. https://doi.org/10.1002/spe.1019.

[Bar+11] Clark Barrett, Christopher L. Conway, Morgan Deters, Liana Hadarean, Dejan Jovanovic, Tim King, Andrew Reynolds, and Cesare Tinelli. "CVC4". In: *Proceedings of the 23rd International Conference on Computer Aided Verification, CAV*. 2011, pp. 171–177.

[Bec08] Steffen Becker. *Coupled Model Transformations for QoS Enabled Component-Based Software Design*. Universitätsverlag Karlsruhe, 2008. https://publikationen.bibliothek.kit.edu/1000009095.

[Ber+08] Bernard Berthomieu, Jean-Paul Bodeveix, Patrick Farail, Mamoun Filali, Hubert Garavel, Pierre Gaufillet, Frederic Lang, and François Vernadat. "Fiacre: an Intermediate Language for Model Verification in the Topcased Environment". In: *4th European Congress ERTS Embedded Real Time Software*. Jan. 2008, 8p. https://hal.inria.fr/inria-00262442.

[Bey16] Dirk Beyer. "Partial Verification and Intermediate Results as a Solution to Combine Automatic and Interactive Verification Techniques". In: *Leveraging Applications of Formal Methods, Verification and Validation: Foundational Techniques*. 2016, pp. 874–880.

[BGM20] Silvia Bonfanti, Angelo Gargantini, and Atif Mashkoor. "Design and validation of a C++ code generator from Abstract State Machines specifications". In: *Journal of Software: Evolution and Process* 32.2 (2020). https://doi.org/10.1002/smr.2205.

[BGS05] Xavier Blanc, Marie-Pierre Gervais, and Prawee Sriplakich. "Model Bus: Towards the Interoperability of Modelling Tools". In: *European Workshop on Model Driven Architecture*. 2005, pp. 17–32. https://doi.org/10.1007/11538097_2.

[BK96] Johannes Aldert Bergstra and Paul Klint. "The ToolBus coordination architecture". In: *Coordination Languages and Models*. 1996, pp. 75–88. https://doi.org/10.1007/3-540-61052-9_40.

[BMW97] Volker Braun, Tiziana Margaria, and Carsten Weise. "Integrating tools in the ETI platform". In: *International Journal on Software Tools for Technology Transfer* 1.1-2 (Dec. 1997), pp. 31–48. https://doi.org/10.1007/s100090050004.

[Bob+12] François Bobot, Jean-Christophe Filliâtre, Claude Marché, and Andrei Paskevich. "Why3: Shepherd Your Herd of Provers". In: *Boogie 2011: First International Workshop on Intermediate Verification Languages* (May 2012).

[Cav+14] Roberto Cavada, Alessandro Cimatti, Michele Dorigatti, Alberto Griggio, Alessandro Mariotti, Andrea Micheli, Sergio Mover, Marco Roveri, and Stefano Tonetta. "The nuXmv Symbolic Model Checker". In: *Computer Aided Verification*. 2014, pp. 334–342.

[CDT13] Alessandro Cimatti, Michele Dorigatti, and Stefano Tonetta. "OCRA: A Tool for Checking the Refinement of Temporal Contracts". In: International Conference on *Automated Software Engineering*. 2013, pp. 702–705.

[Cim+02] Alessandro Cimatti, Edmund M. Clarke, Enrico Giunchiglia, Fausto Giunchiglia, Marco Pistore, Marco Roveri, Roberto Sebastiani, and Armando Tacchella. "NuSMV 2: An

OpenSource Tool for Symbolic Model Checking". In: *14th International Conference on Computer Aided Verification, CAV, Proceedings*. 2002, pp. 359–364.

[CKL04] Edmund Clarke, Daniel Kroening, and Flavio Lerda. "A Tool for Checking ANSI-C Programs". In: *Tools and Algorithms for the Construction and Analysis of Systems*. Vol. 2988. 2004, pp. 168–176.

[Cru+13] Simon Cruanes, Gregoire Hamon, Sam Owre, and Natarajan Shankar. "Tool Integration with the Evidential Tool Bus". In: *International Workshop on Verification, Model Checking, and Abstract Interpretation*. 2013, pp. 275–294. https://doi.org/10.1007/978-3-642-35873-9_18.

[DE10] Matthew B. Dwyer and Sebastian Elbaum. "Unifying verification and validation techniques". In: *Proceedings of the FSE/SDP workshop on Future of software engineering research*. 2010. https://doi.org/10.1145/1882362.1882382.

[Dut14] Bruno Dutertre. "Yices 2.2". In: *Computer Aided Verification*. 2014, pp. 737–744.

[Far+06] Patrick Farail, Pierre Gaufillet, Agusti Canals, Christophe LE Camus, David Sciamma, Pierre Michel, Xavier Crégut, and Marc Pantel. "The TOPCASED project: a Toolkit in Open source for Critical Aeronautic SystEms Design". In: *European Congress on Embedded Real Time Software*. 2006. https://hal.archivesouvertes.fr/hal-02270461.

[FGH06] Peter Feiler, David Gluch, and John Hudak. *The Architecture Analysis & Design Language (AADL): An Introduction*. Tech. rep. CMU/SEI-2006-TN-011. Software Engineering Institute, Carnegie Mellon University, 2006. http://resources.sei.cmu.edu/library/asset-view.cfm?AssetID=7879.

[For+20] Giorgio Forcina, Ali Sedaghatbaf, Stephan Baumgart, Ali Jafari, Ehsan Khamespanah, Pavle Mrvaljevic, and Marjan Sirjani. "Safe Design of Flow Management Systems Using Rebeca". In: *J. Inf. Process*. 28 (2020), pp. 588–598.

[FP13] Jean-Christophe Filliâtre and Andrei Paskevich. "Why3— Where Programs Meet Provers". In: *European Symposium on Programming Languages and Systems*. 2013, pp. 125–128. https://doi.org/10.1007/978-3-642-37036-6_8.

[GLO11] Matthias Güdemann, Michael Lipaczewski, and Frank Ortmeier. "Tool Supported Model-Based Safety Analysis and Optimization". In: *Proceedings of the 17th IEEE Pacific Rim International Symposium on Dependable Computing*. Jan. 1, 2011. http://ieeexplore.ieee.org/abstract/document/6133100/.

[GRS08] Angelo Gargantini, Elvinia Riccobene, and Patrizia Scandurra. "A Metamodel-based Language and a Simulation Engine for Abstract State Machines". In: *Journal of Universal Computer Science* 14.12 (2008), pp. 1949–1983. https://doi.org/10.3217/jucs-014-12-1949.

[Hei+21] Robert Heinrich, Francisco Durán, Carolyn L. Talcott, and Steffen Zschaler (eds.) *Composing Model-Based Analysis Tools*. Springer, 2021. https://doi.org/10.1007/978-3-030-81915-6.

[Hol03] Gerard Holzmann. The Spin Model Checker: *Primer and Reference Manual*. Addison-Wesley Professional, 2003.

[KNP11] Marta Kwiatkowska, Gethin Norman, and David Parker. "PRISM 4.0: Verification of Probabilistic Real-time Systems". In: *Proc. 23rd International Conference on Computer Aided Verification*. Vol. 6806. 2011, pp. 585–591.

[Mar05] Tiziana Margaria. "Web services-based tool-integration in the ETI platform". In: *Software & Systems Modeling* 4.2 (May 2005), pp. 141–156. https://doi.org/10.1007/s10270-004-0072-z.

[MB08] Leonardo de Moura and Nikolaj Bjørner. "Z3: An Efficient SMT Solver". In: *Tools and Algorithms for the Construction and Analysis of Systems*. 2008, pp. 337–340.

[MNS05] Tiziana Margaria, Ralf Nagel, and Bernhard Steffen. "jETI: A Tool for Remote Tool Integration". In: *Tools and Algorithms for the Construction and Analysis of Systems*. 2005, pp. 557–562. https://doi.org/10.1007/978-3-540-31980-1_38.

[MVR14] Zaur Molotnikov, Markus Völter, and Daniel Ratiu. "Automated domain-specific C verification with mbeddr". In: *International Conference on Automated Software Engineering*. 2014, pp. 539–550. https://doi.org/10.1145/2642937.2642938.

[Obj12] Object Management Group. OMG Systems Modeling Language (OMG SysML), *Version 1.3*. 2012. http://www.omg.org/spec/SysML/1.3/.

[Obj15] Object Management Group. *UML 2.5*. Tech. rep. formal/2015-03-01. Object Management Group, 2015.

[Rat+12a] Daniel Ratiu, Bernhard Schaetz, Markus Voelter, and Bernd Kolb. "Language engineering as an enabler for incrementally defined formal analyses". In: *1st International Workshop on Formal Methods in Software Engineering: Rigorous and Agile Approaches*. 2012, pp. 9–15. https://doi.org/10.1109/FormSERA.2012.6229790.

[Rat+12b] Daniel Ratiu, Markus Voelter, Zaur Molotnikov, and Bernhard Schaetz. "Implementing Modular Domain Specific Languages and Analyses". In: *Proceedings of the Workshop on Model-Driven Engineering, Verification and Validation*. 2012, pp. 35–40. https://doi.org/10.1145/2427376.2427383.

[Rat+13] Daniel Ratiu, Markus Voelter, Bernd Kolb, and Bernhard Schaetz. "Using Language Engineering to Lift Languages and Analyses at the Domain Level". In: *NASA Formal Methods Symposium*. 2013, pp. 465–471. https://doi.org/10.1007/978-3-642-38088-4_35.

[Reb19] Rebeca. *Afra Tool*. http://rebeca-lang.org/alltools/Afra.2019.

[Reu+16] Ralf H. Reussner, Steffen Becker, Jens Happe, Robert Heinrich, Anne Koziolek, Heiko Koziolek, Max Kramer, and Klaus Krogmann. *Modeling and Simulating Software Architectures – The Palladio Approach*. MIT Press, 2016. https://mitpress.mit.edu/books/modeling-and-simulating-software-architectures.

[RGS19] Daniel Ratiu, Marco Gario, and Hannes Schoenhaar. "FASTEN: An Open Extensible Framework to Experiment with Formal Specification Approaches: Using Language Engineering to Develop a Multi-Paradigm Specification Environment for NuSMV". In: *Proceedings of the 7th International Workshop on Formal Methods in Software Engineering*. 2019, pp. 41–50. https://doi.org/10.1109/FormaliSE.2019.00013.

[RU19] Daniel Ratiu and Andreas Ulrich. "An integrated environment for Spin-based C code checking - Towards bringing model-driven code checking closer to practitioners". In: *International Journal of Software Tools for Technology Transfer* 21.3 (2019), pp. 267–286. https://doi.org/10.1007/s10009-019-00510-w.

[Rus05] John Rushby. "An Evidential Tool Bus". In: *Formal Methods and Software Engineering*. 2005, pp. 36–36. https://doi.org/10.1007/11576280_3.

[Sir+04] Marjan Sirjani, Ali Movaghar, Amin Shali, and Frank S. de Boer. "Modeling and Verification of Reactive Systems using Rebeca". In: *Fundamenta Informaticae* 63.4 (2004), pp. 385–410.

[Sir+19] Marjan Sirjani, Giorgio Forcina, Ali Jafari, Stephan Baumgart, Ehsan Khamespanah, and Ali Sedaghatbaf. "An Actor-Based Design Platform for System of Systems". In: *43rd IEEE Annual Computer Software and Applications Conference*. 2019, pp. 579–587.

[SK16] Marjan Sirjani and Ehsan Khamespanah. "On Time Actors". In: *Theory and Practice of Formal Methods - Essays Dedicated to Frank de Boer on the Occasion of His 60th Birthday*. 2016, pp. 373–392.

[SMB97] Bernhard Steffen, Tiziana Margaria, and Volker Braun. "The Electronic Tool Integration platform: concepts and design". In: *International Journal on Software Tools for Technology Transfer* 1.1-2 (Dec. 1997), pp. 9–30. https://doi.org/10.1007/s100090050003.

[Som15] Ian Sommerville. *Software Engineering*. Pearson, 2015.

[TO17] Okan Topçu and Halit Oğuztüzün. *Guide to Distributed Simulation with HLA*. Springer, 2017. https://doi.org/10.1007/978-3-319-61267-6.

[Voe+12] Markus Voelter, Daniel Ratiu, Bernhard Schaetz, and Bernd Kolb. "Mbeddr: An Extensible C-Based Programming Language and IDE for Embedded Systems". In: *3rd Annual Conference on Systems, Programming, and Applications: Software for Humanity*. 2012, pp. 121–140. https://doi.org/10.1145/2384716.2384767.

Chapter 6
Continual Model-Based Analysis

Kenneth Johnson, Marc Zeller, Arthur Vetter, and Daniel Varro

Abstract In this chapter, we describe the *continual model-based analysis* (CMBA) framework as an approach for analysing a system under continual change. We give a formal specification of the CMBA framework and apply it to case studies from incremental verification, safety-critical systems, and business processes.

This core chapter addresses Challenge 3 introduced in Chap. 3 of this book (*continual model-based analysis*).

6.1 Introduction

Model-driven engineering (MDE) facilitates the intensive use of models throughout the entire life-cycle of systems design. Model-based analysis aims to reduce development costs and increase the understanding of engineers by highlighting design flaws early. For example, when developing safety-critical systems in avionics, railway, or automotive domains, the risk to harm humans needs to be analysed. Techniques such as Failure Mode and Effect Analysis [Int91] help engineers justify if derived safety requirements of the system are provenly met. However, new components are added with increasingly complex dependencies, thus interconnect-

K. Johnson (✉)
Auckland University of Technology, Auckland, New Zealand
e-mail: kenneth.johnson@aut.ac.nz

M. Zeller
Siemens AG, Munich, Germany
e-mail: marc.zeller@siemens.com

A. Vetter
Dr. Ing. h.c. F. Porsche AG, Stuttgart, Germany
e-mail: arthur.vetter@porsche.de

D. Varró
McGill University, Montreal, QC, Canada
e-mail: daniel.varro@mcgill.ca

© The Author(s), under exclusive license to Springer Nature Switzerland AG 2021
R. Heinrich et al. (eds.), *Composing Model-Based Analysis Tools*,
https://doi.org/10.1007/978-3-030-81915-6_6

97

ing previously isolated safety-critical functions. To ensure compliance with safety standards, the system must be analysed after each change.

This chapter introduces the *continual model-based analysis* (CMBA) conceptual framework for re-establishing compliance by efficiently identifying and re-assessing only those system components impacted by change. At the heart of our framework is a general formulation of the system and requirements, models, and analysis tools. The CMBA framework is applied to a model-driven engineering domain and establishes concepts of dependency in system and requirements artefacts. The framework uses the system's architecture to quantify change impact and aims to perform a minimal re-analysis after a change to re-establish requirements compliance, reusing previous analysis results whenever possible.

We validate the CMBA conceptual framework using disparate case studies based on the authors' experience in safety-critical systems, service-based systems, and business processes. The case studies in this chapter highlight a key technical challenge for applying model-based analysis for evolving systems: Analysis results become meaningless if changes in the system are not appropriately mirrored in their models. Our aim is to support practitioners for integrating specific formalisms, models, and domain-specific modelling languages into the CMBA framework.

The remainder of this chapter is structured as follows. Section 6.2 gives an algebraic specification of the continual model-based analysis framework, building on modelling notions described in Chap. 2 of this book [Hei+21] and outlines the model-based analysis techniques used when applying the CMBA framework to case studies. Section 6.3 instantiates the CMBA framework in the context of incremental verification and is used for runtime probabilistic verification of a service-based system. Section 6.4 instantiates the CMBA framework for a case study in safety-critical systems and Sect. 6.5 for business processes in IT management. Section 6.6 outlines the composition of CMBA frameworks for probabilistic model checking and *satisfiability modulo theories* (SMT) solving to analyse candidate deployment configurations of service-based systems. Lastly, we give concluding remarks in Sect. 6.7 and outline areas for future work.

6.2 Algebraic Specification of the Continual Model-Based Analysis Framework

Model-based analysis is performed to answer questions about properties of interest of a system under study as discussed in the Foundations chapter of this book [Hei+21]. Continual model-based analysis repeats model-based analysis after a change in the system under study occurs. In the event of a change, the system models and properties used to perform an analysis may be rendered obsolete due to changes in the structure of the system. System changes must be reflected as changes in models and properties so that when the analysis is repeated, the results reflect the new system. Throughout the lifecycle of the system, global changes are rare and therefore previous analysis results from unaffected portions of the system are re-used whenever possible.

To give a concrete example, if the development team of a safety-critical system decides to modify the design of a component affecting several dependent components, then continual model-based analysis is necessary to provide safety assurances of the updated design. Both the change to design and re-analysis results should be documented to be used as an auditable record to promote confidence in the system for all stakeholders such as developers and assessors. Continual model-based analysis is also an important tool for runtime maintenance of an operational system. In this context, changes may occur from unexpected component failures, e.g., stemming from faulty hardware or through managerial decisions modifying the system configuration. In both cases, system administrators may need to quickly carry out re-analysis to prove *quality-of-service* (QoS) compliance of a cloud-deployed system to customer *service level agreements* (SLAs).

Both scenarios feature high-level and domain-specific requirements from stakeholders that need to be formalised into system properties. This general problem is found across a wide range of domains.

6.2.1 Descriptive Models of the System

We suppose that each component of the system has a corresponding *descriptive model* that abstractly describes the component in terms of *attributes* of interest. Let S be the set of all descriptive models of the system.

The notion of *system change* is formalised by defining operations to be applied to elements of S, forming an algebra. In a practical sense, the elements of S may be objects written in a general-purpose object-oriented programming language such as Java. The operations are methods that change values stored in instance variables. More abstractly, description models of the system can be specified as a term algebra in which basic description models are constant symbols, and more complex descriptions are built up by applying operation symbols to simpler terms.

Terms have a natural tree structure to express dependencies between system components, and this dictates the order in which analysis is performed [JCK13]. More generally, a partial ordering can be defined on S arising from component *dependencies* in the system. In symbols, $s < s' \iff s'$ is dependent on s for elements s and s' in S.

6.2.2 Structural, Behavioural, and Quality Models

The descriptive models in S form an abstraction of the system. This model is appropriate to analyse the system at a structural level, where the dependency relationship over S is easily visualised as a graph. However, to analyse *behaviour* or *quality* properties of the system, we shall consider appropriate models of the system; state-based models, for example. Let M denote the set of such models. We specify a model translation $\alpha : S \rightarrow M$ such that the equation $\alpha(s) = m$ means descriptive model $s \in S$ is transformed to the model $m \in M$ by α. In general, transformations are performed by hand by an expert, and the models reflect current values of the system description. When a system description is modified by the operation $f : S \rightarrow S$ modelling a system change, we have a corresponding operation $g : M \rightarrow M$ on models in M, forming an algebra. We expect α enjoys homomorphic properties such that changes in S are mirrored in M. In symbols: $\alpha(f(s)) = g(\alpha(s))$.

6.2.3 Domain-Specific Requirements

It is often the case that system requirements are expressed by domain-experts using natural language. This is slightly risky as the requirements can pick up ambiguities inherent in the language making it difficult to analyse formally. Formal requirement specification can mitigate this risk by devising restricted natural languages using grammars giving it precise unambiguous semantics. Patterns often express commonly occurring requirement specifications.

Let Q be the set of words accepted by grammar and P the set of properties to analyse on models in M. We specify property translation by the function $\beta : Q \rightarrow P$ is defined such that the equation $\beta(q) = p$ means property p is translated from requirement q. For probabilistic model checking, Q is a formal language defining patterns for probabilistic requirements and P the set of *probabilistic computation tree language* (PCTL) formulae [Gru08, DAC99].

6.2.4 Model-Based Analysis

The foundations chapter of this book [Hei+21] describes analysis as a judgement of a model satisfying a property, from which we obtain an answer. When applied to practical software engineering in a safety-critical system, analysis is rarely automated. Model checkers, however, are software tools capable of automating analysis of state-based models. To capture a range of analysis techniques, we formalise model-based analysis as the mapping $analysis : M \times P \rightarrow A$ such that

$$analysis(m, p) = a \qquad (6.1)$$

performs an analysis of property $p \in P$ on model $m \in M$ to obtain an answer $a \in A$. For the remainder of this section, we introduce several instantiations of (6.1).

Model Checking

Given a p from the set $P = CTL$ of linear and computation tree temporal logic formulae and an m from the set $M = LTS$ of labelled transition systems, $analysis(m, p) = a$ evaluates the satisfiability relationship $m \models p$ to yield a binary yes or no answer $a \in \mathbb{B}$. In this case, the set of model checking answers is the set of Booleans such that $A := \mathbb{B}$.

Probabilistic Model Checking

Let $P = PCTL$ be the set of temporal logic formulae extended to include probabilistic computation tree logic and let $M = MC$ be the set of discrete and continuous Markov-chain models. Probabilistic model checking is given by $analysis : MC \times PCTL \rightarrow \mathbb{P}$ such that $analysis(m, p) = v$ is the probability v that the satisfiability relationship $m \models p$ is true. In this case, the set A contains Boolean truth values and real number values measuring probabilities.

Model-Based Safety Analysis

Traditionally, safety analysis consists of bottom-up safety analysis approaches, such as *failure mode and effect analysis* (FMEA) [Int91], and top-down ones, such as *fault tree analysis* (FTA) [Ves+81, Int90, RS15], to identify failure modes, their causes, and effects with impact on the system safety. The result of a (quantitative) analysis is a set of failure rates for the hazardous events which are used for the verification of the safety requirements. The use of models in safety analysis processes has gained increasing attention in research within the last decade [MK06, LSK10, LKN11, Sha+15]. Models used in safety analysis annotate the system models with failure propagation models. This enables the construction of the safety analysis model in a structured way.

   Component fault trees (CFTs) is a model- and component-based methodology for fault tree analysis [KLM03, Höf+18, Kai+18]. In CFTs, a Boolean model (the so-called CFT element) $m_i \in M$ is related to a system component $s_i \in S$. The failure behaviour represented by the CFTs includes the internal failures of the components (with the failure rates) and the propagation of failures within the system. The inter-component propagation follows the structural description of the safety-critical system which is for instance expressed by any *model-based systems engineering* (MBSE) methodology (such as SysML [Obj12], Capella [Roq16], etc.). Failures that are visible at the outport of a component are models using Output Failure Modes which are related to the specific outport. To model how specific failures propagate from an import of a component to the outport, Input Failure Modes are used. The internal failure behaviour that also influences the output failure modes is modelled using the Boolean gates such as OR and AND as well as Basic Events.

Let P be a set of quantitative safety requirements (e.g., in form of Tolerable Hazard Rates, THR) and $M = CFT$ a set of CFT models describing the failure behaviour and propagation of a system. The FTA is given by $analysis : CFT \times THR \rightarrow \mathbb{B}$, a binary yes or no answer, if the given safety requirements are satisfied or not.

6.2.5   Composition Model-Based Analysis and Results Reuse

A variety of analysis compositions, including traditional assume-guarantee verification and Hoare logic for sequential programs are described in this book [Hei+21]. This kind of composition has greatly expanded the range of systems capable of being analysed using model-based approaches.

A key challenge in continual model-based analysis is the notion of change: The system and therefore models change and require re-analysis. To minimise computation time, we define the notion of a repository $r : M \times P \rightarrow A$ that stores answers for a given analysis technique. Then $r(m, p) = a$ if, and only if analysis of property p is performed on model m, resulting in $a \in A$ using the technique. Let $R = [M \times P \rightarrow A]$. Extending Eq. (6.1) we have $analysis : M \times P \times R \rightarrow A$ such that the equation

$$analysis(m, p, r) = a \tag{6.2}$$

means analysis of property p on model m utilising results in repository r yields answer a.

6.2.6   Summary

To summarise our current position, we presented the theoretical underpinnings of the conceptual continual model-based analysis framework to support the analysis of component-based systems undergoing change during development and runtime phases. We hinted at some analysis instantiations of the framework which we shall develop later in this chapter. Figure 6.1 presents the key elements of the CMBA framework and their relationships which form the tuple $C = (S, Q, \alpha, \beta, analysis)$ comprising

- Structural system model S with component dependencies;
- High-level system requirements Q;
- Transformation $\alpha : S \rightarrow M$ for models from the set M;
- Transformation $\beta : Q \rightarrow P$ for properties from the set P; and
- An analysis technique capable of utilising previous analysis answers in A from a repository in R, specified by the mapping $analysis : M \times P \times R \rightarrow A$.

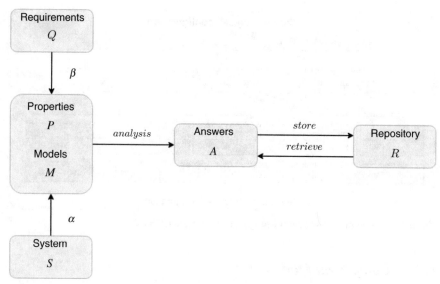

Fig. 6.1 Elements of the CMBA framework

6.3 Incremental Verification of Service-Based Systems

Service-based systems (SBSs) operate in a dynamic environment. The likelihood of the system failing over a specific time period may therefore vary as the system's operational profile changes during runtime. Formal verification techniques such as probabilistic model checking have been used extensively for analysing the health of a system at runtime. Requirements, formulated as temporal logic formulae, are verified against a model of the system to provide evidence of compliance. While this approach is compelling, there are two key challenges for verifying service-based systems. First, most systems are simply too big to apply state based verification techniques. Interactions between even a handful of components results in a huge monolithic model and causes the well-known state explosion problem. Secondly, changes are typically localised within the system, such as a single component failure, a hardware upgrade, or addition of new functionality. Verification therefore should be applied selectively, and reuse previous results whenever possible to re-establish compliance of those aspects of the system affected by a change.

To address these challenges, the key elements of the continual model-based analysis framework developed in Sect. 6.2 are instantiated with probabilistic assume-guarantee reasoning [Kwi+10] to verify the reliability of an SBS deployed over physical servers in a cloud data-centre and show how CMBA can identify regions of the system affected by a runtime change. Hence, we apply the conceptual continual model-based analysis framework to the case study original developed in [JCK13]. This chapter extends the original case study by using a directed-acyclic graph to describe the system.

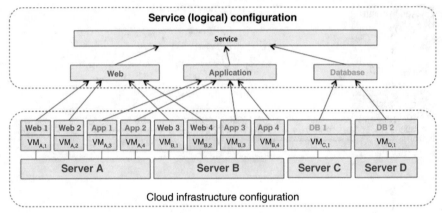

Fig. 6.2 Cloud-deployed service-based system, taken from [JCK13]

6.3.1 Component Models

Consider the service-based system `service` which Fig. 6.2 depicts an architecture diagram of a cloud-deployed service-based system. The `service` comprises functionality `web`, `app`, and `db`, deployed across four cloud infrastructure servers A to D. The number of instances and their deployment within the cloud determines the service's configuration. To improve reliability the configuration comprises four instances of `Web`, two on A and two on B, four instances of `app`, with two on A and two on B, and two instances of `db`, with one on C and one on D.

To apply the CMBA framework, we define the set

$$S = \{A, B, C, D, \text{waA}, \text{waB}, \text{dbC}, \text{dbD}, \text{wa}, \text{db}, \text{service}\} \qquad (6.3)$$

of descriptive models of components in Fig. 6.2. Our component models are designed to analyse deployment reliability. For example, the server models A to D maintain attributes *disks*, *cpus*, and *mem* that record the number of operational hard disks, CPUs, and memory units, respectively. When the server component issues a unit failure notification the appropriate attribute is decreased. The remaining component models keep track of functionality dependencies. For example, `wa` is dependent on `waA` and `waB` that model deployment of `web` and `app` on servers A and B, respectively. The component model `service` represents the complete system.

Component models in S form a *dependency graph*: a directed-acyclic graph where system models are nodes and edges formalise dependencies as shown in Fig. 6.3.

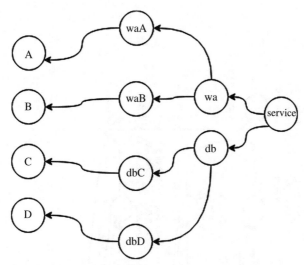

Fig. 6.3 Dependency graph of components descriptions in S

6.3.2   Probabilistic Automatons for SBSs

To analyse probabilistic behaviour, we define the mapping $\alpha : S \rightarrow M$ such that $\alpha(s)$ is a probabilistic automaton in M modelling $s \in S$. When no ambiguities arise, we will simply write s to denote its model $\alpha(s)$. Figure 6.4 presents the probabilistic automaton of cloud server A. If multiple disk, CPU, or mem unit failures are detected, the server issues a warn signal. However, with probability 0.1 it will fail to issue a warning. The model has a state corresponding to every possible value of the server's attributes. Each state is labelled with an atomic proposition true in that state. In the initial state, all units are operational and is labelled with propositions $disk = 4$, $cpus = 4$, and $mem = 4$. State transitions are probability distributions labelled with an action. From the initial state, the action `disk_op` labels the probability distribution modelling the likelihood that a disk unit operation fails (probability 0.005) or succeeds (probability 0.995). At the end of the analysis time period, the server model is in either one of two states as identified in Fig. 6.4: the `succ` state where at least one of each kind of unit is operational or the `fail` state where the server fails after successive failures of all disk or CPU or mem units.

6.3.3   Assume-Guarantee Model Checking of SBSs

Assume-guarantee model checking is a step-wise verification process to verify local properties of components that form assumptions which are used to guarantee properties of the complete system.

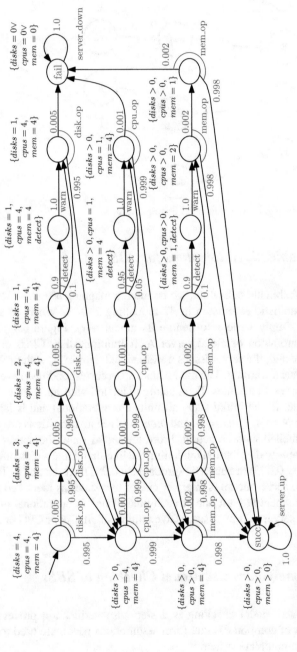

Fig. 6.4 Probabilistic automation modelling cloud server A, modified from [JCK13]

To apply an assume-guarantee reasoning to determine the probability that system failure will occur within a 1-month time period, we formalise an assume-guarantee model checker by the function $mc : M \times P \times R \rightarrow V$ where the equation

$$v = mc(m, \phi, r) \tag{6.4}$$

means the result value $v \in V$ obtained by verifying the temporal logic formula $\phi \in P$ on model $m \in M$, assuming results in the repository $r \in R$. The CMBA-framework analysis technique given by Eq. (6.2) is instantiated by mc, and r contains the assumptions that mc uses to verify m.

We specify the *store* $: R \times [M \times P \rightarrow V]$ operation which adds the verification result computed in (6.4) to the repository r. In symbols, we write $store(r, m, p, v) = r \cup \{(m, p) \rightarrow v\}$. As shown in Fig. 6.1, the model checker mc may invoke the *retrieve* operation to obtain existing verification results corresponding to a model and property analysis step.

The temporal logic formula ϕ verifies a *probabilistic safety property*: a regular safety property as a *deterministic finite automata* (DFA) p and probability bound v, written $\langle p \rangle_{\geq v}$. The alphabet of p contains actions from its component's model. Words accepted by p correspond to prefixes of paths that *do not* satisfy the safety property. Let P be the set of all probabilistic safety properties. Probabilistic safety properties represent a range of important component properties. For example, *the probability of the cloud server* A *going down without warning is at most* v_1 is represented by safety property pA with alphabet $\{server\_down, warn\}$. Accepting words are defined by the regular expression $server\_down(warn|server\_down)^*$ and correspond to paths through the parallel model A $\|$ pA where the property is violated. Here, A is the probabilistic model of the physical server shown in Fig. 6.4. We invoke

$$mc(\text{A} \| pA, P_{=?}[F\, fail], \langle true \rangle) \tag{6.5}$$

to verify formula $P_{=?}[F\, fail]$ yielding the probability 1.2326e$-$6 of reaching a *fail* state A $\|$ pA, for the vacuous assumption $\langle true \rangle$. We create a repository of assumptions of the form $r := \text{A} \rightarrow \langle pA \rangle_{\geq v_1}$ to be used in subsequent verification steps, setting $v_1 := 1 - 1.2326$e-6.

Now, the web and application functionality modelled by a probabilistic model waA can fail due to server A experiencing a hardware or VM failure. We formalise these errors by the safety property $\langle pwaA \rangle_{\geq v_2}$.

Using the assumption obtained in Step (6.5) we invoke

$$mc(pA \| pwaA \| \text{waA}, P_{=?}[F\, fail], r) \tag{6.6}$$

to compute the minimum probability of reaching the accepting *fail* states of $pwaA$ on model waA. Steps (6.5) and (6.6) compute the probabilistic assume-guarantee rule

$$\frac{\langle true \rangle \text{ A } \langle pA \rangle_{\geq v_1}, \ \langle pa \rangle_{\geq v_1} \text{ waA } \langle pwaA \rangle_{\geq v_2}}{\langle true \rangle \text{ A } \| \text{ waA } \langle paA \rangle_{\geq v_2}} \tag{6.7}$$

modularising verification of a large model a $\|$ waA into two smaller, and separate, verification steps.

6.3.4 Verification Tasks

Each step of assume-guarantee model checking is a verification *task* of the form $T = M \times P$ such that the pair $t = (m, p)$ in T means property $p \in P$ is to be verified against component model $m \in M$. Clearly, the *order* of verification tasks plays a critical role. If we think of the edges in the dependency graph as defining a relationship between components such that $s < s'$ if, and only if, $s \leftarrow s'$ then $(S, <)$ defines a partial ordering over component models in S. For example, the directed edge wa $\leftarrow$ service in Fig. 6.3 means wa $<$ service. The $<$ relationship extends to $\leq$ (reflexive, antisymmetric, transitive) when we consider equality of descriptive models. If the modelling function $\alpha : S \rightarrow M$ is monotonic such that $s \leq s' \implies \alpha(s) \leq \alpha(s')$, then we can define a partial ordering on models in M. By the linear-extension property of partial orders, we form a total ordering which induces a verification sequence $\tau = m_1, m_2, \ldots$ as having the property that for any pair of models m_i and m_j in τ if $m_i < m_j$ then $i < j$. This is essentially a topological sorting of the system's dependency graph. Lifting this ordering to verification tasks in T, we define the set *Seq* of *valid* verification task sequences. For example, a topological sorting of the graph in Fig. 6.3 yields the valid sequence

$$A, \text{waA}, B, \text{waB}, \text{wa}, C, \text{dbC}, D, \text{dbD}, \text{db}, \text{service}. \tag{6.8}$$

The set *Seq* is formed by induction:

Base Cases
- Empty sequence () is in *Seq* and
- (t) is in *Seq* for each task $t \in T$.

Inductive Case for $\tau \in Seq$ and $t \in T$

- $\tau \frown (t)$ is in *Seq*

where $\frown$ is the sequence concatenation operation.

6.3.5 Incremental Verification

Compositional verification model checks tasks in a valid verification sequence in *Seq* such as (6.8) and outputs a repository of verification results.

Mathematically, we define the compositional verification algorithm as a function $cv : Seq \times R \rightarrow R$ by induction over sequences in *Seq*:

Base Cases Let $r \in R$ be a repository.

(i) For the empty verification sequence ϵ the algorithm leaves the repository unchanged: $cv(\epsilon, r) = r$.
(ii) For the sequence (t) containing a single verification task $t = (m, p)$ the equation $cv((t), r) = store(r, m, p, v)$ stores the verification result $(m, p) \rightarrow v$, to r.

Inductive Step Let $\tau' \in Seq$. For $(t) \frown \tau'$ we define $cv((t) \frown \tau', r) = cv(\tau', cv((t), r))$. We write $cv(\tau)$ when no existing verification results are required to verify τ.

Small, localised change during runtime is commonplace in cloud-deployed systems. New components may be added and existing ones removed or modified. We define steps in an *incremental verification algorithm* that selectively applies compositional verification on changed components:

1. *Identify the change.* We assume components in the service-based system contain monitors that identify a range of change behaviours on components that are in turn represented mathematically as operations acting on attributes in S.
2. *Determine affected components.* Any dependent of a component affected by a change is also affected. To formalise this, we adopt standard order-theoretic principles such that if $s \in S$ is affected by a change, then the upset $\uparrow s = \{u \in S \mid s \leq u\}$ contains s and all its dependent descriptive models. For each $u \in \uparrow s$ let $t = (\alpha(u), \beta(u))$ be its associated verification task.
3. *Re-verify affected components.* From the linear-extension property, we form a sequence $\tau \in Seq$ from associated verification tasks of elements in $\uparrow s$. Given the repository $r \in R$ of verification results from previous steps, compositional verification $cv(\tau, r)$ is applied.

6.3.6 Change Scenarios

We demonstrate the incremental verification framework using change scenarios on the service-based system case study. In these scenarios, compositional verification has been performed on Sequence (6.8) and the results stored in repository $r \in R$.

Server Hard-Disk Failure

Suppose server A experiences a hard-disk failure. In the associated descriptive model, the value in the *disks* attribute is decreased by one. To determine how this affects the system, we re-verify the server's associated probabilistic automaton and models of any affected component, given by ↑A. From the linear-extension property we form the sequence $\tau = (A, waA, wa, \texttt{service})$ associated verification tasks to re-verify and compute $cv(\tau, r)$.

Server Memory Upgrade

Suppose server B has scheduled maintenance, whereby two more memory units are added. In the associated descriptive model, the value in the *mem* attribute is increased by two. To determine how this affects the system, we re-verify the server's associated probabilistic automaton and models of any affected component, given by ↑B. However, after completing the verification step for B the verification result is compared to the existing result stored in the repository and shows *the probability of cloud server B going down without a warning* has decreased. Hence, we can be certain $\texttt{service}$ is still compliant to its requirements, and we can stop the re-verification after a single step.

Adding New Functionality Components

Suppose new functionality *fun* is introduced to the system to extend the functionality offered by $\texttt{service}$. The descriptive models of components to be added to S are:

- E, of a cloud server,
- funE, comprising two deployed instances of *fun* on E, and
- fun the descriptive model of the functionality *fun*.

Dependencies between these components are given by the partial order relationship such that E < funE and funE < fun. We apply compositional verification $\tau = (E, funE, fun)$ such that $r' = cv(\tau)$. When fun is added to $\texttt{service}$, the relation fun < $\texttt{service}$ is added to S; e.g., an edge between the components is created in the dependency graph. The results in r' are merged into repository r. The $\texttt{service}$ component is re-verified as it is the only affected component contained in the *strict upset* of fun.

Removing Deployed Functionality

We suppose the redundant database functionality on server C is no longer required. The set of component descriptive models to be removed from S are $X = \{C, dbC\}$. The affected components in S are those elements in the strict upset of the maximum element of X, namely $\text{dbC} \uparrow= \{\text{db}, \text{service}\}$. Compositional verification $cv((\text{db}, \text{service}), r)$ updates the verification results for db and service in the repository r.

6.3.7 Summary

We instantiated the continual model-based analysis framework with a probabilistic model checker to support runtime verification of a cloud-deployed system. To summarise, we specify

$$C_{cv} := (S, Q, \alpha, \beta, cv) \tag{6.9}$$

such that the structural system model S is a dependency graph where models keep track of operational states and current deployment configurations. The map $\alpha : S \rightarrow M$ assigns elements in S to probabilistic finite-state models in M, and $\beta : Q \rightarrow P$ assigns QoS properties in Q to probabilistic temporal logic formulae in P, forming verification tasks. Tasks are analysed by the probabilistic assume-guarantee model checker cv. The resulting CMBA framework is extended to perform selective, incremental verification.

6.4 Continuous Analysis of Safety-Critical Systems

Safety-critical systems (SCS) are omnipresent in many application domains of software-intensive embedded systems, such as aerospace, railway, health care, and automotive. SCS is a class of systems whereby a malfunction may result in the death or serious injuries of humans. Therefore, the development of such systems has to comply with domain-specific safety standards (such as IEC 61508 [Int98], ISO 26262 [Int11], or ARP 4761 [Soc96]): They require stringent safety assurance processes to justify safety compliance. The engineering of safety-critical systems includes various aspects (or viewpoints) as described in safety standards. Figure 6.5 provides an overview of the steps needed in a generic safety engineering life-cycle. The goal of the safety assurance process is to identify all failures that cause hazardous situations and to provide a sound argumentation that the system is sufficiently safe. This argumentation is based on evidence gathered during the system engineering and assessment process (e.g., to demonstrate that the probabilities of the hazards are sufficiently low).

The first step in the safety engineering life-cycle is the item definition, in which the item (along with its purpose and functionality) considered by the safety engineering process is defined, and dependencies between the item and its environment are described. Based on a clear system definition, a *hazard analysis and risk assessment* (HARA) is performed. This analysis tries to identify potential hazards

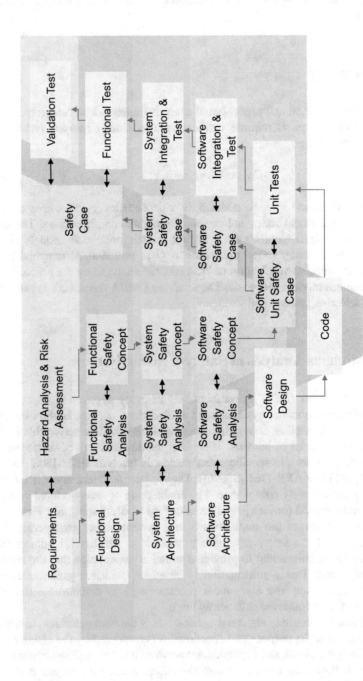

Fig. 6.5 Generic safety engineering life-cycle, after [Tra16]

that can be caused by the system and to assess the associated risks. Different safety standards generally agree on common HARA techniques [Mac+12]. However, the quantification of the risk differs in each domain. As the next step, a system architecture is defined and a so-called *Safety Concept* is derived. The safety concept is defined as the specification of the safety requirements, their allocation to system elements, and their interactions necessary to achieve safety goals [Int11]. Therefore, safety standards demand a complete and deterministic system architecture. Today, the system architecture is often described using MBSE techniques (e.g., SyML). Moreover, the potential causes and the cause-effect-relationships must be evaluated. Therefore, different safety analysis techniques (such as FTA [Ves+81, Int90, RS15] or FMEA [Int91]) are used that evaluate the risk that arises from potential failures and other malfunctions that have been identified as causes for hazards. With CFTs, there is a model- and component-based methodology for fault tree analysis, which allows a modular and compositional safety analysis strategy. CFTs are Boolean models associated with system development elements such as components [KLM03, Adl+11].

Along with the growing system complexity, the effort needed for safety assurance is increasing drastically in order to guarantee the high quality demands of SCS. On the other hand, industry aims to reduce development costs and time-to-market of new products. Therefore, iterative, incremental, or even agile development methodologies known from software engineering are introduced in the systems engineering domain. However, in order to speed up the development of SCS, also the safe assurance process must be accelerated.

In industrial development projects, change requests during the development can come from various stakeholders such as the client, certification authorities, or development teams of the different subprojects. But changes can also be a part of a development strategy, if an existing product can be evolved in a new system in an incremental manner with small changes and adjustments.

To ensure compliance to safety standards (e.g., IEC 61508), the SCS must be analysed in terms of safety after each change. In case of modifications of the system design during the development process, the safety analysis must be adapted accordingly to guarantee that the results of the safety analysis are still valid. Since traceability between the artefacts in the system design and the safety assessment is solely achieved manually in current practice, each change within the system design results in time-consuming manual adjustment performed by the safety engineer. For instance, after each modification all FMEA tables or fault trees of the system must be reviewed and all parts affected by the modification must be adapted manually. In order to decrease the time-consuming adaptation of the safety analyses, traceability between the elements in the safety analysis and the related elements in the system design must be established [Sch+11]. Moreover, automated synchronisation of the safety analysis model with a changing system design in a continuous manner is needed to achieve continual analysis of SCS [ZH16].

The use of models can help to cope with these requirements along two directions. Firstly, it makes safety engineering as a standalone subtask of system development more efficient. Secondly, and even more important, this is an essential step towards a holistic model-based development approach which closes the gap between functional development and safety assurance. Reusing development models for safety analyses and feeding back the results of safety analyses in the development models is a key step for reaching synergies. Hence, *model-based safety assurance* (MBSA) [Jos+05, LKN11, Sha+15] provides promising approaches to enable analysis of systems in terms of safety when combined with MBSE methodologies [RFB12].

In this section, CMBA is instantiated for the development of safety-critical systems. By using CMBA we can avoid performing safety analysis for the entire system each time the system design is changed.

6.4.1   Instantiation of the CMBA for Safety-Critical Systems Development

We instantiate the CMBA framework presented in Sect. 6.2 for the development of safety-critical systems as follows:

- S = SCS consisting of a set of components $\{s_1, s_2, \ldots, s_n\}$ (software, hardware, or mechanical components) forming a component-based system.
- M = Set of safety analysis model of S describing the failure behaviour of each of the components of the system S in form of CFTs where

$$\forall s_i \in S : \quad M_i = \alpha(s_i)$$

- $\alpha(S)$ = Creation of a set of safety analysis models M by a safety expert, which describe the failure behaviour of the system S. Thereby, a safety analysis model $m_i \in M$ is created for each of the components s_i of the safety-critical system S.
- Q = Set of safety requirements (high-level safety goals or technical safety requirements), which must be fulfilled by the system.
- $\beta(Q)$ = Refinement of the safety requirements and the allocation of the requirements to system components, e.g., by specific *safety integrity levels* (SILs) or *tolerable hazard rates* (THRs) which must be fulfilled by the system.
- P = Set of (quantitative) safety properties the system must fulfil/guarantee, e.g., the THR of a specific function performed by S which is allocated to one or a set of components.
- *Analysis* : $M \times P \rightarrow A$ = the quantitative safety analysis of the failure behaviour of the system S in form of a fault tree analysis. Since the safety requirements are allocated on specific components of the systems, pairs of the respective CFT models and the safety properties which need to be fulfilled are created with *analysis* (m_i, p_i). This result is a failure rate λ or a *mean time between failure* (MTBF) value $a \in A$. The result of the fault tree analysis *analysis* $(m_i, p_i) = a$ using the CFT model $m_i \in M$ is used to check if the

property $p_i \in P$ is satisfied or not by the system design (e.g., by checking if a failure rate is less or equal to a tolerable hazard rate). Moreover, the result of each analysis can be stored in a repository R, for instance in a database.

6.4.2 Change Scenarios

Any change of the SCS (during development time or during operation) needs to be analysed, answering the question of whether the change has influence on the system safety or not. This *change impact analysis* (CIA) is defined as "identifying the potential consequences of a change in a system, or estimating what needs to be modified to accomplish a change" [Arn96]. Especially, safety concepts and the safety case must be revised after each change. Therefore, the safety analyses need to be adapted to the changed SCS and performed again to reassess the SCS in terms of safety and to show that the probability of potential hazardous system behaviour is sufficiently low.

In the following, we are applying the concept of the CMBA to changes during the development of SCS.

Thereby, the change Δ within the SCS S represents a change within a component:

$$s_i \xrightarrow{\Delta} s_i'$$

This can be for instance a bug-fix related to a security issue, which does not change the functions of the system or the exchange of a component with a different one (e.g., use of fixed-point arithmetic to speed-up processing time of specific calculations). After the change, the safety of the system must be re-assessed to determine the consequences of the change on the system's safety. Therefore, also the safety analysis model $m_i \in M$ of the component $s_i \in S$ is updated:

$$m_i \xrightarrow{\Delta} m_i'$$

The modified CFT element m_i' of the changed component s_i' may consist of new failures, modified failures, or updates of the failure rates of the component's internal failures. If new failure modes are added at the interfaces of the component, also other CFT elements $m_j \in M, m_j \neq m_i$, may need to be adjusted.

Based on the modified safety analysis models, the respective analysis task(s) are adapted as follows $analysis\ (m_i', p_i)$. The analysis $analysis\ (m_i', p_i) = a'$ is then executed, starting with the analysis of the modified (software) component s_i'. If the results of the newly performed analysis a' is different to the value stored before ($a \neq a'$; e.g., the resulting failure rate $a' = \lambda > p_i = THR$), the analysis must be done for the components, which exchange information with s_i'. Otherwise the analysis can be stopped.

6.5   Business Processes

This section describes the usage of continual model-based analysis for business processes.

6.5.1   Background

Efficient business processes are a key success factor for every company and describe the flow of work in a company in order to achieve the company's goals. Business process management is the discipline which seeks to design, administrate, configure, enact, and analyse business processes [Wes12]. The foundation of business process improvement is a model of the business process itself, which represents the actual business process and can describe different process perspectives like function, information, resource, and organisation (perspective names according to the ISO standard 19439:2006 [ISO06]). Traditionally, process models were and still are often created manually in practice, leading to several shortcomings for analysis purposes. When creating process models from scratch, usually persons who are involved in the business processes are interviewed and observed by the modeller in order to understand how such a business process is executed. This procedure can lead to some of the following errors, which hinders the usage of the process models for deeper analysis methods:

- Humans could lie, because they are maybe afraid of losing their job if they reveal that some tasks in a process are not performed in the way they actually should be performed.
- Humans could forget to mention activities, leading to erroneous omissions of activities. This may happen when a task is so obvious that the person is not aware of it and therefore does not mention it.
- Humans could rate things biased/Humans are not objective. When a modeller asks about frequencies, people can make unintentionally wrong estimates.
- Humans just make errors. The modeller itself, who creates the process model can make errors during the modelling process or during the observation leading to wrong conclusions and faulty models.
- Modellers could abstract too much from details in the process, which leads to an easy understandable process model for humans but leaves out a lot of potential for automated analysis methods like process simulations.

Therefore, the outcome of a manually created model rarely reflects the real world in such accuracy that it is useful for model-based analysis methods like simulations. New techniques like process mining (for an overview see [Aal16]) allow the creation of process models based on data, which is created by IT systems and reflects actions executed automatically or manually executed actions, which are recorded by IT systems. Models created through process mining are much more detailed and are a perfect basis for different model-based analysis methods like simulations [MDC16]. At the beginning of process mining research it was mainly used in an offline mode in order to discover process models based on complete log traces, but not in an online mode, that is used to improve currently running process instances [APS10]. If process mining is used in an online mode, parts of currently running traces can be used to analyse business process models continuously, e.g., to react appropriately in a currently running process instance to avoid bottlenecks, inefficiencies, etc.

After the above introduction on business processes and how process mining builds the foundation for continuous model-based analysis, a case study of two main processes (Order2Cash and Procure2Pay), which can be found in enterprises, is used as an example to show the potential of continuous model-based analysis in the domain of business processes.

6.5.2 Business Processes: Order2Cash and Procure2Pay

In this section, we describe use case documents for two processes *Procure2Pay* and *Order2Cash*. Order2Cash describes the process from an order of a customer to the fulfilment of the order and the payment by the customer. It is an important business process in enterprises, because it is the main process for earning money. Procure2Pay describes the process and the activities from creating a demand for one or many goods, e.g., to fulfil an order by a customer, to the purchase of the order and the payment of the order. Both processes are interconnected. In order to execute an order of a customer (Order2Cash) goods of other companies may have to be bought (Procure2Pay) and processed. In the following, both processes and their potential for continuous model-based analysis are described.

Order2Cash A high-level description of the *Order2Cash* process is illustrated in Fig. 6.6.

- **Create order:** The process starts with a customer demand and the creation of a sales order.
- **Fulfil order:** As the core compound activity, the order then has to be fulfilled in a series of activities.

  - **Workforce Management:** This business process is responsible for assigning a worker to handle a particular sales order.
  - **Schedule appointment:** Depending on the company, e.g., if it is a company, which fixes products in a shop, an appointment has to be scheduled with the customer. This activity depends on the worker assigned to the order by the Workforce Management business process.
  - **Check needed goods:** A worker has to check if all necessary goods in order to fulfil the order are available.
  - **Confirm goods availability:** If all necessary goods are available, then the order can be confirmed immediately.

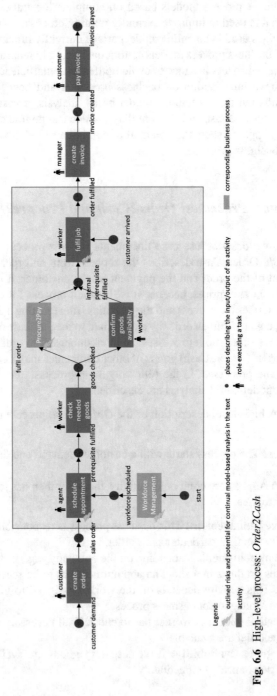

Fig. 6.6 High-level process: *Order2Cash*

Legend:

⟍ outlined risks and potential for continual model-based analysis in the text

● places describing the input/output of an activity   ⬛ corresponding business process

◀ role executing a task

▨ activity

- **Procure2Pay:** If goods are missing, they have to be purchased in advance, which triggers the execution of the Procure2Pay process (see below).
- **Fulfil job:** Finally, the appointment date arrives, the customer shows up in the shop, all necessary goods were received, and the job can be fulfilled by the worker.

- **Create invoice:** After the job is executed, the invoice is created for the customer.
- **Pay invoice:** As the final step of the business process, the customer pays the invoice.

Procure2Pay The Procure2Pay process can be triggered, among other processes, by the Order2Cash process and contains all activities to procure goods and services. The process starts with the creation of a demand and the approval or rejection of the demand. After the demand is approved, the purchase order can be created. Usually a company has a set of chosen suppliers where employees are allowed to order goods and services.

6.5.3 Opportunities for Continual Model-Based Analysis

Many decisions and the consequential activities could conceptually be automated in the underlying IT systems, but automating such steps in a legacy system always incurs substantial costs. Continual Model-Based Analysis could serve as a key technique to reduce such costs.

Legacy and External Data Sources Continuous model-based analysis based on the data of the underlying IT systems creates a potential to push the automation boundaries from highly repetitive tasks further to less repetitive tasks by using Robotic Process Automation or Robotic Process Management [Aal20]. In addition to data from legacy systems, data of other sources could be used for continual model-based analysis like historical customer data, forecast weather data, etc. Model-based analysis allows to analyse consequences of an activity on a whole business process network. Therefore, it enables a more global view on business processes than it is possible within a single IT system, which supports only one business process.

Workforce Management Many things can already go wrong within the Workforce Management process even before the appointment with the customer takes place, which shows the potential of continual business process model-based analysis:

- The customer could get sick and cancel the appointment, leading to unnecessary costs if the ordered goods cannot be cancelled or it was forgotten to cancel the goods.
- The execution of the Procure2Pay process could be delayed and therefore the needed goods would not be available in time for the job fulfilment. In this case, the customer has to be called to rearrange the appointment, already ordered goods

have to be cancelled and so on. The Procure2Pay process is described in more detail later on.

- The worker, who was planned for the job gets sick and it has to be decided if the appointment with the customer has to be rescheduled, which could lead to a cancelled order, if the customer decides to switch to a competitor. On the other hand, a worker could be rescheduled from another shop to this one, trying to minimise the negative effects of personal shortage.

Procurement In big companies there can be even several systems which allow to create orders. Continual model-based analysis can be used to audit, that purchase orders were sent to the correct supplier, otherwise discounts could not be used or products with insufficient quality could be ordered. If purchase orders are created correctly, the orders have to be checked regarding quality and completeness upon receiving. Insufficient product quality can lead to return deliveries to suppliers and can have consequently negative effects on a production line. In this case continual model-based analysis could help to analyse the overall effects and help to decide if a change in the production line could help to reduce negative effects.

User Monitoring Continual model-based analysis could also be used, e.g., to monitor every task, which is performed by the worker and check it for conformance to the to-be process model for the fulfilment of the job. If a deviation is detected in the model-based analysis, the worker can be warned and get a notification about the next step in order to align again with the to-be process model. A big challenge in this scenario would be to detect the task a worker is performing. If the task is a digital one, e.g., to write source code in order to fix the broken product this would be quite easy, because the written source code could be analysed. However, if the fulfilment task is an analogue one it is harder to get the necessary data for continual model-based analysis. In this case, augmented reality in conjunction with machine learning could be a potential use case to get analysable data.

6.5.4 Instantiation of the CMBA for Business Processes

We instantiate the CMBA framework presented in Sect. 6.2 for the analysis of business processes as follows:

- S = Set of system model components used to describe a business process comprising roles, employees, activities, objects, IT components, etc. It is assumed components are recorded in an IT system and can be extracted automatically. Additionally, the system model consists of components describing business process records like it is done, e.g., by the IEEE Standard for *eXtensible Event Stream* (XES) [IEE16].
- M is the set of business process models of S. There is a wide range of modelling formalisms to describe control flow, data flow, organisational view,

and previously executed activities of S. For example, the control flow can be modelled through high-level Petri nets [Sch+16].

- $\alpha(S)$ is the creation of a set of business process models M which represent the current state of the business process S. The business process model can be created by a domain-expert experienced with modelling or automatically through process mining like described in 6.5.1
- Q = Set of business requirements, which must be fulfilled by the business process S, e.g., service level agreements, compliance requirements, etc.
- $\beta(Q)$ = is the modelling process of business requirements expressed over the set of meta-model components. For service level agreements that could be, e.g., throughput times, response times, solution times, waiting times. For compliance requirements that could be specific organisational requirements, e.g., separation of duties.
- P = Set of properties the business process must fulfil.
- *analysis* : $M \times P \rightarrow A$ is the analysis of the business process model. Analysis techniques for business process models can be mainly divided in verification approaches and performance approaches. Verification approaches are concerned with the correctness of a business process. Performance approaches are concerned with the performance of a business process mainly in terms of quality, time, and cost [Aal13]. Usually simulations are used to analyse performance properties.
- A is the execution of the business process model-based analysis leading to a result value $v \in V$. The result value can be, e.g., a simulated average throughput time or a detected deviation of a running business process instance from the to-be business process model.

6.5.5   Change Scenarios

A business process can change during its lifetime because of different reasons. It can be changed from top down in a way that the business process model M is changed in order to improve the business process. The change is first implemented in the business process model in order to analyse if the proposed change has a positive outcome regarding time, quality, or costs of the business process. In this case, the business process model is updated:

$$m_i \xrightarrow{\Delta} m_i'$$

Such a planned change is than propagated to the actual business process S leading to:

$$s_i \xrightarrow{\Delta} s_i'$$

Such changes are easy manageable changes for a process modeller, because he is aware of the change.

However, bottom-up changes are harder manageable, because they have to be detected in S first and then they have to be reflected accordingly in M. Therefore, M has to be adapted in order to represent S accordingly again. Such changes can be concept drifts [Gam+14]. Situations like this occur easily in organisations, when the business process was there first and the business process model second. In this case, the business process model is created to describe the already existing business process and not used to design the business process from scratch and use the business process model as governance tool. Bottom-up changes can be, e.g., seasonal patterns, which are not reflected in M. However, changes can also occur during the execution of a business process and therefore influence a currently running model-based analysis A, which is used, e.g., to predict the next process step.

6.6   Composition of CMBA Frameworks

When *software as a service* (SaaS) solutions are to be deployed on cloud infrastructure, engineers must consider trade-offs on a range of deployment requirements such as having functional redundancies across servers, combining functionalities with high interdependency, and excluding some kinds of functionality from specific servers. Candidate deployment configurations satisfying these requirements can be analysed further to determine compliance to QoS requirements, such as reliability.

In this section, we compose two CMBA frameworks C_{smt} for SMT solving [MB08] with probabilistic assume-guarantee model checking C_{cv} developed in Sect. 6.3 to realise these complex analysis scenarios. These ideas originate from earlier papers [JCK13] and [JC14] and are combined here for the first time.

6.6.1   Logical Deployment Configuration Models

A *deployment configuration* of a Service-Based System associates instances of the service's functionality with one or more physical servers within a cloud data-centre. For example, Fig. 6.2 of the `service` case study depicts a deployment configuration such that four instances of `web` and `app` are deployed across server's A and B, and two instances of `db` are deployed on servers C and D.

We formalise deployment configurations as an assignment function $a : Z \rightarrow \mathbb{Z}$ of integer values in $\mathbb{Z}$ representing the amount of functionality instances to variable symbols in the countable set Z. For example, the assignment $zwebA := 2$ for $zwebA \in Z$ means there are two instances of `web` on server A. The deployment configuration for Fig. 6.2 is given by the assignment such that

$$zwebA := 2 \quad zappA := 2 \quad zdbC := 1$$
$$zwebB := 2 \quad zappB := 2 \quad zdbD := 1$$

All other variables are assigned the value 0 and are omitted.
    Variables in subsets

$$Z_{web} = \{zwebA, zwebB, zwebC, zwebD\}$$

$$Z_{app} = \{zappA, zappB, zappC, zappD\}$$

$$Z_{db} = \{zdbA, zdbB, zdbC, zdbD\}$$

of Z model the deployment configuration of web, app, and db, respectively, across servers A to D. Variables in the set $Z_S = Z_{web} \cup Z_{app} \cup Z_{db}$ is a model for the deployment configuration of service.
    Suppose we have requirements for deploying service as follows:

R1   between two and four instances of each functionality must be deployed,
R2   web and app functionalities have the same number of deployed instances per server, and
R3   db cannot be deployed on server D.

Requirements are formalised as first-order logic formulae that constrain the values assigned to variables in Z_S. Table 6.1 gives the translation of each requirement as a logical formula over the variables in Z, using the following abbreviations:

$$Web := zwebA + zwebB + zwebC + zwebD$$

$$App := zappA + zappB + zappC + zappD$$

$$Db := zdbA + zdbB + zdbC + zdbD.$$

Let P be a subset of first-order formulae over variables in Z. Given the logical formulae we form the constraint $\phi \equiv \phi_1 \wedge \phi_2 \wedge \phi_3$ in P which acts as input to an SMT solver [MB08] that automatically calculates a satisfiable assignment. An SMT solver is specified in the CMBA framework by the function $smt : P \rightarrow [Z \rightarrow \mathbb{Z}]$

Table 6.1 Mapping β translating requirements to logical formulae

Requirement	Logical formula
R1	$\phi_1 \equiv (Web \geq 2 \wedge Web \leq 4) \wedge (App \geq 2 \wedge App \leq 4) \wedge (Db \geq 2 \wedge Db \leq 4)$
R2	$\phi_2 \equiv (zwebA = zappA) \wedge (zwebB = zappB) \wedge$
	$(zwebC = zappC) \wedge (zwebD = zappD)$
R3	$\phi_3 \equiv (zdbD = 0)$

where $a = smt(\phi)$ is an assignment of values in $\mathbb{Z}$ to variables occurring in ϕ such that the formula is satisfied. In symbols: $[\![\phi]\!](a) = true$.

To summarise, we list the elements of the CMBA framework tuple $C_{smt} = (S, Q, \alpha, \beta, smt)$ instantiated with SMT solving:

- $S :=$ {web, app, db, service}, of component descriptions
- $M := \mathscr{P}(Z)$ where models are finite subsets of variables in Z,
- $\alpha : S \rightarrow M$ assigns $\alpha(\text{web}) := Z_{web}$, $\alpha(\text{app}) := Z_{app}$, $\alpha(\text{db}) := Z_{db}$ and $\alpha(\text{service}) := Z_S$
- $Q := \{R1, R2, R3\}$ is the set of deployment requirements for service
- P is a subset of first-order logic formulae over Z
- $\beta : Q \rightarrow P$ is specified by the entries in Table 6.1
- An SMT solving analysis technique $smt : P \rightarrow [Z \rightarrow \mathbb{Z}]$

6.6.2 Reliability Analysis of Satisfiable Deployment Configurations

Using the CMBA Framework C_{smt}, suppose the assignment

$$zwebA := 3, zappA := 3, zdbA := 2, zdbC := 2 \qquad (6.10)$$

is computed by smt analysis satisfying $\phi_1 \wedge \phi_2 \wedge \phi_3$. What is the reliability of this configuration? To answer this question, we compose the analysis results from C_{smt} with the CMBA framework C_{cv} defined in (6.9). This composition requires an appropriate system description S of the cloud deployment output by C_{smt}. To this end, we

1. Define component models for servers A, C (omitting B and D)
2. Define component models that keep track of dependencies corresponding to functional deployment:

   - wadA, for web, app and db deployed on server A
   - dbC, for db, deployed on server C
   - wad and db collecting dependencies for deployment of service

We assume α and β are parameterised to handle model generation for Markov models in M. This typically varies according to the functionality name and dependencies within S. Once the mappings to the models and temporal logics have been defined, compositional verification of the cloud deployment is performed on the verification task sequence (A, C, wadA, dbC, db, wad, service) yielding a probability measuring the service's reliability. This composition can be extended to consider a set of deployment configurations obtained by smt to be analysed by cv and ranked according to reliability. These kinds of analysis are particularly useful to determine deployment configurations after a system change or change in requirements.

6.7 Conclusion

In this chapter, we gave an algebraic specification of the CMBA framework as a means to continually analyse a system during its design and runtime development phases. Our approach was applied to a range of case studies from formal verification, model-based engineering, and IT process management. We outline a case study involving the compositional of CMBA frameworks to provide complex analysis of candidate cloud deployments.

The CMBA framework can be developed in a number of directions. On the more theoretical side, we may provide a full treatment using the algebraic theory of data types to study homomorphisms between algebras representing the system and domain-specific operations and model transformations. Practically speaking, there is a plethora of model-driven engineering case studies, modelling paradigms, and implemented tools in the chapters of this book to which the CMBA framework can be readily applied.

References

[Aal13] Wil van der Aalst. "Business process management: a comprehensive survey". In: *ISRN Software Engineering* 2013 (2013). https://doi.org/10/gb67c5.

[Aal16] Wil van der Aalst. *Process Mining: Data Science in Action*. Springer, 2016.

[Aal20] Wil van der Aalst. "Academic View: Development of the Process Mining Discipline". In: *Process Mining in Action: Principles, Use Cases and Outlook*. 2020, pp. 181–196. https://doi.org/10.1007/978-3-030-40172-6_21.

[Adl+11] Rasmus Adler, Dominik Domis, Kai Höfig, Sören Kemmann, Thomas Kuhn, Jean-Pascal Schwinn, and Mario Trapp. "Integration of Component Fault Trees into the UML". In: *Models in Software Engineering*. 2011, pp. 312–327. https://doi.org/10.1007/978-3-642-21210-9_30.

[APS10] Wil van der Aalst, Maja Pesic, and Minseok Song. "Beyond Process Mining: From the Past to Present and Future". In: *Advanced Information Systems Engineering*. 2010, pp. 38–52. https://doi.org/10/fnr6t8.

[Arn96] Robert S. Arnold. *Software Change Impact Analysis*. IEEE Computer Society Press, 1996.

[DAC99] Matthew B. Dwyer, George S. Avrunin, and James C. Corbett. "Patterns in Property Specifications for Finite-State Verification". In: *21st International Conference on Software Engineering, ICSE, Proceedings*. 1999, pp. 411–420. https://doi.org/10.1145/302405.302672.

[Gam+14] João Gama, Indré Žliobaité, Albert Bifet, Mykola Pechenizkiy, and Abdelhamid Bouchachia. "A Survey on Concept Drift Adaptation". In: *ACM Comput. Surv.* 46.4 (2014), 44:1–44:37. https://doi.org/10.1145/2523813.

[Gru08] Lars Grunske. "Specification Patterns for Probabilistic Quality Properties". In: *30th International Conference on Software Engineering, ICSE, Proceedings*. 2008, pp. 31–40. https://doi.org/10.1145/1368088.1368094.

[Hei+21] Robert Heinrich, Francisco Durán, Carolyn L. Talcott, and Steffen Zschaler (eds.) *Composing Model-Based Analysis Tools*. Springer, 2021. https://doi.org/10.1007/978-3-030-81915-6.

[Höf+18] Kai Höfig, Andreas Joanni, Marc Zeller, Francesco Montrone, Martin Rothfelder, Rakshith Amarnath, Peter Munk, and Arne Nordmann. "Model-based Reliability and Safety: Reducing the complexity of safety analyses using component fault trees". In: *Annual Reliability and Maintainability Symposium, RAMS*. 2018, pp. 1–7. https://doi.org/10.1109/RAM.2018.8463058.

[IEE16] IEEE. "IEEE Standard for eXtensible Event Stream (XES) for Achieving Interoperability in Event Logs and Event Streams". In: (Nov. 2016). https://doi.org/10/gdcf76.

[Int11] International Organization for Standardization (ISO). *ISO 26262: Road vehicles— Functional safety*. 2011.

[Int90] Int. Electrotechnical Commission (IEC). *IEC 61025: Fault Tree Analysis (FTA)*. 1990.

[Int91] Int. Electrotechnical Commission (IEC). *IEC 60812: Analysis Techniques for System Reliability - Procedure for Failure Mode and Effects Analysis (FMEA)*. 1991.

[Int98] International Electrotechnical Commission (IEC). *IEC 61508: Functional safety of electrical/electronic/programmable electronic safety related systems*. 1998.

[ISO06] ISO. *ISO 19439: 2006: Enterprise Integration-Framework for Enterprise Modelling*. 2006.

[JC14] Kenneth Johnson and Radu Calinescu. "Efficient Re-Resolution of SMT Specifications for Evolving Software Architectures". In: *10th International ACM Sigsoft Conference on Quality of Software Architectures, QoSA, Proceedings*. 2014, pp. 93–102. https://doi.org/10.1145/2602576.2602578.

[JCK13] Kenneth Johnson, Radu Calinescu, and Shinji Kikuchi. "An Incremental Verification Framework for Component-Based Software Systems". In: *Proceedings of the 16th International ACM Sigsoft Symposium on Component-Based Software Engineering*. 2013, pp. 33–42. https://doi.org/10.1145/2465449.2465456.

[Jos+05] Anjali Joshi, Steven P. Miller, Michael Whalen, and Mats P.E. Heimdahl. "A proposal for model-based safety analysis". In: *24th AIAA/IEEE Digital Avionics Systems Conference*. 2005. https://doi.org/10.1109/DASC.2005.1563469.

[Kai+18] Bernhard Kaiser, Daniel Schneider, Rasmus Adler, Dominik Domis, Felix Möhrle, Axel Berres, Marc Zeller, Kai Höfig, and Martin Rothfelder. "Advances in Component Fault Trees". In: *Safety and Reliability – Safe Societies in a Changing World, ESREL, Proceedings*. 2018, pp. 815–823. https://www.taylorfrancis.com/books/e/9781351174664/chapters/10.1201/9781351174664-103.

[KLM03] Bernhard Kaiser, Peter Liggesmeyer, and Oliver Mäckel. "A New Component Concept for Fault Trees". In: *8th Australian Workshop on Safety Critical Systems and Software*. 2003, pp. 37–46.

[Kwi+10] Marta Kwiatkowska, Gethin Norman, David Parker, and Hongyang Qu. "Assume-Guarantee Verification for Probabilistic Systems". In: *16th International Conference on Tools and Algorithms for the Construction and Analysis of Systems, TACAS, Proceedings*. Vol. 6105. 2010, pp. 23–37.

[LKN11] Oleg Lisagor, Tim Kelly, and Ru Niu. "Model-based safety assessment: Review of the discipline and its challenges". In: *9th International Conference on Reliability, Maintainability and Safety*. 2011, pp. 625–632. https://doi.org/10.1109/ICRMS.2011.5979344.

[LSK10] Oleg Lisagor, Linling Sun, and Tim Kelly. "The Illusion of Method: Challenges of Model-Based Safety Assessment". In: *28th International System Safety Conference*. 2010.

[Mac+12] Joseph Machrouh, Jean-Paul Blanquart, Philippe Baufreton, Jean-Louis Boulanger, Hervé Delseny, Jean Gassino, Gérard Ladier, Emmanuel Ledinot, Michel Leeman, Jean-Marc Astruc, et al. "Cross domain comparison of System Assurance". In: *Embedded Real Time Software and Systems, ERTS*. 2012. https://hal.archives-ouvertes.fr/hal-02170444.

[MB08] Leonardo de Moura and Nikolaj Bjørner. "Z3: An Efficient SMT Solver". In: *Tools and Algorithms for the Construction and Analysis of Systems*. 2008, pp. 337–340.

[MDC16] Niels Martin, Benoît Depaire, and An Caris. "The Use of Process Mining in Business Process Simulation Model Construction". In: *Business & Information Systems Engineering* 58.1 (2016), pp. 73–87. https://doi.org/10/f8f39n.

[MK06] John McDermid and Tim Kelly. *Software in safety critical systems: Achievement and prediction*. 2006. https://doi.org/10.1680/nuen.2006.2.3.140.

[Obj12] Object Management Group. *OMG Systems Modeling Language (OMG SysML), Version 1.3*. 2012. http://www.omg.org/spec/SysML/1.3/.

[RFB12] Ana Luísa Ramos, José Vasconcelos Ferreira, and Jaume Barceló. "Model-Based Systems Engineering: An Emerging Approach for Modern Systems". In: *IEEE Transactions on Systems, Man, and Cybernetics, Part C (Applications and Reviews)* 42.1 (2012), pp. 101–111.

[Roq16] Pascal Roques. "MBSE with the ARCADIA Method and the Capella Tool". In: *8th European Congress on Embedded Real Time Software and Systems*. 2016.

[RS15] Enno Ruijters and Mariëlle Stoelinga. "Fault tree analysis: A survey of the state-of-the-art in modeling, analysis and tools". In: *Computer Science Review* 15–16 (2015), pp. 29–62.

[Sch+11] Michael Schultz., Lothar Meyer, Boris Langer, and Hartmut Fricke. "Model-based Safety Assessment as Integrated Part of System Development". In: *International Workshop on Aircraft System Technologies*. 2011.

[Sch+16] Andreas Schoknecht, Arthur Vetter, Hans-Georg Fill, and Andreas Oberweis. "Using the Horus Method for Succeeding in Business Process Engineering Projects". In: *Domain-Specific Conceptual Modeling*. 2016, pp. 127–147. https://doi.org/10.1007/978-3-319-39417-6_6.

[Sha+15] Septavera Sharvia, Sohag Kabir, MartinWalker, and Yiannis Papadopoulos. "Modelbased dependability analysis: State-of-the-art, challenges, and future outlook". In: *Software Quality Assurance: In Large Scale and Complex Software-intensive Systems* (2015), pp. 251–278. https://doi.org/10.1016/B978-0-12-802301-3.00012-0.

[Soc96] Society of Automotive Engineers Inc. (SAE). ARP 4761: *Guidelines and Methods for Conducting the Safety Assessment Process on Civil Airborne Systems and Equipment*. 1996.

[Tra16] Mario Trapp. *Assuring functional safety in open systems of systems*. Tech. rep. Fraunhofer IESE, 2016. http://nbn-resolving.de/urn:nbn:de:hbz:386-kluedo-44221.

[Ves+81] William E Vesely, Francine F Goldberg, Norman H Roberts, and David F Haasl. *Fault Tree Handbook*. US Nuclear Regulatory Commission, 1981.

[Wes12] Mathias Weske. *Business Process Management: Concepts, Languages, Architectures*. Springer, 2012.

[ZH16] Marc Zeller and Kai Höfig. "INSiDER: Incorporation of system and safety analysis models using a dedicated reference model". In: *Annual Reliability and Maintain Symposium, RAMS*. 2016, pp. 1–6. https://doi.org/10.1109/RAMS.2016.7448074.

Chapter 7
Exploiting Results of Model-Based Analysis Tools

Francisco Durán, Martin Gogolla, Esther Guerra, Juan de Lara, Houari Sahraoui, and Steffen Zschaler

Abstract Any analysis produces results to be used by analysis users to understand and improve the system being analysed. But what are the ways in which analysis results can be exploited? And how is exploitation of analysis results related to analysis composition? In this chapter, we provide a conceptual model of analysis-result exploitation and a model of the variability and commonalities between different analysis approaches, leading to a feature-based description of results exploitation. We demonstrate different instantiations of our feature model in nine case studies of specific analysis techniques. Through this discussion, we also showcase different forms of analysis composition, leading to different forms of exploitation of analysis results for refined analysis, improving analysis mechanisms, exploring results, etc. We, thus, present the fundamental terminology for researchers to discuss exploitation of analysis results, including under composition, and highlight some of the challenges and opportunities for future research.

This core chapter addresses Challenge 4 introduced in Chap. 3 of this book (*exploiting analysis results*).

F. Durán (✉)
University of Málaga, Málaga, Spain
e-mail: duran@lcc.uma.es

M. Gogolla
Universität Bremen, Bremen, Germany
e-mail: gogolla@uni-bremen.de

E. Guerra · J. De Lara
Autonomous University of Madrid, Madrid, Spain
e-mail: esther.guerra@uam.es; Juan.deLara@uam.es

H. Sahraoui
Université de Montréal, Montréal, QC, Canada
e-mail: sahraouh@iro.umontreal.ca

S. Zschaler
King's College London, London, UK
e-mail: szschaler@acm.org

© The Author(s), under exclusive license to Springer Nature Switzerland AG 2021
R. Heinrich et al. (eds.), *Composing Model-Based Analysis Tools*,
https://doi.org/10.1007/978-3-030-81915-6_7

129

7.1   Introduction

As we have seen in other chapters of this book [Hei+21], the number of situations in which tools may be used in different contexts, for different purposes, is enormous. However, these tools have one thing in common: They produce results that may be directly provided to users or fed into other tools, which may make different uses of them. Indeed, for any analysis to be deemed successful, its results must be able to have an impact on the next steps, in whatever process they are involved.

When we come to tool composition, the situation is not different. Previous chapters of this book [Hei+21] have shown that we may be composing tools in parallel or sequentially (see Chap. 5 on tool integration and orchestration), we may be composing models on which tools operate (see Chap. 4 on composition of languages, models, and analyses), or decomposing them to also decompose the analyses they perform, we may deal on views of a bigger system, or construct them from pieces. There is however one aspect common to all forms of composition: No matter how you compose/decompose your inputs or produce your outputs, you *have* such inputs and outputs, and the main purpose of the tool composition is to add value in the form of results of the analysis.

Two words come as key notions into this process: *purpose* and *interpretation*. Depending on the goals of a tool, its inputs will take one form or another. Depending on what is going to be done with them, its outputs will be ones or others, and produced in one way or another. Hence, the purpose of a tool will condition its inputs, its outputs, and the process to generate the latter from the former. If we see the results of a tool as inputs to other tools, or as information to provide to final users, the question might then be reduced to how this communication happens. But this is of course a giant beast. From an engineering point of view, we need to care about the representation of results as much as on their potential interpretation. As inputs, data are interpreted and then turned into some other format so that the final user or target tool may make use of such results as expected. Notice that this is a key assumption. We may be expecting a specific result interpretation, but the final user or subsequent tool getting these results as inputs might interpret them differently. When your favourite weather prediction tool tells you that the probability of rain in your town tomorrow is 70%, how do you interpret it? Is it a confidence measure? Do I need my umbrella? Even if you know what this number means, as a user, you might be providing an alternative meaning: Your experience tells you that in most cases it means that there is a good chance of getting rain in the nearby mountains, but that it will most probably not rain down in the coast. See Chap. 8 of this book [Hei+21] for more on uncertainty.

The way engineers have come to tackle both purpose and interpretation is the use of precise and unambiguous models with clear and formal semantics. The interchange of such models between tools may be considered as a formal problem where interpretations may be fixed and solved. The results however may be subject to interpretation by a user. For obvious reasons, tools will try to present their results in a way that is comprehensible to their users. However, what is being presented to the users may not be simple. Hence, tools may require *lifting* the analysis results from their internal representation to a suitable format to be presented to the user. Next, we analyse some factors that characterise/differentiate the difficulty of lifting between one representation and another.

One first differentiating factor in this lifting might be the structural/semantic distance between the representation being manipulated/conceptualised by the user and the representation used for analysis. Using this criterion, we may differentiate three levels: static syntactic/type-level analysis, semantic analysis for functional correctness properties, and system-level analysis of quality properties (typical - *ilities*). The lifting faces fundamentally different challenges at each of these three levels.

At the level of *static syntactic/type-level analysis*, the representation that is manipulated/conceptualised by the user is near identical to that being analysed. As a result, lifting is not actually needed. However, the lack of a separate specification implies that we can only analyse the extension of what has been represented, but not the intention behind it. For example, as we will see for the case of a tool to help novice programmers in Sect. 7.4.4, an additional analysis tries to "guess" the intention and then suggests possible actions to bring the extension closer to that intention. Challenges are, hence, that several possible changes can lead to the correction of an error.

At the level of *semantic analysis for functional correctness properties*, lifting becomes harder: The representation that we analyse (e.g., a set of traces) is markedly different from the representation the user is manipulating/conceptualising (program source code, a model diagram, etc.). As a result, we need to translate from one representation to the other [Heg+10]. This translation needs to identify the source of any semantic concepts, errors, etc. This source can be in several places: The requirements/tests can be wrong, the implementation can be wrong, or the language execution semantics could be wrong. However, it is normally possible to identify which of these parts is to "blame", so that the issue can be narrowed down to a localised part. The challenge lies in the translation of the analysis results into the formalism of the model under manipulation.

At the level of *system-level analysis of quality properties (-ilities)*, the gap between model and analysis format is even bigger [CMI07]. For example, an architecture model largely differs from the Markov chain used for reliability analysis [RRU05]. Lifting a problem identified in a Markov-chain model back to an architecture model is very difficult. Moreover, these properties are system properties: They depend on the software structure as well as on a range of other factors, including the execution environment and usage platform. As a result, normally it is not possible to identify the specific part of the overall model that is to "blame", and even when this is possible, the root cause is rarely narrowly located. Hence, a fix cannot be made just by the consideration of the model under manipulation.

In the rest of the chapter, we will first introduce a general model of the uses that we may have of the analysis tools' results. In Sect. 7.2, we will present the main pathways where this impact could manifest. Section 7.3 then provides a feature model of results-exploitation approaches. Several sample cases are presented in Sect. 7.4 to illustrate the alternative uses of outputs we may find in existing tools. Although the instantiation of the feature model is discussed for each tool in its corresponding section, the coverage of the feature model is discussed as a whole in Sect. 7.4.10. Finally, Sect. 7.5 summarises the discussion and highlights an open challenge.

7.2 A General Model of Results Exploitation

Figure 7.1 depicts the different pathways we have identified in which existing tools use their results. This general model has been built based on the expertise of the authors in building analysis tools (e.g., see USE in Sect. 7.4.3, ANATLYZER in Sect. 7.4.8 and Chap. 12 of this book [Hei+21], and *GTSMorpher* in Chap. 9), as well as in their experience as users of a wide range of existing tools for model-based analysis in different domains (e.g., process modelling in Sect. 7.4.1 or counterexample-guided abstraction refinement techniques in Sect. 7.4.9). Each pathway brings its own challenges:

1. In its simplest form, analysis results may be presented to the users (e.g., developers, domain experts) to help them *explore* and *interpret* the system model or the model itself further—for example, to identify the root cause of a problem or to better understand a scientific hypothesis. Challenges in this pathway include:

    • Lifting low-level analysis results back up to the domain level so that they can be understood by domain stakeholders.

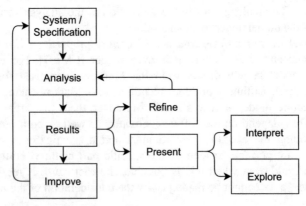

Fig. 7.1 How to use analysis results

- Selecting which analysis results are most important/useful to present in a given situation—this is closely connected to the original purpose for which the analysis was undertaken.
- Enabling users to drill down, possibly interactively, into the analysis results— for example, to enable root-cause analysis.

2. Analysis results can also be exploited to *improve* systems or their specifications/models. Examples of this include model/program repair, refactoring, or refinement. The changes made to a system or its specification, in response to some analysis, can be done automatically as well as manually. Challenges in this pathway include:

- How far can this be automated for different properties of interest?
- Is there a generic automatic mechanism or does each property require its own mechanism?
- Can we learn automated exploitation mechanisms by observing how expert domain users respond to different types of analysis results?
- Is it possible to undertake repair or similar in relation to multiple properties of interest at the same time (i.e., can repair be composed)?

3. Finally, analysis results may be used to *refine* the analysis process itself. For example, by asking the analysis to focus on a particular aspect of the system model in more detail, by tuning some parameters, or by learning an analysis from a set of expert-provided examples of inputs and expected results. Challenges in this pathway include:

- How to enable users to understand the analysis results and provide suitable feedback to the learning algorithm.
- How to model this feedback so that it can be effectively used for improving the analysis. Relevant examples include the classical *counterexample-guided abstraction refinement* (CEGAR) methodology [Cla+00] (see Sect. 7.4.9), from the model-checking area, or approaches to search-based refactoring [Oun+16].
- How to automate the learning process, and to which extent this is even possible.

Overarching these pathways, there is a challenge of how to choose properties, analysis pathways, and combinations thereof to form an overall *argument of fitness-for-purpose* of the system as a whole. Goal-Question-Metric, safety cases, goal-oriented modelling (e.g., the NFR framework [Chu+00]) appear to have building blocks for answering this challenge, but as far as we are aware, there is currently no integrated approach for this purpose.

From this analysis of the conceptual space, we derive a feature model of techniques for using and composing analysis results in Sect. 7.3, which is then exemplified and validated across a large range of case studies in Sect. 7.4. The coverage of the feature model by these case studies is discussed in Sect. 7.4.10.

7.3 A Feature Model of Results-Exploitation Approaches

Figure 7.2 shows a feature model breaking down the three pathways of results presentation, improvement, and analysis refinement from Fig. 7.1 into more specific options. In Sect. 7.4, we will briefly discuss several examples showcasing different configurations of this feature model. Here, we describe the different options more generally.

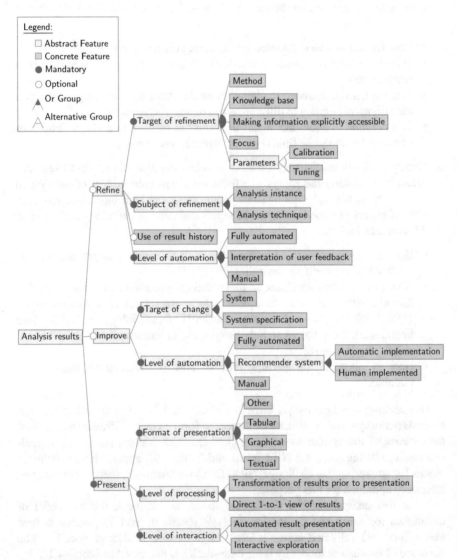

Fig. 7.2 Feature model expressed in FeatureIDE

As we described in Fig. 7.1, analysis results can be used along three different pathways, each corresponding to a top-level feature in our feature model.

1. Results *must* be *presented* to users in some form to enable exploration and interpretation. We differentiate *exploration* and *interpretation*: The former refers to the process by which a user looks at analysis results over time; it is a process largely controlled by the analysis tool. Interpretation, on the other hand, is what happens in an analysis user's brain to transform the results shown into understanding and, possibly, actionable plans. Analysis tools will aim to support this by carefully presenting results in ways that make useful interpretation easier and avoid misinterpretation, but, ultimately, results interpretation is out of the control of the analysis tool developer. In our feature model, we differentiate three aspects of how results presentation can support exploration and interpretation:

   (a) *Level of interaction.* Analysis tools may provide an automated, static presentation of the results—in effect making a static determination what will be the best data to show and how to best show it to the user. On the other end of the spectrum, analysis tools may enable users to interactively explore the analysis results, including options for zoom-in/zoom-out, filtering, searching, etc.
   (b) *Level of processing.* Analysis tools may simply present the results directly as given by the analysis. However, in many cases, it may be more appropriate to pre-transform the results to make them easier to interpret for the user. For example, analysis may have required the system specification to be transformed into a representation that can be processed by the analysis results, in which case the results will need back-translating into the original domain [Fri+08, Gue+09]. Alternatively, it may be useful to compose the original analysis with a further, secondary analysis of the results (see, e.g., Sect. 7.4.4). This transformation may also include aggregation of results into higher-level summary presentations in support of interactive exploration with zoom-in/zoom-out.
   (c) *Format of presentation.* Results can be presented as text, in graphical form, as a table, or in other forms (e.g., as document annotations).

2. Results *may* be used to *improve* the system being analysed. We differentiate two aspects of improvement:

   (a) *Level of automation.* In the simplest case, analysis tools simply present the analysis results and leave it to the *human* user to figure out how these results might be used to improve the system. This requires in-depth domain understanding and, often, some understanding of the analysis method itself for users to be able to make meaningful decisions about system improvement. At the other end of the scale, the analysis tool might directly implement improvement in a *fully automated* manner, without consultation with the user. System adaptation in the context of models@runtime [BGS19] is a good example here. In between these two extremes, there are improvement mechanisms that are partially automated; we label these as *recommender systems* and differentiate two types: *human-implemented* recommender systems present actionable suggestions to users but rely on users to implement these manually, while systems with *automated implementation*—for example, quick-fix systems in IDEs—provide a choice of options to the user and automatically implement the improvement once the user has made a selection [Fur+17, SGL18].

(b) *Target of change.* System improvement may happen in two ways: by changing the *system* directly or by changing the *system specification* and relying on other processes to eventually change the system. The latter is, for example, a suitable approach where the actual system does not yet exist and we are analysing a (prescriptive [AZW06, Sei03]) design model of the system. Equally, in a models@runtime approach, improvement would typically change the specification and rely on reflection mechanisms for these changes to be effected in the actual underlying system.

3. Results *may* be used to *refine* the analysis itself, establishing a feedback process by which the analysis tool learns over time. Refinement can also be interpreted as a form of analysis composition: We can think of the analysis that is being refined as the system, and the results from that analysis as the system specification, for a secondary analysis (a "meta-analysis") which leads to improvements of the original analysis (so we could think of refinement as "meta-improvement"). Consequently, the level of automation is also an important classification aspect for refinement. The target of change is always the system, as there is no meaningful "system specification" of the analysis. Below, we use the category "target of refinement" to further break down the different aspects of an analysis that can be refined by composing a meta-analysis. In addition, there are two further aspects of interest:

(a) *Level of automation.* The simplest form of analysis refinement is *manual*; that is, where a human analyses results from one analysis run or across runs and implements a refinement of the original analysis. For example, in the ANATLYZER tool [SGL17] for the static analysis of model transformations (see Sect. 7.4.8 and Chap. 12 of this book [Hei+21]), the developer may manually disable certain types of checks, for example, if many false positives are reported in the current analysis. On the other end of the spectrum there is *full automation*, where the analysis self-adapts fully automatically. Again, in ANATLYZER, some static analysis results need to be confirmed by a more costly analysis based on model finding. This extra analysis can be run automatically, or required to be explicitly triggered by the user. Recommender systems (as in *improvement*) are less relevant for analysis refinement. However, there is an intermediary automation level, where analysis is refined based on explicitly given user feedback on previous analysis results. CEGAR [Cla+00] is an example that has seen a lot of research interest for model-checking-based analyses (see Sect. 7.4.9).

(b) *Use of result history.* Analysis refinement may build on information about previous analysis results. Such refinement is typically based on multiple sets of previous results (e.g., the trace of results inspected in an interactive exploration session).

(c) *Subject of refinement.* We distinguish two subjects of refinement: refinement may apply to a single *analysis instance* only, implying any refinements do not transfer (and in fact may not even be conceptually transferable) to other runs of the same analysis technique applied to other system specifications. For example, this is the case with CEGAR, where refinements are made based on counterexamples derived from the current analysis run. Refinements of the *analysis technique* on the other hand do transfer to all future analysis runs and often entail a change to the analysis algorithm.

(d) *Target of refinement.* The most invasive refinement changes the overall analysis *method*, while the least invasive refinement may only adjust analysis *parameters* for purposes of *tuning* or *calibration*. Other refinement targets include making information explicit so that it becomes more directly accessible to the analysis (again, CEGAR is an example) or to change the *focus* of the analysis—for example, by analysing different parts of a large search space.

We, next, describe several examples of analyses, paying particular attention to how they fit into the classification scheme provided by our feature model. The feature model and the configurations for each example are also available in FEATUREIDE [Mei+17] format on Github.[1]

7.4 Example Cases

This section presents nine sample cases to illustrate the different alternative uses of outputs we may find in analysis tools. We instantiate our feature model for each case in its corresponding section, and then, we discuss the coverage of the feature model as a whole in Sect. 7.4.10.

The presentation of each case is divided into four parts: (a) "Objective" discussing the goals of the performed analysis, (b) "Analysis description" presenting some details about which technical steps in the applied tool have been taken during the analysis, (c) "Results exploitation" explaining how the analysis results are presented and can be employed in the development process for improvement, and (d) "Instantiation of feature model" considering how the developed feature model for result exploitation is instantiated and which parts of it are used. The different selected tools for analysis cover a wide range of tasks in the development process, are based on a wide spectrum of underlying analysis technologies, and yield a broad collection of results for improving the development. The range is demonstrated in the spectrum of options in the established feature model.

---

[1] The feature model and the configurations for each example are available at https://github.com/szschaler/dagstuhl19418.analysis_results.

7.4.1 Soundness and Safeness of Business Processes

When modelling a business process, many crucial questions arise from a correctness and optimisation point of view. For example, is the workflow precisely modelling what is intended? Is the workflow free of errors and bugs? Are certain properties of interest preserved? Are there bottlenecks and, if so, where? Formal verification and optimisation of business processes aim at, respectively, ensuring correct behaviour and improving these processes, by effectively answering the above questions, with the final goal to reduce costs and augment efficiency. Nonetheless, process correctness and optimisation are far from being simple questions to answer, particularly when modelling complex combinations of tasks, nesting of gateways, cyclic behaviour, and quantitative aspects.

The *business process model and notation* (BPMN 2.0) [OMG11] is a widely accepted language for modelling business processes. Several properties have been introduced in the literature to guarantee process correctness (see, e.g., [Dum+13]). In this section, we focus on tools for the verification of properties such as soundness and safeness of BPMN models.

Objective A model is said to be sound if (i) any process instance always completes once started, (ii) when a process ends there is no activity still running, and (iii) a process does not contain activities that will never be executed. A process model is said to be safe if none of its activities will ever be executed in more than one instance concurrently.

Analysis Description Tools such as Woflan [VA00], ProM [Don+05], or WoPeD [Fre+17] provide different forms of verification of business processes based on mappings into a transition based formalism (e.g., Petri nets), where the analysis is performed. Other tools perform the analysis using other formalisms. For instance, BProVe [Cor+17] and [DRS18] map BPMN processes into rewriting logic, and use tools in the Maude [Cla+07] formal environment to perform the analyses. Specifically, both of these two tools perform their analysis using Maude's *linear temporal logic* (LTL) model checker. Correctness properties encoded in LTL formulae are evaluated and the result is then presented to the user. Figure 7.3 depicts the process.

Results Exploitation BProVe takes results from the analysis back to the original model, so that diagnostic information is reported on the model in a way that is understandable by process stakeholders (who then explore the presented results). The integration of BProVe into Apromore allows model designers to use the Apromore [Ros+11] BPMN editor to design models and to interact with BProVe to verify properties of the designed model. The results are shown graphically on top of the process model, so as to highlight behavioural paths that violate the correctness properties. Designers can then easily identify the violation and repair their model accordingly.

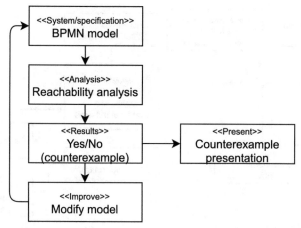

Fig. 7.3 Soundness and safeness of business processes

Instantiation of Feature Model The tool presents the result directly on the original business process so that the user can *explore it interactively*, but there is no prior elaboration of the results other than gathering the counterexample information back onto the user process (*Direct 1-to-1 view of results*). Improvement is totally *manual* by the user, who may gather information from the presented data to modify the business process accordingly (*system specification* as *target of change*).

7.4.2 Analysis of API Usage

In modern software development, achieving any meaningful task of non-trivial complexity requires developers to reuse software from APIs, libraries, and services. Such libraries usually require that client applications obey assumed constraints and usage patterns. Unfortunately, usage patterns are rarely well documented. Identifying them automatically is a good way to address this lack of documentation.

The detection of usage patterns depends on the nature of these patterns. In the case of unordered patterns, the identification consists in finding subsets of API methods that are frequently called together by client methods (see, for example, [Zho+09, Sai+15]). Identifying temporal patterns, i.e., latent temporal properties of APIs, is more complex. It consists in deriving temporal formulas as in [Sai+20].

Objective The goal of this analysis is to identify temporal usage patterns of an API from execution traces of clients using this API.

Analysis Description This analysis consists in using genetic programming, an evolutionary method, to mine temporal patterns from execution traces [Sai+20]. The search process builds gradually LTL formulas, representing candidate usage

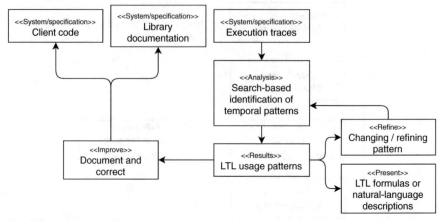

Fig. 7.4 Analysis of API usage

patterns, by combining API method calls with logical and temporal operators. The search-space exploration is guided by the conformance of candidate patterns with execution traces of client programs using the targeted API. The process of identifying and using temporal usage patterns is shown in Fig. 7.4.

Results Exploitation The usage patterns mined can serve different purposes. They can help library developers better document their code. They can also be used as an input for the analysis of a client code to assist developers to correctly integrate the API in their code. Finally, the mined patterns can serve to refine the analysis itself in different ways. For example, if mined patterns are too complex to be humanly understandable, the parameters, involved in the identification, can be tuned to reduce the pattern complexity.

Instantiation of Feature Model Results are presented for *interactive exploration* with no elaborate processing (*direct 1-to-1 view of results*). Results are presented textually with possibly a table that shows some metrics about the patterns such as the frequency in the traces and the confidence score. The system recommends changes, which can automatically implement, but user interaction is required (*recommender system* with *automatic implementation*). The target of change is the client code and its documentation (*system specification*). The system may analyse the information provided by users (*interpretation of user feedback*) to refine its analysis technique by improving its knowledge base.

7.4.3 Diversity-Aware Model Finding with USE

The context for this example are validation and verification in general class models in the *Unified Modeling Language* (UML) [Obj15] utilising attributes, associations, and generalisation relationships, together with *object constraint language* (OCL) [Obj14] constraints. In order to give feedback to the developer on the class model properties, typical satisfying or violating object models can be checked against the implicit UML class model requirements and the explicit OCL constraints. For example, validation aims at showing automatically constructed object models for giving feedback about the possible interplay of constraints. Verification, e.g., of satisfiability, can be achieved by constructing a satisfying, non-empty object model.

Objective The overall process for exploiting results in this example is displayed in Fig. 7.5. Specifically, here class models are made precise with OCL invariants, and so-called classifying *OCL terms* (CTs) are used for the result construction. The purpose of the analysis is to build a collection of diverse UML object models that are instantiations (object models) of the given UML and OCL class model. The process is realised in the tool *UML-based specification environment* (USE) [GHD18].

Analysis Description The UML and OCL model including the OCL invariants is handed over to an analysis tool based on Kodkod [TJ07]. The analysis tool returns an object model satisfying the OCL invariants. The object model is chosen from a previously specified finite search space limiting the number of objects in a class, the attribute values, and the link values. A *diverse* object model collection is achieved when each two distinct object models show substantially different characteristics, e.g., in the object or link structure or in the attribute value combinations or in both. Criteria for diversity are directed by the developer through specifying so-called classifying terms [Gog+15, Hil+18], i.e., a collection of closed, general Boolean or Integer valued OCL terms that describe formal properties of the desired object models. For example, in a class model with classes A and B, the two classifying terms `ctA = A.allInstances()->size()` and

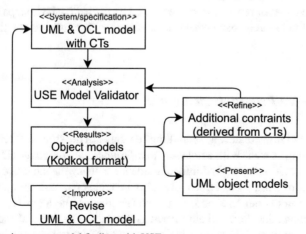

Fig. 7.5 Diversity-aware model finding with USE

`ctB = B.allInstances()->isEmpty()` could deliver a collection of six object models, each showing a different combination for the values of the two classifying terms (`ctA in {1,2,3}`, `ctB in {false,true}`), provided a finite search space is given limiting the number of A objects to be in the interval `1..3` and the number of B objects to be in `0..4`. In order to achieve diversity, the analysis is refined in an iterative way by providing additional constraints to the analysis tool.

Results Exploitation After a single solution in the form of an object model has been found, the classifying terms are evaluated in the last found object model, and a constraint excluding the particular found combination of the classifying term values is added. In the next iteration, the analysis tool will either construct a new solution with a new combination of values for classifying terms or stop in the case no further solution is possible. The process of adding new object models will always terminate, because the finite search space guarantees that only a finite number of solutions exists. Summarising, one can say that the intermediately found analysis results are exploited in order to find further new results and to assess whether the model describes only results that the developer is considering as valid.

Instantiation of Feature Model The presentation of results uses *interactive exploration* for the resulting object model collection, because each single object model can be accessed together with the values of the classifying terms. Results are presented as *UML object models* that can be presented with an automatic layout. Improvement is by *manual* changes of the *system specification* (the UML and OCL class model). Refinement of the original analysis is *fully automated:* The new constraints arising from the classifying terms in the found solutions are automatically added to the internal set of Kodkod constraints and respected in the following steps. *Multiple prior states* are used in the analysis refinement, as the collection of constraints is extended in every step. The level of refinement is the *analysis instance:* By adding the constraints, only the current analysis run will be affected. The target of refinement is the *focus,* i.e., further analysis steps are directed to the part of the search space where no solutions with satisfying classifying terms are present.

7.4.4 Novice Programmer Errors

While this is not immediately a "modelling" example in the strict sense, it is applicable to modelling as well: With a *domain-specific modelling language* (DSML) many users will be novices, so need additional guidance in using the language, identifying errors, and correcting them effectively. This becomes particularly challenging as the DSML grows larger and more complex. Lessons can be learned from the area of programming education and automated assessment. Here, one of the challenges for novice programmers is getting their own code to compile and interpreting the error messages produced by the compiler to "fix" their code. Typically, a compiler analyses the source code and reports errors where it finds an inconsistency. A problem for novice programmers is that the compiler can produce many error messages as a result of a single error (e.g., a missing semicolon or a mistyped variable name) and that these error messages may be associated with many different locations in the source code. Finding the root cause of these errors and fixing it can be challenging when programmers are still struggling to understand the core concepts of the language itself. This creates a challenge for automated assessment systems: How to best report compiler error messages to enable novice programmers to find effective solutions efficiently while learning to use compiler errors directly without additional help from the assessment system.

Objective The purpose of this analysis is to enable novice programmers to effectively identify and fix errors in their programs.

Analysis Description The Nexus system [Zsc+18] has experimented with composing the analysis provided by the compiler with a secondary automated analysis of the error messages to give more directive support to students. For example, where the compiler reports that it does not know a name used in an expression, the Nexus system identifies similarly named objects (variables, methods, etc.) in the program code using Levenshtein editing distance and suggests to students that they may wish to use one of those names instead. The analysis process is depicted in Fig. 7.6.

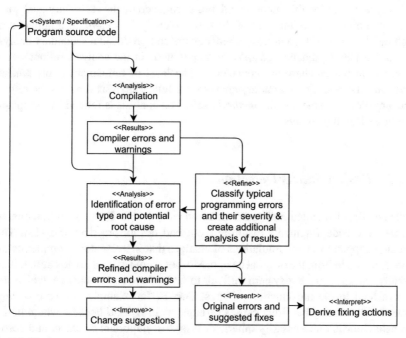

Fig. 7.6 Novice programmer errors

Results Exploitation The error messages reported in this way are meant to help novice programmers get better at understanding and fixing compiler errors. While, in principle, it may be possible to provide automated fixes for at least a subset of the errors (*improve*), this is not desirable here: Automated improvement of the original code would prevent learning by the novice programmer, effectively tying them to the scaffolding provided by the automated platform. Instead, Nexus chooses how to *present* the results to enable novice programmers to better *interpret* them and then manually *improve* their program and fix the errors, based on actionable proposals generated by the secondary analysis. This is an example of how a basic analysis can be *refined* by composing it sequentially with an analysis of the original analysis results. Many studies have been undertaken trying to understand typical mistakes made by novice programmers; most recently, McCall and Kölling [MK19] have undertaken a large-scale analysis of BlueJ data to classify errors by frequency and severity (how difficult the error is for a novice programmer to correct). Such data can then be used to identify which error messages are particularly useful to focus on in a post-analysis as well as providing a good data set of example occurrences of the error to support the development of useful secondary analysis.

Instantiation of Feature Model The presentation of results uses *automated result presentation* without any interactivity using *transformation of results prior to presentation* via the secondary analysis. Results are presented as *text*. Improvement is by *human-implemented recommender system* requiring the novice programmer to interpret the actionable recommendations produced by the secondary analysis. It changes the *system*. Refinement of the original analysis is *manual:* a human analysed the database of typical programmer errors and produced a secondary analysis to provide better guidance. *Results history* is used in the analysis refinement, as all errors in the database are considered. The level of refinement is the *analysis technique:* By adding a secondary analysis, all future analysis runs will be refined. The target of refinement is the *method* itself: The analysis is refined by composing it with a secondary analysis.

7.4.5　Design Smells Detection

Code smells, also called anti-patterns, anomalies, design flaws, or bad smells, are problematic code fragments resulting from bad design practices [Fow18]. They can also happen from accumulations of changes that increase code complexity and deviate the code from the original design. Most of them are unlikely to cause failures directly, but they make a system difficult to understand and to change, which may in turn lead to the introduction of bugs. This is, for example, the case of *large classes*. Others may be direct causes of bugs, as in *refused bequest* where part of the behaviour is unnecessarily inherited. It is then important to detect and correct them.

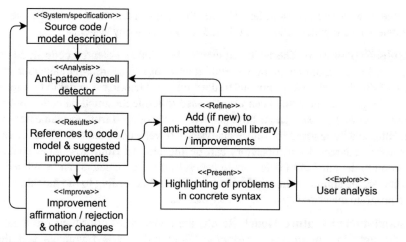

Fig. 7.7 Smells detection

Detecting such smells automatically is not obvious because their manifestation involves many factors that are difficult to quantify or explicit. The detection techniques are generally based on smell definitions that involve quantitative, structural, architectural, and linguistic aspects. For example, a *Blob* smell is a large class that monopolises most of the processing and uses other classes, mainly as data structures. Some techniques use thresholds of design metrics as in [Mar04]—for example, class size larger than some value α. Others combine these metric thresholds with linguistic search—for example, the class name should also include terms like "controller" or "manager" [Moh+10]. Alternative techniques use visualisation features to semi-automatically detect smells [DSP08], rely on change histories [Pal+13], or exploit search-based techniques [KVS10]. The latter uses the analysis process depicted in Fig. 7.7.

Objective   The goal of this analysis is to detect design smells in the code using the artificial immune system metaphor [KVS10].

Analysis Description   The detection process is based on the assumption that the more code deviates from good practices, the more likely it contains code smells. This process has two main steps: detector generation and risk estimation. The generation of detectors is done using a genetic algorithm. Starting from a set of reputedly well-designed systems, the algorithm evolves a population of artificial code fragments, i.e., potential detectors, with the aim of maximising their difference with the good code, using a distance measure.

The second step of the detection process consists of comparing the code to evaluate with the detectors. A code fragment that exhibits a similarity with a detector is considered as likely to contain a code smell. The higher the similarity according to the distance measure, the more a code fragment is considered risky. Only code fragments with a detector similarity higher than a given threshold are kept. Note that the detectors are generated once and used to evaluate many systems.

Results Exploitation The code fragments identified as potential code smells are presented to the maintainers in descending order of risk score. Maintainers inspect each of the flagged code fragments to decide if a refactoring is suitable to improve the code quality. The results can also be used to refine the smell detection process in many ways. For example, if false positives are produced from the same detector, the latter can be ignored for future analyses. Conversely, in the case of many false negatives, a larger set of detectors can be regenerated from new good code. In addition to the number of detectors to generate, other parameters can be refined. In particular, the similarity threshold can be calibrated according to the global quality of a program measured by some quality metrics.

Instantiation of Feature Model Results are transformed prior their presentation to the user for *interactive exploration*. Both risky code fragments and their corresponding detectors are presented textually. Each flagged code is also presented in a table with its risk score. The tool recommends the fragments to change, but to automatically implement the changes, the analysis should be composed with a refactoring analysis (*recommender system* with *automatic implementation*).

7.4.6   Visual-Based Identification of Object-Churn Sources

Object churn is a common performance problem in framework-intensive applications. It consists of an excessive use of temporary objects. Temporaries can impose a significant overhead during the execution, not only because of the increased pressure on the garbage collector, but mostly due to increased initialisation costs.

Objective The goal of this analysis is to identify and understand the sources of churn in the code.

Analysis Description In [DDS12], the authors combine automated static and dynamic analysis with interactive visualisation to identifying the methods responsible for temporary object creations. Automated analysis helps derive *calling context trees* (CCTs), a concise representation of call trees. The CCTs are completed, in each node, with object creation metrics. The metrics are obtained using an escape analysis which determines the bounds on created object dynamic lifetimes. Objects with short lifetimes are considered as potential temporaries. A CCT is then mapped to a sunburst-like visualisation. The final analysis step is the interaction with the visual representation to locate the most significant source of churn. Interactions involve navigation and filtering actions to local interesting regions as well as access to contextual information and view switch (to explore different metrics) to deepen the understanding. The analysis process is depicted in Fig. 7.8.

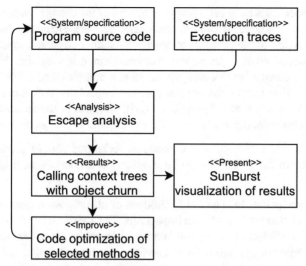

Fig. 7.8 Identification of object-churn sources

Results Exploitation The identification of object-churn sources is an interactive visualisation task. Consequently, the visualisation environment is used to present intermediate as well as final results. It is also used to progressively refine the analysis by applying filters and modifying the mapping functions between the metrics and the graphical attributes. The boundaries between the analysis itself and its refinement are then not as clear as for fully automated analysis tasks. Finally, when the sources of churn are identified, the corresponding program fragments can be analysed in order to optimise the code.

Instantiation of Feature Model Results are presented to the user for *interactive exploration* with various transformations such as aggregations (*Transformation of results prior to presentation*). Additionally, results are mapped to graphical representation using a *visual metaphor*. The system points out potential problems, which may be used by the user to improve the code. The results are used to refine the *analysis instance* thanks to, among others, the application of new filters.

7.4.7   Change Impact Analysis

When a change on a program is requested, it is important to understand its implications to make informed business and technical decisions. One of the most crucial aspects to analyse is the impact at the code level. In this context, a common practice is to predict the set of program elements (the impact set) that should be modified in order to accommodate the change request, and hence assist maintainers in estimating the consequences and cost of a given change [RCR06].

Various techniques have been proposed to predict the change impact set [Li+13]. Some of these techniques exploit dependencies between elements, extracted from the current version of the program to change by static or dynamic analysis. Others rely on elements' co-changes in the program change history. For both families of techniques, change impact analysis remains a complex and uncertain activity. Indeed, in the first family, the accuracy of the impact prediction is restricted by the limitations of static and dynamic analysis, whereas in the second family, the limitation comes from the availability of a representative change history.

Objective An ideal change impact analysis technique should predict for each program element the probability to be modified to accommodate a given change request.

Analysis Description In [Abd+15], Abdeen et al. propose a machine learning-based approach that predicts change impact sets. The approach consists in two steps: learning and prediction. First, it learns a set of Bayesian classifiers to predict the impact of atomic change types. These classifiers are trained with a mix of program dependencies and change dependencies extracted from the histories of a sample of programs. Each classifier estimates the probability that a program element will be impacted by a specific type of atomic change performed on another element, knowing the dependencies between the two.

For the prediction step, when a change is requested, it is decomposed into atomic changes to perform on the program. The trained classifiers are then used to predict the probability of each element in the program to be impacted by each atomic change. Then the atomic change probabilities are combined using different integration strategies to derive the probabilities of each element to be impacted by the whole change request. The elements with probabilities higher than a given threshold form the impact set. The analysis process is depicted in Fig. 7.9.

Results Exploitation The presentation of the impact set with the impact probabilities allows the maintainer to estimate the cost of implementing the change. Such an estimation can be used for different purposes—for example, revise the change request or implement the change. When the decision to implement the change is made, the impact results are further used for pricing, resource allocation, and test plan, among others. The analysis results can also be used to refine the analysis itself. This can be done by retraining the classifiers with new feedback, choosing the right integration strategy, or deciding for an appropriate impact probability threshold.

Instantiation of Feature Model Results are presented to the user for *interactive exploration* with no elaborate transformation (*direct 1-to-1 view of results*). Results, which are presented textually, can be used for both manual and automatic improvement of both the system and its specification. The analysis technique can be refined fully automatically using previous results for the tuning of probability thresholds.

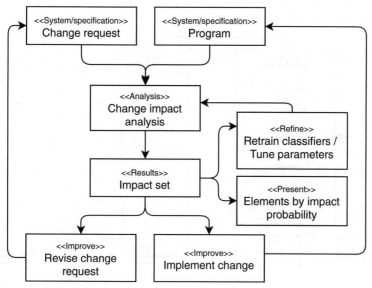

Fig. 7.9 Change impact analysis

7.4.8 ATL Transformations

Model transformations are a key component in any model-based or model-driven solution, as they permit automating the manipulation of models for a wide range of purposes such as model refactoring, model simulation, or model refinement. Given their importance, many model transformation languages have been proposed for transformation development. Among them, ATL [Jou+08] stands out for being one of the most widely used [Bru+20]. It has a hybrid style whereby transformation specifications consist of declarative rules which can include imperative constructs. However, ATL is prone to errors, likely because it is dynamically typed [SGL17].

Objective This analysis scenario encompasses two goals and respective analysis techniques: uncovering errors in ATL model transformations via static analysis, and providing a ranked list of fixes for the detected errors via speculative analysis.

Analysis Description ANATLYZER [SGL17] is a static analysis tool for ATL transformations which covers the above-mentioned objectives. Next, we briefly report on its analysis and reporting capabilities in relation to the feature model of results-exploitation approaches (cf. Fig. 7.2), and refer to Chap. 12 of this book [Hei+21] for a detailed presentation of the tool.

ANATLYZER comprises the steps and produces the results in Fig. 7.10. To uncover errors in transformations, ANATLYZER annotates the nodes of the transformation *abstract syntax tree* (AST) with their type, and then, it builds a so-called *dependency graph* that makes explicit the transformation data flow and rule dependencies. This

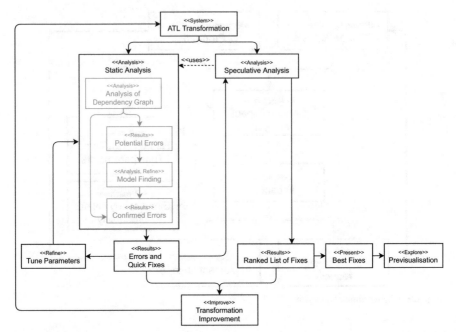

Fig. 7.10 Analysis of ATL transformations

dependency graph is analysed to detect errors (e.g., unresolved bindings or rule conflicts). However, some of the identified errors may not happen in practice—for example, if the transformation logic prevents the error. In those cases, using model finding, the analysis tool tries to find an input model which forces the execution of the problematic statement when fed to the transformation. For this purpose, it builds an OCL expression which characterises such a class of input models, and relies on USE [KG12] (cf. Sect. 7.4.3) to find a witness model that confirms the error (or falsifies the error if no model is found). Hence, the analysis based on the dependency graph is *refined* by a more costly analysis based on model finding.

In addition, ANATLYZER provides a list of quick fixes for each detected error, ranked using speculative analysis [SGL18]. Speculative analysis [Bru+10] performs an analysis of the possible future states of the evolution of a program (an ATL transformation in our case) in order to gather information about the resolution or introduction of errors when applying a quick fix. This way, the quick fixes that repair more errors without introducing new ones appear in the first positions of the ranking.

Results Exploitation The detected errors are presented in the ATL editor, underlined with error markers (*present and explore*). This way, developers can locate the errors within their context and proceed to correct them (*improve*). The results of the speculative analysis help developers select the most appropriate fix by creating a dynamic ranking of fixes (*present*), reporting on the consequences of applying a quick fix (*present and explore*), and providing a previsualisation of each quick fix application (*explore*).

Instantiation of Feature Model The quick fix previsualisation options provide some degree of *interactive exploration* of results. There is *transformation of results prior to presentation*. Results are presented in different formats, including *graphical* (e.g., rule dependencies can be visualised as a graph), *tabular* (e.g., errors and quick fixes are displayed in a table), and *other* (e.g., errors are shown underlined in the transformation code). Exploitation of results is by an *automatic implementation recommender system* which automatically applies the selected quick fix upon user selection. The target of change is the *system*. There is room for the *manual* improvement of an *analysis instance* by *tuning* its parameters (e.g., disable classes of errors or adjusting the model finder search scope). Moreover, the analysis results based on the dependency graph may need to be refined using model finding, which is *fully automated*.

7.4.9   Counterexample-Guided Abstraction Refinement

Abstraction is considered to be the most general and flexible technique for handling the state explosion problem in model checking. Intuitively, abstraction amounts to removing details of the original specification that are irrelevant to prove or disprove the property under consideration.

Objective CEGAR [Cla+00, Cla+03] is a technique that iteratively refines an abstract model using counterexamples. The technique is based on the idea that by simplifying the model too much we may be obtaining wrong results, which are provided in the form of counterexamples that witness a property violation.

Analysis Description The technique is described in Fig. 7.11. In software verification, counterexamples are paths that violate properties. With CEGAR, we start with the most abstract model and check if an error path can be found. If the analysis of the abstract model does not find an error path, the analysis terminates, reporting that no violation exists. However, if the analysis finds an error path, then it is checked whether the path is executable according to the concrete program semantics, that is, its feasibility is checked. If the error path is infeasible, the violation is due to a too coarse abstract model. In this case, the infeasible error path is used to automatically refine the current abstraction, and the analysis proceeds. However, if the error path is feasible, the analysis terminates. An error path in the program has been identified, and is reported as a violation of the property, together with the error path that works as a witness of the problem.

Results Exploitation Error paths are used to either refine the abstraction or to report a problem. If there is a problem in the program, it is reported as a

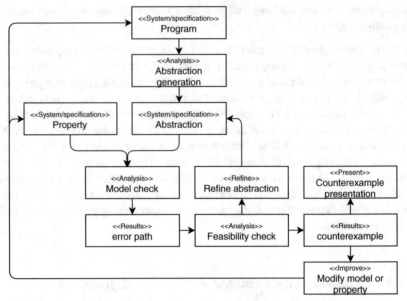

Fig. 7.11 Counterexample-guided abstraction refinement

counterexample, which the user may use to identify and correct it. It might also happen that the problem is in the property being verified.

Instantiation of Feature Model The technique refines the analysis instance fully automatically. The process terminates either succeeding or presenting a counterexample to the user. In case of the provision of a counterexample, the user may interact with it to get enough understanding to improve either the model or the property. In the core technique, the improvement is manual.

7.4.10 Summary of Example Cases

Table 7.1 summarises the examples that we have discussed in relation to the feature model presented in Fig. 7.2. These examples provide good coverage of the features.

Regarding the *Present* task, most tools do not offer interactive exploration of results, but do offer automated result presentation. In this case, results are often 1-to-1 translations of analysis results, while the most commonly found format is text.

The *Improve* task is mostly done manually, or with recommendations automatically suggested, but manually implemented. This means that human intervention is most of the time advisable. Since we have revised model-based analysis tools, the improvement normally leads to a modification of a specification of the system, and not to the system itself. We have not shown an example of analysis that provides

Table 7.1 Summary of examples

Feature	Business process analysis	Analysis of API usage	Model finding in USE	Novice programmer errors	Design smells detection	Object churn	Change impact analysis	ATL transformations	CEGAR
Present	✓	✓	✓	✓	✓	✓	✓	✓	✓
Level of interaction	✓	✓	✓	✓	✓	✓	✓	✓	✓
Interactive exploration	✓						✓	✓	✓
Automated result presentation		✓	✓	✓	✓			✓	
Level of processing	✓	✓	✓	✓	✓	✓	✓	✓	✓
Direct 1-to-1 view of results	✓	✓		✓				✓	✓
Transformation of results prior to presentation		✓			✓	✓	✓		
Format of presentation	✓	✓	✓	✓	✓	✓	✓	✓	✓
Textual		✓	✓	✓	✓		✓		✓
Graphical	✓		✓			✓	✓		
Tabular		✓			✓		✓	✓	
Other								✓	
Improve	✓	✓	✓	✓	✓	✓	✓	✓	✓
Level of automation	✓	✓	✓	✓	✓	✓	✓	✓	✓
Manual	✓		✓			✓			✓
Recommender systems		✓		✓	✓		✓	✓	
Human implemented				✓	✓		✓		
Automatic implementation		✓			✓			✓	
Fully automated									
Target of change	✓	✓	✓	✓	✓	✓	✓	✓	✓
System specification	✓	✓	✓		✓		✓		✓
System				✓		✓	✓	✓	
Refine		✓	✓	✓	✓	✓	✓	✓	✓
Level of automation		✓	✓	✓	✓	✓	✓	✓	✓
Manual				✓	✓	✓		✓	
Interpretation of user feedback		✓							
Fully automated			✓				✓	✓	✓
Usage of result history			✓	✓					
Subject of refinement		✓	✓	✓	✓	✓	✓	✓	✓
Analysis technique		✓		✓	✓				
Analysis instance			✓			✓	✓	✓	✓
Target of refinement		✓	✓	✓	✓		✓	✓	
Parameters		✓			✓		✓	✓	
Tuning		✓					✓	✓	
Calibration					✓				
Focus			✓						
Making information explicitly available									✓
Knowledge base		✓			✓				
Method				✓					

fully automated improvement, as we have been focusing on design-time analyses. Here, even analyses that could improve the system fully automatically, normally include an interaction with a human designer, so that we have classified these as automatically implemented recommender systems. Fully automated improvement based on analysis results can typically be found in adaptive systems (e.g., based on the models@runtime paradigm [BGS19]), where analysis of the system state (represented in model form) leads to automated improvement allowing the system to adapt to changing environment conditions. Chapter 6 of this book [Hei+21] discusses some of the issues in runtime analysis in more detail. Compiler optimisations are another example where analysis leads to automated improvement. Here, the compiler analyses the program source code and identifies, for example, dead code which it then automatically removes to improve the final machine-code program.

Finally, most tools support some mechanism to *Refine* the analysis given the results, by some kind of feedback loop. However, in the majority of the cases it is not fully automated and the subject of change is the analysis instance.

Overall, we have seen that mechanisms for *improving* the system and *refining* the analysis are generally required by analysis tools, while requiring from interactivity to support human intervention. Interactive exploration of results presentation improves the user experience, but currently remains as a challenge for tool builders, since many times results are presented textually with no further processing.

7.5 Conclusions

Previous chapters discussed how analysis formalisms and tools can be composed. Instead, in this chapter, we have considered the important question of what happens *after* an analysis has been performed. Hence, we identified how analysis composition can be used to provide better (i.e., more actionable, more easily interpretable) analysis results to analysis users.

To understand this, we have first introduced a generic model of the post-analysis pathways that analysis results can take. We noticed that results can be presented to analysis users for their interpretation and exploration. Analysis results can also be used to improve the system under study. Finally, analysis results may be used to refine the analysis itself, so that better analysis results can be produced in the future.

As a next step, we broke down these three pathways further, classifying the different options into a feature model. We then briefly described nine examples to show how different choices of analysis features lead to different forms of analysis. In Table 7.1, we have briefly summarised how these examples cover the feature model.

The examples also show different ways in which analyses are composed to provide better results to analysis users: Parallel composition of analyses led to richer results in ANATLYZER (Sect. 7.4.8 and Chap. 12 of this book [Hei+21]), sequential analyses composition was used for producing increasingly better focused results (e.g., in USE, Sect. 7.4.3) or for improving the analysis technique as a whole (e.g., Sect. 7.4.4).

In this chapter, we have explored the framework of exploitation pathways for analysis results by discussing specific examples. A question that remains open is how these pathways mesh *in general* with the different forms of analysis composition and tool orchestration for the provision of efficient and effective model-based system analysis.

References

[Abd+15] Hani Abdeen, Khaled Bali, Houari Sahraoui, and Bruno Dufour. "Learning dependency-based change impact predictors using independent change histories". In: *Information and Software Technology* 67 (2015), pp. 220–235. https://doi.org/10.1016/j.infsof.2015.07.007.

[AZW06] Uwe Aßmann, Steffen Zschaler, and Gerd Wagner. "Ontologies, Meta-Models, and the Model-Driven Paradigm". In: *Ontologies for Software Engineering and Technology*. 2006, pp. 249–273. https://doi.org/10.1007/3-540-34518-3_9.

[BGS19] Nelly Bencomo, Sebastian Götz, and Hui Song. "Models@run.time: a guided tour of the state of the art and research challenges". In: *Software and Systems Modeling* 18 (2019), pp. 3049–3082. https://doi.org/10.1007/s10270-018-00712-x.

[Bru+10] Yuriy Brun, Reid Holmes, Michael D. Ernst, and David Notkin. "Speculative analysis: exploring future development states of software". In: *FSE/SDP Workshop on Future of Software Engineering Research*. 2010, pp. 59–64. https://doi.org/10.1145/1882362.1882375.

[Bru+20] Jean-Michel Bruel, Benoît Combemale, Esther Guerra, Jean-Marc Jézéquel, Jörg Kienzle, Juan de Lara, Gunter Mussbacher, Eugene Syriani, and Hans Vangheluwe. "Comparing and classifying model transformation reuse approaches across metamodels". In: *Software and Systems Modeling* 19.2 (2020), pp. 441–465. https://doi.org/10.1007/s10270-019-00762-9.

[Chu+00] Lawrence Chung, Brian A. Nixon, Eric Yu, and John Mylopoulos. *Non-Functional Requirements in Software Engineering*. Springer, 2000. https://doi.org/10.1007/978-1-4615-5269-7.

[Cla+00] Edmund Clarke, Orna Grumberg, Somesh Jha, Yuan Lu, and Helmut Veith. "Counterexample- guided abstraction refinement". In: *Int'l Conf. Computer Aided Verification, CAV*. 2000, pp. 154–169. https://doi.org/10.1007/10722167_15.

[Cla+03] Edmund M. Clarke, Orna Grumberg, Somesh Jha, Yuan Lu, and Helmut Veith. "Counterexample-guided abstraction refinement for symbolic model checking". In: *Journal of the ACM* 50.5 (2003), pp. 752–794. https://doi.org/10.1145/876638.876643.

[Cla+07] Manuel Clavel, Francisco Durán, Steven Eker, Patrick Lincoln, Narciso Martí-Oliet, José Meseguer, and Carolyn L. Talcott. *All About Maude—A High-Performance Logical Framework, How to Specify, Program and Verify Systems in Rewriting Logic*. Vol. 4350. Springer, 2007.

[CMI07] Vittorio Cortellessa, Antinisca Di Marco, and Paola Inverardi. "Integrating performance and reliability analysis in a non-functional MDA framework". In: *10th International Conference Fundamental Approaches to Software Engineering*. 2007, pp. 57–71. https://doi.org/10.1007/978-3-540-71289-3_6.

[Cor+17] Flavio Corradini, Fabrizio Fornari, Andrea Polini, Barbara Re, Francesco Tiezzi, and Andrea Vandin. "BProVe: A formal verification framework for business process models". In: *32nd IEEE/ACM International Conference on Automated Software Engineering*. 2017, pp. 217–228. https://doi.org/10.1109/ASE.2017.8115635.

[DDS12] Fleur Duseau, B. Dufour, and Houari Sahraoui. "Vasco: A visual approach to explore object churn in framework-intensive applications". In: *28th IEEE International Conference on Software Maintenance.* 2012, pp. 15–24. https://doi.org/10.1109/ICSM.2012. 6405248.

[Don+05] Boudewijn F. van Dongen, Ana Karla A. de Medeiros, H. M. W. Verbeek, A. J. M. M. Weijters, and Wil M. P. van der Aalst. "The ProM framework: A new era in process mining tool support". In: *26th International Conference Applications and Theory of Petri Nets.* 2005, pp. 444–454. https://doi.org/10.1007/11494744_25.

[DRS18] Francisco Durán, Camilo Rocha, and Gwen Salaün. "Stochastic analysis of BPMN with time in rewriting logic". In: *Science of Computer Programming* 168 (2018), pp. 1–17. https://doi.org/10.1016/j.scico.2018.08.007.

[DSP08] Karim Dhambri, Houari A. Sahraoui, and Pierre Poulin. "Visual detection of design anomalies". In: *12th European Conference on Software Maintenance and Reengineering.* 2008, pp. 279–283. https://doi.org/10.1109/CSMR.2008.4493326.

[Dum+13] Marlon Dumas, Marcello La Rosa, Jan Mendling, and Hajo A. Reijers. *Fundamentals of Business Process Management.* Springer, 2013.

[Fow18] Martin Fowler. *Refactoring: improving the design of existing code.* Addison-Wesley Professional, 2018.

[Fre+17] Thomas Freytag, Philip Allgaier, Andrea Burattin, and Andreas Danek-Bulius. "WoPeD—A "proof-of-concept" platform for experimental BPM research projects". In: *BPM Demo Track and BPM Dissertation Award.* 2017. http://ceurws.org/Vol-1920/ BPM_2017_paper_190.pdf.

[Fri+08] Mathias Fritzsche, Jendrik Johannes, Steffen Zschaler, Anatoly Zherebtsov, and Alexander Terekhov. "Application of tracing techniques in model-driven performance engineering". In: *4th ECMDA Traceability Workshop.* 2008. https://doi.org/10.1.1.148. 4702.

[Fur+17] Carlo A. Furia, Martin Nordio, Nadia Polikarpova, and Julian Tschannen. "Auto- Proof: auto-active functional verification of object-oriented programs". In: *International Journal Software Tools Technology Transfer* 19.6 (2017), pp. 697–716. https://doi.org/ 10.1007/978-3-662-46681-0_53.

[GHD18] Martin Gogolla, Frank Hilken, and Khanh-Hoang Doan. "Achieving Model Quality through Model Validation, Verification and Exploration". In: *Journal on Computer Languages, Systems and Structures* 54 (2018), pp. 474–511. https://doi.org/10.1016/ j.cl.2017.10.001.

[Gog+15] Martin Gogolla, Antonio Vallecillo, Loli Burgueno, and Frank Hilken. "Employing Classifying Terms for Testing Model Transformations". In: *18th International Conference Model Driven Engineering Languages and Systems.* 2015, pp. 312–321. https:// doi.org/10.1109/MODELS.2015.7338262.

[Gue+09] Esther Guerra, Juan de Lara, Alessio Malizia, and Paloma Díaz. "Supporting userori- ented analysis for multi-view domain-specific visual languages". In: *Information and Software Technology* 51.4 (2009), pp. 769–784. https://doi.org/10.1016/j.infsof.2008. 09.005.

[Heg+10] Ábel Hegedüs, Gábor Bergmann, István Ráth, and Dániel Varró. "Back-annotation of simulation traces with change-driven model transformations". In: *8th IEEE International Conference on Software Engineering and Formal Methods.* 2010, pp. 145–155. https://doi.org/10.1109/SEFM.2010.28.

[Hei+21] Robert Heinrich, Francisco Durán, Carolyn L. Talcott, and Steffen Zschaler (eds.) *Composing Model-Based Analysis Tools.* Springer, 2021. https://doi.org/10.1007/978- 3-030-81915-6.

[Hil+18] Frank Hilken, Martin Gogolla, Loli Burgueno, and Antonio Vallecillo. "Testing models and model transformations using classifying terms". In: *Software and Systems Modeling* 17.3 (2018), pp. 885–912. https://doi.org/10.1007/s10270-016-0568-3.

[Jou+08] Frédéric Jouault, Freddy Allilaire, Jean Bézivin, and Ivan Kurtev. "ATL: A model transformation tool". In: *Science of Computer Programming* 72.1-2 (2008), pp. 31–39. https://doi.org/10.1016/j.scico.2007.08.002.

[KG12] Mirco Kuhlmann and Martin Gogolla. "From UML and OCL to relational logic and back". In: *15th International Conference on Model Driven Engineering Languages and Systems*. 2012, pp. 415–431. https://doi.org/10.1007/978-3-642-33666-9_27.

[KVS10] Marouane Kessentini, Stéphane Vaucher, and Houari A. Sahraoui. "Deviance from perfection is a better criterion than closeness to evil when identifying risky code". In: *25th IEEE/ACM International Conference on Automated Software Engineering*. 2010, pp. 113–122. https://doi.org/10.1145/1858996.1859015.

[Li+13] Bixin Li, Xiaobing Sun, Hareton Leung, and Sai Zhang. "A survey of code-based change impact analysis techniques". In: *Software Testing, Verification and Reliability* 23.8 (2013), pp. 613–646. https://doi.org/10.1002/stvr.1475.

[Mar04] Radu Marinescu. "Detection strategies: Metrics-based rules for detecting design flaws". In: *International Conference on Software Maintenance*. 2004, pp. 350–359. https://doi.org/10.1109/ICSM.2004.1357820.

[Mei+17] Jens Meinicke, Thomas Thüm, Reimar Schröter, Fabian Benduhn, Thomas Leich, and Gunter Saake. *Mastering Software Variability with FeatureIDE*. Springer, 2017.

[MK19] Davin Alexander McCall and Michael Kölling. "A new look at novice programmer errors". In: *Transactions of Computing Education* 19.4 (2019). https://doi.org/10.1145/3335814.

[Moh+10] Naouel Moha, Yann-Gaël Guéhéneuc, Laurence Duchien, and Anne-Françoise Le Meur. "DECOR: A Method for the Specification and Detection of Code and Design Smells". In: *IEEE Transactions on Software Engineering* 36.1 (2010), pp. 20–36. https://doi.org/10.1109/TSE.2009.50.

[Obj14] Object Management Group. *Object Constraint Language 2.4*. Tech. rep. formal/14-02-03. Object Management Group, 2014.

[Obj15] Object Management Group. *UML 2.5*. Tech. rep. formal/2015-03-01. Object Management Group, 2015.

[OMG11] OMG. *Business Process Model and Notation (BPMN)—V 2.0*. 2011.

[Oun+16] Ali Ouni, Marouane Kessentini, Houari A. Sahraoui, Katsuro Inoue, and Kalyanmoy Deb. "Multi-criteria code refactoring using search-based software engineering: An industrial case study". In: *ACM Transactions on Software Engineering and Methodology* 25.3 (2016), 23:1–23:53. https://doi.org/10.1145/2932631.

[Pal+13] Fabio Palomba, Gabriele Bavota, Massimiliano Di Penta, Rocco Oliveto, Andrea De Lucia, and Denys Poshyvanyk. "Detecting bad smells in source code using change history information". In: *28th IEEE/ACM International Conference on Automated Software Engineering*. 2013, pp. 268–278. https://doi.org/10.1109/ASE.2013.6693086.

[RCR06] Xiaoxia Ren, Ophelia C. Chesley, and Barbara G. Ryder. "Identifying failure causes in Java programs: An application of change impact analysis". In: *IEEE Transactions on Software Engineering* 32.9 (2006), pp. 718–732. https://doi.org/10.1109/TSE.2006.90.

[Ros+11] Marcello La Rosa, Hajo A. Reijers, Wil M. P. van der Aalst, Remco M. Dijkman, Jan Mendling, Marlon Dumas, and Luciano García-Bañuelos. "APROMORE: An advanced process model repository". In: *Expert Systems with Applications* 38.6 (2011), pp. 7029–7040. https://doi.org/10.1016/j.eswa.2010.12.012.

[RRU05] Genaina Nunes Rodrigues, David S. Rosenblum, and Sebastián Uchitel. "Reliability prediction in model-driven development". In: *8th International Conference Model Driven Engineering Languages and Systems*. 2005, pp. 339–354. https://doi.org/10.1007/11557432_25.

[Sai+15] Mohamed Aymen Saied, Omar Benomar, Hani Abdeen, and Houari Sahraoui. "Mining multi-level API usage patterns". In: *IEEE 22nd International Conference on Software Analysis, Evolution, and Reengineering*. 2015, pp. 23–32. https://doi.org/10.1109/SANER.2015.7081812.

[Sai+20] Mohamed Aymen Saied, Erick Raelijohn, Edouard Batot, Michalis Famelis, and Houari Sahraoui. "Towards assisting developers in API usage by automated recovery of complex temporal patterns". In: *Information and Software Technology* 119 (2020), p. 106213. https://doi.org/10.1016/j.infsof.2019.106213.

[Sei03] Ed Seidewitz. "What models mean". In: *IEEE Software* 20.5 (2003), pp. 26–32.

[SGL17] Jesús Sánchez Cuadrado, Esther Guerra, and Juan de Lara. "Static analysis of model transformations". In: *IEEE Transactions on Software Engineering* 43.9 (2017), pp. 868–897. https://doi.org/10.1109/TSE.2016.2635137.

[SGL18] Jesús Sánchez Cuadrado, Esther Guerra, and Juan de Lara. "Quick fixing ATL transformations with speculative analysis". In: *Software and System Modeling* 17.3 (2018), pp. 779–813. https://doi.org/10.1007/s10270-016-0541-1.

[TJ07] Emina Torlak and Daniel Jackson. "Kodkod: A relational model finder". In: *13th International Conference on Tools and Algorithms for the Construction and Analysis of Systems*. 2007, pp. 632–647. https://doi.org/10.1007/978-3-540-71209-1_49.

[VA00] Eric Verbeek and Wil M. P. van der Aalst. "Woflan 2.0: A Petri-net-based workflow diagnosis tool". In: *21st International Conference Application and Theory of Petri Nets*. 2000, pp. 475–484. https://doi.org/10.1007/3-540-44988-4_28.

[Zho+09] Hao Zhong, Tao Xie, Lu Zhang, Jian Pei, and Hong Mei. "MAPO: Mining and recommending API usage patterns". In: *European Conference on Object-Oriented Programming*. 2009, pp. 318–343. https://doi.org/10.1007/978-3-642-03013-0_15.

[Zsc+18] Steffen Zschaler, Sam White, Kyle Hodgetts, and Martin Chapman. "Modularity for automated assessment: A design-space exploration". In: *Workshop Software Engineering für E-Learning-Systeme*. 2018. http://ceur-ws.org/Vol-2066/seels2018paper02.pdf.

Chapter 8
Living with Uncertainty in Model-Based Development

Simona Bernardi, Michalis Famelis, Jean-Marc Jézéquel, Raffaela Mirandola, Diego Perez Palacin, Fiona A. C. Polack, and Catia Trubiani

Abstract Uncertainty is present in model-based developments in many different ways. In the context of composing model-based analysis tools, this chapter discusses how the combination of different models can increase or decrease the overall uncertainty. It explores how such uncertainty could be more explicitly addressed and systematically managed, with the goal of defining a conceptual framework to deal with and manage it. We proceed towards this goal both with a theoretical reasoning and a practical application through an example of designing a peer-to-peer file-sharing protocol. We distinguish two main steps: (i) software system modelling and (ii) model-based performance analysis by highlighting the challenges related to the awareness that model-based development in software engineering needs to coexist with uncertainty. This core chapter addresses Challenge 5 introduced in Chap. 3 of this book (*living with uncertainty*).

S. Bernardi
University of Zaragoza, Zaragoza, Spain
e-mail: simonab@unizar.es

M. Famelis
Université de Montréal, Montréal, QC, Canada
e-mail: famelis@iro.umontreal.ca

J.-M. Jézéquel
IRISA, University of Rennes, Rennes, France
e-mail: jezequel@irisa.fr

R. Mirandola
Polytechnic University of Milan, Milan, Italy
e-mail: raffaela.mirandola@polimi.it

D. Perez-Palacin (✉)
Linnaeus University, Växjö, Sweden
e-mail: diego.perez@lnu.se

F. A. C. Polack
Keele University, Newcastle-under-Lyme, UK
e-mail: f.a.c.polack@keele.ac.uk

C. Trubiani
Gran Sasso Science Institute, L'Aquila, Italy
e-mail: catia.trubiani@gssi.it

8.1 Introduction

The identification and handling of uncertainties is an important concern for the composition of models and for the combination of model-based analysis results. Engineers who work with different models and use results from different analyses need to be able to ask and understand whether composed analysis results are more or less trustworthy than those achieved from independent models.

Engineering can then be seen as the science of containing both complexity and uncertainty, creating systems that are predictable, within the limits of the engineering. This is easy to see in mechanical and civil engineering: the system is created so that if the real world (the materials it is made of and the context in which it operates) behaves in the way the engineers expect, the system will do what it is supposed to do. However, real-world situations that are outside the envisaged "operational envelope" cause failures: buildings do not withstand all earthquakes; machines suffer from metal fatigue, etc.

What is outside a known operational envelope is infinite and, to a large extent unknowable. That is quite often not a problem in practice: the classic example is that Newtonian physics works fine so long as your level of abstraction is at a scale somewhere between small creatures and solar systems. It is a different story at very small scales, where currently unpredictable quantum effects dominate, or at the very large scales, e.g., cosmology. But every now or then, something unpredicted or unpredictable from a practically irrelevant scale impinges on an engineered system. The biggest source of real-world uncertainty in software is humans (software and system designers, intended and unintended users, etc.).

Another view of an engineered system that helps to distinguish between engineered (complicated systems) and other (complex) systems defines an engineered system as a system that can be taken apart and put back together, and will then work as originally intended. If you dismantle a bridge and reconstruct it, or put the classes of a Java file into separate files and then recombine them, the system does what the original did.

Software systems are engineered systems. The platforms they run on are engineered systems. We are well aware that we can create complexity by linking together computers (e.g., the global internet), but we often overlook complexity when engineering software. In short, software systems are full of uncertainties because (1) they interact with the real world, including humans and sensors and (2) they run on computers, which are themselves physical artefacts subject to failures and nondeterministic behaviour.

In order to start to understand uncertainties in software systems, we can consider where uncertainties come from. One approach is as follows:

- **Above**: The software design and realisation make assumptions about the world that the software interacts with, including rules and human behaviour. In software engineering, recording of ever changing requirements and assumptions is typically quite rough, usually implicit, and thus does not adequately address corner cases.
- **Inside**: Beyond rare cases of software (and compilers/hardware) proven correct with respect to some specific properties, it is difficult, or even undecidable, to know whether a given implementation fulfils its requirements.
- **Below**: Our questionable software, with its approximate implementation (possibly meeting not-so-well-defined requirements), has to run on a physical platform, which itself is subject to uncertainties and failures. Examples of uncertainties from below include issues with hardware, operating systems, and compilers and the unforeseen side effects of running alongside other software on general-purpose/high-performance computers and (complex) networks.
- **Outside**: Software typically operates on externally provided data, whose fidelity, availability, and quality can vary. Some outside interaction is initiated maliciously or accidentally: sabotage, cyber attacks, or external interfaces accepting something that the software allows but does not handle appropriately.

Engineers typically deal with these uncertainties by first trying to reduce them as much as possible and then most often just ignoring them (unless they work in safety-critical domains). Recognising the presence of uncertainties can contribute to reducing their influence and increasing the level of trust in a given software. Within the software modelling community, researchers have started to focus on identification and modelling of uncertainties, and recognised that not all uncertainties can be traced to their origin, eliminated, or accounted for.

In this chapter, we explore how uncertainty could be more explicitly addressed and systematically managed in modelling. In the context of composing model-based analysis tools, we discuss how the combination of different models can increase or decrease the overall uncertainty.

We proceed towards this goal both with a theoretical reasoning and a practical application through an example of designing a peer-to-peer file-sharing protocol. We distinguish two main steps and highlight the challenges related to the uncertainty: (i) software system modelling and (ii) model-based analysis.

A wide range of models have been proposed and used to support software engineering. They vary according to the level of formality and precision, the aspects they intend to describe, and the kind of reasoning they support. Often they are used in combination to show how different aspects of a system can interact. As illustration, our example consists of six heterogeneous model types, which span different lifecycle phases.

Model-based analysis is challenging due to the complexity of keeping control of the possible uncertainties and their propagation to analysis results. A possible way of classifying existing methods is based on how uncertainty is described, e.g., probabilistic, i.e., the probability density functions of the uncertain parameters are assumed to be known; and possibilistic, i.e., uncertain parameters are described with fuzzy boundaries. Other approaches involve the use of model averaging, model discrepancy, sensitivity analysis, and so on. Sometimes, it is enough to acknowledge that uncertainty is known to exist, without quantification or mitigation.

The next section motivates and illustrates, using simple examples, the existence and importance of the uncertainty when part of the development process requires a composition of models. To make things more concrete, Sect. 8.3 details the modelling of a peer-to-peer file-sharing case study and discusses the various places where uncertainty creeps in. Based on this example, Sect. 8.4 covers model-based performance analysis, and Sect. 8.5 discusses some of its main challenges, i.e., reducing the uncertainty while analysing the models. We note that, if the combination of models and analysis is not seamless, inconsistencies in the system can appear. This boosts the effect of uncertainties and reduces trust in the obtained results. Section 8.6 discusses related work, and Sect. 8.7 concludes this chapter.

8.2 Uncertainty and Composition of Models

Like other engineers, software engineers who work with different models and use results from different analyses need to be able to ask and understand whether composed analysis results are more or less trustworthy than those achieved from independent models.

The question does not have an unequivocal answer, although a part of the trustworthiness of the results is related to the existence of uncertainty in the steps that achieve them. When model-based analysis is used, there is a relation between the trust in results and the uncertainty surrounding its inputs and assumptions. Trustworthiness is affected by the amount, types, and severity of uncertainty introduced by the utilisation of multiple models, by the process of analysing multiple models together, and by the process of combination of results.

Composition of models and analysis can *reduce the uncertainty*. This occurs, for instance, if the multi-model design or its analysis allows generation of more accurate input parameter values than would be possible using information from only one model. Mitigation of uncertainty can also come from the utilisation of alternative analyses, as described in the strategy *portfolio* in Chap. 5 of this book [Hei+21].

Example 1 (Replacement of Guesses) The engineer's original analysis typically includes some guessed parameter values, which are thus considered uncertain. The engineer can reduce the inherent uncertainty of the results by replacing guessed parameters with more informed values from a different analysis. Here, the reduced uncertainty of the analysis derives from the implicit or established trustworthiness (and appropriateness) of the replacement values.

Example 2 (Use of Alternative Analysis) When the engineer is not confident of the adequacy of the model and the analysis method, a multiple analysis approach can be used to shed light on the trustworthiness of results. Each analysis method executes its own implementation, under its own assumptions. The different results can establish bounds or intervals of values for a known unknown. Moreover, even if the results from the different analyses vary or suggest a wide interval, the engineer may be able to identify that some of the assumptions underpinning the model or analysis have a strong influence on the results—which could, in turn, become a further uncertainty challenge. This case also applies to the aforementioned *portfolio* strategy.

Composition of models and analyses can also *increase the uncertainty* in the results. This can happen when different aspects of the system are analysed in specific tools, and then the results are aggregated. One such approach is described by the strategy *combined analysis orchestration* in Chap. 5. Increased uncertainty also arises when an analysis develops a chain of results—for instance when one analysis takes as input some parameters calculated in a previous analysis, as described in the strategies *cooperating analysis orchestration* and *sequential analysis orchestration*, described in Chap. 5. A similar situation arises when a parameter that is not accurate but is bounded is replaced as an input to a model-based analysis with an input generated in an earlier analysis, of which the trustworthiness is reduced or unknown.

Example 3 (Replacement of Bounded-Error Parameters) The engineer's original analysis takes into account that only part of the reality was used to produce results, and this uncertainty is reflected in the confidence of the obtained results. For example, the current obtained point estimate may have low reliability, but the accompanying error interval gives precise bounds about the location of the actual result. This allows the engineer to manage a "known unknown". Again, some guessed parameters are replaced by values from a different analysis. Even though the point estimate provided by a new analysis may, in fact, be closer to the real value, the information on the accuracy and trustworthiness of the new results is not available. Therefore, the error is no longer bounded, the previous "known unknown" is no longer there, and the engineer cannot assess the effect on the uncertainty of the results. This causes an increase in the overall uncertainty.

This case could be handled by performing both the original and new analyses using the *combined analysis orchestration* strategy— the engineer can use the new analysis to provide the point estimate and the original analysis to provide the bounds.

Despite the possibility to capture the rationale underpinning the trustworthiness of models, parameters, analysis, and results, there is no existing general guidance on how to combine uncertainties during model or analysis composition.

Example 4 (Composition of Results) The engineer needs to take design decisions and wants to have as much information as possible to support decision-making. A range of analysis tools are used, each with its own results, accuracy, and bias. In this case, the engineer follows the *separate parallel analysis orchestration* strategy described in Chap. 5, manually aggregating the results to take an informed decision. However, the manner in which the engineer weights and aggregates the results of the different analyses may add uncertainty to the decision-making process. The utilisation of multiple sources of information does not automatically lead to more certain results. For example, incorporating more information sources that share a common bias into the decision-making process may increase the likelihood of a wrong decision.

Example 5 (Results Originate from a Chain of Analysis) In this example, the engineer applies the *sequential analysis orchestration* strategy described in Chap. 5. The final result comes from a sequence of black-box analyses, where the output of one analysis is an input to a subsequent analysis tool. The black-box view of analysis tool composition focuses on the connections that are possible between tools, not on the realisation. Even assuming a perfect separation of concerns in each analysis tool, the abstracted chaining of analyses propagates uncertainty. In practice, however, analyses are not independent. In the black-box view of sequential analysis, concepts such as the model of network delays are typically required in more than one analysis in the chain. The final results may thus over-represent the effect of the concept on the system, increasing the uncertainty of the chained analysis result. A white-box analysis, which looks more carefully at the structure and content of models and the generation of results, may at least identify where concepts are over- or under-represented in the analysis chain, and should be able to establish better confidence in results than a black-box approach. However, such an approach also identifies more potentially uncertain elements and exacerbates the problem of how to combine uncertainties or derive trustworthiness.

8.3   Software System Modelling

To perform a quantitative evaluation of, for instance, performance or dependability, a software engineer needs both structural and behavioural views of the software design. Such views, or models, provide useful information for the construction of formal models on which analysis tools run, such as *queuing networks* (QNs) or stochastic Petri nets [CDI11, BMP13].

In the following, we analyse the types of uncertainties that arise in different model views, and, as elsewhere in the book, we use the *Unified Modeling Language* (UML) [OMGb] as the modelling language. In principle, other structural and behavioural models could be used. The UML supports many model notations; within a model-based development setting, the UML specification of a software system is done as a composition of complementary views. The set of these views can also be viewed and managed as a multi-model. UML structural views focus on classes, objects, components or nodes, and their relationships, whereas the behavioural views convey the permitted or required behaviours of the system. Such views are created and used in various stages of software lifecycle. For example, they can help developers explore system design in the early phases of the system's development.

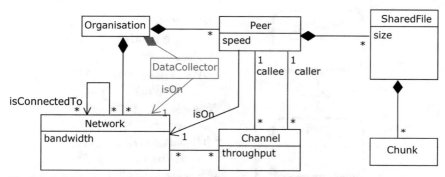

Fig. 8.1 PtP domain model. Coloured elements indicate the presence of uncertainty

Here, we particularly focus on the views that are typically used as input artefacts for the construction of a formal performance model (discussed in Sect. 8.4).

To better illustrate our ideas, we use an example first developed in [FSC12] of a company developing a peer-to-peer document-sharing protocol, called PtP. At the start of our scenario, the company has developed some incomplete structural and behavioural models. In the diagrams that follow, elements with black borders indicate aspects of the system for which the developers are already certain at the start of our scenario. Coloured elements indicate aspects about which the developers are uncertain and whose ultimate role in the system is contingent on some design decision.

The class diagram in Fig. 8.1 shows the protocol that allows peers that are members of an organisation to share files, by establishing direct communication channels with each other on the organisation's network. The files are shared by chunks. The diagram also contains the class `DataCollector` that is responsible for logging. However, its ultimate inclusion in the model is the subject of a design decision, as described later in the section.

The company has also created a preliminary version of the behavioural view of the protocol for each peer, shown in Fig. 8.2 based on certain assumptions, as follows:

- Peers are initially in the `Idle` state, in which no documents are being shared.
- Peers that are in the `Leeching` state are trying to download but do not have a complete version of the `SharedFile`. They are connected with other peers and trying to download the chunks of the document that they are missing. They can also share the chunks they already have.
- Peers that are in the `Seeding` state possess complete copies of the `SharedFile`. Other peers can download chunks that they lack from a `Seeding` peer.

The developers of PtP could face uncertainty in any number of features across the multi-model. Here, we focus on uncertainty in the required behaviours. When

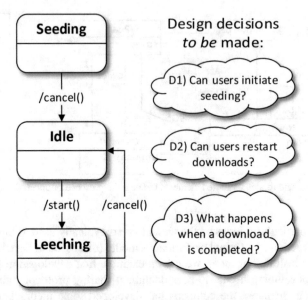

Fig. 8.2 Overview of the initial, incomplete behaviour of the PtP example. Important information (e.g., event triggers) is missing and some design decisions remain to be made

developing Fig. 8.2, the developer is uncertain about some important design decisions:

D1 Should peers be allowed to start `Seeding` without first `Leeching`?
D2 Should peers be allowed to re-download an already-complete `SharedFile`?
D3 What should happen when a peer completes downloading a `SharedFile`?
    There are three possible scenarios under consideration:

    D3.1 "Selfish" scenario: Peers disconnect as soon as they have finished downloading.
    D3.2 "Benevolent" scenario: Peers that finish a download become seeds.
    D3.3 "Compromise" scenario: Any peer already connected can complete a download, but no new connection is allowed.

The alternative scenarios can be expressed using additions to the state diagrams.

We assume that the developers decide not to permit re-download of an already-complete `SharedFile` (D2), and permit all three alternatives for D3; Fig. 8.3b elaborates the required logging behaviour. The revised models are shown in Fig. 8.3. The models support two alternative scenarios for D1: the original option (Fig. 8.2) that does not allow seeding without previous leeching, and the revised option that allows seeding before leeching, supported by adding a transition `Share` from `Idle` to `Seeding`.

Figure 8.1 is a UML class diagram that specifies the **domain model**—a visual representation of conceptual classes or real-world objects in a domain of interest [MO97] (a structural view). Such a domain model is typically constructed during

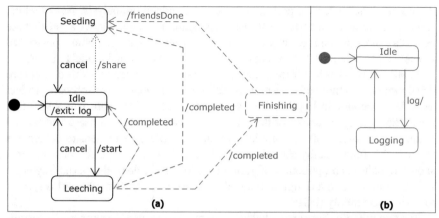

Fig. 8.3 PtP state machines. (**a**) State machines of the peers. Blue dotted line supports the alternative decision for D1; green dashed portion represents the three scenarios of D3. (**b**) State machine of the `DataCollector` class. The existence of this state machine is contingent upon a design decision

the requirement and business modelling activities and sets a common vocabulary among the system stakeholders. The abstraction level of the domain model leads to several uncertainties.

Some uncertainties can be directly expressed in the UML notation, by giving a context-dependent interpretation [Sal+18] to multiplicity constraints of association ends. Multiplicity constraints allow specifying that an association end can have an allowed number (an exact value, a range, or a set of disjoint values) of target class instances (i.e., objects) that may be associated with a source instance. Uncertain bounds are denoted as * either alone or in a range that identifies an exact lower bound (e.g., 1..*). Most association ends in Fig. 8.1 are uncertain: for example, the * number of `peers` within an organisation gives rise to an input parameter of the performance model and needs to be resolved to a specific value or range to allow performance analysis.

Other uncertainty cannot be expressed in the notations. Consider the types specified for class attributes, which also give rise to input parameters for performance analysis. A primitive type—such as integer or real—does not convey the information needed for quantitative analysis of software systems; the type alone says nothing about the unit of measurement or any statistical qualifier—minimum, mean, maximum, stochastic distribution, etc. For example, in Fig. 8.1, it is not resolved whether the network `bandwidth` and the peer `speed` have the same units of measurement.

The modelling notations can be extended to elaborate types with such information, using notes, comments, profiles, etc. Indeed, there are several extensions or proposals to extend the UML to support the specification of non-functional requirements (e.g., the OMG standard UML profile MARTE (*Modeling and Analysis of Real-Time Embedded system*) [OMGa]) that could be applied to reduce some of the uncertainties affecting performance and dependability analysis. Nevertheless, from our experience in performance and dependability modelling, we argue that the necessary information is usually not available during domain modelling, postponed to later stages when the analyst has to decide the type of formal model to build.

Finally, variability is a form of uncertainty that arises in many forms of software development, and thus software models, notably in development of software product lines. For example, in Fig. 8.1, the class DataCollector represents a variation point: the logging capability of the PtP example can be considered as an additional feature of the basic software product. In our example, it is unclear to developers whether this functionality should be added by default to the system, or whether it should remain as an optional configuration option. The role of this variability point is thus contingent on a design decision that the developers must take and is subject to design uncertainty [FC19].

Turning to **state diagrams**—behavioural models are used to express the permitted behaviours of objects over their lifetimes—Fig. 8.3 illustrates a way to model two main forms of uncertainty: (in)completeness of the design specification and alternative design choices.

To understand better the forms of uncertainty (not) expressible in a state diagram, we need to consider state diagram semantics. A state represents a situation during the life of the object in which it either satisfies some condition, or it performs some action, or it waits for some event to occur (e.g., the Idle state of the peer). A transition is a response to an event that triggers specific actions, provided that the relevant condition is satisfied. In general, a transition is labelled as an *event-name [guard-condition]/action* expression. A transition is triggered by at most one event, such as a signal or a request to invoke a specific operation. A transition with no explicit trigger event is called a completion transition and fires only after all the events and actions (e.g., do-activities) present in the current state are completed. A guard is a Boolean expression that provides control over the firing of a transition. When the transition fires, an action may be performed.

Incompleteness may cause nondeterminism in the state machine model due to the use of completion transitions, outgoing from the same state, without guards, or due to several transitions from the same state with the same trigger event. Indeed, the UML state machine execution semantics for making the selection of the transition to execute is undefined [OMGb]. Typical examples, in Fig. 8.3a, are the transitions labelled share and start, from the state Idle.

To resolve nondeterministic, guards could be used. However, accurate specification of guards typically requires more detailed knowledge of the design than is available at this stage.

Nondeterminism is also introduced in Fig. 8.3 by representing alternative design choices. These can be resolved by establishing a single design, but again, it may not be possible to resolve the design at this point—indeed the performance analysis may be needed to make that design decision.

Incompleteness also arises from the absence of information about the environment and how the environment interacts with the state machine. For example, what is going to trigger the cancel transitions in the Seeding/Leeching states?

Finally, when considering performance evaluation, the workload aspect needs to be considered. For instance, in the PtP example, are seeding/leeching requests sent in batch? Is there a fixed number of users that periodically ask for leeching? Clearly, also a model of the environment could help in reducing this type of uncertainty.

We can start to address environmental uncertainty using a view such as a UML **deployment model**, a structural view that specifies the physical hardware configurations at runtime and the allocation of software to hardware.

Figure 8.4 shows a runtime configuration of the PtP example. Nodes represent the physical structure of a system, modelling execution environments, or devices (processors on which software executes, disks, or I/O devices). Artefacts represent files containing the code of subsystems and/or components that are deployed on nodes.

Here again, uncertainties are apparent. The forms of uncertainty in this model view are related to the abstraction level, the node characteristics, and variability.

The precise network topology is a design decision that has impact on the system's overall performance. However, deployment diagrams can be used either to capture a specific deployment or to show a generic network that connects different nodes, focusing on the mapping of the software components on the execution platform. In Fig. 8.4, a new uncertainty is introduced: does the system consist of exactly three peers (and corresponding nodes) or is Fig. 8.4 simply an example runtime configuration? It is obviously possible to refine the network nodes to represent

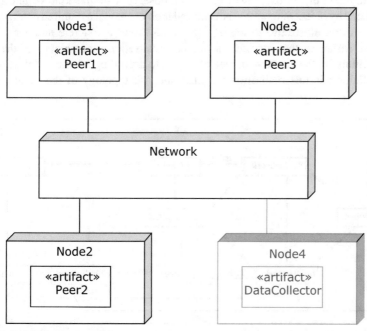

Fig. 8.4 PtP deployment model

a specific topology if the number of network nodes is relatively small. However, the refinement does not reduce the uncertainty about whether the model view is the required configuration or an illustrative example.

Deployment diagrams are also prone to the forms of uncertainty noted for class attributes in the domain model view, above. In particular, a deployment model needs to resolve input parameters that have an impact on communication delays [CM00], such as network bandwidth. As for class diagrams, this form of uncertainty can be addressed by annotating the deployment diagram or by applying suitable profiles, such as UML MARTE [OMGa].

Variability has also been discussed in relation to the domain model view. In the deployment view, there is variability uncertainty concerning any of the variation points in the runtime configuration of the software components, such as the DataCollector.

Finally, we can consider using an **object model**—a structural view that represents a specific configuration, or instance, of a class diagram. For example, Fig. 8.5 is an instance of the domain model in Fig. 8.1, expressing a specific topology of three peers communicating through specified channels.

This model view is often used to explore the meaning of the modelled relationships between class instances. For example, modelling scenarios using object models can be used in resolving uncertainty over (*) multiplicities in the domain model.

The object diagram supports modelling at a lower level of abstraction than class or deployment diagrams. However, we can observe a similar kind of uncertainty introduced by object diagrams—is a particular object model a required configuration instance or an illustrative example? Figure 8.5 shows a concrete number of links between instances that represent a possible realisation (not unique) of the class associations in the domain model of Fig. 8.1, according to the association-end multiplicities: is this realisation the final network topology of the system under

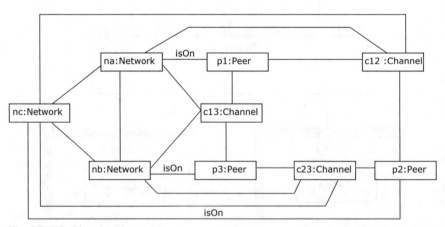

Fig. 8.5 PtP object model

analysis or is this a possible network configuration during the operational life of the PtP?

The discussion in this section is by no means a comprehensive review of the forms of models or the forms of uncertainty that arise in software specification: we do not, for instance, consider sequence diagrams, widely used in the design of system components "interactions".

Table 8.1 summarises the forms of uncertainties discussed for each model view (first column) that the developers need to consider while developing the PtP system. Each form of uncertainty (second column) is also classified according to its origin (third column), and specific examples from the PtP system are given (fourth column).

The classification by origin uses the terms introduced in Sect. 8.1, specifically, in this example the *Above* and *Below* origins. For example, the *variability* in the domain and deployment models is related to assumptions made by the designers, so its origin can be placed in the *Above* class, while the *association multiplicities* in the domain model and the *abstraction level* in the deployment model are related to the platform characteristics, so their origin belongs to the *Below* class. We do not have, at this level, uncertainties whose origin belongs to the *Inside* or *Outside* classes, because we are not referring to specific implementations or specific workload.

These are the kinds of uncertainties encountered by the developer up to this point in the scenario. In a typical development, later iterations elaborate models through more thorough requirements analysis, resolution of options, and the results

Table 8.1 Example uncertainties captured in different model views

Model view	Uncertainty	Origin	Examples from P2P
Domain model	Association multiplicities	Below	How many peers within the organisation?
	Attribute values	Below	Do speeds of the peers and network bandwidth have the same unit?
	Variability	Above	Is a `DataCollector` concept needed?
State machine	Incompleteness (design specifications)	Above	`share` and `start` transitions: which one is going to fire?
	Design alternatives	Above	`completed` transitions: which one is eventually considered?
	Incompleteness (interacting environment)	Below	What triggers the `cancel` transition (e.g., input from a user or another system, or a time trigger)?
Deployment model	Abstraction level	Below	Network topology, number of peers/nodes.
	Node characteristics	Below	Network bandwidth.
	Variability	Above	`DataCollector` and `Node4`.
Object model	Abstraction level (low)	Below	Is this the actual network topology or an example?

of analysis. While further analysis resolves some uncertainties using newly acquired information, it also exposes new uncertainties (e.g., about how to deal with errors such as peer crashes).

8.4 Model-Based Performance Analysis

The challenges of model-based performance analysis under uncertainty can be considered under three headings: (i) the choice of the model formalism, (ii) the definition of the model structure, and (iii) the values of parameters and their propagation to the analysis results.

We can classify uncertainty due to choice of model formalism, using the classification in Sect. 8.1, in two ways. If we see the choice of model formalism as part of the development process, the origin of uncertainty belongs to the *Above* class; on the other hand, if we look at choice of model formalism as pertaining to implementation, then the origin of uncertainties is in the *Inside* class.

Again, uncertainties related to the model structure can belong to either the *Above* and *Below* classes since both design and deployment assumptions are made at this level to be able to build a model. Model parameters express uncertainties related both to external data and to the platform characteristics so their origin can be placed in the *Outside* or in the *Below* classes. An ideal solution is to be able to record uncertainty systematically when modelling software systems and embed uncertainty analysis in development. Research in this area typically explores uncertainty classification and analysis [PM14b].

Here, we select a specific formalism, QNs, and explore uncertainty in performance modelling and analysis of the PtP case study described in Sect. 8.3. We discuss how challenges concerning (ii) the definition of the model structure and (iii) the values of parameters and their propagation to the analysis results impact the performance evaluation, and propose ways to mitigate uncertainty in performance analysis. QNs have been widely applied to represent and analyse resource-sharing systems [Kle75]. A QN represents a collection of interacting service centres (i.e., system resources) and a set of jobs (i.e., the requests). Each service centre is composed of a server and, except in the special case of a delay centre, a queue; service centres are connected through links that represent the network topology. Each server picks a job from its queue (if not empty), processes it, and selects one link that routes the processed request to another service centre. The time spent in every server by each request is modelled by an exponential distribution. Jobs are generated by source nodes regulating the rate of arrival requests. A QN is thus a directed graph whose nodes are service centres and edges are connections between centres. Jobs follow the graph's edge set to model the behaviour of customers' service requests. A QN thus models an instance of a state machine, in the way that an object model is an instance of a class diagram.

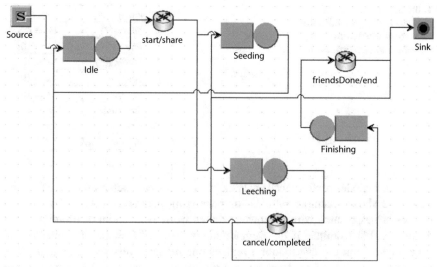

Fig. 8.6 PtP example: QN model, derived from the state machine, Fig. 8.3a

Figure 8.6 depicts the QN model built for the case study example. With respect to the uncertainties in the model structure (see Table 8.1), in this QN model, we have the following assumptions:

- The model refers to the behaviour of a single peer and includes the three alternative completion scenarios (regulated by probability values) discussed in Sect. 8.3.
- The network delay is not represented for sake of simplicity.
- The data collector is not included for sake of clarity.

The source node regulates the arrival requests. The request activity starts in the *idle* state. Requests are then routed (via the *start/share* routing station) to either the *seeding* or the *leeching* queues. After leeching, there is a *cancel/completed* routing station that determines whether requests go back to idle (due to cancel/completed events) or are routed to the *seeding* or *finishing* queues. The *friendsDone* event causes a request to either go back to the seeding queue or terminate in the *sink* node.

The uncertain parameters for this QN model are as follows:

- Source arrival rate: inter-arrival time distribution among multiple requests generated by the source node
- Idle, seeding, leeching, and finishing service time distributions: duration of actions related to the corresponding operations
- (Start/share, cancel/completed, friendsDone/end) Routing probabilities: how often requests are routed to the different queues, and what is the probability that requests terminate

Table 8.2 Examples of parameters in the QN model. Results are illustrated for variation of parameters marked (*)

Parameter	Value
Source(*)	$\lambda = 0.5$
Idle	$\lambda = 10$
Seeding(*)	$\lambda = 10$
Leeching	$\lambda = 10$
Finishing	$\lambda = 10$
Start/share	$\pi = 0.5$
Cancel/completed	$\pi = 0.25$
FriendsDone/end	$\pi = 0.5$

To run a model performance analysis, we first set parameter values for the QN. Table 8.2 shows example settings for generating parameter values. The service centres are associated with parameters drawn from exponential distributions with average λ. For example, if the *source* node is assigned $\lambda = 0.5$, the inter-arrival time drawn from the distribution averages one request every two time units. The QN centres (*idle*, *seeding*, *leeching*, and *finishing*) all have $\lambda = 10$, so timings are drawn from an exponential distribution with average $\lambda = 10$. By varying λ, we can run QN analysis with parameters representing a range of different timings.

For the QN analysis, all routings have equal probability, defined by π. Thus, *start/share* has two connections (*seeding* and *leeching*) giving a probability of $\pi = 0.5$, whereas *cancel/completed* has four options, so it is set to $\pi = 0.25$. Note that from *leeching* requests are routed back to *idle* either with *cancel* or *completed*, so the probabilities are summed and set to $\pi = 0.5$.

Figures 8.7 and 8.8 show the impact of the uncertainty in the parameters on the overall system quality.

Figure 8.7 presents preliminary simulation results for the timing analysis, varying the *source* parameter for the request-arrival rate, on the x-axis, between $\lambda = 0.05$ and $\lambda = 0.5$. As expected, the system response time, on the y-axis, increases as the request-arrival rate increases; more specifically, the system response rises from 3.9 to 12.1 time units. The detailed analysis is shown in the bottom part of Fig. 8.7: the header row shows the request-arrival rate (λ) setting, while the table shows values of mean, maximum system response time, determined by the confidence intervals from the corresponding simulation. For example, a request-arrival rate $\lambda = 0.5$ results in a mean response time of 11.8 time units and max and min values estimated to be 12.1 and 11.4, respectively.

Figure 8.8 shows the result of varying the service rate for the *seeding* node from $\lambda = 5$ (0.2 s in average) to $\lambda = 10$ (0.1 s in average), modelling the system response time variation as the *seeding* operation takes longer while increasing the corresponding rate of the queueing centre. The plot shows that a service time 0.17 or higher (service rate 1/0.17 or lower) results in a steep rise in the response time, indicating a software bottleneck.

A second QN model has been derived to explore some of the uncertainties in the model structure summarised in Table 8.1. In particular, we consider:

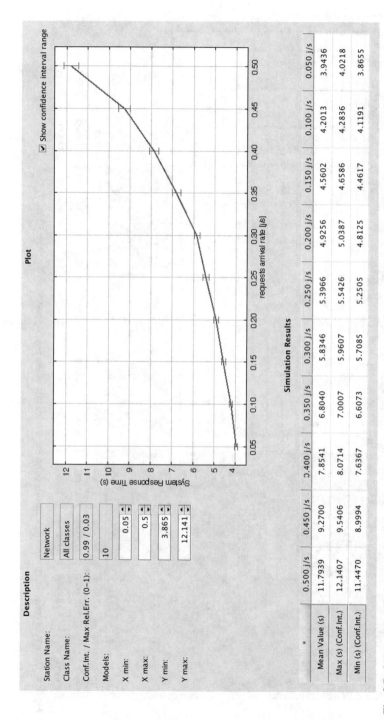

Fig. 8.7 QN model preliminary simulation results, with the arrival rate of the *source* node varying from 0.05 to 0.5

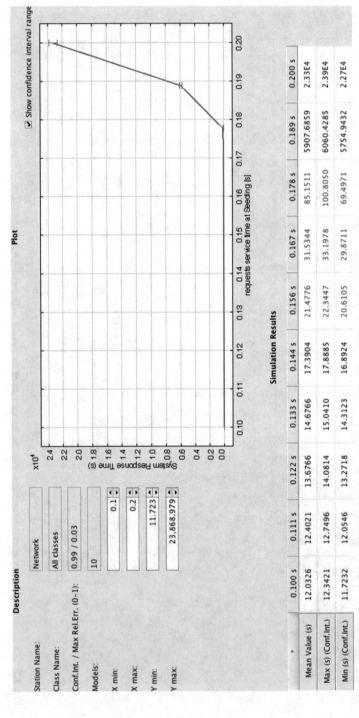

Fig. 8.8 QN model preliminary simulation results (with the service rate of the *seeding* node varying from 10 to 20)

The simulation results table from the figure:

	0.100 s	0.111 s	0.122 s	0.133 s	0.144 s	0.156 s	0.167 s	0.178 s	0.189 s	0.200 s
Mean Value (s)	12.0326	12.4021	13.6766	14.6766	17.3904	21.4776	31.5344	85.1511	5907.6859	2.33E4
Max (s) (Conf.Int.)	12.3421	12.7496	14.0814	15.0410	17.8885	22.3447	33.1978	100.8050	6060.4285	2.39E4
Min (s) (Conf.Int.)	11.7232	12.0546	13.2718	14.3123	16.8924	20.6105	29.8711	69.4971	5754.9432	2.27E4

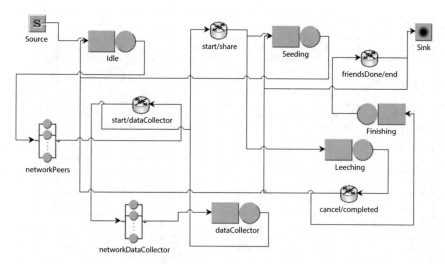

Fig. 8.9 QN model for the PtP example considering two peers and the data collector

- Two peers communicating through a network.
- The network delay is represented.
- The data collector is included.

The derived QN model is shown in Fig. 8.9. The uncertainties related to parameters follow the same assumptions as for the earlier QN, Fig. 8.6, as summarised in Table 8.2. The *source* node collects all incoming requests and dispatches them among the peers, which initially are all in the idle state. Each peer may decide to interact with the data collector or proceed with internal computations. This is modelled through the *start/dataCollector* routing node, by which peers either (i) communicate with the *data collector* with the *network* modelled as a delay node (there is no queue, but a waiting time expresses the network-related latency) or (ii) proceed with internal computations regulated by the routing centre *start/share* node (similarly to the previous QN model, see Fig. 8.6). There are further queueing centre nodes (i.e., *networkPeers*, *networkDataCollector*, *dataCollector*) to represent the communication among peers and the interaction with the data collector.

Figure 8.10 summarises the system response time analysis for the QN including two peers and a data collector. As for the first QN analysis, the peer(s) arrival rate λ ranges from 0.05 to 0.5 jobs/time unit (x-axis). The resulting system response times (y-axis) reflect the increased complexity of the system, rising from 9.6 up to 18.3 s, and these values may not meet the end-user requirements.

Summarising, these model-based performance results show the advantage of providing an understanding of the software behaviour, thus to support a quantitative evaluation of system uncertainties.

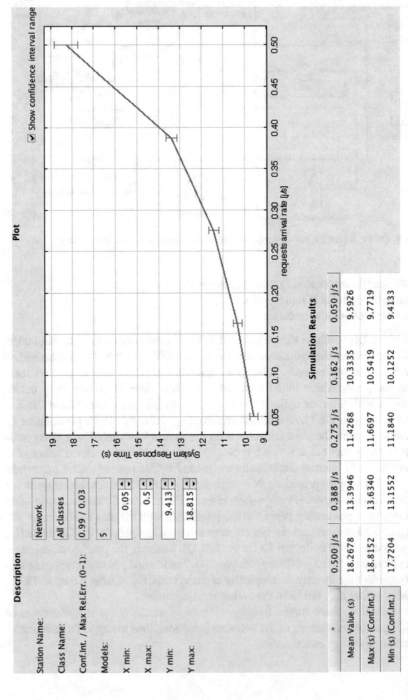

Fig. 8.10 QN model preliminary simulation results for the more complex case

8.5   Discussion of Challenges

Model-based developments need to take into account the uncertainties that arise in the process, from system elicitation to the software delivery, analysis, and presentation of results.

The running PtP example has explored and illustrated several challenges in the analysis and development of software systems that arise from the existence of uncertainties. The challenges reflect the developers' level of understanding and concern: the moment at which uncertainties are recognised (represented) in the system description; the way that uncertain concepts can be represented or recorded; the propagation of uncertainty across models, model composition, and analysis; how using a multi-model representation of the system affects uncertainty and its handling; how to select suitable values for uncertain parameters during performance analysis; the type of each uncertainty and how much it can be mitigated by applying appropriate methods; and, from a research perspective, some agreement on the semantics of uncertainty terminology.

The moment at which uncertainties are recognised is addressed in Sect. 8.3. The PtP example illustrates uncertainties about behaviour from the initial stages of system development and modelling (e.g., D1 and D2), and uncertainties about the behaviour of users. We have shown some ways in which the former affects the decisions that have to be taken during the first system analysis. Many of these early uncertainties would be mitigated in later phases of development, as the product owner provides more detail, allowing engineers to produce a more detailed design. However, our analysis results suggest that an early exploration of performance and response time can help to inform developers and the product owner of the consequences of different resolutions of uncertainty.

Uncertainties about the users also affect decisions that have to be taken during the system development, but these uncertainties are hard to mitigate before the first release of the system, because they concern future user behaviour. The development team has to live with these uncertainties during the whole development.

Section 8.3 also illustrates that *uncertainties can be generated by the modelling language*. For instance, UML accommodates uncertainty in representations (multiplicities, types), and the model semantics do not give a unique interpretation of what the domain model (or any other model) represents. Therefore, already in the initial requirement elicitation and business modelling activities, engineers must be aware that:

- They may not have completely understood how the system is expected to be developed (known unknowns).
- As development proceeds, or even once software is deployed, there may appear new concepts that are not understood (current unknown unknowns).
- For the part of the system that the developers have understood, what they have represented in their models may not be fully or accurately captured by the modelling language.

Management of uncertainties, whether arising at elicitation stage or later in the development, can only be achieved if there is explicit recognition and representation of uncertainty, which requires training and procedures for software development that force consideration of uncertainties. In software development, *uncertainties should be explicitly represented and documented*—it is not useful to have important information about uncertainty residing only in the mind of an engineer. There is ongoing research on the challenge of representing uncertainty in modelling, e.g., [Ber+18, Zha+19] propose uncertainty models and language extensions for representing uncertainty using UML.

Having made uncertainty explicit, processes and procedures need adjusting to take them into account, for instance in design decisions and other decision-making activities of different people. Software engineering needs to adopt uncertainties as first class citizen in models and to accept that the use of modelling languages generate *per se* new uncertainties.

There is an inherent contradiction between representing uncertainty in models and models that are themselves uncertain representations of the reality or developer intentions. As so often in engineering, there is a trade-off and a balance to be struck, with more research needed.

The specification of a software system can be seen as multi-model consisting of a group of complementary—but potentially overlapping—views. The challenges related to the *multi-model representation of systems* reside in: (a) inconsistencies in or different granularities of overlapping models and (b) for the non-overlapping parts, different assumptions made in each model about the characteristics of the other models. Section 8.2 delves into the evolution of uncertainties when composing models and model-based analyses.

In model-based software development, the model-based *system analysis phase also introduces uncertainty-related challenges*. Analysis requires an analysable model, which may differ from the models used to communicate the system design—such as the QN used for analysis of the PtP example. Model-driven engineering provides the foundations for automatic transformation from source to target models, and it is commonly used for transforming design models into analysable models (e.g., [Per+19]). However, unless the information in the target model is a subset of the information in the source model, there is an information gap that requires the making of assumptions; the assumptions are then captured in the transformation model, which, in practice, can hide the assumptions from the engineers. For the PtP case study, the challenges of uncertainty in the definition of a model structure are elaborated in Sect. 8.4. As noted above, uncertainties, and thus the information gap, can be mitigated as more data becomes available; model calibration to reduce uncertainty by eliminating poor choices of parameter and bad modelling decisions can also reduce the risks inherent in embedding assumptions in transformation rules.

In transformation, the target model needs to be able to represent information in the source model that is uncertain: the parts of the system that are not completely understood (system behaviour, known unknowns); the parts of the models in the source where the modelling language results in uncertainty of representation, even where the design or reality is fully understood by developers; and the parts of the development that depend on the future user behaviour (known unknowns about the user). The transformation should also avoid semantics mismatch, i.e., the translated model still needs to capture the original modeller intentions. Section 8.4 exemplifies some of these challenges, through the analysis of the system considering parameters with unknown specific values.

Although in specific cases uncertainty can be studied and mitigated, in the general case this is not guaranteed. Most commonly, when an engineer identifies a known unknown, it is not straightforward to act upon it. The proposal of a *systematic methodology to handle identified uncertainties* remains an open challenge. Such methodology could assist engineers in handling uncertainties once they have been identified and modelled. For instance, processes and techniques could be provided to support mitigation of different forms or occurrences of uncertainty.

Some uncertainty, notably uncertainties relating to (currently) unknowable features of the domain or eventual system context and usage, cannot be mitigated by design methodology. In these cases, it may be possible to qualify, or even quantify, the uncertainty importance or the potential effect of uncertainty (e.g., studying the associated risks). Even if nothing can be done to resolve uncertainty, it is important to document its existence. In the PtP example, for instance, it is important to record that the object, deployment, and QN models are intended only as indicative instances and do not represent anything about the eventual deployment and operation of the system. More generally, research in a variety of uncertain domains proposes taxonomies of uncertainties to support association of handling techniques to different classes of uncertainty [PM14a, PM14b].

The area of model-based analysis under uncertainty encounters additional challenges. For example, other open challenges in this area are: (i) usage of machine learning techniques to save computational effort in the analysis; (ii) visualisation of analysis-based issues to track the most critical input parameters; (iii) proactive reconfiguration of systems when uncertainties lead to overloaded resources/failures.

8.6   Related Work

There is a lot of general research on *types of uncertainty*. Jousselme et al. [JMB03] review many existing hierarchies and ontologies and propose definitions from a situational analysis perspective such as ignorance (a state of mind) and uncertainty (a consequence of limitations in observation). Padulo and Guenov [PG12] also review existing research, deriving a summary that sees the design problem as separable into uncertainty about and uncertainty within the problem.

A useful classification of the different types of uncertainty is given by Esfahani and Malek [EM13]. They describe it in terms of two axes: (a) *reducible* versus *irreducible* and (b) *aleatory* versus *epistemic*. The authors clarify that *"aleatory and epistemic represent the essence of uncertainty, while irreducible and reducible represent the managerial aspect of uncertainty"*. They add that the distinction between epistemic and aleatory uncertainty *"is motivated by the location of the uncertainty—in the decision-maker or in the physical system"*. We further clarify these concepts below.

Irreducible uncertainty refers to cases where uncertainty persists even in the presence of complete information. Such phenomena are inherently unknowable. Reducible uncertainty, on the other hand, refers to cases where more knowledge can be gathered, ultimately eliminating all uncertainty. An example of irreducible uncertainty in software engineering occurs when a developer is restricted to a high level of abstraction but is uncertain about what takes place at a low level of abstraction. Consider an Enterprise Java developer who is interested in the use of individual CPU registers. Even with complete information available at her level of abstraction (the Java runtime, etc.), there is no way to access information about machine code execution since that is hidden by the operating system. This can be mitigated by lifting the restriction to a specific level of abstraction, in which case uncertainty becomes reducible. However, lifting the restriction may not be feasible or desirable.

Aleatory uncertainty is *"caused by randomness and is typically modelled with probabilities"* [EM13]. Epistemic uncertainty in contrast is the result of insufficient knowledge. Statistical prediction models typically contain aleatory uncertainty, e.g., predicting the network load of a server. In contrast, if a developer is uncertain about a concept, e.g., which XML library is more reliable, that uncertainty is epistemic: it can be resolved by learning more about the available options.

The literature on *model-based analysis under uncertainty* includes several approaches defined to measure the impact of uncertain input parameters on the system output. The Object Management Group initiative on uncertainty modelling brings together a range of industrial and academic experts; the publications include a metamodel of uncertainty in cyber-physical systems [Zha+19] that aims to capture the (un)certainty of the modeller, by expressing beliefs about information. More generally, a possible way to classify existing methods is based on how uncertainty is described. The main categories are: (i) *probabilistic*, e.g., the probability density functions of the uncertain parameters are assumed to be known [Mee+11, Tru+13]; (ii) *possibilistic*, e.g., uncertain parameters are described with fuzzy boundaries [ACT15, Jam+16]; and (iii) *interval analysis*, i.e., the limits of variation are investigated to deduce best/worst cases [Etx+14, Car+18]. More recently, some approaches have been defined to reduce the uncertainty [TM17, Cám+18]; this way the complexity in handling variations is also smoothed.

Traditional approaches of handling uncertain input parameter values of a model are uncertainty quantification and sensitivity analysis. Both approaches typically rely on executing the model many times, varying input parameter values. Uncertainty quantification determines the likelihood of different model outputs given the uncertainty in the values of the input variables and can be carried out using Monte Carlo methods [Cun+14]. Sensitivity analysis is aimed at determining the degree to which an input parameter influences the output, and there are a number of different techniques that can be used to perform sensitivity analysis, e.g., the Sobol sensitivity analysis [Sob01], the Morris method [CCS07], and the Feature Importance method [RXZ17]. Such techniques can be used to rank the input parameters and to determine the most and least sensitive input parameters. The methods consider different metrics to rank the input parameters.

8.7 Conclusion

In this chapter, we have explored how uncertainty could be more explicitly addressed and systematically managed, with the goal of defining a conceptual framework to deal with and manage uncertainty. We have presented how uncertainty exists in model-based developments and that the composition of models during the system development can affect the uncertainty in both directions: the composition can reduce or increase the uncertainty. We have also shown that the complete elimination of uncertainty during the development of a software system is unrealistic. Instead, engineers need to live with uncertainty during model-based system development. We have proceeded towards these goals both with theoretical reasoning and a practical application through an example of designing a peer-to-peer file-sharing protocol. We have distinguished two main steps: (i) software system modelling and (ii) model-based performance analysis by highlighting the challenges related to the awareness that model-based development in software engineering needs to coexist with uncertainty. Although the exemplified model-based analysis dealt only with performance, other kinds of analysis would also have their issues with uncertainty.

Further research on this area can explore the capture of uncertainty aspects in the system design, which includes leaving options open as far as possible and incorporating belief values into the design. Another relevant research direction is the dynamic handling of uncertainties of data-driven models, such as deep learning, in safety-critical context, in particular in the autonomous driving domain. Research attention on the field of complex systems and deep uncertainty is also increasing, for instance, on appropriately interpreting results and understanding system behaviours. In Part II of this book [Hei+21], a range of case studies are presented that address some of the challenges in Part I. The challenges posed by uncertainty are not considered directly, though many of the case studies would be amenable to the sort of analysis presented in this chapter. Indeed, reasoning about operational semantics (GTS, Chap. 9) and the modular syntax approach of MontiCore (Chap. 10) offer many potential sources of uncertainty. Also potential sources of uncertainty need to be considered in modelling and analysing software architectures (Chap. 11).

References

[ACT15] Davide Arcelli, Vittorio Cortellessa, and Catia Trubiani. "Performance-Based Software Model Refactoring in Fuzzy Contexts". In: *International Conference on Fundamental Approaches to Software Engineering, FASE*. 2015, pp. 149–164.

[Ber+18] Manuel F. Bertoa, Nathalie Moreno, Gala Barquero, Loli Burgueño, Javier Troya, and Antonio Vallecillo. "Expressing Measurement Uncertainty in OCL/UML Datatypes". In: *Modelling Foundations and Applications*. 2018, pp. 46–62.

[BMP13] Simona Bernardi, José Merseguer, and Dorina C. Petriu. *Model-Driven Dependability Assessment of Software Systems*. Springer, 2013.

[Cám+18] Javier Cámara, Wenxin Peng, David Garlan, and Bradley R. Schmerl. "Reasoning about sensing uncertainty and its reduction in decision-making for self-adaptation". In: *Science of Computer Programming* 167 (2018), pp. 51–69.

[Car+18] Valeria Cardellini, Tihana Galinac Grbac, Matteo Nardelli, Nikola Tankovic, and Hong-Linh Truong. "Qos-based elasticity for service chains in distributed edge cloud environments". In: *Autonomous Control for a Reliable Internet of Services*. 2018, pp. 182–211.

[CCS07] Francesca Campolongo, Jessica Cariboni, and Andrea Saltelli. "An effective screening design for sensitivity analysis of large models". In: *Environmental Modelling & Software* 22.10 (2007), pp. 1509–1518. ISSN: 1364-8152. https://doi.org/10.1016/j.envsoft.2006.10.004.

[CDI11] Vittorio Cortellessa, Antinisca DiMarco, and Paola Inverardi. *Model-Based Software Performance Analysis*. Springer, 2011. https://doi.org/10.1007/978-3-642-13621-4.

[CM00] Vittorio Cortellessa and Raffaela Mirandola. "Deriving a Queueing Network based Performance Model from UML Diagrams". In: *Second International Workshop on Software and Performance, WOSP*. 2000, pp. 58–70.

[Cun+14] Americo Cunha, Rafael Nasser, Rubens Sampaio, Hélio Lopes, and Karin Breitman. "Uncertainty quantification through the Monte Carlo method in a cloud computing setting". In: *Computer Physics Communications* 185.5 (2014), pp. 1355–1363. https://doi.org/10.1016/j.cpc.2014.01.006.

[EM13] Naeem Esfahani and Sam Malek. "Uncertainty in Self-Adaptive Software Systems". In: *Software Engineering for Self-Adaptive Systems II*. 2013, pp. 214–238.

[Etx+14] Leire Etxeberria, Catia Trubiani, Vittorio Cortellessa, and Goiuria Sagardui. "Performance-based selection of software and hardware features under parameter uncertainty". In: *International Conference on Quality of Software Architectures, QoSA*. 2014, pp. 23–32.

[FC19] Michalis Famelis and Marsha Chechik. "Managing design-time uncertainty". In: *Software & Systems Modeling* 18.2 (2019), pp. 1249–1284.

[FSC12] Michalis Famelis, Rick Salay, and Marsha Chechik. "Partial models: Towards modeling and reasoning with uncertainty". In: *34th International Conference on Software Engineering, ICSE*. 2012, pp. 573–583.

[Hei+21] Robert Heinrich, Francisco Durán, Carolyn L. Talcott, and Steffen Zschaler (eds.) *Composing Model-Based Analysis Tools*. Springer, 2021. https://doi.org/10.1007/978-3-030-81915-6.

[Jam+16] Pooyan Jamshidi, Amir Sharifloo, Claus Pahl, Hamid Arabnejad, Andreas Metzger, and Giovani Estrada. "Fuzzy self-learning controllers for elasticity management in dynamic cloud architectures". In: *International Conference on Quality of Software Architectures, QoSA*. 2016, pp. 70–79.

[JMB03] Anne-Laure Jousselme, Patrick Maupin, and éloi Bossé. "Uncertainty in a situation analysis perspective". In: *6th International Conference of Information Fusion*. 2003, pp. 1207–1214. https://doi.org/10.1109/ICIF.2003.177375.

[Kle75] Leonard Kleinrock. *Queueing Systems Vol. 1:Theory*. Wiley, 1975.

[Mee+11] Indika Meedeniya, Irene Moser, Aldeida Aleti, and Lars Grunske. "Architecture-based reliability evaluation under uncertainty". In: *International Conference on Component-Based Software Engineering and Software Architecture, CompArch*. 2011, pp. 85–94.

[MO97] James Martin and James J. Odell. *Object-Oriented Methods: a Foundation*. 2nd Edition. Prentice Hall, 1997.

[OMGa] OMG. *UML Profile for MARTE*. Version 1.2, formal/19-04-01, April 2019. Object Management Group.

[OMGb] OMG. *Unified Modeling Language*. Version 2.5.1, formal/17-12-05, December 2017. Object Management Group.

[Per+19] Diego Perez-Palacin, José Merseguer, José I. Requeno, M. Guerriero, Elisabetta Di Nitto, and D. A. Tamburri. "A UML Profile for the Design, Quality Assessment and Deployment of Data-intensive Applications". In: *Software & Systems Modeling* 18.6 (2019), pp. 3577–3614. https://doi.org/10.1007/s10270-019-00730-3.

[PG12] Mattia Padulo and Marin D. Guenov. "A methodological perspective on Computational Engineering Design under uncertainty". In: *European Congress on Computational Methods in Applied Sciences and Engineering*. 2012, pp. 7509–7528. https://eccomas2012.conf.tuwien.ac.at/.

[PM14a] Diego Perez-Palacin and Raffaela Mirandola. "Dealing with Uncertainties in the Performance Modelling of Software Systems". In: *10th International ACM Sigsoft Conference on Quality of Software Architectures, QoSA*. 2014, pp. 33–42. https://doi.org/10.1145/2602576.2602582.

[PM14b] Diego Perez-Palacin and Raffaela Mirandola. "Uncertainties in the Modeling of Self-Adaptive Systems: A Taxonomy and an Example of Availability Evaluation". In: *5th ACM/SPEC International Conference on Performance Engineering, ICPE*. 2014, pp. 3–14. https://doi.org/10.1145/2568088.2568095.

[RXZ17] Alaleh Razmjoo, Petros Xanthopoulos, and Qipeng Phil Zheng. "Online Feature Importance Ranking Based on Sensitivity Analysis". In: *Expert Systems with Applications* 85.C (2017), pp. 397–406. https://doi.org/10.1016/j.eswa.2017.05.016.

[Sal+18] Tiago Prince Sales, Fernanda Baião, Giancarlo Guizzardi, João Paulo A Almeida, Nicola Guarino, and John Mylopoulos. "The common ontology of value and risk". In: *International Conference on Conceptual Modeling*. 2018, pp. 121–135.

[Sob01] Ilya M. Sobol. "Global sensitivity indices for nonlinear mathematical models and their Monte Carlo estimates". In: *Mathematics and Computers in Simulation* 55.1 (2001), pp. 271–280. https://doi.org/10.1016/S0378-4754(00)00270-6.

[TM17] Catia Trubiani and Raffaela Mirandola. "Continuous Rearchitecting of QoS Models: Collaborative Analysis for Uncertainty Reduction". In: *European Conference on Software Architecture (ECSA)*. 2017, pp. 40–48.

[Tru+13] Catia Trubiani, Indika Meedeniya, Vittorio Cortellessa, Aldeida Aleti, and Lars Grunske. "Model-based performance analysis of software architectures under uncertainty". In: *International Conference on Quality of Software Architectures, QoSA*. 2013, pp. 69–78.

[Zha+19] Man Zhang, Shaukat Ali, Tao Yue, Roland Norgren, and Oscar Okariz. "Uncertainty-Wise Cyber-Physical System test modeling". In: *Software & Systems Modeling* 18.2 (2019), pp. 1379–1418. https://doi.org/10.1007/s10270-017-0609-6.

Part II
Case Studies

Chapter 9
GTSMorpher: Safely Composing Behavioural Analyses Using Structured Operational Semantics

Steffen Zschaler and Francisco Durán

Abstract We are seeing an increase in the number of different languages and design tools used for designing and implementing such systems, fuelled by research in domain-specific modelling languages leading to increasingly more reliable and production-ready environments for *language-oriented programming* (LOP). While LOP has undeniable benefits for the efficiency and effectiveness of software development, it creates new problems for software analysis: most existing analysis tools are tied to a specific representation of the software to be analysed. LOP is predicated on developing bespoke representations for each type of problem. This requires analysis tools to be, at least partially, reimplemented and adapted for each new such language.

One approach is to build transformations that compile a model in a given language into a representation that can be handled by a given analysis tool (cf. Chap. 5 of this book). A key challenge here is to ensure that these transformations correctly reflect the semantics of the original language in the analysis-tool-specific representation. This is non-trivial and becomes even more challenging when more than one analysis tool is to be applied to a given system design.

In this chapter, we present a different approach, where analyses are directly represented as *executable domain-specific modelling languages* (xDSMLs), making their operational semantics explicit as graph-transformation rules. Powerful composition operations provide support for the independent and reusable development of analysis tools and languages, which can then be woven at will. In previous work, we have developed the formal foundations for this approach and have shown the conditions under which such composition is safe, even when combining multiple different analyses. In this chapter, we introduce *GTSMorpher*, a software tool that allows xDSMLs and their compositions to be expressed in the context of the

S. Zschaler (✉)
King's College London, London, UK
e-mail: szschaler@acm.org

F. Durán
University of Málaga, Málaga, Spain
e-mail: duran@lcc.uma.es

© The Author(s), under exclusive license to Springer Nature Switzerland AG 2021
R. Heinrich et al. (eds.), *Composing Model-Based Analysis Tools*,
https://doi.org/10.1007/978-3-030-81915-6_9

189

Eclipse Modelling Framework. We demonstrate the use of *GTSMorpher* through case studies.

This case-study chapter illustrates concepts introduced in Chap. 4 and addresses Challenge 1 in Chap. 3 of this book.

9.1   Introduction

Quality properties of software-intensive systems are increasingly important. At the same time, we are seeing an increase in the number of different languages and design tools used for designing and implementing such systems, fuelled by research in *domain-specific modelling languages* (DSMLs) leading to increasingly more reliable and production-ready environments for *language-oriented programming* (LOP) [War94]. LOP takes Naur's insight that all programming is theory building [Nau86] and follows it to its natural consequence, contending that software should be developed in problem-specific languages rather than general-purpose programming languages. While LOP has undeniable benefits for the efficiency and effectiveness of software development, it creates new problems for software analysis: most existing analysis tools are tied to a specific representation of the software to be analysed. LOP, on the other hand, is predicated on developing bespoke representations for each type of problem. This requires analysis tools to be, at least partially, reimplemented and adapted for each new such language.

One approach is to build transformations that compile a model in a given language into a representation that can be handled by a given analysis tool (cf. Chap. 5 of this book [Hei+21], [GM04]). A key challenge here is to ensure that these transformations correctly reflect the semantics of the original language in the analysis-tool-specific representation. This is non-trivial and becomes even more challenging when more than one analysis tool is to be applied to a given system design.

In this chapter, we present an alternative approach, predicated on the idea that modelling a language's semantics explicitly—producing an *executable domain-specific modelling language* (xDSML)—makes it possible to reason about these semantics when developing analysis tools. We introduce *GTSMorpher*, a tool, and DSML for specifying graph-transformation systems and their algebraic composition. We use graph transformations [Cor+97] to capture a language's operational semantics and then combine and reuse them with semantic guarantees. The approach indeed enables a modular approach to analysis (see Chaps. 4 and 5 of this book [Hei+21]), in which different analyses can be combined into one modelling language, so that different analyses can be enabled depending on what a project requires.

Graph-transformation systems (GTSs) were proposed in the late seventies as a formal technique for the rule-based specification of the dynamic behaviour of systems [Ehr79]. Recent uses of GTSs in the context of *model-driven engineering* (MDE) have proposed more practical uses of different forms of parametric GTSs for reusing model transformations, and reusing and composing DSML definitions. For example, in [LG13], de Lara and Guerra propose the use of transformation templates expressed over *metamodel concepts* that can then be instantiated. A metamodel concept defines structural requirements on a metamodel that allow a transformation to be executed. Metamodel semantics are not captured by metamodel concepts. In [DZT13, Dur+17], Durán et al. propose a more general form of parametrised GTSs where the parameter is not just a type graph, but a complete GTS, and where composition of GTSs is based on a GTS amalgamation construction. In the same way metamodel concepts gather the structural requirements, the set of rules of parameter GTSs are behavioural requirements over the concrete GTSs used in their instantiation. Thus, parametrised GTSs extend the metamodel concept notion to include the behavioural semantics of the metamodels.

GTS morphisms (see, e.g., [Eng+97, Ehr+06, GPS98b, EHC05]) are a key ingredient of GTSs and GTS compositions. The use of GTS morphisms enables useful syntactic and semantic guarantees. For example, morphisms are used in [LG13] so that transformations can be guaranteed to be syntactically reusable. In the case of [Dur+17], the use of suitable morphisms enables guarantees on behaviour protection of amalgamated GTSs. However, graph morphisms and GTS morphisms require a strong structural similarity between source and target graphs and GTSs, which hinders their applicability.

The need for powerful and flexible mechanisms for relating GTSs, to broaden opportunities for GTS reuse, has been attempted to solve in different ways. In the case of models, represented as graphs, this has been resolved more or less pragmatically by supporting a specific, fixed set of adaptations to be applied prior to applying the morphism (see, e.g., [LG13, Lar+07, DMC12, LG14]). To support complete GTSs, rules must also be related in a flexible manner. In [GPS98a, GPS98b], Große-Rhode et al. introduce temporal and spatial refinement relations, in which rules are refined into either sequences or amalgamations of rules. However, despite the introduction of derived attributes and links as in [DMC12] or [LG14], and the behavioural relations provided for GTS morphisms as in [Dur+17], we do not find a satisfactory solution until the proposal of *GTS families* in [ZD17].

Often, even where there is an intuitive match, no morphism can be established, due to structural mismatches. In [ZD17], Zschaler and Durán propose the use of *GTS transformers* to refactor GTSs with the goal of resolving these mismatches between source and target GTSs so that GTS morphisms can be defined. GTS transformers are basically functions and can successively be applied to our source GTS to find the one on which the morphism can be defined. This basic idea is systematised with the notion of GTS families. Given a set of transformers T, the T-family of a GTS GTS_0 is the set of GTSs reachable from GTS_0 using the transformers in T. The problem of defining a mapping morphism between a GTS GTS_0 and a target GTS GTS_1 then amounts to finding a GTS in the family of GTS_0 from which the morphism can be defined. This way, the problem becomes a model-based search problem [Joh+19]. In this chapter, however, instead of blindly searching for such matches, we use the capabilities of the *GTSMorpher* tool to specify the explicit transformation steps to be applied.

This approach offers a powerful reuse opportunity for model-based analysis tools when systems are developed using xDSML-based specifications. The possibilities for the modularisation of analyses as a parametrised GTS have been previously shown in, e.g., [Dur+17]. In [Mor+14], Moreno-Delgado et al. showed how the approach can be applied to reimplement the analysis provided by the Palladio simulator (see [Reu+16] and Chap. 11 of this book [Hei+21]). However, while the theory has been developed, for this approach to become practically viable, tool support is required. In this chapter, we introduce *GTSMorpher*, a tool, and DSML for specifying graph-transformation systems and their algebraic composition. We show how *GTSMorpher* can be used to specify weavings of simple graph-transformation systems as per [Dur+17] as well as of GTS families [ZD17]. A new case study in Sect. 9.4 shows a reimplementation of the Karlsruhe Architectural Maintainability Prediction (KAMP) approach [Ros+15] using the *GTSMorpher* tool. The tool ensures the correctness of weaving specifications and outputs GTSs in the Henshin format [Str+17] that can be executed or analysed further.

We have shown in previous work [Dur+17] that the same composition mechanism can also be used to combine multiple analyses on top of one xDSML. For example, [DZT13] shows an example of capturing performance analysis in this form. Generally, we encode analyses using the idea of history-determined variables [AL94]—variables whose current value can be inferred from the current and past values of other variables. In an MDE context, we encode these as observer objects in our models, using additional *Observer* metaclasses or metaassociations in the metamodel as suggested by Troya in [Tro+13]. This is combined with an operational semantics expressed using graph-transformation rules specifying how model state changes over time (which is similar to Abadi/Lamport's temporal logic of actions (TLA) [Lam94] approach). As in TLA, updates to the observers (history-determined variables) are simply included in the update parts of the graph-transformation rules giving the xDSML's operational semantics. This way, properties such as performance, reliability, efficiency, etc. of a modelled system can easily be read off at any point by inspecting the values captured by observer objects and links.

In the remainder, Sect. 9.2 gives a motivating example, which we will use in Sect. 9.3 to introduce the *GTSMorpher* tool. In Sect. 9.4 we walk through a more complex case study before concluding in Sect. 9.5.

9.2 Motivating Example

In this section, we present a simplified example of how a model-based analysis can be modelled using an xDSML in a way where this can be safely composed into different xDSMLs and, thus, easily reused.

Consider the example of a simple xDSML specifying production-line systems. Figure 9.1 gives an overview of the language's metamodel. It can be seen that in the language we can specify production-line systems by connecting various types

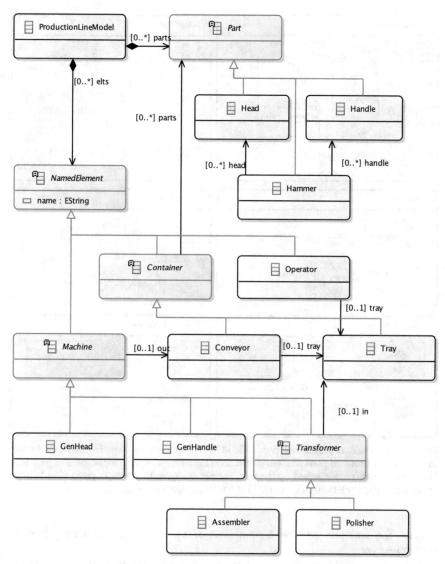

Fig. 9.1 Metamodel for the PLS xDSML

of machines via different kinds of containers. Different kinds of parts are produced and manipulated by the machines and transported via the containers. The operational semantics of this xDSML can be captured using several graph-transformation rules. Figure 9.2 shows such rules, specifying operational semantics of the *production-line system* (PLS) language. In particular, the behaviour of the Polisher machine is specified by the Polish rule (in the bottom right corner of Fig. 9.2). From these rules,

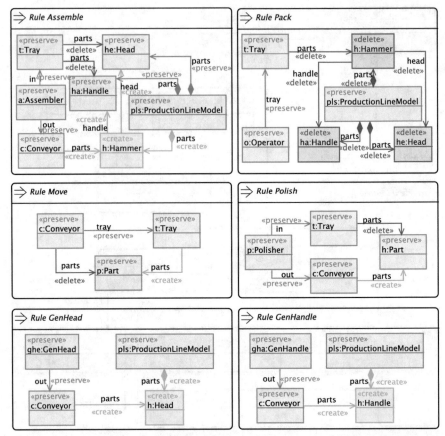

Fig. 9.2 PLS's rules expressed in Henshin [Str+17]. Henshin uses colour coding and textual labels to compactly present all parts of a graph-transformation rule. Elements represented in grey (and labelled preserve) are matched by the rule, but not changed. Elements in green (and labelled create) are added, while elements in red (and labelled delete) are removed

we can, for example, generate a simulation of a given production-line system for further analysis.

Let us now consider specifying an analysis of production-line systems. As a very simplistic example, we will specify an analysis that allows to keep track of parts manipulated by a specific machine. This can, for example, be used to track reliability or performance of any given machine. Rather than changing the PLS xDSML to introduce the relevant observer objects and associations directly, we want to specify our analysis in a reusable format that can be woven into the PLS xDSML, but also into other xDSMLs. Figure 9.3 shows how we might capture this in a metamodel. Note the green association (made) indicating the new observer association we need to add to the metamodel to capture elements manipulated by a given server. In the following, we will consider everything in the metamodel not coloured in green

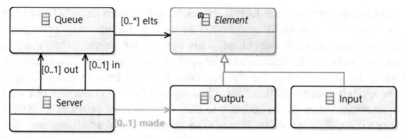

Fig. 9.3 Analysis metamodel

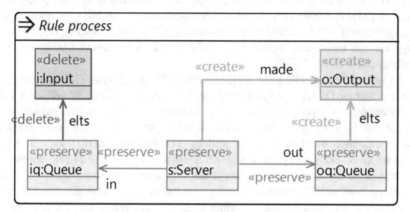

Fig. 9.4 Rule specifying the analysis based on the abstract server metamodel

the interface of our analysis xDSML (and, technically, will annotate it with the @Interface annotation). To compose our analysis into the PLS xDSML, we will need to establish a mapping instantiating every interface concept with a concept in the PLS metamodel. Figure 9.4 shows a rule specifying the semantics of our analysis: whenever a Server produces a part on its out Queue, it will record this fact by establishing a made link.

In Sect. 9.3, we introduce our *GTSMorpher* tool and show how it can be used to specify these xDSMLs and their composition so that the analysis is included in the result. After that, we will walk through a more complex analysis composition and reuse case study.

9.3   The *GTSMorpher* Tool

In this section, we give a brief walk-through of *GTSMorpher* using the example from Sect. 9.2, before we apply *GTSMorpher* to a new example of analysis composition in the next section.

GTSMorpher supports the formal specification and analysis of GTSs and morphisms between them (*GTS morphisms*) as well as the automated composition of GTSs based on GTS morphisms. This enables the existing theory on GTS morphisms and GTS amalgamation to be applied to real-world GTSs, which would otherwise be impractical as the size and complexity of even simple GTS specifications quickly make it difficult for a human to validate correctness or compute amalgamations manually. In addition to this, *GTSMorpher* provides a number of features to simplify the specification of GTS morphisms and amalgamations: Code-completion support makes it easier to correctly reference various constituent parts of a GTS, while morphism auto-completion, interface morphisms, and GTS-family support [ZD17] allow very compact specifications of complex morphisms and amalgamations. Where analyses are specified as GTSs (or xDSMLs), *GTSMorpher* supports the automated weaving of analyses into arbitrary xDSMLs, enabling analysis reuse across DSMLs.

To support the specification of GTSs and GTS morphisms, *GTSMorpher* provides a textual DSML for specifying algebraic manipulations of GTSs. A GTS is encoded as a type graph (an Ecore metamodel [Ste+09]) and, optionally, a module of Henshin graph-transformation rules [Str+17]. *GTSMorpher* supports the specification of plain GTSs as well as GTS families [ZD17], as well as the expression of GTS morphisms and GTS amalgamations [Dur+17], which can be reused as inputs for further morphism and amalgamation definitions. GTSs produced from any *GTSMorpher* specification can be exported as Ecore metamodels and Henshin modules for use in further analysis and execution. *GTSMorpher* has been developed in the Xtext language workbench and can be obtained from its Github repository.[1]

The foundation of safe composition of GTSs lies in the notion of GTS morphisms—mappings between the elements of two GTSs that ensure the structure of the GTSs is preserved. We, therefore, start by showing how a GTS morphism is expressed in the *GTSMorpher* DSML. On top of GTS morphisms, we can weave GTSs by computing the pushout of a suitable span of GTSs and GTS morphisms. In this section, we show how this can be expressed and controlled in *GTSMorpher*.

9.3.1   Specifying GTS Morphisms

GTSs and GTS morphisms are expressed in .gts files. These are text files using the syntax below (syntax completion is available throughout the Eclipse editor).

---

[1] *GTSMorpher* is available at https://github.com/gts-morpher/gts_morpher.

Basic GTS Syntax

The easiest way to specify a GTS is through a GTS literal as below:

```
gts PLS {
   metamodel: "pls"
   behaviour: "plsRules"
}
```

Here, PLS can be an arbitrary, optional name for the GTS that may later be used to reference the GTS. The **metamodel** clause references an Ecore package defining the metamodel of the GTS. The **behaviour** clause references a Henshin module the rules of which are considered to be the rules of the GTS. It is acceptable to leave out the behaviour clause. Some alternative forms of specifying GTSs exist; these all differ primarily by what is specified between the curly braces: we will discuss GTS families and GTS amalgamation later.

Any GTS specification may be annotated with two modifiers:

1. **export**: This annotation indicates that the .ecore (and optionally the .henshin) file of the GTS should be generated into the src-gen/ folder of the containing Eclipse project.
2. **interface_of**: These GTSs are formed from the original metamodel and rules by only considering a sub-GTS typable over the metamodel elements explicitly annotated with @Interface. This is particularly useful for GTS amalgamation as described below.

Finally, a GTS specification can reference another named GTS. This is particularly useful when referencing a pre-defined GTS from a mapping specification.

Basic Morphism Syntax

A GTS morphism is specified as a mapping between two GTSs, using a **map** clause as shown in Listing 9.1.

Here, **from** and **to** each specify a GTS. The block in curly braces after **from** and **to** is actually a GTS specification (see above) with the **gts** keyword left out.

The mandatory **type_mapping** section describes the type-graph morphism part of the GTS morphism by providing a clan morphism between the two metamodels [Lar+07]. This is achieved through a list of mapping statements that map a class, reference, or attribute.[2]

Similarly, the optional **behaviour_mapping** section describes rule mappings. If the GTSs do not have rules, the **behaviour_mapping** clause should also be left out and the file only specifies a clan morphism between the metamodels. Each rule mapping is started using the keyword rule followed by the name of the rule in the source GTS,

---

[2] The careful reader will have noticed the metaclasses InputQueue and OutputQueue being referenced here. These will be explained later, when we introduce the definition of GTS families.

```
map {
  from interface_of {
    Server
  }

  to {
    metamodel: "pls"
    behaviour: "plsRules"
  }

  type_mapping {
    class server.Server    => pls.Polisher
    class server.InputQueue  => pls.Tray
    class server.OutputQueue => pls.Conveyor
    // reference  YYY => XXX
    // attribute  YYY => XXX
    // ...
  }

  behaviour_mapping {
    rule process to polish {
      object iq => t
      object o  => pt2
      object s  => p
      object oq => c
      link [s->iq:in]   => [p->t:in]
      link [oq->o:elts]  => [c->pt2:parts]
      link [iq->i:elts]  => [t->pt:parts]
      link [s->oq:out]   => [p->c:out]
      object i => pt
    }
  }
}
```

Listing 9.1 Syntax for specifying GTS morphisms

the keyword **to**, and the name of the rule in the target GTS. Each rule mapping again contains a list of mappings for objects, links, and slots (attribute constraints) in the rule as well as for rule parameters.

Extensive validation is performed for any mapping specification, including to check whether it represents a (potential) GTS morphism. Eclipse error and warning markers provide information and hint about the results of these checks. Slot mappings are considered valid if the associated expressions are syntactically identical, subject to parameter renaming.

Morphism Auto-Completion and Unique Auto-Completion

The system will create error markers if type or behaviour mappings are not complete. As it can be quite tedious to type out all parts of the mapping, it is possible to ask the system to automatically complete a partial mapping by adding the keyword **auto–complete** at the start of the specification:

```
auto−complete map { ... }
```

As long as the mappings specified do not break the conditions for a GTS morphism, the system will attempt to complete the morphism automatically. The user can request for the completed morphisms to be exported as .gts files for inspection. Auto-completion uses a backtracking algorithm tentatively adding mappings and checking if morphism properties are still maintained. Mappings are not selected randomly: the structure of the metamodel and rules and existing mappings are taken into account to identify mappings that are likely to maintain morphism properties.

Users can claim that only a unique auto-completion to a morphism exists by adding the **unique** keyword:

```
auto−complete unique map { ... }
```

Checking whether a unique auto-completion exists is expensive as it may require searching the complete space of possible mappings (as opposed to checking if a completion is possible, where we can stop once one completion has been found). To avoid interfering with the editing experience, *GTSMorpher* will initially only add a warning marker to the **unique** keyword to show that this claim has not been checked yet. To check unique completability, users must explicitly request a validation. If auto-completion is not unique, an error marker will be added to the file. This provides quick-fix suggestions for mappings to add to sufficiently constrain the possible auto-completions. Suggestions are provided in order of potential impact; the top suggestion should offer the quickest path to unique auto-completion.

Mapping with Virtual Rules

When a rule in the source GTS cannot be mapped to any rule in the target GTS, it can be mapped to a virtual rule, automatically generated by *GTSMorpher*. This is useful, for example, where we want to produce amalgamations that introduce new rules into an existing GTS. In such a case, there is no rule that can be mapped to, but the amalgamation still requires a complete morphism. Mapping a rule to a virtual rule is indicated using a rule mapping of the following form (we will call such mappings "to-virtual mappings"):

```
rule init to virtual
```

Note that **virtual** is a language keyword, rules named "virtual" are not supported. From such a rule mapping, *GTSMorpher* will generate a virtual rule with the same structure as the source rule and use that in the mapping. Note that to-virtual rule mappings cannot specify any element mappings; these are all implicit, because the rule is dynamically generated only when needed. At the same time, there is only one valid mapping between source rule and virtual rule, so there is no need to specify any explicit element mappings.

Mapping to arbitrary virtual rules may affect behaviour-preservation properties of the morphism [Dur+17]. To ensure behaviour in the target GTS is preserved, it is possible to constrain virtual rules to be identity rules; that is their left- and right-hand sides must be identical. Adding an identity rule to a GTS does not change the behaviours modelled apart from adding stuttering steps. Only identity rules can be mapped to virtual identity rules, of course, and the tool will check this. To specify a rule mapping to a virtual identity rule (a "to-identity rule mapping") the following form of rule mappings should be used (where init is the name of a rule in the source GTS):

---

rule init **to virtual identity**

Note that the word **identity** is a keyword in the morphism language. It is therefore not possible to map rules named "identity".

Where possible, auto-completion will consider completing by introducing to-virtual or even to-identity rule mappings. This behaviour can be restricted by claiming auto-completion is possible using only to-identity rule mappings or without using to-virtual mappings at all, to ensure behaviour preservation:

- **auto−complete to−identity−only map** { ... } claims that only to-identity mappings might need to be introduced.
- **auto−complete without−to−virtual map** { ... } claims that no to-virtual mappings will need to be introduced to complete the morphism.

Conversely, rule mappings can be established from virtual empty source rules. This is useful where the target GTS contains rules that cannot be matched by any of the source rules—for example where the target GTS contains more rules than the source GTS, as is the case when reusing the specifications of non-functional properties as described in [DZT13]. There is no need to consider identity source rules or any other more complex source rules: For empty source rules rule morphisms trivially exist.

A rule mapping from an empty source rule (a "from-empty rule mapping") is defined as follows:

---

rule empty to do

---

where do is the name of a rule in the target GTS. **empty** is a keyword in the language and cannot be the name of a rule.

Auto-completion can consider introducing from-empty rule mappings automatically. Note that this is very likely to reduce the chances of producing *unique* auto-completions as from-empty mappings can be trivially introduced and can be trivially complemented with to-virtual mappings to ensure all rules in both GTSs have a mapping. In order to produce more intuitive behaviour, *GTSMorpher* will

```
gts_family ServerFamily {
   {
      metamodel: "server"
      behaviour: "serverRules"
   }

   transformers: "transformerRules"
}
```

Listing 9.2 Syntax for specifying GTS families

(1) not try to introduce from-empty mappings if a mapping with an actual source rule can be found, and (2) only try to introduce from-empty rule mappings if explicitly instructed to do so. The following syntax allows from-empty mappings to be included:

```
auto−complete allow−from−empty map { ... }
```

9.3.2 GTS Families

You can specify that the source or target of a GTS morphism should be taken from a GTS family by providing the definition of the family and the sequence of transformers to apply to the family's root GTS when picking the GTS you actually want. GTS families are described in more detail in [ZD17]. Intuitively, the T-GTS family of a GTS GTS_0 is the set of GTSs reachable from GTS_0 using the transformers in T.

To specify a GTS family, replace the GTS specification with one that follows the format shown in Listing 9.2. In it, **metamodel** and **behaviour** describe the root GTS of the family as usual. Although the transformers introduced in [ZD17] can be specified in different ways, here we restrict ourselves to transformers specified using Henshin rules. **transformers** references a Henshin module (typed over Ecore and Henshin) with the transformer rules of the GTS family. GTS family specifications can be used anywhere a GTS is expected.

We can then specify a specific GTS in this family by specifying the sequence of transformers to be applied on the root GTS of the family. Listing 9.3 shows this in an example. AdaptedServer picks a specific variant of our Server GTS that can be mapped cleanly onto the PLS xDSML. The **using** clause indicates the sequence of transformer applications, including their actual parameters, to be used in deriving the correct GTS from inside the family. Specifically, it introduces the separate InputQueue and OutputQueue subclasses of Queue that are needed for mapping to Tray and Conveyor. We do not show the transformers used in this example here. These

```
gts AdaptedServer {
  family : ServerFamily

  using [
    addSubClass ( server . Queue , "InputQueue" ),
    addSubClass ( server . Queue , "OutputQueue" ),
    reTypeToSubClass ( serverRules . process , server . Queue ,
                        server . InputQueue , "iq" ),
    reTypeToSubClass ( serverRules . process , server . Queue ,
                        server . OutputQueue , "oq" ),
    mvAssocDown ( server . Server . in , server . InputQueue ),
    mvAssocDown ( server . Server . out , server . OutputQueue )
  ]
}
```

Listing 9.3   AdaptedServer is a GTS in the ServerFamily GTS family

```
gts ServerPLS {
  weave ( dontLabelNonKernelElements , preferMap2TargetNames ): {
    map1 : interface_of ( AdaptedServer )
    map2 : Server2PLS
  }
}
```

Listing 9.4   Syntax for GTS amalgamation

can be found on the *GTSMorpher* repository. Examples of some other transformers will be shown later.

9.3.3   GTS Amalgamation

Once a valid morphism has been described (either as a complete map or by using unique auto-completion), GTS amalgamation can be performed (as per [Dur+17]). Where the source GTS is declared using **interface_of**, amalgamation will assume an inclusion to be defined by the @ Interface annotations.

GTS amalgamation is specified in a special form of GTS specification shown in Listing 9.4. **map1** and **map2** are expected to, together, define a *span*; that is both mappings must have the same source GTS. No further checks of the morphisms are undertaken, and no guarantees are given w.r.t. semantics preservation of the amalgamation step (although we are working on supporting this in future versions of *GTSMorpher*). Both **map1** and **map2** can be defined either by referencing an existing named mapping or by using the **interface_of** keyword.

The **weave** clause can be extended with parameters specifying the rules to use when generating names for the amalgamated model elements. By default, weaving will preserve the names of all model elements that contributed to a given woven element. If these names are all identical, the new model element will have the same name. Otherwise, all names will be joined together using underscores as the separator. Names of model elements that are not mapped from the kernel GTS will be prefixed with left__ (for **map1**) or right__ (for **map2**), respectively, to indicate their provenance. Through parameters, **weave** can be instructed to give preference to names defined in one of the GTSs involved. If any naming option leads to names that are not unique within their scope, the weaver will fall back to the default naming strategy for these elements. The choices we have made in the example above will result in the woven xDSML to use the PLS names wherever possible.

9.4   An Application Example

This section shows how the mechanisms introduced in the previous sections may be useful in the development of generic tools with minimal effort. Specifically, we illustrate how to exploit the capabilities of GTSMorpher by developing an alternative implementation of the *Karlsruhe Architectural Maintainability Prediction* (KAMP) approach [Ros+15]. KAMP evaluates the maintainability of IT systems based on the metamodel of their architectures. More precisely, assuming a component-based architecture, and given an initial request for change, it predicts the change propagation in the software architecture model. In the KAMP approach, components are considered black boxes. Although no knowledge about component internals is required, the model of the software architecture is supposed to include information on both technical and organisational tasks—including source code files, test cases, build configurations, etc.—and contain explicit interface specifications that bind them in the software process. This information and change propagation rules are then used by KAMP to calculate the change propagation in the software architecture automatically. As a result of the process, KAMP gives a list with all the structural and organisational tasks to execute the change request.

A complete implementation of the approach requires a detailed distinction of elements and tasks, so that specific and friendly information is provided to the final user. However, the core of the tool is quite simple; it just "taints" those elements affected by a given change. By using the propagation rules, this "tainting" of elements leads to the identification of all elements affected by an initial change request. However, given a DSML description, possibly including both a metamodel and transformation rules describing its behaviour, the application of the approach would require the modification of the model on which the propagation is to be performed. This is, for example, the approach followed to implement the technique on the Palladio system (cf. [Ros+15]).

To define the KAMP approach generically, so that we can apply it to any DSML description, we just need the possibility of tainting elements and propagating such tainting. In other words, the KAMP approach is defined just by the DSML defined by the metamodel in Fig. 9.5 and the propagation rule in Fig. 9.6. To be able to

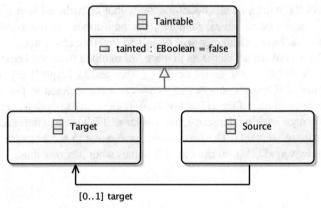

Fig. 9.5 KAMP's metamodel (kamp)

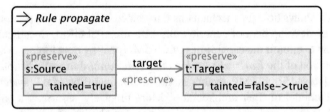

Fig. 9.6 KAMP's rules (kampRules)

propagate the tainting on any specific system, we just need to be able to instantiate the KAMP DSML on the specific places on which change is propagated in the system. The good news is that we only need to indicate the specific propagation points, since the propagation will happen always in the same way. Even more, we can assure that the modified system thus obtained behaves in exactly the same as the original system.

9.4.1 Making PLS Taintable

Instead of using a complex system, we show in the rest of the section how to apply the KAMP approach to the PLS language introduced in Sect. 9.2. To do it, we need to first extend the PLS language so that elements may be tainted, and then introduce the propagation rules on any specific propagation point. Notice that if the attribute was introduced together with the propagation rules, we would get a different attribute on each instantiation. Instead, we first introduce the attribute, a boolean attribute tainted, and then each propagation rule operating on such same attribute. With the machinery provided by GTSMorpher this is very simple. We just

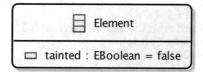

Fig. 9.7 Taintable's metamodel (taintable)

```
auto−complete unique allow−from−empty map ITaintable2PLS {
  from interface_of { Taintable }
  to PLS
  type_mapping {
    class taintable . Element => pls . NamedElement
  }
}
```

Listing 9.5 GTS morphism to enable PLS to become taintable

need a GTS with the metamodel depicted in Fig. 9.7 and no rules. In this metamodel, the only element not annotated with @Interface is precisely the tainted attribute.

```
gts Taintable {
  metamodel: "taintable"
}
```

To be able to taint any element of the PLS language we just need to instantiate the generic Taintable GTS with the PLS, and specifically by mapping the Element class to the NamedElement class, thus giving the tainted attribute to all named elements of the PLS. Given the PLS GTS defined as

```
gts PLS {
  metamodel: "pls"
  behaviour: "plsRules"
}
```

we can instantiate the Taintable generic GTS just by providing the GTS morphism ITaintable2PLS from the GTS interface_of {Taintable} to the PLS GTS that maps the class Element to the class NamedElement as shown in Listing 9.5. Notice the use of the allow-from-empty directive. GTS morphisms require injective and surjective mappings between the two rule sets. That is, for each rule in the target GTS—the PLS in this case—we need a rule in the source GTS. Since there are no rules in the interface of the Taintable GTS, empty rules are used instead. To simplify the exhaustive definition of these mappings, the combined use of the allow-from-empty and auto-complete directives automatically generates all these required mappings.

Given the ITaintable2PLS morphism and the inclusion of the interface of Taintable into itself, the amalgamation GTS TaintablePLS is constructed as shown in Listing 9.6.

```
export gts TaintablePLS {
  weave(dontLabelNonKernelElements , preferMap2TargetNames ): {
    map1: interface_of (Taintable )
    map2: ITaintable2PLS
  }
}
```

Listing 9.6   Constructing TaintablePLS

The TaintablePLS GTS is as the PLS GTS but with an additional attribute tainted in the NamedElement class, which is inherited by all its subclasses, which can now be "tainted".

9.4.2   Adding Taint Propagation

The following step is to instantiate the KAMP GTS with the PLS using different mapping morphisms specifying the different links on which we want to propagate the tainting. Notice that now the tainted attribute is part of the interface, and therefore, it will be mapped into the homonymous attribute in the TaintedPLS GTS. In what follows we are going to carry on several instantiations to illustrate different cases.

The KAMP GTS Family

Assume we are interested in specifying change propagation due to the parts being generated. If a machine changes, the tray on which the parts generated by it are placed requires change. The transformers taking parts from such trays, as well as operators, will also need to adjust to change. This change needs to be propagated along the structure of specific instance models, since the change required by a machine implies the change on a subsequent tray, which changes transformers and operators taking parts from them. In turn, change in these transformers, which are themselves machines, will require change in subsequent trays, transformers, and operators. Notice however that the conveyors between machines and trays do not require change, since they are just moving bands to transport objects. Given the nature of the KAMP approach, tainting may be propagated as required using the relations between these elements. First, we need to define the KAMP GTS:

```
gts kampGTS {
  metamodel: "kamp"
  behaviour: "kampRules"
}
```

However, these relations are not always direct, nor mimic the pattern provided by the KAMP rules. In other words, no morphism can directly be defined for any of these links, and therefore all these instantiations require the introduction of GTS transformers through appropriate GTS families.

Consider for example the in association of the Machine class. In the KAMP's propagation rule, the tainting goes from Source to Target, whilst we are interested in the opposite direction for the in association of the Transformer class, since we want it to propagate from the tray objects to the subsequent transformers taking pieces from them. The same situation is found for the tray association of the Operator class. Moreover, the multiplicity of this association is 0..*, whilst the target association of the Source class in KAMP's metamodel (see Fig. 9.5) has multiplicity 0..1. Finally, the relation between a machine and its subsequent tray is not direct, since it happens through an intermediate conveyor. Of course, we could define a more general metamodel with alternative cases and corresponding alternative rules, but we do not need to. This is precisely the reason for transformers and families, to be able to specify the nature of an abstraction as the one provided by KAMP, manage the variability of situations through transformers, and then adjust the source GTS so that the instantiation may take place.

Figures 9.8, 9.9, and 9.10 define several transformer rules. The addPathElement transformer allows us to introduce an intermediary class between the source and target classes; the reverseReference transformer allows us to reverse a link; and adjustMultiplicity allows us to change the multiplicity of a link. Although some familiarity with Henshin's metamodel and with its way of specifying transformation rules is required to understand them, these rules just define changes on the metamodels and rules of the GTSs on which they are applied. For example, the adjustMultiplicity rule just specifies a change in the multiplicities of the reference specified as parameter. The most complex one of these three transformers is the addPathElement one. Given an EReference instance srcRef, between a source class srcClass and a target class tgtClass, it introduces a new class newClass as target of srcRef, and a new reference newRef from this newClass to tgtClass. Correspondingly, all those rules in which the reference appears are modified introducing new intermediate nodes of class newClass appropriately linked.

The KAMP family is then defined as the family of GTSs reachable from the KAMP GTS using the transformer rules. In general, one would want to provide a set of general transformers and expect the *GTSMorpher* tool to search for the right version of the source GTS so that the instantiation may take place. Instead, here, we explicitly control the application of transformers as pointed out above.

```
gts_family KAMPFamily {
  kampGTS
  transformers: "transformerRules"
}
```

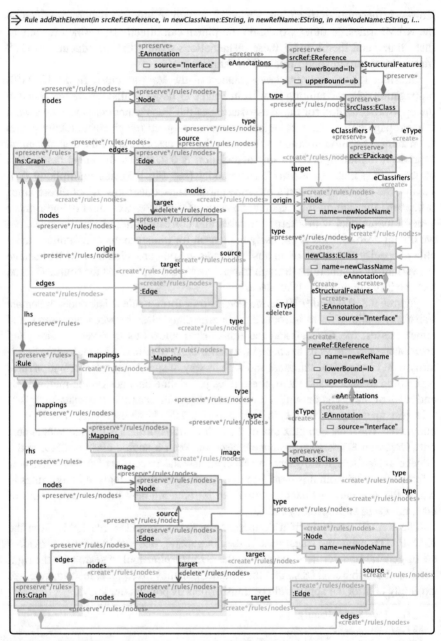

Fig. 9.8 addPathElement transformer (transformerRules)

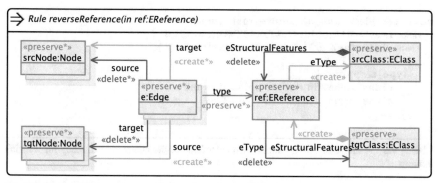

Fig. 9.9 reverseReference transformer (transformerRules)

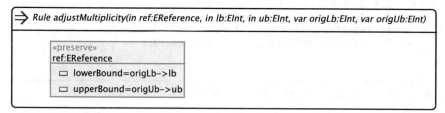

Fig. 9.10 adjustMultiplicity transformer (transformerRules)

Instantiating the Propagation Rules

To propagate the tainting from a machine to its subsequent tray, we can use the addPathElement transformer. Basically, this transformer modifies the source GTS by introducing a new class between two classes linked by some association and updates any rules referencing this association. This transformer takes as arguments the name of the association to operate on, plus identifiers for the new class, reference and node, together with the multiplicity for the additional association. The following GTS PatternMachineOutTray (cf. Listing 9.7) is the result of applying this transformer on the target association of the Source class using the addPathElement transformer of the KAMPFamily family.

```
export gts PatternMachineOutTray {
   family: KAMPFamily
     using [
        addPathElement(kamp.Source.target, "newClass", "newRef",
        "newNode", 0, 1)
     ]
}
```

Listing 9.7 Constructing PatternMachineOutTray

```
auto−complete unique allow−from−empty
  map IPatternMachineOutTray2TaintablePLS {
  from interface_of { PatternMachineOutTray }
  to TaintablePLS
    type_mapping {
      class kamp.Source => pls.Machine
      class kamp.Target => pls.Tray
    }
}
```

Listing 9.8 A morphism from PatternMachineOutTray to the taintable PLS, ready for weaving tainting

```
export gts TaintedPLSMachineOutTray {
  weave ( dontLabelNonKernelElements , preferMap2TargetNames ): {
    map1: interface_of ( PatternMachineOutTray )
    map2: IPatternMachineOutTray2TaintablePLS
  }
}
```

Listing 9.9 Constructing TaintedPLSMachineOutTray

All elements in KAMPS's metamodel are annotated as interface. New elements introduced by transformers are also annotated as interfaces. To construct new GTSs as a result of the amalgamation of previously defined GTSs, we need to define morphisms from a kernel interface to the system on which we wish to act, in this case the TaintablePLS GTS that resulted from the previous amalgamation. The instantiating morphism can now be defined from the interface of the PatternMachineOutTray GTS to the TaintablePLS GTS as shown in Listing 9.8.

Notice the use of the auto-complete directive, with which the mapping for other elements in the interface sub-GTS is automatically calculated. In particular, notice that we do not need to provide an explicit mapping for the new path element introduced. Notice also the use of the allow-from-empty directive as above.

We can now amalgamate this morphism and the inclusion of the interface of the PatternMachineOutTray GTS into itself to generate the TaintedPLSMachineOutTray GTS as shown in Listing 9.9.

The in link of the Transformer class goes from Transformer into Tray. However, we want the tainting to propagate following the inverse direction. We can get the required instantiation of the propagation rule by using the reverseReference transformer rule to reverse the link in the source rule. As before, once the source GTS is obtained we can define the morphism and then the amalgamation GTS (cf. Listing 9.10).

The tray link of the Operator class presents a new challenge. So far, we just needed to apply one transformer to be able to build the required morphism, but in this case, we need to both reverse the link and change its multiplicity. We just need

```
export gts PatternTransformerIn {
  family : KAMPFamily
  using [
    reverseReference (kamp.Source.target)
  ]
}

auto−complete unique allow−from−empty
  map PatternTransformerIn2PLSMachineOutTray {
  from interface_of{PatternTransformerIn}
  to TaintedPLSMachineOutTray
  type_mapping {
    class kamp.Target => pls.Transformer
    class kamp.Source => pls.Tray
  }
}

export gts TaintedPLSTransformerIn {
  weave(dontLabelNonKernelElements , preferMap2TargetNames ): {
    map1 : interface_of (PatternTransformerIn)
    map2 : PatternTransformerIn2PLSMachineOutTray
  }
}
```

Listing 9.10   Construction of the TaintedPLSTransformerIn GTS

to specify the sequence of transformers that lead to the intended target as shown in Listing 9.11.

9.4.3   The Final Taint-Propagating PLS

After the consecutive instantiation of the Taintable GTS and of the KAMP GTS on the specific links specified in the morphisms, we get an extended PLS GTS in which the metamodel includes a tainted attribute in the NamedElement class and propagation rules propagating the tainting along the links between named elements. The extended PLS protects the semantics of the original PLS language, but in addition it now provides this additional functionality to identify the part of the model affected by any potential change as specified. In addition to the original rules in Fig. 9.2, the extended PLS GTS now also includes the rules depicted in Fig. 9.11. The application of these rules on an instance model in which some element is tainted, specifying a change, would result in an instance model in which all elements affected by the change are tainted, in accordance to the specified tainting propagation rules.

```
export gts PatternConveyorTray {
  family: KAMPFamily
  using [
    adjustMultiplicity (kamp.Source.target, 0, -1),
    reverseReference (kamp.Source.target)
  ]
}

auto-complete unique allow-from-empty
  map PatternOperatorTray2TaintedPLSConveyorTray {
  from interface_of{PatternConveyorTray}
  to TaintedPLSTransformerIn
  type_mapping {
    class kamp.Source => pls.Tray
    class kamp.Target => pls.Operator
  }
}

export gts TaintedPLSOperatorTray {
  weave(dontLabelNonKernelElements, preferMap2TargetNames): {
    map1: interface_of(PatternConveyorTray)
    map2: PatternOperatorTray2TaintedPLSConveyorTray
  }
}
```

Listing 9.11 Constructing TaintedPLSOperatorTray

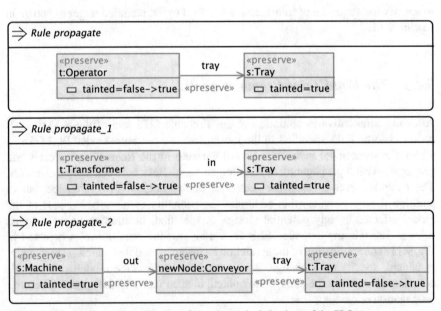

Fig. 9.11 The amalgamation adds these four rules to the behaviour of the PLS

9.5   Conclusions and Outlook

In this chapter, we have shown a tool and case study showing how the explicit specification of a language's operational semantics with graph transformations can make
it possible to reuse analysis techniques for different domain-specific modelling
languages. This approach allows the reuse of analysis techniques across different
domain-specific languages reducing the effort required for different domains to
benefit from particular analysis expertise. Because it enables a modular approach
to analysis (as discussed also in Chaps. 4 and 5 of this book [Hei+21]), different
analyses can be combined into one modelling language, so that different analyses
can be enabled depending on what a project requires.

References

[AL94]   Martin Abadi and Leslie Lamport. "An Old-Fashioned Recipe for Real Time". In: *ACM
          Transactions on Programming Languages and Systems* 16.5 (Sept. 1994), pp. 1543–
          1571.
[Cor+97] Andrea Corradini, Ugo Montanari, Francesca Rossi, Hartmut Ehrig, Reiko Heckel,
          and Michael Löwe. "Algebraic approaches to graph transformation I: Basic concepts
          and double pushout approach". In: *Handbook of Graph Grammars and Computing by
          Graph Transformation, Volume 1: Foundations*. 1997. Chap. 3.
[DMC12]   Zinovy Diskin, Tom Maibaum, and Krzysztof Czarnecki. "Intermodeling, Queries, and
          Kleisli Categories". In: *Conf. Fundamental Approaches to Software Engineering*. 2012,
          pp. 163–177. https://doi.org/10.1007/978-3-642-28872-2_12.
[Dur+17] Francisco Durán, Antonio Moreno-Delgado, Fernando Orejas, and Steffen Zschaler.
          "Amalgamation of Domain Specific Languages with Behaviour". In: *Journal of Logical
          and Algebraic Methods in Programming* 86 (1 2017), pp. 208–235. https://doi.org/10.
          1016/j.jlamp.2015.09.005.
[DZT13]   Francisco Durán, Steffen Zschaler, and Javier Troya. "On the Reusable Specification
          of Non-functional Properties in DSLs". In: *5th Int'l Conf. on Software Language
          Engineering, SLE. 2013*, pp. 332–351. https://doi.org/10.1007/978-3-642-36089-3_19.
[EHC05]   Gregor Engels, Reiko Heckel, and Alexey Cherchago. "Flexible Interconnection
          of Graph Transformation Modules". In: *Formal Methods in Software and Systems
          Modeling*. 2005, pp. 38–63. https://doi.org/10.1007/978-3-540-31847-7_3.
[Ehr+06] Hartmut Ehrig, Karsten Ehrig, Ulrike Prange, and Gabriele Taentzer. *Fundamentals
          of Algebraic Graph Transformation*. Springer, 2006. https://doi.org/10.1007/3-540-
          31188-2.
[Ehr79]   Hartmut Ehrig. "Introduction to the algebraic theory of graph grammars". In: *1st Graph
          Grammar Workshop*. 1979, pp. 1–69. https://doi.org/10.1007/BFb0025714.
[Eng+97] Gregor Engels, Reiko Heckel, Gabriele Taentzer, and Hartmut Ehrig. "A Combined
          Reference Model- and View-Based Approach to System Specification". In: *Interna-
          tional Journal of Software Engineering and Knowledge Engineering* 7.4 (1997), pp.
          457–477. https://doi.org/10.1142/S0218194097000266.
[GM04]   Vincenzo Grassi and Raffaela Mirandola. "A Model-driven Approach to Predictive Non
          Functional Analysis of Component-based Systems". In: *Proc. Workshop on Models for
          Non-Functional Aspects of Component-Based Software*. 2004.

[GPS98a] Martin Große-Rhode, Francesco Parisi-Presicce, and Marta Simeoni. "Refinements of Graph Transformation Systems via Rule Expressions". In: *6th Int'l Workshop Theory and Application of Graph Transformations*. 1998, pp. 368–382. https://doi.org/10.1007/978-3-540-46464-8_26.

[GPS98b] Martin Große-Rhode, Francesco Parisi-Presicce, and Marta Simeoni. "Spatial and Temporal Refinement of Typed Graph Transformation Systems". In: *23rd Int'l Symposium Mathematical Foundations of Computer Science*. 1998, pp. 553–561. https://doi.org/10.1007/BFb0055805.

[Hei+21] Robert Heinrich, Francisco Durán, Carolyn L. Talcott, and Steffen Zschaler (eds.) *Composing Model-Based Analysis Tools*. Springer, 2021. https://doi.org/10.1007/978-3-030-81915-6.

[Joh+19] Stefan John, Alexandru Burdusel, Robert Bill, Daniel Strüber, Gabriele Taentzer, Steffen Zschaler, and Manuel Wimmer. "Searching for Optimal Models: Comparing Two Encoding Approaches". In: *Journal of Object Technology* 18.3 (2019), 6:1–22. https://doi.org/10.5381/jot.2019.18.3.a6.

[Lam94] Leslie Lamport. "A Temporal Logic of Actions". In: *ACM Transactions on Programming Languages and Systems* 16.3 (1994), pp. 872–923.

[Lar+07] Juan de Lara, Roswitha Bardohl, Hartmut Ehrig, Karsten Ehrig, Ulrike Prange, and Gabriele Taentzer. "Attributed Graph Transformation with Node Type Inheritance". In: *Theoretical Computer Science* 376 (2007), pp. 139–163. https://doi.org/10.1016/j.tcs.2007.02.001.

[LG13] Juan de Lara and Esther Guerra. "From Types to Type Requirements: Genericity for Model-Driven Engineering". In: *Software and Systems Modelling* 12.3 (2013), pp. 453–474. https://doi.org/10.1007/s10270-011-0221-0.

[LG14] Juan de Lara and Esther Guerra. "Towards the flexible reuse of model transformations: A formal approach based on graph transformation". In: *Journal of Logical and Algebraic Methods in Programming* 83.5–6 (2014). 24th Nordic Workshop on Programming Theory (NWPT 2012), pp. 427–458. issn: 2352-2208. https://doi.org/10.1016/j.jlamp.2014.08.005.

[Mor+14] Antonio Moreno-Delgado, Francisco Durán, Steffen Zschaler, and Javier Troya. "Modular DSLs for Flexible Analysis: An e-Motions Reimplementation of Palladio". In: *Proc. 10th European Conf. on Modelling Foundations and Applications)*. 2014, pp. 132–147. https://doi.org/10.1007/978-3-319-09195-2_9.

[Nau86] Peter Naur. "Programming as Theory Building". In: *Microprocessing and Microprogramming* 15 (1986), pp. 253–261. https://doi.org/10.1016/0165-6074(85)90032-8.

[Reu+16] Ralf H. Reussner, Steffen Becker, Jens Happe, Robert Heinrich, Anne Koziolek, Heiko Koziolek, Max Kramer, and Klaus Krogmann. *Modeling and Simulating Software Architectures: The Palladio Approach*. MIT Press, 2016.

[Ros+15] Kiana Rostami, Johannes Stammel, Robert Heinrich, and Ralf H. Reussner. "Architecture-based Assessment and Planning of Change Requests". In: *11th International ACM SIGSOFT Conference on Quality of Software Architectures*. 2015, pp. 21–30. https://doi.org/10.1145/2737182.2737198.

[Ste+09] Dave Steinberg, Frank Budinsky, Marcelo Paternostro, and Ed Merks. EMF: *Eclipse Modeling Framework*. Addison-Wesley Professional, 2009.

[Str+17] Daniel Strüber, Kristopher Born, Kanwal Daud Gill, Raffaela Groner, Timo Kehrer, Manuel Ohrndorf, and Matthias Tichy. "Henshin: A Usability-Focused Framework for EMF Model Transformation Development". In: *10th Int'l Conf on Graph Transformations*. 2017, pp. 196–208.

[Tro+13] Javier Troya, Antonio Vallecillo, Francisco Durán, and Steffen Zschaler. "Model-Driven Performance Analysis of Rule-Based Domain Specific Visual Models". In: *Information and Software Technology* 55.1 (2013), pp. 88–110. https://doi.org/10.1016/j.infsof.2012.07.009.

[War94] Martin P.Ward. "Language-oriented programming". In: *Software-Concepts and Tools* 15.4 (1994), pp. 147–161. URL: http://www.gkc.org.uk/martin/papers/middle-out-t. pdf.

[ZD17] Steffen Zschaler and Francisco Durán. "GTS Families for the Flexible Composition of Graph Transformation Systems". In: *20th Int'l Conf. Fundamental Approaches to Software Engineering*. 2017, pp. 208–225. https://doi.org/10.1007/978-3-662-54494-5_12.

Chapter 10
Compositional Modelling Languages with Analytics and Construction Infrastructures Based on Object-Oriented Techniques—The MontiCore Approach

Arvid Butting, Katrin Hölldobler, Bernhard Rumpe, and Andreas Wortmann

Abstract Composing modelling languages and analysis tools still require significant efforts to properly consider syntax and semantics as well as related analyses and syntheses. This composition ideally should be defined on individual language components that can be composed when needed. Only when model-based analysis infrastructures can be composed in accordance to their related language definitions and can be reused in a black-box fashion without modification, can we foster automation in language engineering and integration. In this chapter, we demonstrate object-oriented language engineering concepts that enable composing models of heterogeneous languages using the language workbench MontiCore. This composition includes the concrete syntax and abstract syntax as well as analysis infrastructures and analyses. We demonstrate in detail how the MontiCore infrastructure enables (de)composing languages and related model-based analysis techniques such that the analyses can be reused with other languages with minimal effort. Several of the provided techniques are based on adaptations of the well-known concepts of object-oriented development, such as inheritance and the extension and the visitor patterns. This can reduce the effort of engineering truly domain-specific modelling languages significantly.

This case-study chapter illustrates concepts introduced in Chap. 4 and addresses Challenge 1 in Chap. 3 of this book.

A. Butting · K. Hölldobler · B. Rumpe (✉)
RWTH Aachen, Aachen, Germany
e-mail: butting@se-rwth.de; hoelldobler@se-rwth.de; rumpe@se-rwth.de

A. Wortmann
Universität Stuttgart, Stuttgart, Germany
e-mail: andreas.wortmann@isw.uni-stuttgart.de

217

10.1   Introduction

Many engineering domains moved to use explicit modelling languages to enable domain experts to contribute to the engineering of systems. Ideally, these modelling languages and their parts can be reused in and tailored to different contexts, such that deploying precise *domain-specific modelling languages* (DSMLs) becomes less challenging. Despite efforts in software language engineering [Kle08, HRW18], the composition of modelling languages, especially their analyses and syntheses, is far from solved in general (cf. Chap. 3 of this book [Hei+21]) and still requires significant manual efforts. This hinders the deployment of the most suitable domain-specific modelling languages for experts, who instead have to cope with overly generic modelling languages, such as the *unified modeling language* (UML) [Obj15] or the *systems modeling language* (SysML) [Obj12], and tailor these through profiles or modelling guidelines. Both introduce a conceptual gap [FR07] between the experts' problem domain of discourse (e.g., material science, kinematics, geometry) and the solution domain of software engineering through which the domain experts need to work around the limitations of these languages.

The efforts for efficiently engineering DSMLs can be reduced if the languages support modularity and their infrastructure follows this modularity. When the infrastructure for analyses is derived in ways that foster modularity, composition of this infrastructure can be automated as well. This eases reusing DSML (parts) and their analysis in the context of other languages and can foster the application of DSMLs in general. In this chapter, we therefore demonstrate core concepts to compose models from heterogeneous sublanguages. This includes the syntax (concrete and abstract) as well as the infrastructures to define the syntax and the analyses to operate on these composed languages. We demonstrate in detail how the MontiCore infrastructure allows to decompose a number of analysis techniques, both for functional and for extra-functional properties.

The contributions of this chapter, hence, are:

- A method for engineering modelling languages based on modular syntax definitions
- Generation of a visitor-based framework for modular model-based analyses
- Families of modular languages for expressions and literals

In the remainder, Sect. 10.2 introduces MontiCore, before Sect. 10.3 applies it to engineering modular languages and analysis infrastructures. Section 10.4 highlights related work, and Sect. 10.5 discusses our approach. Section 10.6 concludes.

10.2 Preliminaries

This section introduces the MontiCore [HR17] language workbench [Erd+15] and its features used for engineering compositional languages as explained in subsequent sections.

MontiCore is a language workbench that provides an EBNF-like grammar format to define languages from which it generates much of the infrastructure necessary to efficiently engineer modular languages. It has been applied to the engineering of modelling languages for a variety of domains, including automotive [Dra+19], cloud services [Eik+17], robotics [Ada+17b], systems engineering [Dal+19], and more.

For a given grammar, MontiCore generates infrastructure for the language. This includes parser and lexer, Java classes for the *abstract syntax tree* (AST), an infrastructure to implement context conditions (language well-formedness rules), visitors [Hei+16] to develop and compose analyses, and symbol tables [HMR15, MRR15, MRR16] to combine models of different languages. The general procedure to process a model is depicted in Fig. 10.1. First, the model is transferred to its internal representation, i.e., the AST, by the parser and lexer. Next, the AST is processed by functions, which can include well-formedness checks, analyses, or transformations. The resulting AST as well as the analysis results are used to produce the output, which can be generated code, models, or analysis reports.

A MontiCore grammar defines the abstract and concrete syntax of a language. It consists of productions that define nonterminals. A production consists of a *left-hand side* (LHS) and a *right-hand side* (RHS) separated by an = sign. The LHS is the nonterminal that the production defines, while the RHS is the production's body and defines both the abstract and concrete syntax. Figure 10.2 depicts a MontiCore grammar of a compact language for finite automata, while Fig. 10.3 shows a corresponding automaton model. This grammar consists of three productions defining the nonterminals Automaton, State, and Transition. MontiCore generates one AST class for each production. Its attributes are defined by the production body. Stored terminals map to attributes, while nonterminal usages map to compositions.

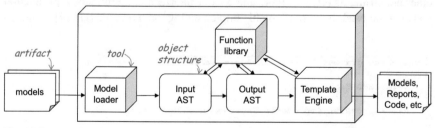

Fig. 10.1 MontiCore's tool chain for processing models comprises fully generated components (parser, lexer, etc.) and modular infrastructures for tools that are handcrafted (well-formedness rules, model transformations)

```
1  grammar Automata extends ExpressionsBasis,
2                            CommonLiterals {
3    Automaton = "automaton" Name "{"
4                 (State | Transition)* "}" ;
5
6
7    State = ["initial"]? ["final"]? "state" Name ";";
8
9    Transition = from:Name "-" ("[" guard:Expression "]")?
10                 input:Name ">" to:Name ";";
   }
```

Fig. 10.2 Exemplary grammar of an automata language

```
1  automata PingPong {
2    initial state Ping;
3    state Pong;
4
5    Ping - [ballHit] returnBall > Pong;
6
7    Pong - returnBall > Ping;
   }
```

Fig. 10.3 Exemplary automaton for the language of Fig. 10.2

The body of a production consists of terminals and nonterminals. Terminals are surrounded by quotation marks, e.g., `"automaton"` in line 3 of Fig. 10.2. Both terminals and nonterminals can have different multiplicities, i.e., by appending a question mark ? it becomes optional, while * allows arbitrarily many (including zero) occurrences and + enforces at least one occurrence. Alternatives are separated by |, and grouping can be achieved by parenthesising parts using round brackets. Terminals whose presence is relevant for the abstract syntax can be parenthesised in square brackets, yielding a Boolean attribute in the abstract syntax. Optionals are mapped to Java optionals and multiple occurrences to Java lists.

Besides "normal" nonterminals, MontiCore provides interface, abstract, and external nonterminals. Abstract and external nonterminals are not detailed here, but detailed information on these is available in [HR17]. Interface nonterminals are marked using the keyword interface (cf. Fig. 10.4, line 3). They do not specify concrete syntax themselves. Instead, interface nonterminals are implemented by other nonterminals (cf. Fig. 10.4, line 5). For interface nonterminals, a production body can be used to restrict possible implementing nonterminals [HR17]. Concep-

```
1  component grammar ExpressionsBasis extends LiteralsBasis {
2
3    interface Expression;
4
5    NameExpression implements Expression<350> = Name;
6
7
8    LiteralExpression implements Expression<340> = Literal;
   }
```

Fig. 10.4 Component grammar providing basic syntax elements for expressions

tually, interface nonterminals are an extension of alternatives. Whenever interface nonterminals are used in a production body, every interface implementation is possible. Thus, instead of A = B | C; one can use interface nonterminals to define interface A; B implements A; C implements A;. The concrete syntax for these two examples does not differ. However, for interface nonterminals, an AST interface instead of a class is generated and the relation between A and B and A and C is mapped to inheritance instead of composition in the abstract syntax.

Using MontiCore, languages can be developed efficiently by reusing the modular (parts of) other languages. To this end, MontiCore provides grammar extension mechanisms. As depicted in Fig. 10.2 line 1, the grammar of the automata language already uses this concept. By using the keyword extends followed by one or multiple comma-separated grammars, a grammar can extend other grammars. As a consequence, all nonterminals defined by productions of the inherited grammars (also referred to as super grammars) are available in the current grammar. In the automata language, this is used for the transition production as it uses the nonterminals Expression that is not defined locally but defined in the super grammar ExpressionsBasis. If a grammar is designed for reuse only and does not define a language itself, it can and should be marked as a component grammar by adding the keyword component (cf. Fig. 10.4, line 1).

The start nonterminal of a grammar is by default the first nonterminal in the grammar [HR17]. However, there are situations in which this is not feasible, e.g., when extending an existing grammar and one of its nonterminals should be the start nonterminal of the currently developed language. To address this, it is possible to configure the start nonterminal explicitly as follows: start State. In this case, State is used as the start nonterminal.

When extending a grammar, it is possible to extend productions of the super grammars. This is possible for normal as well as for interface productions. In both cases, conceptually a new alternative to the existing body resp. implementations is created. Thus, all nonterminals and especially interface nonterminals can serve as extension points. To further control the priority of the newly added alternative, it is possible to add a priority in angle brackets (cf. Fig. 10.4, line 5). The higher the number within the brackets, the higher is the alternative's priority in the generated parser.

10.3 Compositional Language Engineering

MontiCore provides means to support modular definition of languages and means to realise language composition [HR17]. Modularisation fosters language reusability and reduces co-evolution, as the commonalities in different languages can be extracted to individual language modules that multiple languages rely on.

Grammar inheritance can be leveraged to decompose the syntax of a language into modules (cf. Sect. 10.2). Further, MontiCore supports the definition of component grammars to indicate that a grammar contains a reusable collection of pieces of syntax rather than a complete language. For instance, the automata grammar presented in Fig. 10.2 uses grammar inheritance to decouple the definitions of the automata language syntax in terms of states and transitions from the syntax of expressions and of literals. This is realised by extending the grammars ExpressionsBasis and CommonLiterals. A language module, also referred to as language component, is defined by its grammar but also contains all artefacts generated from the grammar, all handwritten extensions to the generated artefacts, and handwritten language tooling such as, e.g., model-based analyses. Therefore, modularisation has to be carried out for all these constituents as well.

As describing modular analyses on languages requires modular language syntax, the following first introduces some of MontiCore's means for modular grammar definitions, before introducing the modular visitor infrastructure. Afterwards, the application of this infrastructure for modular analyses is demonstrated by example.

10.3.1 Modular Syntax Definition

Expressions, types, literals, and statements are typical elements in modelling or programming languages. However, every language requires a well-suited variant of these concepts. Thus, these concepts are natural candidates for being encapsulated into individual language components that can be reused by any language.

To facilitate this, MontiCore offers a multitude of modular base grammars each of which contributes syntax to define expressions, literals statements, or types. Figs. 10.4, 10.5, 10.6, and 10.7 demonstrate this concept. The ExpressionsBasis (Fig. 10.4) and CommonExpressions (Fig. 10.5) grammars provide syntax for expressions.

```
1  component grammar CommonExpressions extends ExpressionsBasis {
2
3    LogicalNotExpression implements Expression <190> =
4      "!" Expression;
5
6
7    PlusExpression implements Expression <170> =
8      left:Expression operator:"+" right:Expression;
9
10   EqualsExpression implements Expression <130> =
11     left:Expression operator:"==" right:Expression;
   }
```

Fig. 10.5 Component grammar describing the syntax of basic expressions

```
1  component grammar LiteralsBasis  {
2    interface Literal;
3  }
```

Fig. 10.6 Grammar providing a syntax extension point for literals

```
1  component grammar CommonLiterals extends LiteralsBasis {
2
3    BooleanLiteral implements Literal =
4      source:["true" | "false"];
5
6
7    SignedNatLiteral implements Literal =
8      (negative:["-"])? Digits;
}
```

Fig. 10.7 Basic Boolean and integer literals

The ExpressionsBasis grammar is a component grammar providing building blocks for the syntax of expressions. At its core, it contains an interface nonterminal Expression acting as extension point for different syntactical constructs that realise expressions. ExpressionsBasis only provides the syntax for names (cf. NameExpression) and values (cf. LiteralsExpression). Name (not depicted) is a token for Java-like identifiers, such as Java method names. Literal is an inherited interface nonterminal provided by LiteralsBasis (cf. Fig. 10.6), which only provides this interface nonterminal but no implementations. Thus, the decision what kind of literals are used and how these are defined is delayed to further grammars extending the ExpressionsBasis grammar.

CommonExpressions extends ExpressionsBasis and adds three novel implementations to the Expression nonterminal providing syntax for some basic expressions. While the LogicalNotExpression and EqualsExpression are commonly used for Boolean expressions, the PlusExpression is commonly used for number expressions. However, it can also be used to represent, e.g., String concatenation. These grammars define only the syntax of the expression; their evaluation is performed at a later stage in language processing.

All three grammar productions in the grammar for common expressions introduce potential left recursion through inheritance with the interface nonterminal Expression. MontiCore can handle the ambiguity introduced by this left recursion, inter alia, through the parser priorities (cf. Sect. 10.2). The grammar CommonLiterals (cf. Fig. 10.7) extends the LiteralsBasis and introduces Boolean literals (ll. 3–4) and integer literals (ll.6–7).

An example of how to use ExpressionsBasis and add pre-built Literal implementations is presented in Fig. 10.2. The automata grammar extends both the ExpressionBasis grammar and the CommonLiterals. Through this multiple inheritance, the Literal nonterminal in the ExpressionsBasis grammar is implemented by the nonterminals introduced in CommonLiterals. An excerpt of the AST data structure that MontiCore produces from the grammar Automata is depicted in Fig. 10.8. As a result of this extension, true and false as well as integer numbers can be used in guards of an automaton through the LiteralExpression.

Other possible extensions are to either add further implementations of interface nonterminals Expression or Literal in the automata grammar or use further pre-built grammars that provide additional implementation such as CommonExpressions. Figure 10.9 gives an overview of MontiCore's pre-built grammars for expressions,

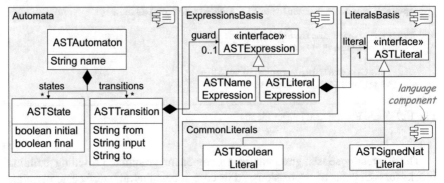

Fig. 10.8 Excerpt from the AST generated from the Automata grammar

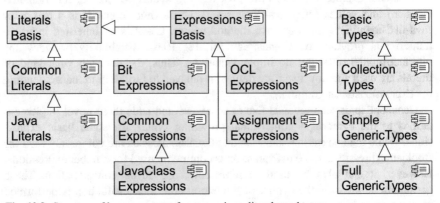

Fig. 10.9 Structure of base grammars for expressions, literals, and types

literals, and types. Types and literals grammars each are in a linear inheritance relationship, where each grammar extends the syntax provided by their parent grammar conservatively [HR17]. To this end, if a language uses types (or literals), it can be post hoc extended with more syntax for types (or literals) by additionally inheriting from a grammar that (transitively) extends the type (or literal) grammar that was originally used.

The various application purposes for expressions prevent a linear inheritance hierarchy for expression grammars: For example, it should be possible for a language to use only the syntax for assignment expressions without bit expressions (which include, e.g., shift operators). At the same time, other languages should be able to use only bit expressions without assignment expressions. However, all expression grammars extend the basis grammar for expressions, and all syntax these add is available by implementing the Expression interface. Therefore, through multiple inheritance with different expression grammars, a combination of expression syntaxes can be made available as well.

In summary, the essence for modular syntax definitions as suggested in this approach is to provide a grammar that only provides an interface nonterminal (in the following called interface grammar). An interface grammar can be extended by other grammars. Hereby, two kinds of extensions are conceivable: (1) Grammars extending the interface grammar can provide further pre-built syntax options that other languages can use. (2) Through inheriting from the interface grammar, a language can delay the decision, which implementations should be used. Languages engineers, thus, can design grammars that extend those interface grammars and by this, specify that some sort of literals, statements, or types are used within their developed language and where they are used. Later, this is resolved through multiple inheritance from this language and the grammar(s) that extend(s) the interface grammars for, e.g., literals, statements, or types. For example, the ExpressionsBasis extends the LiteralsBasis, but through multiple inheritance in the Automata grammar (cf. Fig. 10.2), expressions used in automata can use literals provided by Common-Literals.

Figure 10.10 provides two example language components that utilise the language components shown in Fig. 10.9. RoboJAction is a domain-specific language for modelling actions in the context of service robotics applications similar to this approach [Ada+17a]. The language lends notation elements from Java but only supports basic types, literals of reduced complexity as well as a subset of possible expression implementations. These notation elements are reused by inheriting from several language components. The language further introduces novel syntax elements for realising domain-specific concepts.

The second example is the *object constraint language* (OCL) that combines the language components CommonLiterals, BitExpressions,

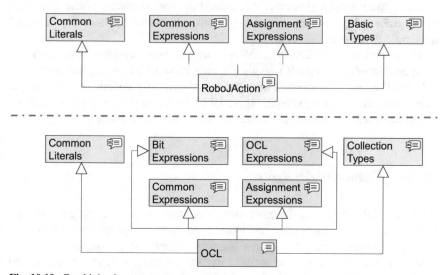

Fig. 10.10 Combining base grammars

`AssignmentExpressions`, `CommonExpression`, `OCLExpressions`, and `CollectionTypes`. `JavaLight` and an `OCL` are considered as complete modelling languages. However, in case more complex types, literals, or expressions are needed, it is possible to extend those languages and combine them with additional language components such as `SimpleGenericTypes` or `JavaLiterals`.

10.3.2 Modular Analysis Infrastructure

The modularity for syntax presented in the previous section would be of limited use without modularity in analyses, transformations, and further operations implemented against the syntax. For this purpose, MontiCore generates composable visitors [Hei+16]. From each grammar, a Visitor interface prefixed with the name of the grammar is generated. This interface provides four methods handle, visit, traverse, and endVisit for each nonterminal of the given grammar. A depth-first traversal of the AST of the grammar is already included via default implementations of the handle and traverse methods. The handle methods encapsulate the handling of the nonterminals and call the corresponding visit, traverse, and endVisit methods for the nonterminals. The traverse method is responsible for traversing child nodes of the nonterminal. To implement an analysis for models of a given language, language engineers can focus on implementing the analysis using the visit and endVisit methods. By default, visit and endVisit methods have an empty default implementation and only have to be implemented if it is intended to use these for the implementation of the analysis. The visitor interfaces provide methods for the current grammar only. However, they extend the corresponding visitor interfaces of all extended grammars, and through this, all visitor methods for inherited nonterminals are available as well.

In addition to visitor interfaces, MontiCore generates delegator visitors that are composed of other visitors. These visitors only handle the traversal themselves but delegate the visit and endVisit to registered visitors. By default, one visitor per super grammar can be registered. Figure 10.11 depicts the visitor interface and the delegator visitor that MontiCore generated for the automata grammar in Fig. 10.2.

10.3.3 Composed Analyses

With the modular analysis infrastructure, MontiCore enables language engineers both (1) to describe monolithic analyses across different syntax modules and (2) to reuse analyses as part of reusing a language component. A monolithic analysis across modular syntax can be realised by implementing a visitor interface and using the visitor methods of all (including inherited) nonterminals. This kind of analysis, thus, enables to optionally reuse all visitor infrastructure parts from

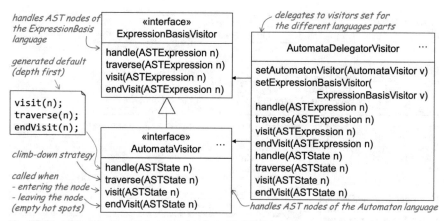

handles AST nodes of the ExpressionBasis language

generated default (depth first)

```
visit(n);
traverse(n);
endVisit(n);
```

climb-down strategy

called when
- entering the node
- leaving the node
(empty hot spots)

«interface»
ExpressionBasisVisitor

handle(ASTExpression n)
traverse(ASTExpression n)
visit(ASTExpression n)
endVisit(ASTExpression n)

«interface»
AutomataVisitor ...

handle(ASTState n)
traverse(ASTState n)
visit(ASTState n)
endVisit(ASTState n)

delegates to visitors set for the different languages parts

AutomataDelegatorVisitor ...

setAutomatonVisitor(AutomataVisitor v)
setExpressionBasisVisitor(
                ExpressionBasisVisitor v)
handle(ASTExpression n)
traverse(ASTExpression n)
visit(ASTExpression n)
endVisit(ASTExpression n)
handle(ASTState n)
traverse(ASTState n)
visit(ASTState n)
endVisit(ASTState n)

handles AST nodes of the Automaton language

Fig. 10.11 Visitors generated for the example in Fig. 10.2

inherited language components while being able to override and customise parts of it whenever this is required or desired. A monolithic analysis is specifically suitable in situations in which the kind of analysis that is required from inherited language parts has a low potential for being reused in different contexts. If analysis parts that operate on inherited language parts are intended to be reused in a different context, we recommend to realise such parts as individual, modular analyses.

An example for a monolithic analysis on the automata language presented in Sect. 10.2 is to calculate the *effective degree* of all states of an automaton model. By effective degree, we denote the number of incoming and outgoing transitions of a state, which have a satisfiable guard condition, i.e., a guard condition that does not always evaluate to *false*. This analysis can be realised as a class EffectiveStateDegrees implementing the interface AutomataVisitor (cf. Fig. 10.11) as depicted in Fig. 10.12. Through transitive inheritance, the visitor methods, e.g., for ASTExpressions, are reused without modification. Only visitor methods that perform parts of the analysis' calculations are overridden. The traverse method for automata is overridden to first handle the traversion of all states of the automaton, before handling all transitions. The purpose of this is that the degree of each state can be initialised with 0 in the visit method of the ASTState. The visit method of ASTTransition is overridden as well. It initialises a Boolean variable isTraversable with *true*. By this, each transition is initially regarded as traversable. If a transition in the model has a guard condition, the AST nodes of this condition are visited by the traversal strategy before invoking the endVisit method of the transition. Thus, by overriding visit methods of expressions and literals, the isTraversable variable can be adjusted specific to each guard. As the automata language in this example uses the ExpressionsBasis language, a guard can only comprise either a single name or a Boolean or integer literal. For this example, we consider expressions comprising either the Boolean value *false* or negative integers as unsatisfiable. This is realised by overriding the visit methods of the respective AST classes in the EffectiveStateDegrees. The overridden endVisit method for transitions increments

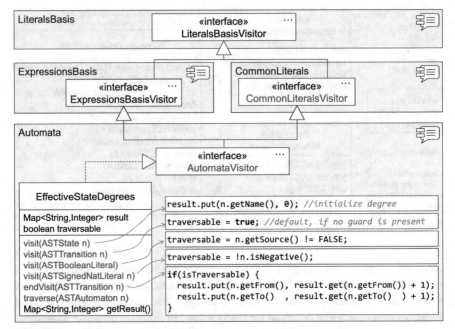

Fig. 10.12 Example for a monolithic analysis across several language components

the degree of source and target states if isTraversable is *true*. As the employed evaluation for expressions has a low potential of being reused in other language components than for automata, the developers decided to realise this as monolithical analysis.

Using delegator visitors enables reusing visitors for the individual language parts involved and, thus, to develop analyses and other operations on the AST modularly. As depicted in Fig. 10.11, a delegator visitor has a setter method for visitors of each (transitive) parent grammar as well as traversal and visit methods for all nonterminals of all grammars. An example for a modular operation on the example automata language is a model complexity analysis as depicted in Fig. 10.13. This analysis counts all instances of abstract syntax elements of a model that introduce

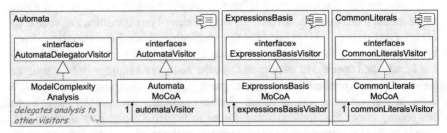

Fig. 10.13 Example for composing modular analyses via delegation visitor

concrete syntax. For each language component in the example that introduces concrete syntax, a class realising the model complexity analysis (suffixed MoCoA) is implemented. These classes implement the visitor interfaces and override their methods to count the syntax elements. The ExpressionsBasisMoCoA, for instance, is capable of counting model elements of expressions only. The CommonLiteralsMoCoA counts boolean and integer values only. The AutomataMoCoA counts all syntax elements of an automaton model except the expressions in the guards.

We distinguish different forms of composing analyses as explained in Chap. 4 of this book [Hei+21]. Combining these modular analyses can be achieved by employing a delegator visitor. In the example, the class ModelComplexityAnalysis extends the delegator visitor for automata and manages delegates for each analysis module. The effect of this is that the delegator visitor delegates the execution of the handle method for an AST node to the delegate, which is responsible for this node. Through this, the model complexity analysis takes into account all automaton model elements including those of the guard condition. Instead of this modular analysis, the ModelComplexityAnalysis could be realised as monolithical analysis as well. But as stated above, this would prevent reusing the analysis modules for literals and expressions for model complexity analyses in other contexts. Furthermore, modular analyses enable reusing foreign analysis parts conveniently. If, for example, the engineers of the automata language decide to use the CommonExpression language component with an individual analysis module instead of ExpressionBasis, the only adjustment in the analysis is to exchange the delegate object.

Conducting analyses can be orchestrated based on different strategies as described in Chap. 5 of this book [Hei+21]. If a composed analysis yields analysis results, these are typically contained in the analysis modules after execution of the analysis. Such results can be exploited in different forms, e.g., to calculate aggregated results or to serve as input for other analyses (cf. Chap. 7 of this book [Hei+21]). In our example, the results are collected from the modules and unified. Each above-mentioned analysis module can yield an integer number representing the number of syntax elements counted during analysis execution. A suitable technique for unifying the partial results in this analysis is to calculate the sum. Sometimes it is useful to exchange information between analysis modules, while the analysis is executed or to collect the analysis results in a common place. This can be realised by sharing a data structure between the analysis modules, e.g., by passing it to the analyses as argument. For instance, the model complexity analysis could store the syntax element counts by their abstract syntax type in a common map. The map could be passed to the analysis modules as argument.

Monolithic analyses can be reused for other analyses by means of delegator visitors as well. For instance, a new complexity analysis can use the analysis results both of the EffectiveStateDegrees analysis and of the ModelComplexityAnalysis. This new analysis can be realised as delegator visitor pointing to both analyses and combine their result. Sometimes, such analyses do not have to be composed at all: If the analyses do not depend on another, it is possible to execute these independently in sequence or parallel and combine their result (cf. Chaps. 4 and 7 of this book [Hei+21]).

10.4   Related Work

Research in software language engineering has produced a wealth of formalisms to define abstract and concrete syntaxes, well-formedness rules, and model transformations [Kle08, HRW18]. These include: (1) The grammar-based integrated syntax formalisms of Neverlang [VC15], Whole Platform [Erd+15], and Xtext [Bet16], as well as the abstract data types Spoofax [KV10] and the metamodels of GEMOC Studio [CBW17] and MPS [Voe11]. (2) Formalisms for the specification of well-formedness, such as OCL [Hei+10] or the Name-Binding Language [WKV14] of Spoofax. (3) Model transformation formalisms, such as ATL [Jou+06], the epsilon transformation language [KPP08], FreeMarker [HR17], or Xtend [Bet16]. Model transformations with ATL are explained in Chap. 12 of this book [Hei+21]. Language workbenches [Erd+15] combine multiple of such formalism to facilitate engineering the constituents of software languages. Yet, the compositionality of the related analyses is limited and rarely directly follows the composition of the syntaxes without severe manual implementation efforts.

For instance, in Neverlang [VC15], DSMLs are defined through language modules comprising grammars describing concrete and abstract syntax as well as through evaluation phases that realise well-formedness checking and syntheses. Extension points of grammars are used, but undefined, production names. While this enables to compose language modules along such extension points, there is no support for automatically composing the languages' analyses accordingly.

SugarJ [Erd+11] serves to specify syntactic extensions for Java that are contained in syntactic sugar libraries. By "desugaring", the extended syntax is transformed into the base syntax. SugarJ uses parsers that are capable of detecting ambiguities, for which they report an error. While it supports importing language modules into another, it does not automatically derive combined analyses from this integration.

The core of the ableC [Kam+17] language framework is an extensible variant of the C language. It uses attribute grammars to describe the syntax of independent language components and provides a composition mechanism for these that guarantees correct composition of the attribute grammars and, therefore, also of the related analyses. As the base language C, however, cannot be exchanged, this, of course, limits the application of ableC. The same holds for mbeddr [Voe+12], a projectional language workbench on top of a C base language.

SDF+FeatureHouse [LDA13] employs superimposition, weaving, and inheritance to compose language modules. While this supports powerful integration of syntaxes, the composition of the related analyses still demands significant effort.

10.5   Discussion

This chapter focuses on modularity in languages foreseen by language engineers; therefore, language components are built as individual units of reuse. In practice, however, this is rarely feasible and requires premature optimisation in identifying such units of reuse. Instead, it occurs that parts of a language component's syntax are identified as units of reuse only once these parts are of use for another language, or if a similarity analysis between language components reveals a potential to extract a common part to a separate component. However, it is possible to modularise an existing MontiCore language with little effort by extracting the nonterminals that should be reused to a separate grammar. The original grammar then extends the new grammar, similar to the "pull-up attribute" refactoring in object-oriented programming.

MontiCore's support for engineering modular languages can be used to build product lines of languages [But+19] in which each feature uses a language component. These foster the reusability of language components for scenarios with a high complexity induced by the number and interrelations of available language components. Through the modular analysis infrastructure, analyses can be defined per feature and then are available for all products of the product line.

Reusing analyses as described in Sect. 10.3 has to be handled with care: If an analysis defined for a language is directly reused in a language that extends the original language, it might yield unintended results. Consider, for example, the automata language presented in Sect. 10.2 and a new HierarchicalAutomata language that extends this language and introduces decomposed states that themselves contain states and transitions. The model complexity analysis for the original automata language, as described in Sect. 10.3, can be applied to the language for hierarchical automata without modification. However, it depends on the realisation of hierarchical states whether these are taken into account or not.

If hierarchical states are introduced through overriding the production for states as depicted in Fig. 10.14a, neither hierarchical nor non-hierarchical states are visited by the visitor as the parser translates both into instances of the new ASTState class. Thus, both are not counted in the analysis. If, however, the hierarchical states are introduced by extending the state production (cf. Fig. 10.14b), non-hierarchical states are visited by the visitor and, thus, taken into account in the analysis.

The techniques described in this chapter can be used to realise both qualitative and quantitative, automated, static analyses as described in Chap. 4 of this book [Hei+21]. Given an AST of the input language as depicted in Fig. 10.1 enables realising analysis on the model/system structure, while the output AST, together with an understanding of the semantic domain, forms a basis for realising behavioural analyses.

MontiCore internally uses the modular analysis framework for each language: Context conditions are realised as Java classes and are checked against the AST using a visitor. Therefore, context conditions can be reused as part of reusing

(a)
```
State = "state" Name ( ("{" (State | Transition)* "}") | ";" );
```

(b)
```
HState extends State = "state" Name "{" (State | Transition)* "}";
```

Fig. 10.14 Adding hierarchical states via (**a**) overriding or (**b**) extending a grammar production

a language component. Similarly, the instantiation of the symbol table of a language [HR17] is performed by a symbol table creator realised as visitor.

10.6   Conclusion

We have presented an approach for compositional language engineering based on modular syntax definitions from which a modular, visitor-based infrastructure for model-based analyses and syntheses is derived. The presented approach relies on language extension and interface productions that can be extended in the extending languages. From this information, visitors for the participating languages are generated that automatically take care of model traversal. Hence, model-based analyses implemented through these visitors can be reused in other language combinations without modification.

The visitor based infrastructure traverses the abstract syntax and can support realising a language's semantics. The applicability of the infrastructure for conceiving novel forms of generator compositions, however, has yet to be evaluated. This fosters not only the reuse of modelling languages and analysis tools but facilitates engineering truly domain-specific modelling languages to integrate experts of the different systems engineering domains more efficiently.

References

[Ada+17a] Kai Adam, Arvid Butting, Robert Heim, Oliver Kautz, Járôme Pfeiffer, Bernhard Rumpe, and Andreas Wortmann. *Modeling Robotics Tasks for Better Separation of Concerns, Platform-Independence, and Reuse*. Shaker, 2017. http://www.se-rwth.de/phdtheses/Modeling-Robotics-Tasks-for-Better-Separation-of-Concerns-Platform-Independence-and-Reuse.pdf.

[Ada+17b] Kai Adam, Katrin Hölldobler, Bernhard Rumpe, and AndreasWortmann. "Modeling Robotics Software Architectures with Modular Model Transformations". In: *Journal of Software Engineering for Robotics* 8.1 (2017), pp. 3–16. https://doi.org/10.1109/IRC.2017.16.

[Bet16] Lorenzo Bettini. *Implementing domain-specific languages with Xtext and Xtend*. Packt Publishing Ltd, 2016.

[But+19] Arvid Butting, Robert Eikermann, Oliver Kautz, Bernhard Rumpe, and Andreas Wortmann. "Systematic Composition of Independent Language Features". In: *Journal of Systems and Software* 152 (2019), pp. 50–69.

[CBW17] Benoit Combemale, Olivier Barais, and Andreas Wortmann. "Language Engineering with the GEMOC Studio". In: *IEEE International Conference on Software Architecture Workshops*. 2017, pp. 189–191. https://doi.org/10.1109/ICSAW.2017.61.

[Dal+19] Manuela Dalibor, Nico Jansen, Bernhard Rumpe, Louis Wachtmeister, and Andreas Wortmann. "Model-Driven Systems Engineering for Virtual Product Design". In: *First International Workshop on Multi-Paradigm Modelling for Cyber-Physical Systems, MPM4CPS*. Sept. 2019, pp. 430–435. https://doi.org/10.1109/MODELS-C.2019.00069.

[Dra+19] Imke Drave, Timo Greifenberg, Steffen Hillemacher, Stefan Kriebel, Evgeny Kusmenko, Matthias Markthaler, Philipp Orth, Karin Samira Salman, Johannes Richen-
hagen, Bernhard Rumpe, Christoph Schulze, Michael Wenckstern, and Andreas Wortmann. "SMArDT modeling for automotive software testing". In: *Software: Practice
and Experience* 49.2 (2019), pp. 301–328. https://doi.org/10.1002/spe.2650.

[Eik+17] Robert Eikermann, Markus Look, Alexander Roth, Bernhard Rumpe, and Andreas
Wortmann. "Architecting Cloud Services for the Digital me in a Privacy-Aware
Environment". In: *Software Architecture for Big Data and the Cloud*. 2017, pp. 207–
226. https://doi.org/10.1016/B978-0-12-805467-3.00012-0.

[Erd+11] Sebastian Erdweg, Lennart CL Kats, Tillmann Rendel, Christian Kästner, Klaus
Ostermann, and Eelco Visser. "Library-based Model-driven Software Development
with SugarJ". In: *Proceedings of the ACM international conference companion on
Object oriented programming systems languages and applications companion*. 2011,
pp. 17–18. https://doi.org/10.1145/2048147.2048156.

[Erd+15] Sebastian Erdweg, Tijs Van Der Storm, Markus Völter, Laurence Tratt, Remi Bosman,
William R Cook, Albert Gerritsen, Angelo Hulshout, Steven Kelly, Alex Loh, et al.
"Evaluating and comparing language workbenches: Existing results and benchmarks
for the future". In: *Computer Languages, Systems & Structures* 44 (2015), pp. 24–47.
https://doi.org/10.1016/j.cl.2015.08.007.

[FR07] Robert France and Bernhard Rumpe. "Model-driven Development of Complex Software: A Research Roadmap". In: *Future of Software Engineering* (May 2007), pp.
37–54. https://doi.org/10.1109/FOSE.2007.14.

[Hei+10] Florian Heidenreich, Jendrik Johannes, Sven Karol, Mirko Seifert, Michael Thiele,
Christian Wende, and Claas Wilke. "Integrating OCL and textual modelling languages".
In: *International Conference on Model Driven Engineering Languages and Systems*.
2010, pp. 349–363. https://doi.org/10.1007/978-3-642-21210-9_34.

[Hei+16] Robert Heim, Pedram Mir Seyed Nazari, Bernhard Rumpe, and Andreas Wortmann.
"Compositional Language Engineering using Generated, Extensible, Static Type Safe
Visitors". In: *Conference on Modelling Foundations and Applications*. 2016, pp. 67–82.
https://doi.org/10.1007/978-3-319-42061-5_5.

[Hei+21] Robert Heinrich, Francisco Durán, Carolyn L. Talcott, and Steffen Zschaler (eds.)
Composing Model-Based Analysis Tools. Springer, 2021. https://doi.org/10.1007/978-
3-030-81915-6.

[HMR15] Katrin Hölldobler, Pedram Mir Seyed Nazari, and Bernhard Rumpe. "Adaptable
Symbol Table Management by Meta Modeling and Generation of Symbol Table
Infrastructures". In: *Domain-Specific Modeling Workshop*. 2015, pp. 23–30. https://doi.
org/10.1145/2846696.2846700.

[HR17] Katrin Hölldobler and Bernhard Rumpe. *MontiCore 5 Language Workbench Edition 2017*. Shaker, 2017. http://www.se-rwth.de/phdtheses/MontiCore-5-Language-
Workbench-Edition-2017.pdf.

[HRW18] Katrin Hölldobler, Bernhard Rumpe, and Andreas Wortmann. "Software Language
Engineering in the Large: Towards Composing and Deriving Languages". In: *Computer
Languages, Systems & Structures* 54 (2018), pp. 386–405.

[Jou+06] Frádáric Jouault, Freddy Allilaire, Jean Bázivin, Ivan Kurtev, and Patrick Valduriez.
"ATL: a QVT-like transformation language". In: *Companion to the 21st ACM SIGPLAN
symposium on Object-oriented programming systems, languages, and applications*.
2006, pp. 719–720. https://doi.org/10.1145/1176617.1176691.

[Kam+17] Ted Kaminski, Lucas Kramer, Travis Carlson, and Eric Van Wyk. "Reliable and
Automatic Composition of Language Extensions to C: The ableC Extensible Language
Framework". In: *Proceedings of the ACM on Programming Languages* 1 (Oct. 2017),
98:1–98:29. https://doi.org/10.1145/3138224.

[Kle08] Anneke Kleppe. *Software language engineering: creating domain-specific languages
using metamodels*. Pearson Education, 2008.

[KPP08] Dimitrios S Kolovos, Richard F Paige, and Fiona AC Polack. "The Epsilon trans-formation language". In: *International Conference on Theory and Practice of Model Transformations*. 2008, pp. 46–60. https://doi.org/10.1007/978-3-540-69927-9_4.

[KV10] Lennart C. L. Kats and Eelco Visser. "The Spoofax Language Workbench. Rules for Declarative Specification of Languages and IDEs". In: *Proceedings of the 25th Annual ACM SIGPLAN Conference on Object-Oriented Programming, Systems, Languages, and Applications*. 2010, pp. 444–463. https://doi.org/10.1145/1869459.1869497.

[LDA13] Jörg Liebig, Rolf Daniel, and Sven Apel. "Feature-oriented Language Families: A Case Study". In: *Seventh International Workshop on Variability Modelling of Software intensive Systems, VaMoS*. 2013, 11:1–11:8. https://doi.org/10.1145/2430502.2430518.

[MRR15] Pedram Mir Seyed Nazari, Alexander Roth, and Bernhard Rumpe. "Management of Guided and Unguided Code Generator Customizations by Using a Symbol Table". In: *Domain-Specific Modeling Workshop*. 2015, pp. 37–42. https://doi.org/10.1145/2846696. 2846702.

[MRR16] Pedram Mir Seyed Nazari, Alexander Roth, and Bernhard Rumpe. "An Extended Symbol Table Infrastructure to Manage the Composition of Output-Specific Generator Information". In: *Modellierung 2016 Conference*. Vol. 254. Mar. 2016, pp. 133–140. https://doi.org/dl.gi.de/20.500.12116/819.

[Obj12] Objcet Management Group. *OMG Systems Modeling Language (OMG SysML), Version 1.3*. 2012. https://www.omg.org/spec/SysML/1.4/.

[Obj15] Object Management Group. *UML 2.5*. Tech. rep. formal/2015-03-01. Object Manage-ment Group, 2015.

[VC15] Edoardo Vacchi and Walter Cazzola. "Neverlang: A framework for feature-oriented language development". In: *Computer Languages, Systems & Structures* 43 (2015), pp. 1–40. https://doi.org/10.1016/j.cl.2015.02.001.

[Voe+12] Markus Voelter, Daniel Ratiu, Bernhard Schaetz, and Bernd Kolb. "mbeddr: an Extensible C-based Programming Language and IDE for Embedded Systems". In: *Proceedings of the 3rd annual conference on Systems, programming, and applications: software for humanity*. 2012, pp. 121–140. https://doi.org/10.1145/2384716.2384767.

[Voe11] Markus Voelter. "Language and IDE Modularization and Composition with MPS". In: *International Summer School on Generative and Transformational Techniques in Software Engineering*. 2011, pp. 383–430. https://doi.org/10.1007/978-3-642-35992-7_11.

[WKV14] Guido H Wachsmuth, Gabriël D P Konat, and Eelco Visser. "Language Design with the Spoofax Language Workbench". In: *IEEE Software* 31.5 (2014), pp. 35–43. https://doi.org/10.1109/MS.2014.100.

Chapter 11
Challenges in the Evolution of Palladio—Refactoring Design Smells in a Historically-Grown Approach to Software Architecture Analysis

Robert Heinrich, Jörg Henss, Sandro Koch, and Ralf Reussner

Abstract In this chapter, we provide insights into Palladio—a tool-supported approach to modelling and analysing software architectures. Palladio serves as a case study for the evolution of historically-grown approaches to model-based analysis. We report about design smells in Palladio's metamodel and simulators caused by evolution and growth over several years. Design smells are structures that require refactoring. Decomposition is key for refactoring these design smells. We discuss how techniques for decomposition and purpose-oriented composition can help refactoring design smells in Palladio's metamodel and simulators.

This case-study chapter illustrates concepts introduced in Chaps. 4 and 5; it addresses Challenge 1 and Challenge 2 in Chap. 3 of this book.

11.1 Introduction and Problem Statement

Palladio is a tool-supported approach to modelling and analysing software architectures for various quality properties [Reu+16]. It is named after the Italian Renaissance architect Andrea Palladio. Initially, Palladio was focused on performance and then has been extended for several quality properties, such as reliability [Bro+12], scalability and elasticity [Leh14], energy consumption [Sti18], security [TH16], confidentiality [SHR19], and maintainability [Ros+15]. With Palladio, costly changes to software after it has been implemented can be avoided by analysing the quality of a software system of a given architecture early in development. Decisions in software design are typically made on the basis of experience

R. Heinrich (✉) · S. Koch · R. Reussner
Karlsruhe Institute of Technology, Karlsruhe, Germany
e-mail: robert.heinrich@kit.edu; sandro.koch@kit.edu; ralf.reussner@kit.edu

J. Henß
FZI Research Center for Information Technology, Karlsruhe, Germany
e-mail: henss@fzi.de

© The Author(s), under exclusive license to Springer Nature Switzerland AG 2021
R. Heinrich et al. (eds.), *Composing Model-Based Analysis Tools*,
https://doi.org/10.1007/978-3-030-81915-6_11

235

or, when lacking those, by making an educated guess. The information provided by the Palladio approach enables to choose the best-suited design alternative and to make trade-off decisions [Hei+18].

The Palladio approach consists of three essential parts that are designed to work hand in hand [Reu+16]. First, the *Palladio Component Model* (PCM) as a domain-specific modelling language defined in the form of a metamodel is targeted at specifying and documenting software architectural knowledge. Second, various analysis techniques ranging from queuing network analysis to discrete-event simulation can be applied to predict the quality of a system modelled based on the PCM. Third, the Palladio approach is aligned with a development process that comprises several developer roles and activities tailored to component-based software design.

In this chapter, we focus on the evolution of the PCM and the associated simulators. We understand the term simulator to be a software tool that implements one or more techniques of simulative analysis for approximating the quality properties of a system under study. We understand the term simulation to be the execution of a stimulative technique using a simulator. Simulation is therefore an example of automated analysis (cf. Chap. 2 of this book [Hei+21]). The PCM is an established and widely used metamodel. The PCM and the associated simulators provide various useful features for quality modelling and analysis of component-based software architectures.

We use the term feature to specify what a modelling language should express and what a simulator should analyse on a conceptual level. A feature of a metamodel (or a modelling language in general) is an abstraction of a thing to be modelled [HSR19]. Examples of language features in Palladio are amongst others those for modelling the component structure, component-internal behaviour, system usage, and performance-related annotation [SHR18]. A feature of a simulator is an abstraction of a property to be analysed by simulation. Examples of simulator features in Palladio are amongst others those for analysing user behaviour, system behaviour, resource usage, and for eliciting performance-related measurements.

The PCM consists of 203 classes dispersed amongst 24 packages [HSR19]. It is organised into five partial metamodels. Since its inception in August 2006, the PCM has a long history of evolution. There are at least 12 documented extensions to the PCM publicly available. However, many more extensions exist that are not publicly available (e.g., student theses, experimental, incubation). Owing to its historically-grown structure, the PCM exhibits some shortcomings such as package structure erosion, uncontrolled growth of dependencies, instance incompatibility, and incompatible extensions. The simulators for reasoning about model instances of the PCM show similar size and complexity. For example, the original simulator SimuCom [Bec08] consists of 231 classes in 50 packages. Due to historical growth, also the simulators show shortcomings such as package structure erosion, uncontrolled growth of dependencies, underdefined semantics, and incompatible extensions.

This chapter provides insights into the evolution of Palladio to serve as a case study for decomposition and composition of model-based analysis. We report about design smells in the metamodel and simulators caused by evolution and growth over several years. Design smells are structures that indicate the violation of fundamental design principles and therefore negatively affect the quality of the metamodel and simulators. Thus, design smells require refactoring. Decomposition is key for refactoring design smells in Palladio's metamodel and simulators. Due to the rigorous quality assurance process of Palladio, most of the design smells have already been addressed. Nevertheless, the design smells reported may provide food for thought for others evolving historically-grown metamodels and simulators and motivate the usage of techniques for decomposition and composition. We discuss how techniques for decomposition and purpose-oriented composition can help refactor design smells in the metamodel and simulators. This chapter, therefore, illustrates concepts discussed in Chaps. 4 and 5 of this book [Hei+21].

The remainder of this chapter is structured as follows. Section 11.2 gives an overview of Palladio's modelling environment—the Palladio-Bench. We report about design smells in the PCM in Sect. 11.3 and in the simulators in Sect. 11.4. The application of techniques for decomposition and composition to resolve design smells is described in Sect. 11.5. This chapter concludes in Sect. 11.6.

11.2 Overview of the Palladio-Bench

Before discussing design smells in the evolution of Palladio, this section gives a detailed overview of the three essential parts of the Palladio approach [Reu+16]— the domain-specific modelling language PCM, the various analysis techniques, and the development process comprising several developer roles. These three parts of the Palladio approach are implemented in the Palladio-Bench that is based on the Eclipse *integrated development environment* (IDE) [Hei+18].

The PCM consists of the partial metamodels shown on the left-hand side in Fig. 11.1 to reflect different architectural views on a software system. The several developer roles use graphical editors provided by the Palladio-Bench [Hei+18] to specify the partial models of the Palladio approach. The component developer designs the software component specifications. The component repository model is created by the component developer to design the software components and their required and provided interfaces stored in a repository. Moreover, the component developer specifies the components' inner behaviour in the form of the so-called *Service Effect Specification* (SEFF). A SEFF expresses internal actions of a component's services typically annotated with quality-specific information depending on its context and external service calls. The software architect designs the software architecture in the system model by assembling components from the repository. Thus, the quality of a system can be estimated with respect to the component assembly described in the system model. The system deployer specifies the execution containers (i.e., servers) including their processing resources

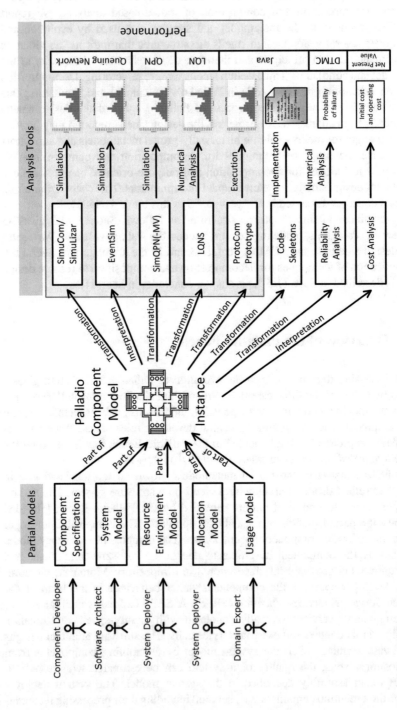

Fig. 11.1 Partial models of the PCM and transformation to analysis tools, extension of [Reu+16]

(i.e., CPU, hard disk, and network) in the resource environment model. For each execution container, quality-relevant properties like processing rate of the CPU are part of the resource environment model. Moreover, the system deployer describes the deployment of the components to the execution containers in the allocation model. The domain expert specifies the workload of the system in terms of user behaviour and usage intensity in the usage model.

The Palladio-Bench offers several analysis tools for reasoning about quality depicted on the right-hand side in Fig. 11.1. Note, although the focus of this chapter is on simulators, we deliberately depict other tools of the Palladio-Bench in Fig. 11.1 to give a comprehensive overview. We therefore introduce the broader term analysis tool here (cf. Chap. 2 of this book [Hei+21]). An analysis tool in the context of the Palladio-Bench is a software tool that implements one or more analysis techniques for approximating the quality properties of a system under study. Analysis tools for estimating the performance of a software system are central to the Palladio-Bench, and a wide range of tools are available. These performance tools are highlighted in the grey box in Fig. 11.1 and differ mainly in their range of functions, result accuracy, and analysis speed. The Palladio-Bench also offers tools for the analysis of reliability [Bro+12] and prediction of costs [Mar+10] as well as various extensions, e.g., for the analysis of energy consumption [Sti18], security [TH16], confidentiality [SHR19], and maintainability [Ros+15], not depicted in the figure.

Palladio's original simulator SimuCom [Bec08] is a discrete-event performance simulator that estimates response times of both, system-level and component-level services, as well as utilisation of processing resources specified in the resource environment. The performance simulator SimuLizar [BLB13] is focused on analysing self-adaptations in cloud computing environments, e.g., when scaling out components by replication. EventSim [MH11] is a discrete-event performance simulator that complements SimuCom in that it primarily addresses highly complex models in simulation by applying event-scheduling simulation techniques. Besides the simulators, the Palladio-Bench offers tools for transforming model instances of the PCM to the formalisms *queuing Petri net* (QPN) and *layered queuing network* (LQN). These are established formalisms and commonly used for software performance prediction independent of the Palladio approach. ProtoCom [Bec08] is a tool provided by the Palladio-Bench to create performance prototypes in the form of Java code that mimic demands to different types of processing resources to evaluate the system performance in a realistic environment.

The reliability analysis tool of the Palladio-Bench estimates software and hardware failure potentials using *discrete-time Markov chain* (DTMC) [Bro+12]. The simple cost analysis provided by the Palladio-Bench allows to assign costs to software components and hardware that is then used to estimate the initial and operating costs of the system [Mar+10].

Referring to the analysis orchestration strategies introduced in Chap. 5 of this book [Hei+21], the Palladio-Bench applies the single analysis orchestration strategy. The aforementioned developer roles use the Palladio-Bench to create a domain-specific model of the system to conduct quality analyses based on one of the aforementioned analysis tools. The Palladio-Bench transforms the domain-specific model into an analysis model specific to the given analysis tool for quality analysis. After the analysis has been finished, the results are lifted back to the Palladio-Bench. The Palladio-Bench in turn displays the results to the developers. There is no interaction between the individual monolithic analysis tools.

11.3   Design Smells in the Palladio Component Model

In this section, we give examples of design smells that occurred in the PCM while it evolved over the course of several years. These design smells serve as motivation for the decomposition and purpose-oriented composition of the PCM to refactor the design smells as described in the following sections.

In object-oriented design, the term design smell is commonly understood as a structure that indicates the violation of fundamental design principles and therefore negatively affects quality properties of the system like maintainability and evolvability. Design smells in object-oriented design are classified as creational, structural, and behavioural smells [GS13].

Design smells not only occur in the object-oriented design of software systems but also in the design of metamodels. Strittmatter [Str19] investigated design smells in metamodels and identified that many structural design smells known in object-oriented design can also be found in metamodel design. This is reasonable as there are many commonalities in object-oriented design and metamodel design from a structural point of view. Both, object-oriented design and metamodel design, specify classes and their attributes, package structures, as well as dependencies between classes [Str19]. Creational and behavioural smells from object orientation cannot be found in metamodels as with respect to these categories object-oriented design and metamodel design differ [Str19].

In the following, we discuss some examples of design smells that refer to the modularity of metamodels and explain their occurrence in the PCM to demonstrate the need for refactoring by decomposition and purpose-oriented composition of the PCM. We thereby focus on design smells on the level of the package structure of the metamodel or on the level of metamodel files. A complete overview of metamodel design smells is given in [Str19].

Language Feature Scattering The content of a metamodel is logically partitioned by its package structure. A language feature is implemented by one or several classes in the metamodel. Language features are hard to grasp, if they are not adequately reflected in the package structure. If classes that constitute a language feature are spread over multiple packages that do not share a meaningful parent, it is defined as *Language Feature Scattering* [Str+16]. When a language feature is scattered over multiple packages, it is hard to understand the purpose of such a package without considering all other dependent packages. Consequently, this smell hampers the comprehensibility of the metamodel. Also the maintainability of the metamodel may be negatively affected. Language Feature Scattering occurs in the

PCM. For example, the language features for modelling the software repository, resource interfaces, middleware infrastructure, events, performance, and reliability (cf. [SHR18]) are all scattered over multiple packages.

Package Blob A package that contains classes of multiple language features is defined as *Package Blob* design smell [Str+16]. The Package Blob smell reduces understandability of the package as one needs to identify and understand all the contained language features and their respective classes in order to understand the package. Furthermore, it unnecessarily increases complexity and negatively affects reusability of the package as it is not possible to selectively depend only on the necessary language features. Examples for the Package Blob smell in the PCM are data types and the abstract component-type hierarchy, which both are located in a single package, namely the repository package.

Metamodel Monolith The *Metamodel Monolith* design smell is defined as a metamodel file that implements multiple language features. This is the analogy of the Package Blob on the level of metamodel files. The Metamodel Monolith smell negatively affects the reusability of the metamodel file as it is not possible to selectively depend only on the necessary language features. The complexity of the metamodel files is unnecessarily increased, and the understandability is reduced due to lack of modularity [Str19]. The Metamodel Monolith smell occurs in the PCM as the entire PCM with all its packages is contained in a single metamodel file.

11.4 Design Smells in the Simulators

In this section, design smells in the Palladio simulators are discussed. These design smells serve as motivation for the decomposition and purpose-oriented composition of the simulators to refactor the design smells as described in the following sections.

Stepney [Ste12] collected smells in scientific simulation. Some of these smells refer to simulator design and can also be found in similar form in the simulators of Palladio. Moreover, we identified additional smells in the Palladio simulators that we could not yet find in the literature. These additional smells result from our professional experience in using the simulators of Palladio both, in academic and industrial projects. In the following discussion, design smells inspired by Stepney are marked by the reference [Ste12].

Amateur Science [Ste12] The *Amateur Science* smell denotes simulator development without the involvement of domain experts, e.g., because the simulator developers assume to be familiar with a given domain, and thus making simplifying assumptions. This smell is represented by modelling languages and simulators that are oversimplified for the given analysis task. This may result in neglected domain knowledge and thus negatively affect the accuracy of the simulation results. In the simulators of Palladio, the simulation of the network resources is implemented in a very simplistic way. The assumption was made that the impact of the network resources on the accuracy of the simulation results would not be of significance. However, with this assumption, we underestimated the impact of network resources on the distortion of service response times [KBH07, Ver+07]. Especially for modern distributed systems, network latency and throughput may have significant impact on the overall system performance. Therefore, network resources need to be adequately considered in simulation to achieve accurate results.

Analysis Paralysis [Ste12] Simulator developers may spend too much time analysing and modelling the domain, trying to get everything perfect, and not getting to the simulation. This is defined as the *Analysis Paralysis* smell. This smell is represented by modelling languages and simulators that are unnecessarily complex or detailed for the given analysis task. As a consequence, developing and maintaining the modelling languages and simulators is more time-consuming and error-prone than actually necessary. The PCM allows the modelling of a component-type hierarchy to provide support for an iterative specification of components. Components can be specified at different levels of abstraction based on the amount of knowledge currently available for these components [Reu+16]. However, for the goal of performance analysis, the structure of the component-type hierarchy has no effects on the simulation. Thus, the PCM is unnecessarily detailed for the task of performance analysis with respect to the component-type hierarchy as it is not used for analysing the performance of the software system in the simulators of Palladio.

Everything but the Kitchen Sink [Ste12] Simulator developers may add irrelevant features not related to the actual analysis task to a modelling language and simulator. This is denoted as the *Everything but the Kitchen Sink* smell. In contrast to the Analysis Paralysis smell, the modelling language and simulator do not show unnecessarily complex or detailed features but features that are not relevant to the analysis task at all, e.g., adding a reliability-related feature to a pure performance simulation. The Everything but the Kitchen Sink smell is represented by convoluted and monolithic modelling languages and simulators with unclear focus and purpose and seldom used or even unused features. As a consequence, developing and maintaining the modelling languages and simulators is more time-consuming and error-prone than actually necessary. The main purpose of Palladio's simulators is software architecture-based performance analysis. However, features like the *Accuracy Influence Analysis* [Gro13] and the *Sensitivity Analysis* [Bro+12] are part of SimuCom. Although these features are seldom used, each change in Palladio (e.g., updating the Java version or changes to the PCM) potentially requires effort to keep them functional. Moreover, the strong interconnection of these features to other features of the simulator may result in negative side effects.

Living Flatland [Ste12] When simulator developers use a wrong level of abstraction like simulating a 2D space and then naively translating the results in a 3D space, it is defined as the *Living Flatland* smell. This smell may negatively affect the accuracy of simulation results. In Palladio, for example, a simple processor-sharing scheduler was implemented in the simulator SimuCom, with the assumption made, that this kind of scheduler is sufficient to approximate all kinds of CPU-scheduling policies. This resulted in inaccurate simulation results and, as a consequence, development overhead, because the *Linux Exact Scheduler* [Hap08] had to be implemented in order to fix shortcomings caused by the initial assumption.

Underdefined Semantics The semantics of the input model of a simulator may not exactly correspond to the semantics actually implemented in the simulator as the simulator's semantics is underspecified. This is denoted as the *Underdefined Semantics* smell. This smell results in gaps in semantics definition of model and simulator, and thus ad hoc definition of semantics during simulator development. Moreover, there is a high risk that the simulation will provide faulty results due to underdefined semantics. Furthermore, underdefined semantics can lead to semantic shifts, rendering older models invalid as they were created with a different understanding of model elements in mind. This can also interfere with the reproducibility of simulation experiments. In the early years of Palladio development, several extensions were made to the PCM without defining a clear semantic mapping to the simulator SimuCom. Examples are the output parameters and the fork join actions. This led to the problem that semantics were defined in an ad hoc way during simulator development and had to be adjusted in several iterations or are still not well defined up to now. The interested reader is referred to Chap. 9 of this book [Hei+21] where further discussion on the topic is given.

Excessive Events/Event Flooding A simulator utilising an unnecessarily large number of events is defined as the *Excessive Events* or *Event Flooding* smell. The massive creation of unnecessary events in simulation largely impacts the execution efficiency. Therefore, simulator developers should try to minimise the number of events to be managed in simulation. In Palladio, we discovered several shortcomings in the realisation of the resource schedulers in SimuCom. Requests created excessive numbers of events when running in fair-share mode in overload scenarios leading to starvation and crashes in simulation.

Simulator Feature Scattering A simulator is logically partitioned by its component structure. A simulator feature is implemented by one or several classes of the simulator. Simulator features are hard to grasp, if they are not adequately reflected in the component structure. Classes that implement a feature of a simulator may be spread over multiple components of the simulator that do not share a meaningful parent. This is defined as the *Simulator Feature Scattering* smell. When a feature of a simulator is scattered over multiple components, it is hard to understand the purpose of such a component without considering all other dependent components. Consequently, this smell hampers the comprehensibility of the simulator. Also, the maintainability of the simulator may be negatively affected. In Palladio's simulator SimuLizar, for example, the simulator feature to handle the language feature *Usage* [SHR18] that contains amongst others the usage model is implemented in 18 classes scattered over three components.

Simulator Component Blob A simulator component that contains classes of multiple simulator features is defined as *Simulator Component Blob* smell. The

Simulator Component Blob smell reduces understandability of the simulator component as one needs to identify and understand all the contained simulator features and their respective classes in order to understand the component. Furthermore, it unnecessarily increases complexity and negatively affects reusability of the simulator component as it is not possible to selectively depend only on the necessary language features. In EventSim, for example, the different features of the simulator like simulation of users, resources, and network are heavily interwoven in the core simulator component [MH11].

Simulator Monolith If there is no decomposition of the simulator at all, we denote this design smell as *Simulator Monolith*. The Simulator Monolith smell negatively affects the reusability of the simulator as it is not possible to selectively depend only on the necessary simulator features. The complexity of the simulator is unnecessarily increased, and the understandability is reduced due to lack of modularity. There is no example of a Simulator Monolith in the Palladio context as all simulators are at least partially decomposed.

Global State Object and God Parameter The state of an entire simulation may be stored in a single object. This is defined as the *Global State Object* smell. A global state object is an object that encapsulates large parts of the world model of a simulator. Thus, it is an instance of a god class [LM06]. Every entity in the simulation has access to this object. Entities in the simulation usually access the global state object directly to query and manipulate the global state of the simulation similar to the blackboard pattern [Bus+96]. When extending the simulator, developers usually add more and more fields to the global state object. This introduces large maintainability problems when changing fields as no clear interfaces and access restrictions exist. This design smell can be accompanied by the *God Parameter* smell, a field in the global state object that can be used to manipulate the behaviour of entities ignoring any existing encapsulation. In SimuLizar, for example, the simulation control information is passed through the whole simulation, if it is required or not.

Intrusive Extension A simulator may have extensions that are tightly coupled into the code base. This is defined as the *Intrusive Extensions* smell. The intrusive extensions can clutter the codebase and introduce technical debts. Furthermore, they may cause dead code in the long term if not used anymore. In SimuCom, the reliability extension [Bro+12] is an example of this design smell. Though being used rarely, it could not be disabled in the generation of SimuCom code and led to several problems and bugs.

11.5 Application of Decomposition and Composition Techniques to Palladio

This section provides insights into the application of decomposition and composition techniques to Palladio. Applying these techniques enables to fix many of the aforementioned design smells in the metamodel and simulators. First, we discuss techniques for the decomposition and composition of the PCM. This serves as a preparatory step for the decomposition and composition of the associated simulators. Then, we discuss the decomposition and composition of the simulators.

11.5.1 Decomposition and Composition of the Palladio Component Model

One way to address the aforementioned design smells in the PCM is the application of techniques for decomposition and composition as known from object-oriented design to metamodels in combination with a reference architecture to structure metamodels and support the decomposition and purpose-oriented composition of metamodels for quality modelling and analysis [HSR19].

Many commonalities in object-oriented design and metamodel design exist from a structural point of view. Both, object-oriented design and metamodel design, specify classes and their attributes, package structures as well as dependencies between classes, may it be for example association or inheritance [Str19]. Encouraged by these commonalities, we transferred established concepts from object-oriented design, such as decomposition and composition, acyclic dependencies, dependency inversion, extension, and layering to metamodels [HSR19].

Also transferring the idea of a reference architecture to metamodels seems reasonable. In our work, we focus on metamodels for quality modelling and analysis of software-intensive systems in different domains like information systems, production automation, and automotive. When comparing metamodels for modelling and analysing different quality properties in these domains, substantial parts of the metamodels exhibit quite similar language features [HSR19].

A Layered Reference Architecture for Metamodels

In [HSR19], we proposed a layered reference architecture for metamodels for quality modelling and analysis of software-intensive systems to address shortcomings in the evolution of metamodels. The reference architecture leverages reoccurring patterns in various domains. We studied different metamodels used for quality modelling and analysis in various domains as well as their extensions and identified that these metamodels reflect in most cases language features from distinct categories—structure, behaviour, and quality. This observation led to the separation of parts of a metamodel into different layers in the reference architecture. A layer is a set of metamodel components. A metamodel component is defined as a container of packages and classifiers that has explicit dependencies. Metamodel components can be extended by lower-level layers and reused in different metamodels [HSR19]. The layers of the reference architecture are dedicated to structure/behaviour, quality, and the corresponding analysis. We further separated the structure/behaviour layer into paradigm and domain to distinguish domain-spanning fundamental concepts from domain-specific concepts. Metamodel components are assigned to one specific layer depending on the features they offer to the language. Based on concepts taken from object-oriented design and detailed application guidelines of these concepts described in [HSR19], the reference architecture supports (a) the top-level decomposition of metamodels for quality modelling and analysis into the four layers—paradigm, domain, quality, and analysis, (b) the decomposition of partial metamodels assigned to one of the layers into reusable metamodel components, and (c) the reuse of metamodel components in different contexts and thus the purpose-oriented composition of metamodels.

In the following, we give more detailed definitions of the single layers of the reference architecture taken from [HSR19] before we describe the application of the reference architecture to the PCM. The *paradigm* (π) layer is the most basic and most abstract layer. The foundation of the language is defined on the π layer by specifying language features for reoccurring patterns of structure and behaviour but without dynamic semantics. Furthermore, π does not carry any domain-specific semantics as this layer is not intended to be used without any additional layer. The *domain* (Δ) layer builds upon the π layer and assigns domain-specific semantics to the abstract first-class language features of π. Therefore, the Δ layer builds upon structural as well as on behavioural language features of π. The *quality* (Ω) layer defines quality-related properties of language features located on previous layers. The analysis layer (Σ) builds upon the previous layers and specifies language features used by analyses. Σ comprises language features to define configuration data, runtime state, output data, and input data that do not belong to Δ language features.

The result of the application of the reference architecture to the PCM is depicted as an excerpt in Fig. 11.2. The figure and the explaining text come from [HSR19]. We split the largest metamodel component of the original PCM into 23 smaller components to separate features properly. The other four metamodel components of the original PCM were already sufficiently modular. The number of classes in the decomposed PCM grew from 203 to 229. This is because during refactoring we split classes and created new containers for extensions. The number of references in the decomposed PCM reduced from 198 to 174. This is because we removed or remodelled redundant dependencies that violated the reference architecture. The decomposed PCM populates the layers π, Δ, and Ω. The Σ layer is populated by analysis-specific extensions of the PCM.

The most important metamodel components of the decomposed PCM are depicted in Fig. 11.2. On the π layer, these are *repository*, *composition*, *control flow*, and *annotations*. *Repository* specifies abstract components, interfaces, and

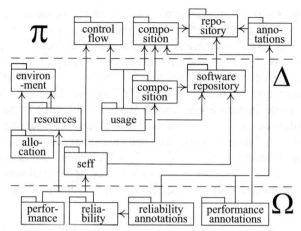

Fig. 11.2 Excerpt of the decomposed PCM. ©2021 IEEE. Reprinted, with permission, from [HSR19]

roles. *Composition* introduces component composition and therefore extends the *repository* metamodel component. *Control flow* defines a structure similar to activity diagrams. *Annotations* contains quality-independent annotations as an extension of the *repository* metamodel component. The domain (Δ) layer comprises the *composition* and *software repository* metamodel components, which extend their counterpart from the π layer and carry additional domain-specific content. This means the specialisation of abstract components to software components is happening in these two metamodel components. The *environment* metamodel component specifies execution containers and network links between the execution containers. The *resources* metamodel component extends the *environment* metamodel component to add hardware resource specifications to the execution containers and the network links. The *allocation* metamodel component enables software component instances (from the *composition* metamodel component) to be deployed on the execution containers of the *environment* metamodel component. The *usage* metamodel component specifies system usage profiles, which can be applied to interfaces from the *software repository* metamodel component. It therefore reuses the *control flow* metamodel component of π, which is also reused by the *seff* metamodel component to define the control flow between component-internal actions and component-external services. The quality (Ω) layer comprises the *performance* metamodel component, which extends the *resources* extension of the *environment* metamodel component by performance-relevant properties. It also extends the *seff* metamodel component by resource demand specifications. The dependencies of the *reliability* metamodel component are analogous. Finally, there are two metamodel components that enable the annotation of both quality properties in a component-based architecture by reusing the abstract definition of *annotations* on the π layer.

For the purpose-oriented composition of metamodel components, different meta-model extension mechanisms are proposed in [HSR19], which serve as composition operators. The concept of extension is well known and established in object-oriented design, for example, by means of stereotyping. However, EMOF on which the PCM is based does not support an extend relation. For this reason, several ways of how to enable the creation of extensions with EMF's Ecore are identified and discussed in [HSR19]. These include EMF Profiles [Lan+11] that enable the support for stereotypes, different kinds of plain referencing in combination with the introduction of new containers or inheritance relations, and cross-module inheritance.

The interested reader may refer to Chap. 2 for foundations of model and analysis composition, to Chap. 4 for general discussion on compositional semantics and to Chap. 9 of this book [Hei+21] for its application in the context of GTSMorpher.

Refactoring Metamodel Design Smells

Based on metamodel decomposition techniques and the reference architecture, detailed guidelines for metamodel refactoring have been proposed in [HSR19]. These guidelines comprise refactorings on metaclass level as well as on metamodel component level. In the following, we describe how the design smells in the PCM discussed in Sect. 11.3 can be refactored.

The Language Feature Scattering smell can be refactored by decomposing metamodel packages and locating all classifiers that implement a specific language feature into a single metamodel package [HSR19]. Classifiers within a metamodel package that are more closely related should be placed into their own subpackage. Details on refactoring metaclass and packages are described in [Str19]. The reference architecture proposed in this chapter helps to distinguish classifiers of fundamental (abstract) language features (π), domain-specific features (Δ), quality-specific features (Ω), and features specific to analyses (Σ). In the decomposed PCM (see Fig. 11.2), all classes for representing the resources feature, for example, have been located in a metamodel package on the Δ layer called resources. All classes for implementing the performance feature and reliability feature, respectively, have been placed into the metamodel packages performance and reliability on the Ω layer and extend the resource-specific classes on the Δ layer.

For resolving the Package Blob smell, the metamodel package must be split so that each package only contains classifiers of a single language feature [HSR19]. Subpackaging may be applied to further decompose metamodel packages. Details on refactoring metaclass and packages are described in [Str19]. The refactored metamodel packages may be located on different layers of the reference architecture depending on the purpose they satisfy. In the decomposed PCM (see Fig. 11.2), the repository package is split to distinguish the various features implemented in this package. A package repository is located on the π layer to implement a domain-independent repository feature that is further subdivided into packages to implement features for component composition and annotation. On the Δ layer, the repository package is extended by domain-specific classes to represent software components.

Representing components of other domains, like electrics/electronics or mechanics, as extension of the domain-independent repository feature is possible on the Δ layer but out of the scope of the original PCM. Extensions to represent performance and reliability are located on the Ω layer.

The Metamodel Monolith smell can be refactored by splitting the metamodel files according to their language features following the metamodel decomposition techniques proposed in this chapter. Each metamodel file then contains a single metamodel component. Based on the language features they provide, the metamodel components can be composed to form a language specific to a given purpose.

11.5.2 Decomposition and Composition of the Simulators

The layered reference architecture for quality modelling and analysis introduced in the previous section cannot only be applied to metamodels but also to simulators working on instances of the metamodels. Simulators may be decomposed into simulator components along the features they provide. We define a simulator component as a container of packages and classes that has explicit interfaces to other simulator components. The individual simulator components may be composed to satisfy a specific purpose for which a system is to be analysed. This requires composition operators for simulators.

Three forms of composition of analyses in general—model composition (white-box composition), result composition (black-box composition), and analysis composition (grey-box composition)—have been introduced in Chap. 4 of this book [Hei+21]. In this chapter, we give concrete examples of how to implement these forms of composition by discussing specific composition operators for simulators in the context of Palladio.

First attempts at composition operators for simulators in the context of Palladio have been described in [Hei+17]. These composition operators are:

- Composition by result exchange between isolated simulators
- Composition by co-simulation
- Composition by transformation into a joint formalism
- Composition by extension of one simulator by another

Composition by result exchange between isolated simulators conforms to the form result composition (black-box composition) in Chap. 4 of this book [Hei+21]. It is the most simple way of simulator composition. This way of composition can only be applied if one simulator requires the results of another simulator, but there is no interaction between the simulators required during simulation. Both simulators are executed in isolation, and information is exchanged ex-post by inserting the results of one simulator as input into another simulator.

Composition by co-simulation conforms to the form analysis composition (grey-box composition) in Chap. 4 of this book [Hei+21]. It enables information exchange during simulation. Simulators are interlinked in order to exchange information during simulation. Co-simulation commonly requires additional efforts, for example, a coordinator for time management, model synchronisation, and connectivity in order to enable coherent simulation.

Composition by transformation into a joint formalism conforms to the form model composition (white-box composition) in Chap. 4 of this book [Hei+21]. It uses model transformations for creating a homogeneous simulation model. A characteristic of this approach is that a single formalism model is used as input to the simulation. Commonly, general-purpose simulation formalisms like Petri nets or queuing networks are used as the target formalism. This way of simulator composition can only be applied if there is a joint formalism to integrate the models of all the simulators (or if such an integrated formalism can be constructed). For Palladio, for instance, transformations to layered queuing networks [KR08] and queuing coloured Petri nets [MKK11] have been developed so far.

Composition by extension is another way to implement the form model composition (white-box composition) in Chap. 4 of this book [Hei+21]. This way of simulator composition is about extending the metamodel and simulation routines of one simulator by the metamodel and simulation routines of another simulator to form an integrated and unified simulator. Composition by extension is applicable if all the simulators build upon the same (or compatible) modelling paradigm and simulation formalism.

In the following, we give examples of the application of the composition operators in the context of Palladio.

IntBIIS

The approach *Integrated Business IT Impact Simulation* (IntBIIS) [Hei+17] is an example of composition by extension. IntBIIS is a composition of Palladio's simulator EventSim [MH11] and a business process simulator by extending the metamodel and simulation routines of Palladio by entities, scheduling policies, and simulation routines specific to business processes. Applying composition by extension in IntBIIS is possible as both simulators, Palladio's EventSim and the business process simulator, adhere to the same modelling paradigm and simulation formalism. IntBIIS extends the usage specification of the PCM by business process constructs. Both, the usage model and the business process model, rely on an activity diagram like modelling paradigm. They specify a certain workload to be processed by resources in the form of sequences of actions (possibly hierarchically nested) and intensity of action execution. Both, Palladio's EventSim and the business process simulator, build upon queuing theory concepts to simulate resources processing aforementioned workload.

An overview of the composed simulators of IntBIIS is given in Fig. 11.3. Blue elements with a stickman symbol indicate modelling constructs and simulation routines introduced as an extension of the original EventSim simulator. The remaining grey elements are those of the original EventSim simulator. A run of the composed simulators starts at the topmost layer with simulating workloads that originate

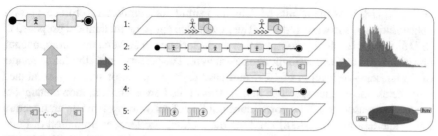

Fig. 11.3 Composition by extension in IntBIIS, after [Hei+17]

from the business process model. For each workload specification, a workload generator spawns a new business process instance in the simulation whenever a certain inter-arrival time has been passed [Hei+17]. A business process instance is the representation of a single enactment of the business process model [Hei+17]. Each business process instance is then simulated individually by traversing the corresponding sequence of actions specified in the business process model (layer 2). When the traversal procedure arrives at an action, basically two cases can be distinguished [Hei+17]: (i) the simulation encounters an actor step or (ii) it encounters a system step (i.e., system entry call).

In case (i), a suitable resource that represents a human actor is requested (layer 5, left) in simulation. If the selected actor is already busy, the actor step is enqueued in its waiting queue. This induces a waiting period not only for the actor step but also for the enclosing business process instance. Based on these concepts taken from queuing theory, we can simulate execution times of actor steps and the entire business process instance as well as utilisation of actor resources depending on a given workload. Simulation results can be visualised in the form of histograms and pie charts for engineers.

In case (ii), resource demands are not issued directly by the business process instance but emerge as the system request propagates through components (layer 3), their service effect specifications (layer 4), down to hardware resources (layer 5, right) [Hei+17]. Similar to actor resources, hardware resources may be busy and therefore block a request. This causes waiting time for the system step and the enclosing business process instance. Based on these concepts taken from queuing theory, we can simulate execution times of system steps and the entire business process instance as well as utilisation of hardware resources depending on a given workload. Simulation results can be visualised again in the form of histograms and pie charts for engineers.

PCA

Composition by result exchange between isolated simulators has been applied in the Palladio context to use Palladio simulator results in other analysis tools as a basis to reason about additional quality properties. The *Power Consumption Analyzer*

(PCA) [Sti18] uses the results of Palladio's simulator SimuLizar to forecast power consumption of software systems. The Power Consumption metamodel proposed in [Sti18] is used to specify consumption characteristics of servers, their components, and connected power distribution infrastructure. The performance simulation results of SimuLizar—utilisation of CPU and hard disk resources of servers—combined with the characteristics specified in instances of the Power Consumption metamodel are used to reason about the power consumption of software systems on architecture level. The analysis in [Sti18] supports the architecture-level examination of both, static and self-adaptive software systems. As shown in Fig. 11.4, the PCA uses measurements from the Palladio Runtime Measurement Model that have been produced by SimuLizar and calculates the power consumption based on its Power State Model. A Power State Model is a stateful power model in the form of a state machine that describes, for example, which servers are in on or off state. The results of the PCA are then accessible in the Palladio Runtime Measurement Model and can be used to trigger self-adaptations in SimuLizar.

OMPCM

An example of composition by co-simulation in the Palladio context is the OM-PCM [HMR13] approach. Modelling and simulation of network communication are limited in Palladio. This weakens not only the prediction accuracy for network-intensive systems [KBH07, Ver+07] but also misses the opportunity to simulate different network configurations and topologies before implementing them. Extensive network communication arises especially within distributed systems, where software components deployed on different hardware nodes work together towards a common goal. OMPCM integrates the OMNeT++-based network simulation

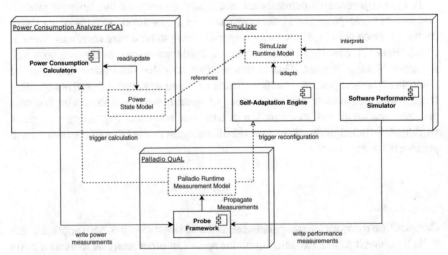

Fig. 11.4 Composition by result exchange in PCA, after [Sti18]

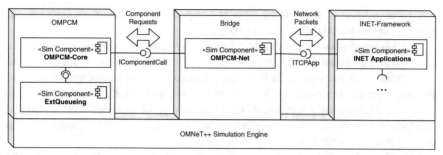

Fig. 11.5 Composition by co-simulation in OMPCM

framework INET with the Palladio architecture-level software performance prediction implemented in the OMPCM-Core and ExtQueueing components to enrich Palladio by more detailed network simulation. OMPCM applies composition by co-simulation by having a dedicated bridge (OMPCM-Net) to manage the translation of events between the OMPCM and the INET simulators. As shown in Fig. 11.5, the OMPCM-Net bridge component accepts events corresponding to the IComponentCall interface. The IComponentCall interface describes the sending and reception of requests and responses on software component level. The bridge component then translates the component-level events to network-level events by resolving remote software components to network nodes and requests/responses to TCP transfers. Implementing the ITCPApp interface of the INET-Framework, the bridge component then sends and receives network-level events to and from the network simulation.

Refactoring Simulator Design Smells

Next, we discuss how aforementioned design smells in the simulators can be resolved.

The Amateur Science smell can be refactored by the proposed simulator composition techniques. The individual simulator components can be developed independently by domain experts for the specific simulator components. The simulator components can then be composed to satisfy a certain analysis goal. In the Palladio context, for example, composition of OMPCM and the OMNeT++-based network simulator INET by co-simulation [HMR13] allows for including detailed network simulation in Palladio, while the INET network simulator has been developed by domain experts independent of Palladio.

The smell Analysis Paralysis can be addressed by decomposing unnecessarily complex or detailed metamodels and simulators and composing the metamodel components and simulator components, respectively, as described in this chapter on an appropriate level of complexity or detail.

The Everything but the Kitchen Sink smell can be addressed by decomposing metamodels and simulators by distinguishing relevant from irrelevant features and composing only relevant metamodel components and simulator components, respectively, as described in this chapter.

The Living Flatland smell can be refactored by enabling the replacement and/or composition of simulator components to consider other and/or additional levels of abstraction in simulation. In Palladio, the simulator component responsible for processor scheduling needs to be replaced so that a new simulator component can provide the scheduling policies needed. Alternatively, the composition of additional simulator components that provide the needed scheduling policies with the existing simulator components is a solution in Palladio.

The Underdefined Semantics smell can be addressed by clearly defining the semantics of metamodel and simulator components and by purpose-oriented composition of only semantically compatible simulator components to satisfy a certain analysis goal. Compositionality of analyses and specific conditions of composition are discussed in Chap. 4 of this book [Hei+21].

The Excessive Events/Event Flooding smell can be refactored by avoiding unnecessary communication via events and using as little events as possible. This can be achieved by aggregating events that happen at the same time instead of sending each event individually. In addition, only time-dependent communication should happen via events, and the temporal resolution can be communicated before starting the simulation to reduce time synchronisation effort via events. Note, the Excessive Events/Event Flooding smell can be caused by simulator composition as each simulator component may have its own event management that needs to be synchronised with others. This synchronisation causes large event communication overhead. This communication overhead needs to be considered in simulator design and avoided as described before or by using a centralised event management like in [IEE10].

The Simulator Feature Scattering, Simulator Component Blob, and Simulator Monolith smells can be refactored by decomposing the simulator into simulator components along the features provided by the simulator following the decomposition techniques proposed in this chapter. The composition techniques described in this chapter enable the interaction between the different simulator components. Adequate decomposition of simulators allows for exchanging and purpose-oriented composition of simulator components.

The Global State Object and God Parameter smells can be resolved by decomposing the simulator into simulator components and following object-oriented design principles [Mar00] to reduce coupling between the simulator components.

The Intrusive Extension smell can be resolved by adequately decomposing the simulator into simulator components along the features it provides. This will lead to an extraction of intrusive simulator extensions into separate simulator components.

11.6   Conclusion and Outlook

This chapter gave insights into Palladio as a case study for evolution of a historically-grown approach to model-based analysis. We provided an overview of the Palladio approach and the associated tooling. We reported about design smells in the metamodel and simulators caused by evolution and growth over several years. We discussed how techniques for decomposition and purpose-oriented composition can help refactoring the metamodel and simulators to avoid these design smells and thus ease the evolution of the Palladio approach in the future.

Techniques for decomposition and composition of modelling languages and analysis tools need to be further investigated in the future to make the concepts discussed in this chapter applicable in a more general way. The application of the decomposition and composition techniques for grammar-based modelling languages would be interesting to investigate in the future. While in this chapter the techniques for decomposition and composition have been discussed in the light of the Palladio approach, we expect these techniques are independent of quality modelling and analysis and can be applied to modelling languages and analysis tools in general. Further, the dependencies between modelling languages and analysis tools on the level of their features and components need to be investigated in the future. Tool support is required for visualising dependencies between modelling languages and analysis tools on feature and component level to simplify working with and configuring large modelling languages and analysis tools.

References

[Bec08] Steffen Becker. *Coupled Model Transformations for QoS Enabled Component-Based Software Design*. Universitätsverlag Karlsruhe, 2008. https://publikationen.bibliothek. kit.edu/1000009095.

[BLB13] Matthias Becker, Markus Luckey, and Steffen Becker. "Performance Analysis of Self-adaptive Systems for Requirements Validation at Design-time". In: *9th International ACM Sigsoft Conference on Quality of Software Architectures*. 2013, pp. 43–52. https://doi.org/10.1145/2465478.2465489.

[Bro+12] Franz Brosch, Heiko Koziolek, Barbora Buhnova, and Ralf Reussner. "Architecture-Based Reliability Prediction with the Palladio Component Model". In: *IEEE Transactions on Software Engineering* 38.6 (2012), pp. 1319–1339. https://doi.org/10.1109/TSE.2011.94.

[Bus+96] Frank Buschmann, Regine Meunier, Hans Rohnert, Peter Sommerlad, and Michael Stal. *Pattern-Oriented Software Architecture—Volume 1: A System of Patterns*. Wiley Publishing, 1996.

[Gro13] Henning Groenda. *Certifying Software Component Performance Specifications*. Vol. 11. KIT Scientific Publishing, Karlsruhe, 2013. https://doi.org/10.5445/KSP/1000036063.

[GS13] Samarthyam Ganesh and Tushar Sharma. "Towards a Principle-based Classification of Structural Design Smells". In: *Journal of Object Technology* 12 (2013). https://doi.org/10.5381/jot.2013.12.2.a1.

[Hap08] Jens Happe. *Predicting Software Performance in Symmetric Multi-Core and Multi-processor Environments*. University of Oldenburg, Germany, 2008. http://oops.uni-oldenburg.de/827/1/happre08.pdf.

[Hei+17] Robert Heinrich, Philipp Merkle, Jörg Henss, and Barbara Paech. "Integrating business process simulation and information system simulation for performance prediction". In: *Software & Systems Modeling* 16.1 (2017), pp. 257–277. https://doi.org/10.1007/s10270-015-0457-1.

[Hei+18] Robert Heinrich, Dominik Werle, Heiko Klare, Ralf Reussner, Max Kramer, Steffen Becker, Jens Happe, Heiko Koziolek, and Klaus Krogmann. "The Palladio-Bench for Modeling and Simulating Software Architectures". In: *40th International Conference on Software Engineering: Companion Proceedings*. 2018, pp. 37–40.

[Hei+21] Robert Heinrich, Francisco Durán, Carolyn L. Talcott, and Steffen Zschaler (eds.) *Composing Model-Based Analysis Tools*. Springer, 2021. https://doi.org/10.1007/978-3-030-81915-6.

[HMR13] Jörg Henss, Philipp Merkle, and Ralf Reussner. "The OMPCM Simulator for Model-Based Software Performance Prediction: Poster Abstract". In: *6th International ICST Conference on Simulation Tools and Techniques*. 2013, pp. 354–357.

[HSR19] Robert Heinrich, Misha Strittmatter, and Ralf Reussner. "A Layered Reference Architecture for Metamodels to Tailor Quality Modeling and Analysis". In: *IEEE Transactions on Software Engineering* 47.4 (2019), pp. 775–800. https://doi.org/10.1109/TSE.2019.2903797.

[IEE10] IEEE. 1516-2010—IEEE *Standard for Modeling and Simulation (M&S) High Level Architecture (HLA)*. Tech. rep. IEEE, 2010, pp. 1–38. https://doi.org/10.1109/IEEESTD.2010.5553440.

[KBH07] Heiko Koziolek, Steffen Becker, and Jens Happe. "Predicting the Performance of Component-Based Software Architectures with Different Usage Profiles". In: *Third International Conference on Quality of Software Architectures*. 2007, pp. 145–163. https://doi.org/10.1007/978-3-540-77619-2_9.

[KR08] Heiko Koziolek and Ralf Reussner. "A Model Transformation from the Palladio Component Model to Layered Queueing Networks". In: *SPEC International Performance Evaluation Workshop*. 2008, pp. 58–78. https://doi.org/10.1007/978-3-540-69814-2_6.

[Lan+11] Philip Langer, Konrad Wieland, Manuel Wimmer, and Jordi Cabot. "EMF profiles: A lightweight extension approach for EMF models". In: *Journal of Object Technology* 11 (2011), p. 8. https://doi.org/10.5381/jot.2012.11.1.a8.

[Leh14] Sebastian Lehrig. "Applying Architectural Templates for Design-Time Scalability and Elasticity Analyses of SaaS Applications". In: *2nd International Workshop on Hot Topics in Cloud Service Scalability*. 2014, 2:1–2:8.

[LM06] Michele Lanza and Radu Marinescu. *Object-Oriented Metrics in Practice: Using Software Metrics to Characterize, Evaluate, and Improve the Design of Object-Oriented Systems*. Springer, 2006. https://doi.org/10.1007/3-540-39538-5.

[Mar+10] Anne Martens, Heiko Koziolek, Steffen Becker, and Ralf Reussner. "Automatically Improve Software Architecture Models for Performance, Reliability, and Cost Using Evolutionary Algorithms". In: *First Joint WOSP/SIPEW International Conference on Performance Engineering*. 2010. https://doi.org/10.1145/1712605.1712624.

[Mar00] Robert C. Martin. *Design Principles and Design Patterns*. Vol. 1. Prentice Hall, 2000.

[MH11] Philipp Merkle and Jörg Henss. "EventSim—An Event-driven Palladio Software Architecture Simulator". In: *Palladio Days 2011*. 2011, pp. 15–22. http://digbib.ubka.uni-karlsruhe.de/volltexte/1000025188.

[MKK11] Philipp Meier, Samuel Kounev, and Heiko Koziolek. "Automated Transformation of Component-based Software Architecture Models to Queueing Petri Nets". In: *19th IEEE/ACM International Symposium on Modeling, Analysis and Simulation of Computer and Telecommunication Systems*. 2011. https://doi.org/10.1109/MASCOTS.2011.23.

[Reu+16] Ralf H. Reussner, Steffen Becker, Jens Happe, Robert Heinrich, Anne Koziolek, Heiko Koziolek, Max Kramer, and Klaus Krogmann. *Modeling and Simulating Software Architectures—The Palladio Approach*. MIT Press, 2016.

[Ros+15] Kiana Rostami, Johannes Stammel, Robert Heinrich, and Ralf Reussner. "Architecture-based Assessment and Planning of Change Requests". In: *11th International ACM SIGSOFT Conference on Quality of Software Architectures*. 2015, pp. 21–30. https://sdqweb.ipd.kit.edu/publications/pdfs/rostami2015a.pdf.

[SHR18] Misha Strittmatter, Robert Heinrich, and Ralf Reussner. *Supplementary Material for the Evaluation of the Layered Reference Architecture for Metamodels to Tailor Quality Modeling and Analysis*. Tech. rep. 11. Karlsruher Institut für Technologie (KIT), 2018. 42 pp. https://doi.org/10.5445/IR/1000089243.

[SHR19] Stephan Seifermann, Robert Heinrich, and Ralf H. Reussner. "Data-Driven Software Architecture for Analyzing Confidentiality". In: *IEEE International Conference on Software Architecture*. 2019, pp. 1–10.

[Ste12] Susan Stepney. "A pattern language for scientific simulations". In: *Workshop on complex systems modelling and simulation*. 2012, pp. 77–103.

[Sti18] Christian Stier. *Adaptation-Aware Architecture Modeling and Analysis of Energy Efficiency for Software Systems*. 2018, p. 262. https://doi.org/10.5445/IR/1000083402.

[Str+16] Misha Strittmatter, Georg Hinkel, Michael Langhammer, Reiner Jung, and Robert Heinrich. "Challenges in the Evolution of Metamodels: Smells and Anti-Patterns of a Historically-Grown Metamodel". In: *10th International Workshop on Models and Evolution*. 2016.

[Str19] Misha Strittmatter. *A Reference Structure for Modular Metamodels of Quality- Describing Domain-Specific Modeling Languages*. Universitätsverlag Karlsruhe, 2019. https://publikationen.bibliothek.kit.edu/1000098906.

[TH16] Emre Taspolatoglu and Robert Heinrich. "Context-based Architectural Security Analysis". In: *13th Working IEEE/IFIP Conference on Software Architecture*. 2016, pp. 281–282.

[Ver+07] Tom Verdickt, Bart Dhoedt, Filip De Turck, and Piet Demeester. "Hybrid performance modeling approach for network intensive distributed software". In: *6th International Workshop on Software and Performance*. 2007, pp. 189–200. https://doi.org/10.1145/1216993.1217026.

Chapter 12
AnATLyzer: Static Analysis of ATL Model Transformations

Jesús Sánchez Cuadrado, Esther Guerra, and Juan de Lara

Abstract This chapter presents ANATLYZER—a tool for the static analysis of the ATL model transformation language. ANATLYZER is able to statically detect more than 50 types of problems in ATL transformation programs using different analysis techniques, some of them used in combination as per Challenge 2 (integrating and orchestrating analysis tools, cf. Chap. 5 of this book). The tool also provides a catalogue of more than 100 quick fixes (including quick fix recommendation via speculative analysis), visualisations and explanations to help understand the errors, and a synthesiser of witness models that permit reproducing the errors found. Altogether, this chapter focuses on how transformation developers can exploit ANATLYZER's output results to understand and fix transformation problems and achieve higher quality transformations.

This case-study chapter illustrates concepts introduced in Chap. 7 and addresses Challenge 4 in Chap. 3 of this book.

12.1 Introduction and Problem Statement

Model-to-model transformations are programs that translate models of one language (e.g., statecharts in the *Unified Modeling Language* (UML) [Obj15]) into models of the same or a different language (e.g., Petri nets). Model transformations are the enablers of automation in model-driven engineering processes, and their correctness is crucial to ensure the quality of model-driven solutions since transformations are typically used many times on many different input models [SK03].

Model transformations are generally built using specialised languages called *model transformation languages*. A prominent example is the *ATLAS transforma-*

J. S. Cuadrado (✉)
Universidad de Murcia, Murcia, Spain
e-mail: jesusc@um.es; Juan.deLara@uam.es

E. Guerra · J. De Lara
Autonomous University of Madrid, Madrid, Spain
e-mail: esther.guerra@uam.es

tion language (ATL) [Jou+08], as it has a large community of users [Bru+20]. However, despite the importance of model transformations, many widely used transformation languages lack user-friendly tools and techniques to help ensuring transformations' correctness, as reported for example in [Kah+19]. In particular, ATL is dynamically typed, which makes its static analysis challenging, and therefore, ATL developers typically rely just on ad hoc, manual testing to validate their transformations. However, exhaustive transformation testing is time-consuming as it entails creating a suitable set of test models that is effective in detecting bugs, executing the transformation under test with the (likely large) test model set, and checking the correctness of the output models produced by the transformation either manually or automatically using an oracle function (e.g., by means of a contract). Moreover, there is a lack of tools for testing transformations [Kah+19, GSL19]. This complexity and effort in transformation testing may be the reason why many ATL transformations found in public repositories contain errors [SGL17].

To alleviate this problem, the ANATLYZER tool for the static analysis of ATL transformations was developed [SGL17, SGL18b]. The tool is integrated within the ATL Eclipse development environment and is able to statically detect more than 50 types of problems, and recommend quick fixes for them using speculative analysis [SGL18b]. Moreover, ANATLYZER provides different visualisations and explanations to help developers understand and fix the errors, including a synthesiser of test models that can be used to reproduce the error, and a high-level visualisation of the transformation rules and their dependencies.

In the rest of this chapter, first, Sect. 12.2 introduces the main features of ATL using a running example. Next, Sect. 12.3 overviews the static analysis and quick fix capabilities of ANATLYZER. Section 12.4 walks through the features of the supporting tool, with a special emphasis on the different kinds of outputs produced and their usefulness for ATL developers. Then, Sect. 12.5 showcases the use of ANATLYZER to find, reason, and fix bugs on the running example. Finally, Sect. 12.6 compares with related works, and Sect. 12.7 concludes the chapter discussing some open challenges in the development of static analysis tools for model transformations.

12.2 Background on ATL

ATL is a rule-based language to define model-to-model transformation programs. These programs receive one or more source models and produce one or more target models, all conformant to their respective metamodels. To illustrate the usage of ATL, we will use as a running example an ATL transformation to reverse engineer Java applications into UML class diagrams. The source code of the Java application is converted into a model using the facilities of the Modisco project [Bru+14], which provides a Java metamodel. Figure 12.1 shows an excerpt of the latter metamodel, while Fig. 12.2 shows a fragment of the UML metamodel relevant for the example.

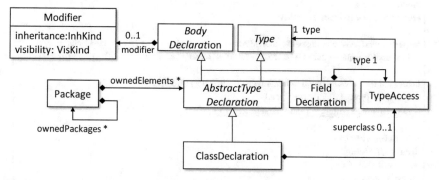

Fig. 12.1 Excerpt of the Java metamodel, as provided by MoDisco [Bru+14]

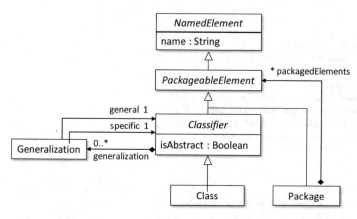

Fig. 12.2 Excerpt of the UML metamodel [OMG17]

Listing 12.1 shows an excerpt of this transformation, which contains some errors that we introduced on purpose to illustrate ANATLYZER. The example is based on the Java2UML benchmark used in [Sán+20].

An ATL program is structured into rules. Rules have a section *from* specifying the type of source objects that the rule will match; an optional *filter* imposing conditions on the matched source objects; a section *to* declaring the objects that the rule application will create; and *bindings* that assign a value to the attributes and references of the created objects. As an example, Lines 21–30 in Listing 12.1 contain the rule Package2Package which, given an object src of type Java Package (Line 22), generates an object tgt of type UML Package. The rule includes a filter to make the rule match only objects which are not proxies, as MoDisco generates extra elements to represent library classes and marks them with $proxy = true$. The type of the objects is prefixed by the metamodel names (JAVA and UML, declared in Line 4). The reference to the metamodels is defined in Lines 1–2. Lines 24–28 contain several bindings that assign a value to the features of the created tgt object.

```
1   -- @nsURI UML=http://www.eclipse.org/uml2/3.0.0/UML
2   -- @nsURI JAVA=http://www.eclipse.org/MoDisco/Java/0.2.incubation/java
3   module java2uml;
4   create OUT : UML from IN : JAVA;
5
6   helper context JAVA!Package def : allNonProxyClassesInPackage : Set(JAVA!ClassDeclaration) =
7     self.ownedElements → select(e | e.proxy = false) → select(e | e.oclIsTypeOf(JAVA!ClassDeclaration));
8
9   helper context JAVA!MethodDeclaration def: isAttribute() : Boolean =
10     self.returnType.isPrimitiveType() and
11     self.name.startsWith('get') and self.name.size() > 4;
12
13  rule Model2Model {
14   from s : JAVA!Model
15   to t : UML!Model (
16    name ← s.name,
17    packagedElement ← s.ownedElements→select(e | not e.proxy)
18   )
19  }
20
21  rule Package2Package {
22   from src : JAVA!Package (not s1.proxy)
23   to tgt : UML!Package(
24    name ← s1.name,
25    packagedElement ← src.ownedPackages→
26      select(e | e.oclIsTypeOf(JAVA!Package)),
27    packagedElement ← src.allNonProxyClassesInPackage,
28    packagedElement ← self.ownedElements
29   )
30  }
31
32  rule Class2Class {
33   from s1 : JAVA!ClassDeclaration(s1.proxy = false)
34   to t1 : UML!Class (
35    generalization ← if not s1.getSuperClass.oclIsUndefined() then
36      thisModule.createGeneralization(s1)
37    else
38     OclUndefined
39    endif,
40    ownedAttribute ← s1.bodyDeclarations→select(d |
41      d.oclIsKindOf(JAVA!MethodDeclaration))→select(m | m.isAttribute(s1)),
42    isAbstract ← if s1.modifier.oclIsUndefined() then
43      OclUndefined
44    else
45      s1.modifier.inheritance = 'abstract'
46    endif
47   )
48  }
49
50  lazy rule createGeneralization {
51    from c : JAVA!ClassDeclaration
52    to g : UML!Generalization (
53      ...
54    )
55  }
```

Listing 12.1 Excerpt of Java to UML transformation. Issues are underlined according to their severity (Error, Warning)

In general, the right-hand side of bindings are *object constraint language* (OCL) expressions that may refer to objects read or created by the rule. Bindings for references (e.g., Lines 25–28) can assign objects of the source model to references in the target model. In such cases, an implicit binding resolution mechanism determines the target objects that were created from the given source objects, and assigns those target objects to the reference. For example, the binding in Line 25 contains objects of type Package in its right-hand side, and so, the Package2Package rule resolves this binding; whereas the binding in Line 27 is resolved by rule Class2Class. In contrast, bindings for attributes (e.g., name ← s1.name in Line 24) are directly assigned.

Rules Model2Model, Package2Package, and Class2Class in the listing are matched rules. A matched rule is applied to each match of its *from* pattern. However, each object in the source model should be translated by one matched rule at most, as otherwise, we obtain a runtime error. ATL also supports other types of rules, like *lazy rules* (Line 50) which are executed only when explicitly called from other rules (e.g., from Line 36). Finally, ATL transformations can include *helpers* to define auxiliary operations written in OCL. For example, helper isAttribute in Lines 9–11 is defined on the context of class MethodDeclaration.

Expressing a model transformation using a dedicated language like ATL has benefits, like the availability of transformation primitives (rules), the integration with navigation and expression languages (OCL) and with an underlying modelling framework (EMF), and a better analysability. However, transformation programs can become large and complex, which make them error-prone without additional support. In the next section, we introduce our approach to tackle these issues.

12.3 Analysing and Fixing Model Transformations

The goal of ANATLYZER is to help developers in the task of building correct ATL model transformations. To this end, ANATLYZER performs a static analysis of a given model transformation and reports information regarding three main questions:

- Q1: Is the transformation correctly typed with respect to the source metamodels?
- Q2: Do the generated models conform to the target metamodel?
- Q3: Do the transformation rules cover all cases?

Answering the first question involves a type checker, whereas answering the second and third questions requires the analysis of the transformation rules using the typing information gathered by the type checker. When a problem is found, it has to be reported to the user in a manner that is comprehensible and helps identify the root cause of the problem. Moreover, ANATLYZER recommends quick fixes that facilitate solving each detected type of problem.

In this section, we first describe our method for the analysis of transformations (Sect. 4.3) and then overview our support for quick fixes (Sect. 12.3.2).

12.3.1 Transformation Analysis

Figure 12.3 depicts ANATLYZER's analysis process [SGL18a]. In a first step—to obtain a more accurate typing—ANATLYZER type-checks the transformation based on a custom, built-in type inference engine for OCL. This process is needed since ATL is a dynamically typed language, and the standard ATL type checker provides scarce typing information. The process annotates each node of the abstract syntax tree of the transformation with the inferred type.

Based on this information, ANATLYZER builds a *transformation dependence graph* (TDG). This is similar to a program dependence graph [FOW87], but it also includes dependency links between each rule binding and all possible rules that can resolve the binding. At this stage, the method produces two types of output: (i) real errors and warnings, which are reported to the user (e.g., the problem in Line 10 of Listing 12.1 signals that MethodDeclaration.returnType might be undefined, in which case calling method isPrimitiveType() would cause a null-pointer exception); and (ii) *"potential problems"* or smells that cannot be confirmed statically to be real errors (e.g., there might be a problem in Line 28 of Listing 12.1 if the available rules do not transform all possible objects that may appear in the binding's right-hand side) but that can be verified using a model finder (a constraint solver over models). To handle this latter case, for each potential problem, its OCL path condition is computed. This is an OCL expression containing the requirements for an input model to make the model transformation fail at the problem's location. Then, this condition is used as input of the model finder. If a model is found, then the problem is confirmed and reported to the user; otherwise, the problem is discarded. A similar approach is used to refine the TDG by removing impossible binding-rule links, which improves the accuracy of the visualisations and program navigation actions (cf. Sect. 12.4).

ANATLYZER detects more than 50 types of errors. Table 12.1 shows some representative ones. The table's columns contain the following information: a description of the error; the kind of error, either typing error, navigation error,

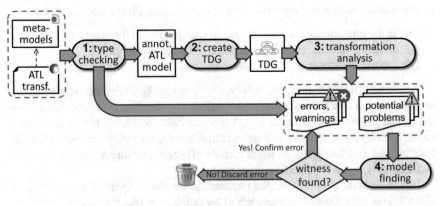

Fig. 12.3 Overview of ANATLYZER's analysis process [SGL18a]

Table 12.1 Some of the problems detected by AnATLYZER

#	Error description	Kind	Time	Solver	Question
1	Feature or operation not found	Typing	Live	No	Q1
2	Incoherent variable declaration	Typing	Live	No	Q1
3	Access over undefined receptor	Navigation	Live	Maybe	Q1
4	No binding for compulsory target feature	Target Integrity	Live	No	Q2
5	Binding resolved by rule with invalid target	Target Integrity	Live	Maybe	Q2
6	Unresolved binding	Rules	Live	Maybe	Q3
7	Rule conflict	Rules	Batch	Maybe	Q3

violation of target metamodel integrity constraint, or rule error; the moment when the error is analysed, either live or batch; whether confirming the error requires using the solver (relevant, as the use of the solver typically incurs in a performance penalty); and the question (Q1–Q3) that the analysis addresses.

The first error in the table is concerned with the usage of features or operations that do not actually exist, and the second one is used to report inconsistencies between the type of a variable and the type of the objects assigned to the variable. Both errors can be checked live—while the transformation is being developed—and do not require the use of the constraint solver. The third error reports whether a navigation expression may contain a *null* reference that produces a null-pointer exception at runtime. This error is also detected live, but in some cases, the solver is needed to confirm that a valid model able to hit the problematic expression exists. Executing the transformation with such a model would make the transformation fail.

Errors 4 and 5 are directed to identify code excerpts that may produce invalid target models (i.e., non-conformant to the target metamodel) when the transformation is executed. Error 4 is reported when a rule does not provide a value for every mandatory slot in a target object. Error 5 occurs when a binding is resolved by a rule that may produce objects with the wrong type (i.e., the rule creates an object whose type is not consistent with the binding left-hand side). If the error is not fixed, then the transformation may yield ill-formed models. Confirming this kind of errors requires the solver.

Errors 6 and 7 are related to well-formedness aspects of the rules. Both are directed to answer Q3 and may need to use the solver. Error 6 is reported when there is no rule to resolve a reference binding. For instance, the binding in Line 25 will be unresolved for Package elements where proxy = true. This is actually reported as warning, since it is only a smell of incompleteness (i.e., a missing rule or the binding needs additional filtering). Error 7 detects if two rules might be applicable to the same source object, which is not allowed in ATL. Since this analysis involves checking conflicts between each pair of rules, it is executed in batch mode when explicitly invoked by the developer. For instance, let us assume that we write a rule to map Java "internal" packages to private UML packages, such as the following:

```
1  rule InternalPackage2Package {
2    from s : JAVA!Package (s.name = 'internal')
3    to  t : UML!Package ( ... )
```

In this case, ANATLYZER will report a rule conflict because a Java package may satisfy the filter expressions of both the Package2Package and InternalPackage2Package rules.

12.3.2 Quick-Fixing ATL Transformations

ANATLYZER also offers an extensible catalogue of quick fixes directed to correct each error type [SGL18b]. Fixes may involve modifying the metamodel, creating or modifying an OCL transformation pre-condition, or modifying the transformation itself. In the latter case, fixes may generate new expressions, adapt an existing expression to a new context, restrict the applicability of expressions, or change operation/feature calls. Rule-related problems are typically fixed by creating or removing rules, modifying rule filters, creating or removing bindings, or modifying the right part of a binding. Other fixes may involve the creation of new helpers or rules, or changing a reference to a different type.

Our fixes can be categorised in three types: *repair*, *heuristic*, and *template*. Repair fixes eliminate the given problem, typically by adding or modifying expressions in certain locations without any additional input from the developer. For example, a fix that corrects the declared type of a variable to match the type of the assigned value is a repair. Heuristic fixes are suggestions, e.g., proposing a valid name for an erroneous collection operation based on string similarity. These fixes choose one among several options based on a heuristic strategy, and may not match the developer expectations. Finally, template fixes generate code that solves the problem, but normally need to be refined by the developer. For example, a fix that creates a new rule typically needs to be completed with appropriate filters and values for the bindings.

Table 12.2 shows some representative quick fixes for the errors described in Table 12.1. For *feature or operation not found*, the table shows 3 possible fixes, even though ANATLYZER actually provides 5 fixes [SGL18b]. The first one heuristically suggests an existing feature or operation based on a suite of string distance metrics. The second fix automatically creates a skeleton for the non-existing operation. Specifically, it creates a new context helper whose context is the class inferred for the receptor object of the call, and its formal arguments are created according to the types of the actual parameters in the call. The last fix modifies the metamodel by adding the required feature to the receptor's object class.

Other quick fixes are repairs. For example, the one suggested for error *incoherent variable declaration* infers the type of the expression assigned to a variable, and

Table 12.2 Some of the quick fixes provided by ANATLYZER

Error description	Quick fixes	Type
Feature or operation not found	Suggest existing feature/operation	Heuristic
	Create context/module helper	Template
	Create feature in metamodel	Template
Incoherent variable declaration	Assign type of variable value to variable	Repair
Access over undefined receptor	Change feature lower bound to 1	Repair
No binding for compulsory target feature	Assign default value (e.g., empty string)	Repair
	Copy and adapt existing expression	Heuristic
	Suggest mapping to similar source feature	Heuristic
Binding resolved by rule with invalid target	Remove guilty rule	Repair
	Choose a different target feature	Heuristic
Unresolved binding	Create new rule	Template
Rule conflict	Modify filter of guilty rules	Repair
	Remove one guilty rule	Repair

assigns this type to the variable. The fix for error *access over undefined receptor* is a repair as well. This changes the metamodel, increasing the lower cardinality of the reference being navigated to 1 to disable undefined values. Detailed information on the other quick fixes of the catalogue is available at [SGL18b].

The application of a quick fix may have side effects, as it may introduce new problems in other locations, and some existing problems may become automatically fixed. Understanding these side effects is important both from the tool perspective (e.g., to provide a rank of quick fixes) and from the developer perspective who would like to make an informed decision when determining the best quick fix to apply. To this aim, ANATLYZER uses *speculative analysis* to help developers understand the *impact* of applying a quick fix. Speculative analysis is a general technique to explore the consequences of modifying a code excerpt before the change actually happens [Bru+10]. In particular, ANATLYZER automatically detects the fixed problems and the newly generated ones after applying a quick fix *without* modifying the transformation program or its metamodels. ANATLYZER uses this information for two purposes: to provide impact information that helps the developer understand the consequences of applying a quick fix, and to rank the applicable quick fixes by positioning the ones that remove more errors first.

12.4 Tool Support

ANATLYZER is available as an Eclipse plug-in that extends the regular ATL *integrated development environment* (IDE) with features to enhance developer productivity [SGL18a]. The installation details, source code and some demonstration screencasts are available at http://anatlyzer.github.io. In this section, we focus on the outputs produced by the tool based on the results of the presented analyses. Developers can exploit this output to improve their transformations. In Sect. 7.4.8 of this book [Hei+21], we provide a summary of these reporting capabilities with respect to the landscape of the existing results-exploitation approaches.

Analysis Information A core feature of ANATLYZER is its ability to perform accurate type checking of ATL transformations and to analyse rule relationships. This information is gathered in the ATL abstract syntax tree by means of additional classes and features that represent type information and the TDG. The output is a formal model which can be consumed by other tools, as ANATLYZER can also be used in standalone batch mode (i.e., without editing support).

Error Reporting As explained in the previous section, ANATLYZER identifies more than 50 problem types based on the result of the type checking phase and the analysis of the TDG. Figure 12.4 shows a screenshot of the IDE for the running example. Code errors are signalled as in any regular programming environment (Label 1): the problematic code is shown underlined in the ATL editor, and a marker indicates whether the problem is either an error that should be fixed or a warning. Warnings typically signal style issues with no impact in the transformation behaviour, or statements that might be optimised.

In addition, ANATLYZER provides a dedicated view to inspect the analysis results, the Analysis View (Label 2). Given that the verification of some types of problems require performing model finding, a concrete problem can be in one of the following four states: *Confirmed*, meaning that a witness model demonstrating the problem has been found; *Discarded*, meaning that no witness model has been found and therefore the problem cannot happen at runtime; *Running*, meaning that the problem is currently being analysed in the background; and *Unknown*, meaning that the problem cannot be evaluated, typically because of limitations in the model finder (e.g., use of non-supported string operations).

The IDE also provides an explanation of the error that novice developers can find useful to learn. Figure 12.5 shows the dialog that gives information about the problem in Line 28 of the running example. Here, developers can inspect a graphical representation of the generated witness models in order to understand the model elements causing a specific problem (Label 2). In this example, the displayed witness model would help the developer understand that the problem is caused by the lack of a rule that considers the cases in which ClassDeclaration.proxy = true. The witness model can be exported into XMI format, which allows executing the transformation with the model to reproduce the error.

ANATLYZER is able to efficiently validate most error types whenever the transformation file is saved. However, there are four error types whose analysis heavily relies on model finding, and therefore, they may take more than a few milliseconds to complete. To avoid interrupting the developer work and improve his/her experience with the IDE, these four analyses are only triggered on demand from the Analysis View, and executed in the background. These four batch analyses are the

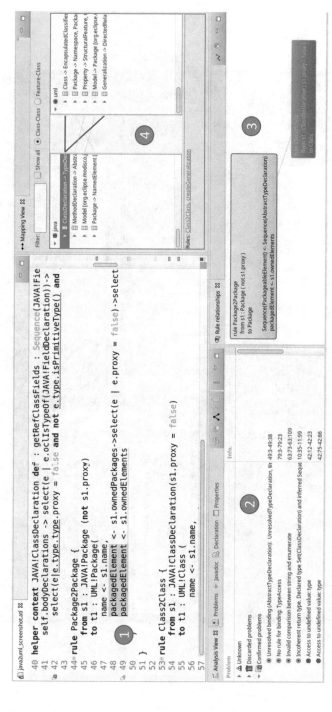

Fig. 12.4 Screenshot of the main interface of AnATLYZER

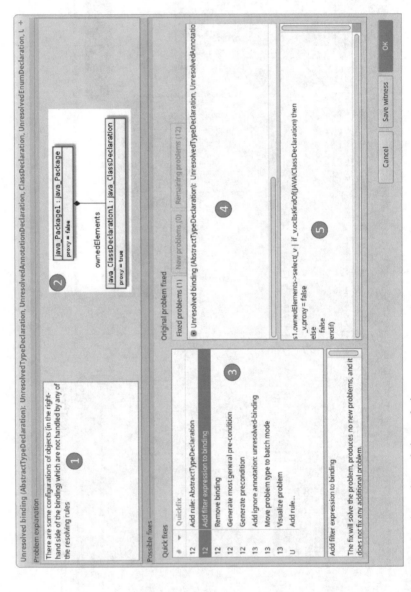

Fig. 12.5 Problem explanation and speculative analysis

following: *rule conflict analysis*, which checks whether two different transformation rules can be applied on the same objects, since ATL disallows it; *target invariant analysis*, which checks that the transformation cannot yield output models that violate the target metamodel invariants or the transformation post-conditions; *child stealing analysis*, which verifies that no object changes its container at runtime; and *unconnected components analysis* to check whether the transformation may yield disconnected graphs, as this may be caused by a buggy rule.

Ranking and Previsualisation of Quick Fixes ANATLYZER incorporates a catalogue of quick fixes to help developers correct the detected problems. Quick fixes are available through the standard facilities provided by Eclipse. This way, developers can ask ANATLYZER to show the available fixes for a reported problem by pressing CTRL+1. Then, selecting a fix applies the fix to solve the problem. A problem may have several possible fixes. Figure 12.6 shows the possible quick fixes for the problem in Line 11. The first solution (illustrated in the figure) is to add a conditional to avoid accessing self.name if it is OclUndefined. Another possibility would be to modify the metamodel to make the feature MethodDeclaration.name mandatory, but this is not appropriate in this case because the MoDisco/Java metamodel is a third-party metamodel. Another possible fix is generating a pre-condition to indicate that the transformation assumes that all method declarations have a name. When looking for witness models, ANATLYZER includes the defined pre-conditions in the model finding process to rule out models not handled by the transformation, which avoids reporting spurious problems.

Another facility of ANATLYZER is speculative analysis [SGL18b], which is used to provide a ranked list of quick fixes (see Fig. 12.6). Quick fixes resolving more problems are ranked first. Moreover, for each quick fix, a previsualisation of the piece of modified code and the status of the transformation (in terms of which problems are fixed and which new problems are introduced) are provided. This helps developers compare the consequences of different quick fixes without actually having to modify the transformation and undo the undesired changes.

High-Level View of Transformation In addition to error detection, the static analysis performed by ANATLYZER is also exploited to produce a high-level graphical representation of the transformation. In this representation, rules are displayed as nodes, bindings are depicted as edges, and rule dependencies due to binding resolutions are shown explicitly. By selecting a rule (i.e., a node in the visualisation) and pressing CTRL+B, it is possible to navigate to the rule's resolving rules. Note that this navigation information is not explicit in the transformation, but ANATLYZER has to discover it by using constraint solving on the TDG. Figure 12.4 illustrates this feature (Label 4).

Tuning of Analysis Parameters There are several configurable parameters in ANATLYZER. First, developers can configure the search scope used in the witness model finding. This is the maximum number of objects and links of each kind a witness model is allowed to have. Smaller search scopes result in more efficient model searches, at the risk of missing witness models that fall outside the selected

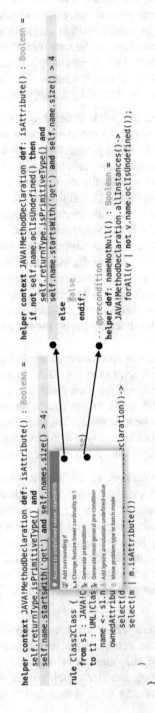

Fig. 12.6 Applying quick fixes to fix "Access to undefined value"

scope. In addition, ANATLYZER permits configuring the error/warning types to analyse whenever the transformation file is saved, specifying the problems to verify in batch mode from the Analysis View, or disabling the analysis of some kinds of errors. For instance, the problem "Binding possibly unresolved" (Line 28) may be frequent depending on the type of transformation and the coding style. Hence, the developer may choose to detect it only in batch mode to avoid distractions.

Tool Integration ANATLYZER offers a Java API that allows invoking the static analysis programmatically, inspecting the results, and obtaining and manipulating an extended version of the syntax tree of ATL transformations enriched with typing information. This simplifies the integration of the analysis output (errors, typing, rule analysis, output of quick fixes) in other tools, and enables the implementation of new kinds of analysis for ATL.

In addition, some parts of ANATLYZER can be extended externally by other developers. First, the static analysis tool is extensible with new kinds of analyses, which can be configured both in standalone mode or using an Eclipse extension point. For instance, in [SGL17], this extension point was implemented to analyse and report errors in ATL transformations related to UML profiles (e.g., incorrect use of stereotypes). The catalogue of quick fixes is also extensible by means of an extension point, which moreover provides several pre-defined abstract quick fixes that simplify the creation of new ones.

As an example of the integration of ANATLYZER with other tools, we can mention the case of WodelTest [Góm+20]. This is a framework to create mutation testing environments for modelling and programming languages. Mutation testing permits estimating the quality of a test set by creating mutants of the tested program, and applying the test set to the mutants. In [Góm+20], WodelTest was used to develop a mutation testing environment for ATL. This environment generates numerous mutants of a given ATL program, and the authors used the API of ANATLYZER programmatically to statically analyse the created mutants and discard the erroneous ones.

Also in the area of mutation testing, in [GSL19], the implementation of ATL mutation operators gets simplified by the integration of ANATLYZER, which permits obtaining typing information of the mutated ATL transformation (e.g., which rules resolve a binding).

12.5   Building Transformations with ANATLYZER in Practice

Next, we showcase the use of ANATLYZER to create and fix the transformation in the running example. We will decompose the three main building blocks to illustrate how the analysis results are made available to developers to assist them in the transformation development process.

12.5.1 Models and Packages

We start building the transformation by identifying the type of the root object in the source models. This is the class Model in the Java metamodel. The natural mapping for this class is UML Model. We specify this mapping by means of the rule in the following listing.

ANATLYZER reports a warning in Line 5 because the transformation has no rule to handle objects of the type in the binding right-hand side. The easiest way to explore the problem is to press CTRL+1 to show the quick fix pop-up dialog. Figure 12.7 shows the process to fix the error. The quick fix dialog includes a brief description of the problem (first line), in this case, that the transformation does not handle objects of type Package. From the list of fixes, we select "Add new rule" since we are interested on mapping Java packages to some UML element. We need to select a concrete UML class, thus a dialog with all UML classes is shown, and we select UML Package. From this information, ANATLYZER generates a new rule called Package2Package and analyses the transformation, which is now free of errors.

12.5.2 Packages and Classes

The next logical step is to complete the Package2Package rule, creating bindings to populate the UML package with the UML classes it contains. Thus, we need a rule to convert Java classes into UML classes. But instead of creating this rule, we may write the binding in Line 6 of Listing 12.3, and use the quick fix facility to generate the Class2Class rule, as before. Listing 12.3 shows a simple, and erroneous, first version of the rule.

The first problem is that we are trying to access a potentially undefined value (s.modifier can be undefined in Line 13). An advantage of ANATLYZER is that it eliminates the burden to continuously inspect the metamodel to check the cardinality of features, which is particularly cumbersome with large metamodels. Instead, we can just write the code in the easiest way, let ANATLYZER pinpoint the cardinality issues, and use quick fixes to automatically generate correct code. Also in Line

```
1  rule Model2Model {
2  from s : JAVA!Model
3  to t : UML!Model (                    Unresolved binding
4    name ← s.name,
5    packagedElement ← s.ownedElements
6  )
7  }
```

Listing 12.2 Rule for mapping Java to UML models (Error, Warning)

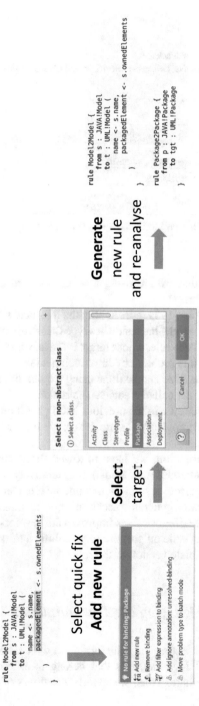

Fig. 12.7 Applying a quick fix to an *Unresolved binding* problem

```
 1  rule Package2Package {
 2    from s : JAVA!Package
 3    to  t : UML!Package (
 4      name ← s1.name,
 5      packagedElement ← s.ownedPackages,
 6      packagedElement ← s.ownedElements→select(e | e.oclIsKindOf(JAVA!ClassDeclaration))
 7    )
 8  }
 9  rule Class2Class {
10    from s : JAVA!ClassDeclaration
11    to  t : UML!Class (      Access to OclUndefined          Invalid comparison: enumeration and string
12      name ← s.name,
13      isAbstract ← s.modifier.inheritance    = 'abstract',
14      generalization ← s.superClass.type
15    )
16  }                              Invalid target assignment
```

Listing 12.3   Rule for mapping Java to UML classes (Error, Warning)

13, the second issue is that we are using a string (i.e., "abstract") instead of an enumeration literal (#abstract).

The third problem in Line 14 is more subtle: the left-hand side of the binding has type Generalization, but the right-hand side has type ClassDeclaration. This latter class is resolved by the Class2Class rule, whose target is Class, which is incompatible with Generalization. We solve this problem by introducing a lazy rule to explicitly create the desired target element. This can be done using a quick fix. Listing 12.4 shows a first version of this lazy rule, called createGeneralization.

The createGeneralization rule in the previous listing has a problem, since it needs to initialise the general compulsory feature. Thus, we introduce a new binding, as the next listing shows.

To create the transformation, we have followed the strategy of starting from the root class of the metamodel (i.e., Model) and iteratively derive new mappings, relying on ANATLYZER to discover relevant metamodel elements and using the quick fix facility to automatically generate pieces of code to make the transformation correct. Moreover, the use of quick fixes improves the developer performance since it allows writing incorrect code on purpose (e.g., calling a missing rule) and rely on the quick fix to get a template version of the rule.

12.5.3   Fixing and Evolving the Transformation

Let us assume that, after testing the transformation with a Java model, we realise that we need to discard Java elements that belong to external Java libraries by checking their proxy attribute. Thus, we modify the filters of the Class2Class and

```
1  rule Class2Class {
2    from s : JAVA!ClassDeclaration
3    to   t : UML!Class (
4      name ← s.name,
5      isAbstract ← if s.modifier.oclIsUndefined() then
6        false
7      else
8        s.modifier.inheritance = #"abstract"
9      endif
10     generalization ← if not s.superClass.oclIsUndefined() then
11       thisModule.createGeneralization(s)
12     else
13       OclUndefined
14     endif
15   )
16 }
17 lazy rule createGeneralization {
18   from c : JAVA!ClassDeclaration
19   to g : UML!Generalization    (
20   )
21 }                   Missing compulsory feature: general
```

Listing 12.4 Rule for mapping Java to UML classes, considering inheritance (Error, Warning)

```
1  lazy rule createGeneralization {
2    from c : JAVA!ClassDeclaration
3    to g : UML!Generalization (
4      general ← c.superClass.type
5    )
6  }
```

Listing 12.5 Rule to create Generalization elements (Error, Warning)

Package2Package rules with not s.isProxy. This will produce several unresolved binding problems, which we can easily fix by applying quick fixes as shown before.

This example shows that using a static analysis tool like ANATLYZER makes evolving a transformation easier. A simple change may affect several parts of a transformation, and without assistance, it can be difficult to identify the impacted parts.

12.6 Related Work

There are some other approaches to the static analysis of rule-base model transformations [RW15]. Next, we analyse the most representative ones with emphasis on how the developers can exploit the analysis results to fix errors.

In graph transformation, critical pair analysis checks pairs of rules to find dependencies (the application of one rule enables another one) and conflicts (applying one rule may disable another one) [Ehr+06]. While this analysis might produce complicated results for the users (pairs of rules may have an extremely high number conflict reasons), in [Lam+18] the authors propose different granularity levels for presenting the conflicts.

Model finders have been extensively used to analyse model transformations [Büt+12, Cab+10b]. Many times, this analysis is based on constructing so-called *transformation models*, made by merging the source and target metamodels, and expressing the transformation rules as declarative (OCL) invariants [Béz+06]. The result of the analysis is typically a model (a witness) that proves the satisfaction (or not) of a property. This method is semi-decidable, since the search is bounded: not finding a model may mean that it does not exist, or that it is outside the search bounds.

In [CT17] the authors use natural deduction and program slicing to analyse ATL model transformations against transformation contracts. The approach was implemented in the VeriATL tool. Different from the model-finding approaches, the outputs of this method are a transformation slice containing the relevant rules for the fault and some *debugging clues*. The authors aim at improving the method usability by automatically generating counterexamples. Contracts are also used in [Oak+18] to analyse ATL model transformations. The technique is based on the translation into the DSLTrans language, and performing model checking. Compared to our approach, the covered subset of the ATL language in these two approaches is smaller (e.g., lazy rules are not covered). Moreover, in our case, we can precisely point to the line of the error (when the analysis based on the dependency graph is enough), or if the model finder is used, we can provide a counterexample model (cf. Fig. 12.5).

Some works combine static analysis with dynamic execution and testing. For example, in [Mot+12] the authors extract a static footprint of the transformation (a reduced input metamodel considering only the elements touched by the transformation). Such footprint is then used to generate input models for testing via the Alloy model finder. In [Tro+18] the authors analyse the testing spectrum (i.e., the rules executed by failing test cases) to locate transformation faults.

With respect to quick fixes, even though many works can be found in the programming community to propose and rank quick fixes [Jef+09, Mus+12], they have been applied seldomly to domain-specific modelling languages [Heg+11], and even more scarcely to model transformations. The closest work are those that derive pre-conditions for graph transformation rules, to limit their applicability (e.g., to avoid violating metamodel integrity constraints) [KLT07, Cab+10a]. In our case, the catalogue of quick fixes is much richer, while the problem is more challenging since ATL is dynamically typed and more expressive.

Overall, the approach of ANATLYZER is unique in that it combines static analysis based on the rule dependency graph with model finding, and provides a catalogue of quick fixes with the possibility of speculative analysis.

12.7 Conclusion and Outlook

In this chapter, we have reviewed the main concepts behind ANATLYZER, a tool for the static analysis and fix of ATL model transformations. The tool is based on the calculation of the transformation dependency graph and on the use of model finders to refine some types of analysis. The tool supports a catalogue of quick fixes and speculative analysis to help the developer choose the most appropriate quick fix.

There are still some open challenges to improve the scope of static analysis tools for model transformations. Techniques to analyse potential errors across transformation chains have been barely developed so far. There are also opportunities to exploit static analysis to optimise the performance of model transformations [Sán+20]. Facilities to integrate ANATLYZER and other similar tools in continuous integration tool chains are needed to make them practical to address industrial projects. Finally, usability studies to assess whether specialised transformation IDEs improve developer performance are also needed [Heb+18].

References

[Béz+06] Jean Bézivin, Fabian Büttner, Martin Gogolla, Frédéric Jouault, Ivan Kurtev, and Arne Lindow. "Model Transformations? Transformation Models!" In: *9th International Conference on Model Driven Engineering Languages and Systems*. Vol. 4199. 2006, pp. 440–453.

[Bru+10] Yuriy Brun, Reid Holmes, Michael D. Ernst, and David Notkin. "Speculative analysis: exploring future development states of software". In: *Workshop on Future of Software Engineering, FoSER*. 2010, pp. 59–64.

[Bru+14] Hugo Brunelière, Jordi Cabot, Grégoire Dupé, and Frédéric Madiot. "MoDisco: A model driven reverse engineering framework". In: *Inf. Softw. Technol.* 56.8 (2014), pp. 1012–1032.

[Bru+20] Jean-Michel Bruel, Benoît Combemale, Esther Guerra, Jean-Marc Jézéquel, Jörg Kienzle, Juan de Lara, Gunter Mussbacher, Eugene Syriani, and Hans Vangheluwe. "Comparing and classifying model transformation reuse approaches across metamodels". In: *Software and Systems Modeling* 19.2 (2020), pp. 441–465.

[Büt+12] Fabian Büttner, Marina Egea, Jordi Cabot, and Martin Gogolla. "Verification of ATL Transformations Using Transformation Models and Model Finders". In: *14th International Conference on Formal Engineering Methods, ICFEM*. Vol. 7635. 2012, pp. 198–213.

[Cab+10a] Jordi Cabot, Robert Clarisó, Esther Guerra, and Juan de Lara. "Synthesis of OCL Preconditions for Graph Transformation Rules". In: *3rd International Conference on Theory and Practice of Model Transformations, ICMT*. Vol. 6142. 2010, pp. 45–60.

[Cab+10b] Jordi Cabot, Robert Clarisó, Esther Guerra, and Juan de Lara. "Verification and validation of declarative model-to-model transformations through invariants". In: *J. Syst. Softw.* 83.2 (2010), pp. 283–302.

[CT17] Zheng Cheng and Massimo Tisi. "A Deductive Approach for Fault Localization in ATL Model Transformations". In: *20th International Conference on Fundamental Approaches to Software Engineering*, FASE. Vol. 10202. 2017, pp. 300–317.

[Ehr+06] Hartmut Ehrig, Karsten Ehrig, Ulrike Prange, and Gabriele Taentzer. *Fundamentals of Algebraic Graph Transformation*. Springer, 2006.

[FOW87] Jeanne Ferrante, Karl J. Ottenstein, and Joe D. Warren. "The Program Dependence Graph and Its Use in Optimization". In: *ACM Trans. Program. Lang. Syst.* 9.3 (1987), pp. 319–349.

[Góm+20] Pablo Gómez-Abajo, Esther Guerra, Juan de Lara, and Mercedes G. Merayo. "Wodel-Test: A model-based framework for language-independent mutation testing". In: *Software and Systems Modeling* (2020). https://doi.org/10.1007/s10270-020-00827-0.

[GSL19] Esther Guerra, Jesús Sánchez Cuadrado, and Juan de Lara. "Towards Effective Mutation Testing for ATL". In: *22nd ACM/IEEE International Conference on Model Driven Engineering Languages and Systems, MODELS.* 2019, pp. 78–88.

[Heb+18] Regina Hebig, Christoph Seidl, Thorsten Berger, John Kook Pedersen, and Andrzej Wasowski. "Model transformation languages under a magnifying glass: a controlled experiment with Xtend, ATL, and QVT". In: *26th ACM Joint Meeting on European Software Engineering Conference and Symposium on the Foundations of Software Engineering.* 2018, pp. 445–455.

[Heg+11] Ábel Hegedüs, ákos Horváth, István Ráth, Moisés Castelo Branco, and Dániel Varró. "Quick fix generation for DSMLs". In: *IEEE Symposium on Visual Languages and Human-Centric Computing, VL/HCC.* 2011, pp. 17–24.

[Hei+21] Robert Heinrich, Francisco Durán, Carolyn L. Talcott, and Steffen Zschaler (eds.) *Composing Model-Based Analysis Tools.* Springer, 2021. https://doi.org/10.1007/978-3-030-81915-6.

[Jef+09] Dennis Jeffrey, Min Feng, Neelam Gupta, and Rajiv Gupta. "BugFix: A learningbased tool to assist developers in fixing bugs". In: *17th IEEE International Conference on Program Comprehension*, ICPC. 2009, pp. 70–79.

[Jou+08] Frédéric Jouault, Freddy Allilaire, Jean Bézivin, and Ivan Kurtev. "ATL: A model transformation tool". In: *Sci. Comput. Program.* 72.1-2 (2008), pp. 31–39.

[Kah+19] Nafiseh Kahani, Mojtaba Bagherzadeh, James R. Cordy, Juergen Dingel, and Dániel Varró. "Survey and classification of model transformation tools". In: *Software and Systems Modeling* 18.4 (2019), pp. 2361–2397.

[KLT07] Christian Köhler, Holger Lewin, and Gabriele Taentzer. "Ensuring Containment Constraints in Graph-based Model Transformation Approaches". In: *Electron. Commun. Eur. Assoc. Softw. Sci. Technol.* 6 (2007).

[Lam+18] Leen Lambers, Daniel Strüber, Gabriele Taentzer, Kristopher Born, and Jevgenij Huebert. "Multi-granular conflict and dependency analysis in software engineering based on graph transformation". In: *40th International Conference on Software Engineering*, ICSE. 2018, pp. 716–727.

[Mot+12] Jean-Marie Mottu, Sagar Sen, Massimo Tisi, and Jordi Cabot. "Static Analysis of Model Transformations for Effective Test Generation". In: *23rd IEEE International Symposium on Software Reliability Engineering, ISSRE.* 2012, pp. 291–300.

[Mus+12] Kivanç Muslu, Yuriy Brun, Reid Holmes, Michael D. Ernst, and David Notkin. "Speculative analysis of integrated development environment recommendations". In: *27th Annual ACM SIGPLAN Conference on Object-Oriented Programming, Systems, Languages, and Applications, OOPSLA.* 2012, pp. 669–682.

[Oak+18] Bentley James Oakes, Javier Troya, Levi Lúcio, and Manuel Wimmer. "Full contract verification for ATL using symbolic execution". In: *Software and Systems Modeling* 17.3 (2018), pp. 815–849.

[Obj15] Object Management Group. *UML 2.5.* Tech. rep. formal/2015-03-01. Object Management Group, 2015.

[OMG17] Object Management Group. *UML 2.5.1 OMG specification.* http://www.omg.org/spec/UML/2.5.1/.2017.

[RW15] Lukman Ab. Rahim and Jon Whittle. "A survey of approaches for verifying model transformations". In: *Software and Systems Modeling* 14.2 (2015), pp. 1003–1028.

[Sán+20] Jesús Sánchez Cuadrado, Loli Burgueno, Manuel Wimmer, and Antonio Vallecillo. "Efficient execution of ATL model transformations using static analysis and parallelism". In: *IEEE Transactions on Software Engineering* (2020).

[SGL17] Jesús Sánchez Cuadrado, Esther Guerra, and Juan de Lara. "Static analysis of model transformations". In: *IEEE Transactions on Software Engineering* 43.9 (2017), pp. 868–897.

[SGL18a] Jesús Sánchez Cuadrado, Esther Guerra, and Juan de Lara. "AnATLyzer: an advanced IDE for ATL model transformations". In: *Proceedings of the 40th International Conference on Software Engineering: Companion Proceedings*, (ICSE'). 2018, pp. 85–88. https://doi.org/10.1145/3183440.3183479

[SGL18b] Jesús Sánchez Cuadrado, Esther Guerra, and Juan de Lara. "Quick fixing ATL transformations with speculative analysis". In: *Software and System Modeling* 17.3 (2018), pp. 779–813.

[SK03] Shane Sendall and Wojtek Kozaczynski. "Model Transformation: The Heart and Soul of Model-Driven Software Development". In: *IEEE Softw.* 20.5 (2003), pp. 42–45.

[Tro+18] Javier Troya, Sergio Segura, José Antonio Parejo, and Antonio Ruiz Cortés. "Spectrum-Based Fault Localization in Model Transformations". In: *ACM Trans. Softw. Eng. Methodol.* 27.3 (2018), 13:1–13:50.

Chapter 13
Using Afra in Different Domains by Tool Orchestration

Ehsan Khamespanah, Pavle Mrvaljevic, Anas Fattouh, and Marjan Sirjani

Abstract The formal modelling and verification of distributed systems represents a complex process in which multiple tools are involved. Rebeca is a language which is developed to make modelling and verification of distributed systems with asynchronous message passing easier. This chapter shows how different tool orchestration methods are used for developing different verification engines for Rebeca models. As the first step, the way of enabling performance evaluation for Rebeca models is shown. To this end, state spaces which are generated for Rebeca models are transformed to the input of a third party tool and the result of the verification is given to the modeller. The second one is developing a search-based optimisation for wireless sensors and actuators applications. Running the model checker in a loop with different input parameters helps in finding the optimum values for parameters with respect to a given optimisation goal. The third one is for safety verification and performance evaluation of collaborative autonomous machines of Volvo car. The verification is done through developing and evaluating models by the model checking tool and Volvo car simulator (VCE Simulator).

This case-study chapter illustrates concepts introduced in Chap. 5 and addresses Challenge 2 in Chap. 3 of this book.

13.1 Introduction

Rebeca is a modelling language which is developed based on Hewitt and Agha's actors [AH87]. The actor model is a well-known model for the development of highly available and high-performance concurrent applications. It benefits from the universal primitives of concurrent computation, called actors. Hewitt introduced the

E. Khamespanah (✉)
University of Tehran, Tehran, Iran
e-mail: e.khamespanah@ut.ac.ir

P. Mrvaljevic · A. Fattouh · M. Sirjani
Mälardalen University, Västerås, Sweden
e-mail: pmc19001@student.mdh.se; anas.fattouh@mdh.se; marjan.sirjani@mdh.se

© The Author(s), under exclusive license to Springer Nature Switzerland AG 2021
R. Heinrich et al. (eds.), *Composing Model-Based Analysis Tools*,
https://doi.org/10.1007/978-3-030-81915-6_13

283

actor model as an agent-based language [Hew72] and is later developed by Agha as a mathematical model of concurrent computation [Agh]. Actors in Rebeca are independent units of concurrently running programs that communicate with each other through message passing. The message passing is an asynchronous non-blocking call to the actor's corresponding message server. Message servers are methods of the actor that specify the reaction of the actor to its corresponding received message. In the Java-like syntax of Rebeca, actors are instantiated from reactive class definitions that are similar to the concept of classes in Java. Actors in this sense can be assumed as objects in Java. Each reactive class declares a set of state variables and the messages to which it can respond.

Rebeca is usable for software engineers and programmers. They are familiar with the Java-like syntax of Rebeca, and with the object-oriented style of programming. For concurrent programming, programmers are mostly using thread-based programming, and the event-based model of computation may not be as widely used by all the programmers. Usually it would be enough to tell them that each actor is one thread of execution, and message servers run atomically with no preemption. Different extensions for Rebeca are proposed to make it more usable for different domains and types of analysis. Timed Rebeca [Rey+14] is an extension on Rebeca with time features which supports modelling and verification of time-critical systems [KKS18, Kha+15, SK16]. Probabilistic Rebeca is another extension of Rebeca which is developed to consider the probabilistic behaviour of actor systems [VK12]. *Probabilistic Timed Rebeca* (PTRebeca) is an extension of Rebeca which benefits from modelling features of Timed Rebeca and Probabilistic Rebeca, combining the syntax of both languages [Jaf+14]. Inheritance for Rebeca is introduced in [You+20] to make modelling easier and enable modellers to define custom communication mechanisms.

Afra is a toolset which is developed for the purpose of providing modelling and verification facilities for Rebeca models and its extensions. Similar to many other Eclipse plugins, Afra contains a set of Eclipse views and editors together with a set of Java components for implementing models and analysing them. Considering the tool orchestration strategies which are presented in Chap. 5 of this book [Hei+21], this chapter shows how Afra is used together with other tools and libraries for the analysis of Rebeca models. We explain how orchestration of Afra with other tools is used in various domains for different purposes like model checking, performance evaluation, or search-based optimisation. Chapter 5 of this book [Hei+21] proposed a reference architecture along with important concepts that can be used to orchestrate analysis tools. Among six different strategies, single analysis orchestration (strategy A), cooperating analysis orchestration (strategy D), and sequential analysis orchestration (strategy E) are used in analysis tools of Rebeca. Single analysis orchestration uses a tool driver to translate the model into a valid input for an external black-box analysis tool. Then the modelling environment translates back the result of the analysis tool by using the tool driver again. Using sequential analysis orchestration the modelling environment invokes one tool, then translates the result into an input to another tool, and then translates the results of the second tool back to the domain-specific model to provide it to the domain expert.

In cooperating analysis orchestration the modelling environment invokes one tool, then translates the result into an input to another tool, and then translates the results of the second tool back into an input of the first tool to run another analysis.

In the rest of this chapter, first, Sect. 13.2 introduces Rebeca modelling language and how correctness properties are defined for Rebeca models using a running example. The main features of Afra are presented in Sect. 13.3. The next four sections show how orchestration of Afra with other tools is used to develop new analysis tools, i.e., Sect. 13.4 for performance evaluation, Sect. 13.5 for schedulability analysis, and Sects. 13.6 and 13.7 for flow management. Finally, Sect. 13.8 concludes the chapter.

13.2 Reactive Object Language (Rebeca)

We illustrate the Rebeca language with the example of a simple ticket service system. The actor model of this system is presented in Fig. 13.1. The model consists of three actors: *Customer, Agent,* and *Ticket Service System. Customer* asks *Agent* for issuing a ticket. The *Agent* actor forwards the request to *Ticket Service System* and it replies to *Agent* by sending a *ticket is issued* response. *Agent* responds to *Customer* by sending the issued ticket information. A Rebeca model has reactive objects with no shared variables, asynchronous message passing with no blocking send and no explicit receive, and unbounded buffers for messages. Objects in Rebeca are reactive and self-contained. Communication takes place by message passing among actors. The unbounded buffer of actors, called message *queue*, is used to store its arriving messages. Actor takes a message—that can be considered as an event—from the top of its message queue and executes its corresponding message server (also called a method). The execution of a message server is atomic which means that there is no way to preempt the execution of a message server of an actor and start executing another message server of that actor.

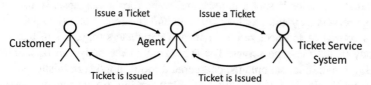

Fig. 13.1 The actor model of Ticket Service System

```
 1  reactiveclass TicketService (3) {    26     }
 2    knownrebecs {Agent a;}             27  }
 3    statevars {                        28  reactiveclass Customer (2) {
 4      int nextId;                      29    knownrebecs {Agent a;}
 5    }                                  30    statevars {
 6    TicketService() {                  31      boolean waiting;
 7      nextId = 0;                      32    }
 8    }                                  33    Customer() {
 9    msgsrv requestTicket() {           34      self.try();
10      delay(?(0.4:2, 0.6:3));          35      waiting = false;
11      a.ticketIssued(nextId);          36    }
12      nextId = nextId + 1;             37    msgsrv try() {
13    }                                  38      waiting = true;
14  }                                    39      a.requestTicket();
15  reactiveclass Agent (2) {            40    }
16    knownrebecs {                      41    msgsrv ticketIssued(byte id) {
17      TicketService ts;                42      waiting = false;
18      Customer c;                      43      self.try() after(30);
19    }                                  44    }
20    msgsrv requestTicket() {           45  }
21      delay(1);                        46  main {
22      ts.requestTicket() deadline(5);  47    Agent a(ts, c):();
23    }                                  48    TicketService ts(a):();
24    msgsrv ticketIssued(byte id) {     49    Customer c(a):();
25      c.ticketIssued(id);              50  }
```

Listing 13.1 The Rebeca model of ticket service system

Listing 13.1 shows the Rebeca model of the ticket service system of Fig. 13.1. A Rebeca model consists of a set of reactive classes (i.e., actor types) and the main block. In the main block, actors which are instances of the reactive classes are declared (lines 47–49). The body of the reactive class includes the declaration of its known actors, state variables, and message servers. For the case of Customer reactive class, its only known actor is an Agent which is accessible by variable a (line 29). As declared in line 31, Customer has one state variable which shows that and actor is sent a request and waits for the response. It also has two message servers try and ticketIssued and one constructor (line 33). Message servers consist of the declaration of formal parameters (e.g., id in line 41) and the body of the message server. The statements in the body can be assignments (line 38), conditional statements, enumerated loops, nondeterministic assignment, and method calls (line 39). Method calls are sending asynchronous messages to other actors (or to itself).

A reactive class has an argument of type integer denoting the maximum size of its message queue (e.g., 2 for Customer as depicted in line 28). Although message queues are unbounded in the semantics of Rebeca, to ensure that the state space is finite, we need a user-specified upper bound for the queue size. The operational semantics of Rebeca has been introduced in [Sir+04] in more detail. In comparison

```
1  property {
2    define {
3       waiting = c.waiting == true;
4    }
5    LTL {
6       NoStarvation : G(waiting -> F(!waiting));
7    }
8  }
```

Listing 13.2   The property file for the Rebeca code in Listing 13.1 stating the safety property as an LTL formula

with the standard actor model, dynamic creation and dynamic topology are not supported by Rebeca. Also, actors in Rebeca are single-threaded.

A Rebeca code can be model checked against a given set of *linear temporal logic* (LTL) properties. These properties specify the correct behaviours/states of the model. For example, in the case of Ticket Service System, one correctness property is that there is no starvation in issuing tickets for customers. This property can be specified in LTL using $\Box(waiting \rightarrow \Diamond(\neg waiting))$ formula which means that now and forever in the future, waiting for a ticket results in not waiting for a ticket (having ticket) eventually in the future.

Listing 13.2 shows how the mentioned LTL property is specified in the Rebeca property file. At the first step, the atomic propositions of the formula are defined in the define section of a Rebeca property file, considering the state variables of the actors (line 3). The name of the atomic propositions is set to waiting and its corresponding formula is put after the equal sign. In the LTL section, the correctness property is specified (line 5). In this example, only one property with the name NoStarvation is defined. Textual presentation of LTL modality $\Box$ (now and forever in the future) is G and $\Diamond$ (eventually in the future) is F in Rebeca property files.

Timed Rebeca [Rey+14] is an extension on Rebeca with time features for modelling and verification of time-critical systems. To this end, three primitives are added to Rebeca to address *computation time, message delivery time, message expiration,* and *period of occurrence of events.* In a Timed Rebeca model, each actor has its own local clock and the local clocks evolve uniformly. Methods are still executed atomically, however passing time while executing a method can be modelled. In addition, instead of a queue for messages, there is a bag of messages for each actor.

The timing primitives that are added to the syntax of Rebeca are *delay, deadline,* and *after.* The *delay* statement models the passing of time for an actor during execution of a message server. The keywords *after* and *deadline* can only be used in conjunction with a method call. The value of the argument of *after* shows how long it takes for the message to be delivered to its receiver. The *deadline* shows the timeout for the message, i.e., how long it will stay valid.

As shown in line 21 of the model of Listing 13.1, processing time of a request in the agent is one time unit. At line 22 the actor instantiated from *Agent* sends a message *requestTicket* to actor *ts* instantiated from *TicketService*, and gives a deadline of five to the receiver to take this message and start serving it. The periodic task of retrying for a new ticket is modelled in line 39 by the customer sending a *try* message to itself and letting the receiver to take it from its bag only after 30 units of time (by stating *after(30))*. Model checker of Timed Rebeca models considers schedulability of message servers. It means schedulability is preserved if none of the specified deadlines of messages is missed.

PTRebeca language supports modelling and verification of real-time systems with probabilistic behaviours [Jaf+16]. PTRebeca introduced probabilistic assignment which is similar to nondeterministic assignment but associate a probability with each value option. In the probabilistic assignment, probabilities are real values between 0 and 1, and sum up to 1. Notably, by using probabilistic assignments, the values of the timing constructs (delay, after, and deadline) can also become probabilistic.

Different probabilistic behaviours can be modelled using the PTRebeca language, depending on the system under study. In the Rebeca code of Listing 13.1, issue time of a ticket in the ticket service system is set to two with the probability of 0.4 and three with the probability of 0.6 (line 10). Finding the expected value of the waiting time for issuing a ticket or computing the probability of deadline misses are two examples of probabilistic analysis which can be done using PTRebeca.

13.3   Afra

Afra is the *integrated development environment* (IDE) for model checking Rebeca and Timed Rebeca models.[1] It is developed as an Eclipse plugin and released as a standalone Eclipse product. It contains a set of Eclipse views and editors together with four Java components for implementing models and analysing them. Afra plugin contains a compiler component for compiling its given models and the *Rebeca model checker* (RMC) component for generating model checking codes for models. Using Afra, syntactically and semantically correct Rebeca models are transformed into a set of C++ source codes which generate the transition system of the model and perform property checking. In other words, running the generated C++ codes provides the model checking result. The working environment of Afra is shown in Fig. 13.2 which contains project explorer, Rebeca code editor, analysis result viewer, and counterexample viewer.

In addition to using Afra for the analysis of Rebeca models, its internal components (i.e., shown in Fig. 13.3) can be orchestrated in collaboration with other components to provide more comprehensive analysis solutions. Having an explicit

---

[1] Afra can be downloaded from http://rebeca-lang.org/alltools/Afra.

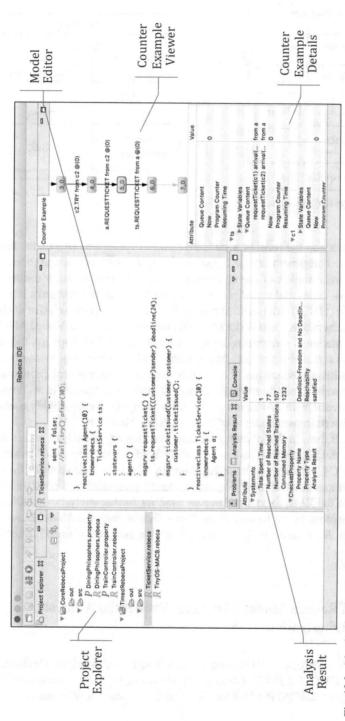

Fig. 13.2 Afra development environment

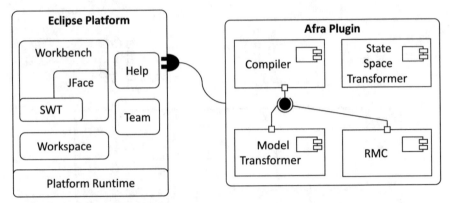

Fig. 13.3 Afra tool architecture

output language in the form of a standard *abstract syntax tree* (AST), the result of the *Compiler* component can be consumed by other components and tools. Using sequential orchestration of the components, the *RMC* component transforms this AST to C++ codes and the *Model Transformer* component transforms it to Real-Time Maude [ÖM07] (for bounded model checking), ROS [Qui+09] (for deploying in autonomous robots), and Akka [Akk09] (for running on Java Virtual Machine). Real-Time Maude is a rewriting-logic-based language which supports the formal specification and analysis of real-time systems. *Robotic Operating System* (ROS) is a robot middleware which has been widely used as an open source framework for the development of robotic applications and has become a standard in academic and industrial environments. Akka is a toolkit for building distributed, highly concurrent and event driven implementation of Hewitt's Actor Model on JVM.

As we will show in the following sections, the majority of analysis orchestrations for Rebeca models are realised by the analysis of the state space of models. By running the C++ codes which are generated by *RMC*, the state space of the model is generated together with applying model checking algorithms. This state space is presented in the XML format and can be used for further analysis, including third party applications or the Rebeca *State Space Transformer* and *Model Transformer* components. How the State Space Analysis tool is used is explained further in this section.

13.4 PTRebeca Model Checking: Sequential Analysis Orchestration

In the model checking of PTRebeca we have **Sequential Analysis Orchestration** strategy of RMC and IMCA (strategy E), shown in Fig. 13.4. *interactive Markov chain analyzer* (IMCA) is a tool for the quantitative analysis of interactive Markov

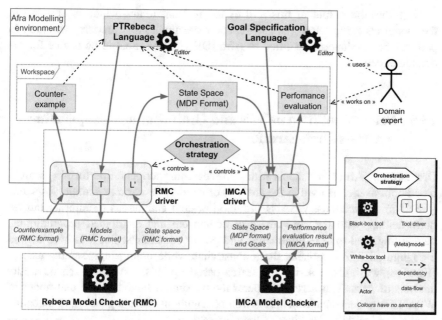

Fig. 13.4 Orchestration of tools and components for the analysis of Probabilistic Timed Rebeca models using IMCA tool

chains. In particular, it supports the verification of interactive Markov chains against reachability objectives, timed reachability objectives, expected time objectives, expected step objectives, and long-run average objectives. Figure 13.4 is developed based on the reference architecture for the integration of analysis tools in Chap. 5 of this book [Hei+21]. In this figure, Afra modelling environment is responsible for both, interacting with analysis tools and interacting with the domain expert. The modelling environment comprises four components: (a) the *domain-specific modelling languages* (DSMLs), (b) a set of tools to create, manipulate, or verify models conforming to these DSMLs, (c) a set of orchestration strategies to manage the interaction with and combination of analysis tools, and (d) the tool drivers that are responsible for actually interacting with the specific analysis tools.

As shown in Fig. 13.4, the modelling environment invokes RMC analysis tool then translates the result into the IMCA [Guc+12] input for performing additional performance analysis. In this case, the modelling DSML is the PTRebeca language and the input PTRebeca model is directly fed to RMC, and running the resulting C++ file, generates the state space of the given model in *time-dependent Markov decision process* (TMDP) format. The *IMCA driver* tool is developed using *State Space Transformer* component to convert the XML file of the TMDP of the model to the input language of IMCA model checker. It also uses the specification of the *goal states* of the model to generate one Markov automaton as the input of the IMCA model checking tool.

Note that the output of this tool as the malfunctioning which is detected in the model checking phase (i.e., RMC counterexample) and property violation in performance evaluation are lifted to Afra IDE viewer format to be usable for the domain expert.

13.5 Schedulability Analysis and Optimisation: Cooperating Analysis Orchestration

Orchestrating Afra components with some searching scripts for performing search-based optimisation is used in the analysis of *wireless sensor and actuator networks* (WSANs) applications. WSANs provide low-cost continuous monitoring but require dealing with the complexity of concurrent and distributed programming, networking, real-time requirements, and power constraints. So, it is hard to find a configuration that satisfies these constraints while optimising resource use. In [Kha+18] we build a script for search-based optimisation using schedulability analysis of Afra. This script computes the maximum sampling rate that nodes of WSAN can collect data from the environment without saturating the communication network and missing deadlines of their internal tasks.

The characteristics of real-time variants of the actor model make them appropriate for using as the DSML of WSAN applications: many concurrent processes with interdependent real-time deadlines. Considering the specification of the WSAN applications, there are many nodes which have the role of data acquisition and data transmission. For data acquisition, nodes have different sensors which periodically acquire data from the environment and send the data to the processing unit of the node. The processing unit validates the data and sends it to a central node using a wireless communication device, which is another actor of the model. As shown in [Kha+18], the node-level Timed Rebeca [Rey+14, KKS18] model of a WSAN application is developed to check for the possibility of deadline violations. Specifically, by changing the timing parameters of the model, the maximum safe sampling rate in the presence of other (miscellaneous) tasks in the node is found. Composing the models of standalone nodes to have a multi-node model requires that the wireless communication protocol is implemented for radio communication devices. Changing the configuration of the network and timing parameters of the model, the new maximum safe sampling rate is found. This optimisation of the sampling rate is implemented by the search-based optimisation technique.

Assigning different values for the parameters of the model, different maximum sampling rates are achieved as the result of the optimisation problem, shown by 3D surfaces in [Kha+18]. This requires running the model checker of Rebeca multiple times and integrating the result. To this end, we developed a script which runs the given model using different configurations to solve the optimisation problem. The script assigns different values for the maximum transmission time of the network,

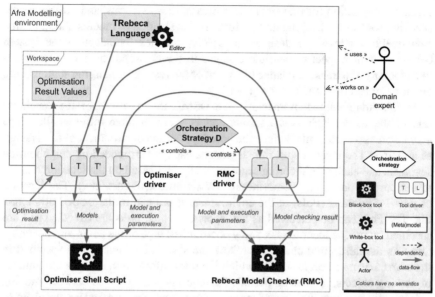

Fig. 13.5 Orchestration of tools and components for the schedulability analysis and optimisation of WSAN models

delay of sensors, the number of nodes in the system, the network packet size, etc. The orchestration of the tools for this problem is shown in Fig. 13.5.

The strategy of orchestration between the optimiser script and *RMC* component is **Cooperating Analysis Orchestration** (strategy D) as the result of the model checking part (RMC) is lifted to be given as the feedback to the optimiser. The result of model checking has to be lifted and transformed to the input of the *Optimiser* and the values which are generated by the *Optimiser* have to be transformed to the input of RMC, which are done by the *Optimiser* and *RMC* drivers, using simple text processing shell scripts. Note that in this tool, Timed Rebeca is the DSML for specifying input models.

13.6 Flow Management: Nested Analysis Orchestrations

AdaptiveFlow [Sir+19, For+20] is an actor-based framework which is used for track-based flow management. There are different track-based flow management systems such as warehouse management systems and transportation systems which play a crucial role in our daily life. All of these systems include a set of moving objects which travel on predefined tracks, e.g., trains on rails, cars on roads, automated vehicles in aisles of a warehouse, and airplanes in predefined airspace-tracks. In this view, the flowing entities move around some environments to transport some assets between some points of interest. AdaptiveFlow as a formal framework provides a common abstraction for movement scenarios in these systems, and utilises model checking for safety checking and performance evaluation of models. Additionally, AdaptiveFlow allows the designer to specify policies for adapting the system behaviour with respect to possible changes in the environment. Sudden changes like blocking of a track, or change of a point of interest like a charging station being out of order can be modelled, too [For+20].

In the AdaptiveFlow framework, the DSML that is used for the specification of the model is in XML format and is given in three different files. The environment.xml file defines the base layer of the environment of the system, as a matrix. The layer is split into segments, each is surrounded by neighbouring segments and each neighbouring segment is labelled based on the location relative to the current one (i.e., NE-northeast, SW-southwest, E-east, etc.). The location of *point of interests* (PoIs) in the environment is defined in the topology.xml file. The PoIs can be perceived as key spots on which tasks are executed and are specified by unique identifiers, x and y coordinates, type of the point, and operating time. As the third input of AdaptiveFlow, the system configuration is specified in the configuration.xml file which includes information such as the number of moving objects, re-sending periods for requests, safe distance between moving objects, etc. The specification of moving objects and their properties are given to AdaptiveFlow using configuration.xml. Each moving object has a list of tasks IDs that are assigned to it, together with its attributes: unique identifiers, machine type, leaving time from parking station, fuel capacity, CO_2 emission, etc.

One round of AdaptiveFlow workflow is split into three phases, shown in Fig. 13.6. The initial phase is the pre-processing phase in which different Timed Rebeca models are generated based on the XML input files (using a Python script) by running the *model generator* script. The second phase consists of formal verification of the generated model by generating the state space [Sir+19]. This verification is performed with model checking tools such as Afra or RMC [Sir+19]. These tools convert Rebeca models to C++ files which are afterwards compiled to an executable file [Sir+19]. Aside from checking regular properties such as deadlock-freedom and safety, AdaptiveFlow also verifies properties like fuel consumption of

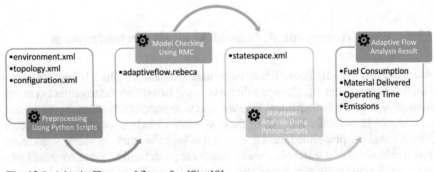

Fig. 13.6 AdaptiveFlow workflow, after [Sir+19]

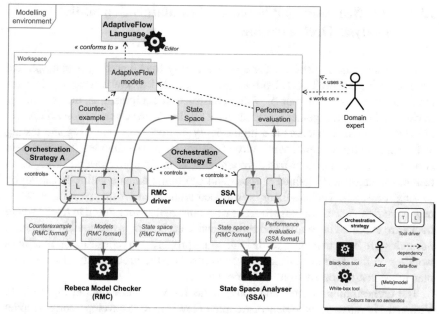

Fig. 13.7 Orchestration of tools and components for AdaptiveFlow (Presented in Fig. 5.4)

machines, correct machine movement, absence of machine collision with obstacles, and no-starvation property [For+20]. Reviewing counterexamples and fixing model errors iteratively, a modeller can develop functionally correct models. As mentioned before, model checking tools also generate state space of models used for the final, post-processing phase. In this phase, a state space which is generated from a functionally correct model goes through the Python script that analyses each state. The state space file, generated by RMC, is analysed with a Python script that extracts the evaluation of performance properties. The performance evaluation includes total CO_2 emissions of machines, the amount of consumed fuel, moved material, and operating time of the collaborative system.

The orchestration of components for AdaptiveFlow is presented in Fig. 13.7 (Note that this figure is the same as Fig. 5.4 in Sect. 5.7 with some minor modifications). As shown in this figure, the orchestration strategy in AdaptiveFlow is nested orchestration strategies; a smaller cycle with **Single Analysis Orchestration** (strategy A) within a larger cycle of **Sequential Analysis Orchestration** (strategy E). The pre-processing python script of AdaptiveFlow works as the transformer component of RMC driver. The lifting component L of RMC driver translates counterexamples from XML format to Afra counterexample viewer format and L' only performs no modification to the state space file. On the other hand, *state space analyser* (SSA) driver components only feed and retrieve data to/from SSA components.

13.7   Safe Scenarios for Volvo CE Simulator: Sequential Analysis Orchestration

AdaptiveFlow can be used for the analysis of any track-based flow management system. In VMap project, AdaptiveFlow is extended to make it appropriate for the analysis of the behaviour of Volvo construction equipment, as an example of track-based flow management systems [Mrv20]. The *Volvo Construction Equipment Simulator*[2] (VCE Simulator) is a high-fidelity platform for simulating and testing Volvo construction equipment in a virtual environment. The simulator's core system is a distributed component-based system that is made up of several tasks. Each task has a single well-defined purpose and can communicate with other tasks by passing messages. The simulator is equipped with an editor that permits to create new scenarios. A scenario is a sequence of actions that are organised in tracks where tracks are executed in parallel and actions inside each track is executed in sequence. Scenarios are built manually for testing some properties of construction machines working on the desired environment or to measure the productivity of a working plan in a construction environment for example.

The orchestration of tools and components for VMap is shown in Fig. 13.8. In VMap, the iterative development of AdaptiveFlow is used to develop a correct model with an acceptable level of performance. Then, XMLs of AdaptiveFlow models are transformed to the VCE simulator input format for the simulation purpose. Finally, the results of the VCE simulator are given as feedback to the designer to improve the model. The scenario in the VCE simulator is described by an XML file, namely `dynamic.content`. The `dynamic.content` file contains a list of the objects inside the scenario, the components of each object with its properties, and the communication between the objects. It could also include links to objects defined in other files.

As a result, the orchestration strategy of AdaptiveFlow and VMap is **Sequential Analysis Orchestration** (strategy E). The transformer of VCE driver is responsible for transforming AdaptiveFlow specifications and other simulation-specific files to the `dynamic.content` format. The lifting component of VCE driver makes the simulation results human readable.

---

[2] VCE   Simulator: https://www.volvoce.com/europe/en/services/volvo-services/productivity-services/volvo-simulators.

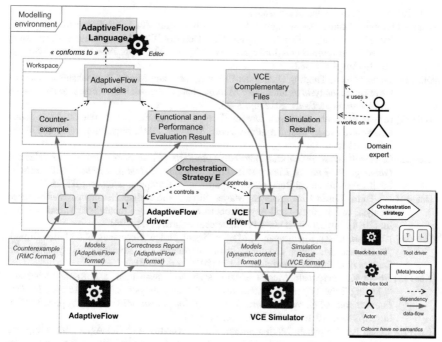

Fig. 13.8 Orchestration of tools and components for VMap

13.8 Conclusion

Different verification engines are developed for Rebeca models using orchestrations of a set of analysis tools. In Chap. 5 of this book [Hei+21], a catalogue of strategies for tools orchestration is proposed. For each of them, strategies name, explanation, and examples are proposed in a systematic way. We studied a few Rebeca analysis tools and classified them as one of the orchestration strategies presented in this catalogue.

Using the proposed patterns makes it easier to reuse the existing tools and put them together in different ways. This way, the future analysis tools of Rebeca will be developed easier and faster. Orchestration strategies also improved the documentation and maintenance of the existing verification engines by furnishing an explicit specification of tools interactions.

References

[Agh] Gul A. Agha. ACTORS - *A Model of Concurrent Computation in Distributed Systems*. MIT Press.

[AH87] Gul Agha and Carl Hewitt. "Concurrent programming using actors". In: (1987), pp. 37–53.

[Akk09] Akka. *Typesafe, Inc. Akka.* 2009.

[For+20] Giorgio Forcina, Ali Sedaghatbaf, Stephan Baumgart, Ali Jafari, Ehsan Khamespanah, Pavle Mrvaljevic, and Marjan Sirjani. "Safe Design of Flow Management Systems Using Rebeca". In: *Journal of Information Processing* 28 (2020), pp. 588– 598. https://doi.org/10.2197/ipsjjip.28.588.

[Guc+12] Dennis Guck, Tingting Han, Joost-Pieter Katoen, and Martin R. Neuhäußer. "Quantitative timed analysis of interactive Markov chains". In: *4th international conference on NASA Formal Methods.* 2012, pp. 8–23.

[Hei+21] Robert Heinrich, Francisco Durán, Carolyn L. Talcott, and Steffen Zschaler (eds.) *Composing Model-Based Analysis Tools.* Springer, 2021. https://doi.org/10.1007/978-3-030-81915-6.

[Hew72] C. Hewitt. *Description and Theoretical Analysis (Using Schemata) of PLANNER: A Language for Proving Theorems and Manipulating Models in a Robot.* MIT Artificial Intelligence Technical Report 258. Department of Computer Science, MIT, 1972.

[Jaf+14] Ali Jafari, Ehsan Khamespanah, Marjan Sirjani, and Holger Hermanns. "Performance Analysis of Distributed and Asynchronous Systems using Probabilistic Timed Actors". In: (2014). http://journal.ub.tu-berlin.de/eceasst/article/view/984.

[Jaf+16] Ali Jafari, Ehsan Khamespanah, Marjan Sirjani, Holger Hermanns, and Matteo Cimini. "PTRebeca: Modeling and analysis of distributed and asynchronous systems". In: *Science of Computer Programming* 128 (2016), pp. 22–50.

[Kha+15] Ehsan Khamespanah, Marjan Sirjani, Mahesh Viswanathan, and Ramtin Khosravi. "Floating Time Transition System: More Efficient Analysis of Timed Actors". In: *12th International Conference Formal Aspects of Component Software.* 2015, pp. 237–255. https://doi.org/10.1007/978-3-319-28934-2_13.

[Kha+18] Ehsan Khamespanah, Marjan Sirjani, Kirill Mechitov, and Gul Agha. "Modeling and analyzing real-time wireless sensor and actuator networks using actors and model checking". In: *International Journal on Software Tools for Technology Transfer* 20.5 (2018), pp. 547–561.

[KKS18] Ehsan Khamespanah, Ramtin Khosravi, and Marjan Sirjani. "An efficient TCTL model checking algorithm and a reduction technique for verification of timed actor models". In: *Science of Computer Programming* 153 (2018), pp. 1–29.

[Mrv20] Pavle Mrvaljevic. *Tool Orchestration for Modeling, Verification, and Analysis of Collaborating Autonomous Machines.* Master Thesis. Mälardalen University, 2020.

[ÖM07] Peter Csaba Ölveczky and José Meseguer. "Semantics and pragmatics of Real-Time Maude". In: *Higher-Order and Symbolic Computation* 20.1-2 (2007), pp. 161–196.

[Qui+09] Morgan Quigley, Ken Conley, Brian Gerkey, Josh Faust, Tully Foote, Jeremy Leibs, Rob Wheeler, and Andrew Y Ng. "Workshop on Open Source Software in Robotics". In: vol. 3. 3.2. 2009, p. 5.

[Rey+14] Arni Hermann Reynisson, Marjan Sirjani, Luca Aceto, Matteo Cimini, Ali Jafari, Anna Ingólfsdóttir, and Steinar Hugi Sigurdarson. "Modelling and Simulation of Asynchronous Real-Time Systems Using Timed Rebeca". In: *Science of Computer Programming* 89 (2014), pp. 41–68.

[Sir+04] Marjan Sirjani, Ali Movaghar, Amin Shali, and Frank S. de Boer. "Modeling and Verification of Reactive Systems using Rebeca". In: *Fundamenta Informaticae* 63.4 (2004), pp. 385–410.

[Sir+19] Marjan Sirjani, Giorgio Forcina, Ali Jafari, Stephan Baumgart, Ehsan Khamespanah, and Ali Sedaghatbaf. "An Actor-Based Design Platform for System of Systems". In: *43rd IEEE Annual Computer Software and Applications Conference.* 2019, pp. 579–587. https://doi.org/10.1109/COMPSAC.2019.00089.

[SK16] Marjan Sirjani and Ehsan Khamespanah. "On Time Actors". In: *Theory and Practice of Formal Methods - Essays Dedicated to Frank de Boer on the Occasion of His 60th Birthday.* 2016, pp. 373–392. https://doi.org/10.1007/978-3-319-30734-3_25.

[VK12] Mahsa Varshosaz and Ramtin Khosravi. "Modeling and Verification of Probabilistic Actor Systems Using pRebeca". In: *14th International Conference on Formal Engineering Methods*. 2012, pp. 135–150. https://doi.org/10.1007/978-3-642-34281-3_12.

[You+20] Farnaz Yousefi, Ehsan Khamespanah, Mohammed Gharib, Marjan Sirjani, and Ali Movaghar. "VeriVANca framework: verification of VANETs by property-based message passing of actors in Rebeca with inheritance". In: *International Journal on Software Tools for Technology Transfer* 22.5 (2020), pp. 617–633. https://doi.org/10.1007/s10009-020-00579-8.

Chapter 14
Conclusion

Francisco Durán, Robert Heinrich, Carolyn Talcott, and Steffen Zschaler

Abstract The final chapter of this book summarises the key challenges in the research area and highlights perspectives for research and practice, including a roadmap of upcoming research challenges.

14.1 Summary

Modelling is a key activity in software development. It enables software engineers to consider in isolation specific aspects of the systems they are developing and, by providing appropriate abstractions, allows engineers to focus on core problems without having to get immersed in every low-level detail. As a result, modelling is a necessary instrument for conquering the complexity and heterogeneity of modern software-intensive systems. Because of the abstraction offered, modelling also enables effective and efficient analysis of properties of the system. This can be done even before the system has been developed (by analysis based on a predictive model), but can also relate to a model representation of an existing system (a descriptive model, cf. also the current discussions around the notion of a "digital twin" [Gri12, *p.* 133]).

F. Durán (✉)
University of Málaga, Málaga, Spain
e-mail: duran@lcc.uma.es

R. Heinrich
Karlsruhe Institute of Technology, Karlsruhe, Germany
e-mail: robert.heinrich@kit.edu

C. Talcott
SRI International, Menlo Park, CA, USA
e-mail: clt@csl.sri.com

S. Zschaler
King's College London, London, UK
e-mail: szschaler@acm.org

For several reasons, analysis of models of real-world systems can rarely be achieved using a single analysis technique. On the one hand, different stakeholders require different perspectives on a system—leading to different models and different analysis needs for each stakeholder. On the other hand, models and properties quickly grow too complex to be efficiently analysed in a single analysis-tool run. This is exacerbated as models change continually. In such a situation, efficient analysis techniques should really only touch those parts of the model that have changed rather than requiring a complete re-analysis of the entire model.

Therefore, to obtain a complete analysis of a system, it is necessary to compose different analyses of (potentially different) models of the system. This book [Hei+21] has provided an overview of the challenges and opportunities related to the composition of model-based analyses and analysis tools. Specifically, we have explored the following challenges:

1. Chapter 4 (*Composition of Languages, Models, and Analyses*) has focused on the foundational challenges of how to compose different models, modelling languages (formalisms), and their semantics, and analyses in ways that ensure meaningful results are produced.
2. Chapter 5 (*Integration and Orchestration of Analysis Tools*) has built on the composition of models, formalisms, and analyses and explored the engineering challenges involved in composing actual analysis *tools* in efficient and effective ways. We have explored basic concepts to integrate analysis tools and a spectrum of strategies to orchestrate analysis tools, and relevant application contexts.
3. Chapter 6 (*Continual Model-Based Analysis*) has explored how composition of analyses can enable incremental continual analysis, but also how the need for continual analysis poses additional challenges for analysis composition.
4. Chapter 7 (*Exploiting Results of Model-Based Analysis Tools*) has explored how analysis composition can improve analysis results, but also how composition of analyses can make it more challenging to efficiently exploit analysis results.
5. Finally, Chap. 8 (*Living with Uncertainty in Model-Based Development*) has explored the impact of uncertainty on analysis results, especially where models and analyses are composed in different ways.

The chapters in the second part of this book have shown some examples of how these challenges have been addressed for specific types of analyses. We have seen examples of modelling-language composition in Chaps. 9 and 10 with an application in the context of a specific modelling environment and specific analysis tools in Chap. 11. Chapter 12 has shown an example of composing multiple analysis tools to enrich analysis results in the context of ATL transformations. Chapter 13 has shown different examples of tool orchestration in the context of actor-based modelling.

14.2 Research Roadmap

Substantial challenges remain, however, before the topic of the book can be considered addressed sufficiently. We collect these challenges in form of a research roadmap in the following. Figure 14.1 shows an overview of how we categorise the challenges on the research roadmap for the composition of model-based analysis tools. We differentiate two orthogonal dimensions: On the one hand, we categorise challenges based on whether they relate to the conceptual foundations, the development of novel tool concepts, or the efficient implementation of analysis-composition support. On the other hand, we categorise challenges based on the thematic area they relate to. Thematically, challenges can relate to composition—which subsumes the composition of models, analyses, or results—to incrementality of analysis, or to uncertainty.

In Fig. 14.1, we have labelled each of the locations in the research-roadmap matrix with a Roman number. Below, we discuss challenges at each of these locations:

I *Foundations of Composition.* Chapter 4 has introduced a foundational understanding of the compositionality of analyses. However, this must be instantiated
for specific properties, requiring further research to understand the *compositionality* of specific properties and analyses. For some properties research
has already advanced well in this area, but many important properties remain

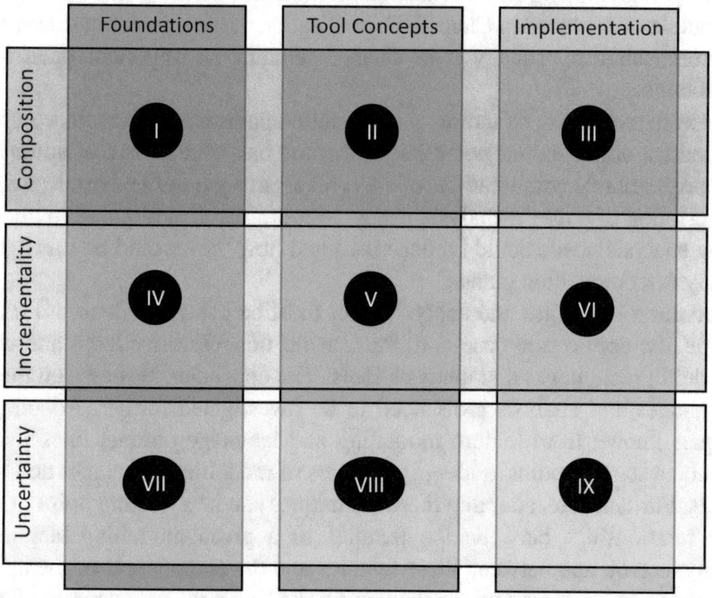

Fig. 14.1 Overview of a research roadmap in the composition of model-based analysis tools. The Roman numbers correlate with the numbers used in the text

for which compositionality is still not well understood. For example, research advances on compositionality of performance properties have been achieved in the last decade (compare also Chap. 11) while compositionality of security properties is still not well understood.

Chapter 4 has also introduced three different forms of analysis composition (black-, white-, and grey-box). Understanding the conditions under which each of them should be used remains an important topic for future research. Again, this will require a detailed understanding of individual properties before a more generalised theory can be hoped to be achieved.

While Chap. 7 has provided the terminology to discuss different ways of exploiting analysis results and how these are affected by analysis composition, this framework has, to date, only been explored through specific examples making specific choices on the spectrum of possible configurations. A systematic understanding of the relationships between the different exploitation pathways and the different forms of analysis composition introduced in Chap. 4 and the orchestration strategies from Chap. 5 would enable more principled choices to be made by analysis users.

II *Tool Concepts for Composition.* While Chap. 5 has introduced general concepts for analysis-tool integration and orchestration, mapping out six different types of orchestration strategies, this list of strategies is by no means complete. A more extensive study of orchestration strategies and the contexts in which these are most appropriate remains for future research. To support this, a further challenge is to create a language providing appropriate primitives for specifying and operationalising new orchestration strategies building on the foundational principles introduced in Chap. 5. Formalisation of the transformations proposed for orchestration strategy F in Chap. 5 remains an important open research challenge.

The systematic understanding of exploitation pathways and results composition called for above, could potentially form the basis for tools that automatically propose suitable combinations of analyses from a pre-defined catalogue given a description of a user's analysis needs. More research is required to understand how analysis needs could be described and how they would be translated into analysis-composition plans.

Modelling languages and analysis tools must be configurable to tailor them to a specific application case and, thus, avoid unnecessarily large and complex modelling languages and analysis tools. The dependencies between modelling languages and analysis tools need to be investigated further. Adapting techniques known from feature modelling and language product lines [Men+16] can be a starting point to identify features of modelling languages and analysis tools. Furthermore, adapting these techniques can be a starting point to identify the relationships between the features of a given modelling language and analysis tool, and between these features and the components of the modelling language or analysis tool implementing the features. Language configuration requires language and analysis artefacts that are ready to be reused in different configurations. A component-based approach to the definition of languages can be a key contribution here. One example of syntactic components is role-based language composition [WTZ10]. An example of semantic components has been discussed in Chap. 9. Moreover, further research on analysis components and their configuration is required. First attempts have been shown in Chap. 11. However, there is still a long way to go to come to the semantically sound configuration and composition of analysis tools.

Tool support is an important means to manage large and complex modelling languages and analysis tools in practical settings. Functionality known from *computer-aided software engineering* (CASE) tools can be adapted for modelling languages and analysis tools, e.g., for detecting and solving design smells, collecting metrics, configuring and managing variants and versions, etc.

III *Implementation of Composition.* Implementing the orchestration strategies proposed in Chap. 5 efficiently requires substantial future research. Some initial progress is currently being made with protocols for language editing[1] or debugging,[2] and the increasing trend towards web-based modelling tools, but substantial challenges remain. For example, modular language development across concrete and abstract syntax as well as semantics can be achieved for specific cases, but a safe general approach is still missing. This becomes even more challenging when model transformations need to be composed, too. An integration of analysis-tool composition into mega-modelling systems (e.g., MMINT [San+15]) will be an important step towards supporting reasoning about analysis configurations. Future progress requires research in language engineering and tool support.

IV *Foundations of Incrementality.* The CBMA framework proposed in Chap. 6 offers a first pragmatic classification of the various components and processes involved in continual analysis under composition. However, a full theory of composition of continual model-based analysis remains an open goal: What are the formal operators involved and how do they interact to form a system of continually updating, composed domain-specific analyses? Invariably, this will require establishing closer links to the formal foundations of analysis and formalism composition as well as to the orchestration of analysis tools. However, the need to support *continual* and *incremental* analysis substantially changes the conceptual framework required as we have demonstrated in Chap. 6.

V *Tool Concepts for Incrementality.* Once we have a clearer understanding of what incremental analysis means in the context of analysis composition, we need to develop tool concepts that allow practitioners to compose incremental analysis tools. For example, designing a tool platform where software designers can indicate a number of orthogonal analysis tools and ask the platform to generate a composed *and* incremental analysis tool can be an important step. This includes investigating what languages are needed for describing software

---

[1] See the language server protocol, https://microsoft.github.io/language-server-protocol/.

[2] For example, through the debug adapter protocol, https://microsoft.github.io/debug-adapter-protocol/, and the GEMOC Studio [CBW17].

designers' analysis needs. Further research is needed on how we can support incremental analysis while continuing to allow flexible composition of model-based analyses, which may require different types of information to be included in a model.

VI *Implementation of Incrementality.* We need to develop efficient algorithms for composed incremental analysis. This includes answering the question of how to efficiently track changes and their analysis implications for large-scale models that are stored in a distributed environment and are manipulated by multiple modellers concurrently. Further, we need to develop appropriate caching and consistency-preservation algorithms in such a setting.

VII *Foundations of Uncertainty.* As we have seen in the example-driven discussion in Chap. 8, uncertainty is an important consideration in any model-based analysis. Composition of model-based analysis can both decrease overall uncertainty and create an additional source of uncertainty. A systematic conceptual framework of the precise relationship between analysis composition and uncertainty remains an open research ambition. Identifying these relationships—whether generally or for specific properties or composition approaches—would be invaluable to software engineers aiming to make informed decisions about the design of complex and heterogeneous software-intensive systems.

We need to further explore the capture of uncertainty aspects in the system design, which includes leaving options open as far as possible and incorporating belief values into the design. Other relevant research directions comprise the dynamic handling of uncertainties of data-driven models, such as deep learning, in safety-critical contexts, e.g., in autonomous driving, and in security-critical contexts, e.g., in production automation and energy supply.

VIII *Tool Concepts for Uncertainty.* We need to get a better understanding of what tools that support uncertainty-awareness for modellers look like in the context of analysis composition. Designing generic tools that can enhance existing model-based analysis tools with an analysis of how uncertainty propagates through the analysis chain can be a step in this direction. We need to investigate what information about uncertainty and about the analysis tools such generic tools would require and how such information would best be captured. Further, we need to investigate effective ways of communicating uncertainty and uncertainty propagation to modellers.

IX *Implementation for Uncertainty.* If generic tools for uncertainty-enhancement of analysis tools and compositions of analysis tools can be designed, we need to investigate what algorithms that efficiently implement the underlying uncertainty propagation can look like. We also need to figure out how these tools can be implemented to cater for large-scale distributed models developed concurrently by multiple developers.

References

[CBW17] Benoit Combemale, Olivier Barais, and Andreas Wortmann. "Language Engineering with the GEMOC Studio". In: *IEEE International Conference on Software Architecture Workshops, ICSAW*. 2017, pp. 189–191. https://doi.org/10.1109/ICSAW.2017.61.

[Gri12] Michael Grieves. Virtually Perfect: *Driving Innovative and Lean Products through Product Lifecycle Management*. Space Coast Press, 2012.

[Hei+21] Robert Heinrich, Francisco Durán, Carolyn L. Talcott, and Steffen Zschaler (eds.) *Composing Model-Based Analysis Tools*. Springer, 2021. https://doi.org/10.1007/978-3-030-81915-6.

[Men+16] David Méndez-Acuña, José A. Galindo, Thomas Degueule, Benoit Combemale, and Benoit Baudry. "Leveraging Software Product Lines Engineering in the development of external DSLs: A systematic literature review". In: *Computer Languages, Systems & Structures* 46 (2016), pp. 206–235. https://doi.org/10.1016/j.cl.2016.09.004.

[San+15] Alessio Di Sandro, Rick Salay, Michalis Famelis, Sahar Kokaly, and Marsha Chechik. "MMINT: A Graphical Tool for Interactive ModelManagement". In: *MoDELS 2015 Demo and Poster Session*. 2015. http://www.cas.mcmaster.ca/~kokalys/files/Models15demo.pdf.

[WTZ10] Christian Wende, Nils Thieme, and Steffen Zschaler. "A Role-Based Approach towards Modular Language Engineering". In: *2nd Int'l Conf. on Software Language Engineering, SLE*. Vol. 5969. 2010, pp. 254–273. https://doi.org/10.1007/978-3-642-12107-4_19.

Printed in the United States
by Baker & Taylor Publisher Services